Praise for Other Books by Kenneth Cloke

"Once again Ken Cloke pushes us to think beyond the conventional boundaries of conflict resolution. This time he goes so far as to propose a unified field theory. His ideas are dangerous. Read them at your own risk — and the reward is great!" —William Ury, co-author *Getting to Yes,* author *Getting to Yes with Yourself*

"There is no one — NO ONE — more deeply versed in conflict resolution, locally and globally, personally and professionally, privately and politically, than Ken. Take his trainings, read his books, hear him speak, participate in his endeavors. I can count on one hand the number of people who have profoundly influenced my life, my career and my course. Ken is one of them. A tough and realistic intelligence coupled with an enormous and generous heart." —Victoria Pynchon, author, *Success as a Mediator for Dummies.*

"Overwhelmed by the politics of our time? Think it's all getting worse? Think again. *Conflict Revolution* will change you profoundly. In the confusions and conflicts of our time lie great opportunities and optimisms. Perhaps even a collective destiny that we can all embrace. If you think that's airy-fairy, think again. Here's a book by someone who has walked the talk, who has been there and done it, who has successfully helped people find resolutions in some of the most trying circumstances imaginable. You would think after 25 years of being in the middle of other people's fights, he would see the world darkly. Quite the opposite. Kenneth Cloke's new book is a lantern. It illuminates and points the way forward. —Peter S. Adler, author, *Eye of the Storm Leadership.*

"... a treasure trove of profound insights and practical wisdom about understanding, addressing, transforming, and transcending conflict.

It will enrich and inspire, and even empower, not only mediators, but anyone who works with conflict, professionally or personally." —Leonard L. Riskin, author, *Managing Conflict Mindfully.*

"Kenneth Cloke proposes that conflict resolution be more than therapeutic talk, and a step from social change to social justice. I have known him since the very beginning of the 1960s, and the insights on these pages come not only from the experience of revolt against the status quo, but the complexities of transforming revolt into reforms in everyday life and long-term reconciliation between antagonists. This wonderful book studies conflict resolution not only between human groupings, but between human beings and the planet we continue to destroy." —Tom Hayden, California State Senator

"A CLASSIC! Full of timeless insights into highly sophisticated mediating. The stories are told in detail, so that moves and responses by the parties and the mediators are apparent. The mediator's exquisite sense of timing and respect for the parties combine to produce often astonishing results. Essential reading for experts as well as novices." —Barbara Ashley Phillips, author, *Finding Common Ground* and *The Field Guide to Mediation*

"A book that is bristling with wisdom and practical advice. There is not a stale or tired thought on any page. In short, the authors have produced a very important book, one that promises to change the entire foundation of what we have wrongly taken as management." —Ian I. Mitroff, author, *Managing Crises Before They Happen,*

"Ken Cloke is a modern-day prophet, speaking the Truth to help us wake up. To everyone who sees the brokenness in our world, I urge you to take heed of his timely and penetrating wisdom." Erica Ariel Fox, Lecturer, Harvard Law School Founder, Harvard Negotiation Insight Initiative; author, *Winning from Within*

"This new book by Dr. Kenneth Cloke, will change your life. You will never view conflict the same way again. If you only read one more book on the theory and practice of Conflict Resolution, make it this one. Dr. Cloke's explorations in mediation, dialogue, and conflict resolution systems are revolutionary." Ron Supancic, Collaborative Lawyer, Rotary Peace Project

"The brilliance of this book is that its lessons apply in any ... setting." —Blenda Wilson, President and CEO, The Nellie Mae Foundation

"Ken Cloke elevates mediation to a fine art that creates opportunities for human growth to rise out of conflict. Cloke demonstrates that mediation is more than a skill set --it can be a journey of connection and growth.... This book links the mediation process to social justice and a transformation of society's basic compact with its citizens. This book is a gift--and should be required reading for anyone entering the field of mediation. Ken Cloke is one of mediation's pioneers and offers insight and guidance to both conflict resolution professionals and people facing conflict." Forrest (Woody) Mosten, author *Complete Guide to Mediation,* and *Making Mediation Your Career* (Jossey Bass)

"For all those who have wrestled with the increasingly problematic fate of humanity in the face of evil, war, injustice and terrorism, Kenneth Cloke's incredible message of hope for rescuing our planet by 'changing the way we change,' and 'transforming the way we think about our opponents, conflicts and resistance to change' — these encourage us not only to transform the world into something better, but as Cloke writes, 'to do so with smiles on our faces and songs in our hearts.'" —A. Marco Turk, J.D., former Program Director, Negotiation, Conflict Resolution & Peacebuilding Program, California State University-Dominguez Hills

"Few people today approach conflict with the wisdom and grace of Kenneth Cloke. Far fewer possess the ability to provide a clear and detailed roadmap for resolution and transformation. Cloke's teachings provide inspiration and courage to those who dream of changing the world, and guidance to those who strive to change themselves. While conflict is a necessary element of the human condition, how we handle it is our choice. This book is a gift to all of us in learning how to make those choices." —Laurel Kaufer, mediator/arbitrator; founder, Mississippi Mediation Project

"Kenneth Cloke's *Conflict Revolution* is a powerful and comprehensive argument for justice, harmony and common sense. This seminal book will help teach our children that we can and must live in peace with each other and with the world we share. *Conflict Revolution* inspires us to aspire to more. Don't just read this book, carry it with you — as I will." —Adam Urbanski, President, Rochester (NY) Teachers Association, vice president American Federation of Teachers, and director of the Teacher Union Reform Network (TURN) of AFT and NEA Locals.

"In this encyclopedic work based on decades of personal experience, Kenneth Cloke offers a way out for our species: interest-based conflict resolution. Otherwise, we may go the way of the Dodo — and for the same reasons: inability to understand and to take concerted action to meet challenges like global warming, global terrorism and globally destructive weapons." —Sidney Rittenberg Sr, President, Rittenberg Associates Inc., China, Visiting Professor, Pacific Lutheran University

"Cloke helps us understand how the authenticity and power of our similarities, our connectedness and our internal technology can resolve conflicts regardless of the venue, type, complexity or people involved. This book gives us a conflict resolution paradigm though which we can see the realities of where are today and the prospect of what we must do for a better tomorrow." —Marvin Johnson, Executive Director, National Center for Alternative Dispute Resolution

THE MAGIC IN MEDIATION

THE MAGIC IN MEDIATION

A Search for Symmetries, Metaphors and Scale-Free
Practices

KENNETH CLOKE

goodmedia PRESS

Dedication

For Joan, who encouraged, supported, participated in, and aided and abetted the many efforts over several decades that culminated in this book, and made it better.

To my children and grandchildren who will hopefully inherit a world that is a little better because of it.

And to my fellow mediators around the world who search courageously every day for ways to make it happen.

GoodMedia Press

An imprint of goodmedia communications, llc

www.goodmediapress.com

Book cover and book layout design by GoodMedia Press.

The text in this book is set in Josefin Sans and Crimson Text.

Manufactured in USA

Names: Cloke, Kenneth, author.

Title: The magic in mediation : a search for symmetries , metaphors and scale-free practices / Kenneth Cloke.

Description: Includes index. | Dallas, TX: GoodMedia Press, 2023.

Identifiers: LCCN: 2023946772 | ISBN: 979-8-9852429-4-2 (paperback) | 979-8-9852429-5-9 (ebook)

Subjects: LCSH Conflict management. | Mediation.| BISAC LAW / Alternative Dispute Resolution | LAW / Arbitration, Negotiation, Mediation

Classification: LCC HM1126 .C56 2023 | DDC 303.69--dc23

Also by Kenneth Cloke

Mediation: Revenge and the Magic of Forgiveness

Mediating Dangerously: The Frontiers of Conflict Resolution

The Crossroads of Conflict: A Journey into the Heart of Dispute Resolution

Conflict Revolution: Mediating Evil, War, Injustice and Terrorism

The Dance of Opposites: Explorations in Mediation, Dialogue and Conflict Resolution Systems Design

Conflict Revolution: Designing Preventative Systems for Chronic Social, Economic and Political Conflicts, Second Edition

Politics, Dialogue and the Evolution of Democracy: How to Discuss Race, Abortion, Immigration Gun Control, Climate Change, Same Sex Marriage and Other Hot Topics

Words of Wisdom: Profound, Poignant and Provocative Quotes for Your Insight and Inspiration

Ordinary Ecstasy: A Meditation Home Companion

Mediation in a Time of Crisis: Pandemic, Prejudice, Police, and Political Polarization

Also by Kenneth Cloke & Joan Goldsmith

Thank God It's Monday: 14 Values We Need to Improve the Way We Work

Resolving Conflicts at Work: A Complete Guide for Everyone on the Job

Resolving Personal and Organizational Conflicts: Stories of Transformation and Forgiveness

The End of Management and the Rise of Organizational Democracy

The Art of Waking People Up: Cultivating Awareness and Authenticity at Work

Resolving Conflicts at Work: Eight Strategies for Everyone on the Job (Second Edition)

Resolving Conflicts at Work: Ten Strategies for Everyone on the Job (Third Edition)

Resolving Organizational Conflicts: A Course on Mediation and Systems Design

Contents

Genuine tragedies in the world are not conflicts between right and wrong. They are conflicts between two rights.

Georg Wilhelm Friedrich Hegel

Conflict is the gadfly of thought. It stirs us to observation and memory. It instigates to invention. It shocks us out of sheeplike passivity, and sets us at noting and contriving.

John Dewey

Somewhere we know that without silence words lose their meaning, that without listening speaking no longer heals, that without distance closeness cannot cure.

Henri J.M. Nouwen

We all carry within us places of exile; our crimes, our ravages. Our task is not to unleash them on the world; it is to transform them in ourselves and others.

Albert Camus

Preface

THE HISTORY AND HOPE THAT HATCHED THIS BOOK

The very least you can do in your life is to figure out what you hope for. And the most you can do is live inside that hope. Not admire it from a distance but live right in it, under its roof.

Barbara Kingsolver

Optimism is a strategy for making a better future. Because unless you believe that the future can be better, it's unlikely you will step up and take responsibility for making it so. If you assume that there's no hope, you guarantee that there will be no hope. If you assume that there is an instinct for freedom, there are opportunities to change things. There's a chance you may contribute to making a better world. The choice is yours.

Noam Chomsky

I know you never intended to be in this world. But you're in it all the same.So why not get started immediately.

Mary Oliver

In his *Theses on the Philosophy of History*, Walter Benjamin famously envisioned "the angel of history":

> His face is turned toward the past. Where we perceive a chain of events, he sees one single catastrophe which keeps piling wreckage and hurls it in front of his feet. The angel would like to stay, awaken the dead, and make whole what has been smashed, but a storm is blowing in from paradise. It has got caught in its wings with such a violence that the angel can no longer close them. The storm irresistibly propels him into the future to which his back is turned, while the pile of debris before him grows skyward. ... The storm is what we call progress.

We can think of this "storm from paradise" as a metaphor for conflict, except that in the world of mediation, the angel is able, somehow, every so often, to magically "awaken the dead, and make whole what has been smashed." This book is a search for ways of describing that magic, unpacking it, transforming it into technique, and discovering ways of practicing and applying it — not only in small-scale interpersonal disputes, but mid- and large-scale political ones as well.

The wreckage caused by "the angel of history" is incalculable, and while it may have decreased in severity over millennia, as Stephen Pinker has argued, the damage it has caused continues to be painful and palpable — and nearly always preventable. And all that is required to dramatically reduce the cost of human conflicts are five relatively simple, inexpensive, easily implementable steps:

1. Mediate *every* conflict on every scale before it escalates and becomes needlessly damaging and costly to resolve.
2. Make conflict resolution skills and services available, affordable, abundant, and ubiquitous.
3. Require first use of mediative methodologies, such as informal problem-solving, conflict coaching, facilitated

dialogue, consensus building, restorative justice, mediation, arbitration, etc., before getting violent or going to court.

4. Train people *globally* in applying these skills and methodologies, and shaping them to fit their cultures and communities.

5. Design preventative dispute resolution systems to assist couples, families, communities, and organizations on all scales to redress the chronic, systemic sources of conflict, *including* those that arise in our social, economic, and political lives.

The goal of these efforts should not be to *eliminate* conflicts, which are simply the unheard, unacknowledged, unaddressed voice of what isn't working and needs correcting, or is ready to evolve and struggling to free itself from what is no longer useful. Instead, it should be to turn the anger and resentment that fuel our repetitive disputes in the direction of creative problem solving, collaborative negotiation, forgiveness, reconciliation, and a continuing, proactive commitment to improving our communications and relationships.

When did the first conflicts begin? With the birth of the universe. The Big Bang created not just matter and anti-matter, quarks and gluons, protons, electrons and neutrons; but *time*–i.e., before, after, and now; *charge*–i.e., positive, negative, and neutral; *space*—i.e., here and there, up and down, back and forth, in and out, and the *infinite* in-between — in other words, *opposites*, and hence conflicts. And with conflicts came unending mediations and the *magic* of emergence—of order out of chaos, evolution, higher forms of complexity, and the *transcendence* of opposites, by means of invention, synthesis, and creative combination.

The history of human conflict and its' resolution through mediation, is rich and ancient, and while we have slaughtered one another mercilessly over the course of millennia for reasons that seem woefully insufficient in hindsight, this is partly because we have lacked a rich, diverse, robust, sophisticated set of skills for bringing people to agreement, resolving the underlying reasons for their disputes, defusing the emotional triggers that kept them stuck, assisting them in reaching forgiveness and reconciliation, and using conflict resolution systems design to prevent hostilities from turning chronic, festering, and escalating.

At least since Mary Parker Follett began writing about conflict resolution in the 1920s, and with increasing depth and sophistication in the 1980s with the advancement of scientific understanding, mediation and its' many sister skills have been transformed into a rapidly growing profession that includes tens of thousands of practitioners world-wide, a vast and impressive literature, scientific research, school programs, academic instruction, large and small mediation organizations, countless trainings and webinars, rich and exciting ideas, and a passion, commitment, and *esprit de corps* that are thrilling and successful.

This rapid growth, richness of ideas, commitment, and success prompt us to ask: "How far can we go?" "What are the limits of our knowledge and skills? "What can we learn and adapt from other fields of knowledge?" and "Is it possible to apply the knowledge and skills we've gained working with small-scale disputes to mid- and large-scale conflicts, including social, economic, political, and environmental disputes?" This book is a search for answers to these questions.

The short answer, I believe, is this: the problems we face as a species are less and less likely to be solved using power-based techniques like military force, or rights-based methods like litigation, and increasingly require advanced, collaborative, complex, multi-dimensional, sophisticated, *interest*-based approaches like mediation, restorative justice, and what I think of as the "conflict resolution arts and sciences." Indeed, without them we may not be able to survive.

To discover, invent, extend, and apply these approaches, it will be important to identify the sources of magic in mediation, to learn from other disciplines and professions, and to search for ways of translating successful small — scale techniques into scale-free methodologies we can apply to mid- and large-scale social, economic, political, cultural, and environmental conflicts.

It is clear that Covid, climate change, ecological destruction, poverty, war, and other crises, have created problems that cannot be resolved or prevented *except* globally, collaboratively, and mediatively using scaled-up, higher order dispute resolution skills. This, I believe, is the core mission and calling of conflict resolvers around the world. And as these problems and conflicts we create have no borders, neither should our efforts to resolve them.

MY PERSONAL HISTORY WITH CONFLICT AND RESOLUTION

For forty years, I have searched for these "scale-free" practices, and tried them out. I have mediated many thousands of disputes on all scales, including small-scale interpersonal and mid-scale community, environmental, public policy, and organizational disputes, and explored how we might go about using these ideas to help resolve large-scale social, economic, political, and environmental disputes.

For my entire adult life, I have been involved in conflicts of various kinds, including (often concurrently) the following, each of which shaped this book:

- 15 years as a full-time political activist, organizer, and leader in the student, civil rights, civil liberties, and peace movements of the 1960's and '70's, consisting of *encouraging* social, economic, political, and environmental conflicts, so as to bring about social change.
- 10 years practicing law of various kinds, consisting of advocating for individuals and political groups in conflict.
- 10 years in law and graduate schools, consisting of studying, researching, writing, and thinking about conflict.

- 8 years as a professor of law, history, political science, and urban studies, consisting of teaching about conflict.
- 5 years as an administrative law judge and judge *pro tem* on the Superior Court, consisting of deciding and settling conflicts.
- 45 years as a labor arbitrator, consisting of issuing awards in labor-management conflicts.
- 30 years as a mediator, consultant, and external change agent, consisting of designing structural, systemic, procedural, and relational alternatives to conflict for small and large organizations, including Fortune 100 companies, non-profits, and governments.
- 30 years as a personal, leadership, and conflict coach, consisting of helping individuals resolve conflicts.
- 42 years as a mediator, dialogue facilitator, speaker, and trainer, consisting of practicing and building skills in conflict resolution.
- 10 years as a professor at various universities, consisting of teaching courses in conflict resolution and writing many books about it.
- 30 years mediating, teaching, facilitating dialogues, consisting of resolving disputes in over 20 countries, and being co-founder and first President of Mediators Beyond Borders.

In these experiences I was not unique, but part of an inspiring and growing community of practitioners. I mention my experience here for three reasons: first, to show how rich, varied, and ubiquitous conflict resolution experiences can be; second, to be transparent and reveal my personal biases and predilections, and the "data" on which my assertions in this book are grounded; and third, to show how history and hope are connected, both personally and politically, in ways that feed into and inform the topics explored in this book, and why I believe it is possible for Benjamin's "angel of history" to *pivot* in a magical direction.

The wonderful artist M. C. Escher wrote that "We adore chaos because we like to restore order." This has certainly been true for me, and I think for many dispute resolvers who derive immense *pleasure* from entering the chaos of conflict and unexpectedly discovering — not only hidden sources of order, but ways of resolving, transforming, and transcending conflicts at their source, ways that always appear magical to those who are stuck in them.

What helps us find, feed, and foment this magic are not just the extraordinary successes, but the inevitable, equally extraordinary *failures* on which most of the ideas in this book are based. Every conflict is *already* a failure, and every mediation starts with failure and continues to fail, until somehow, magically, it doesn't. This reminds me of Douglas Adams' humorous observation in *The Hitchhiker's Guide to the Galaxy*, that the art of flying consists of "learning how to throw yourself at the ground and miss."

This is likely to be my last book on conflict resolution. I am nearing the end of what feels like a lifetime of learning things I could never have imagined about conflict and resolution, neurophysiology and emotional intelligence, apology and forgiveness, transformation and transcendence, and feel a need to express in writing some of the ideas I've thought about, sometimes for decades, but never put in writing.

A caution: each person is different, each moment is different, each conflict is different, and everyone mediates differently. The magic in mediation is therefore not fixed, but constantly moving, and can only be discovered by moving with it, by opening ourselves to it, and by resonating with it. Each chapter is a search for magic in different locations, where it is often hidden in plain sight. Each is entirely separate, yet connected, and none is complete. They are invitations to join the search, to invent and discover the magic yourself, then make it commonplace.

Some of what is written here may be pure fancy, or entirely subjective and personal, or a complete failure–but hopefully, in the generative, creative way of other "noble failures," may lead, in some far-off time or corner of the globe, to a rare flash of insight that, without warning, sees things clearly, and changes everything. The impressionist painter Paul Cezanne said it best: "The day is coming when a single carrot, freshly observed, will set off a revolution."

This book is my search for that carrot.

Kenneth Cloke

Santa Monica, California

ONE

Magic, Metaphor, and Meaning

FROM NEUTRALITY TO OMNI-PARTIALITY

Whatever is magical in the world, whatever brings color and sound and light and joy, was brought into the center of living by those people curious enough—perhaps angry enough—to go to the edge of the town, the forest, the river, and see what else was in the world. Someone recognized the boredom, the waste of sitting in the dark and merely living and invented the story and the song. Someone recognized that the mere act of procreation was insufficient, and love and seduction and play was invented.

Tennessee Williams

Because metaphors are vivid and memorable, and because they are not readily subjected to critical analysis, they can have considerable impact on human judgment even when they are inappropriate, useless, or misleading.

Amos Tversky

A book must start somewhere. One brave letter must volunteer to go first, laying itself on the line in an act of faith, from which a word takes heart and follows, drawing a sentence into its wake. From there, a paragraph amasses, and soon a page, and the book is on its way, finding a voice, calling itself into being.

Ruth Ozeki

WE DO NOT SEE THE WIND, EXCEPT AS IT MOVES THROUGH THE TREES. We do not feel it, except when it caresses our skin. Wind is an *activity* of the air, a verb rather than a noun. It cannot be frozen or pinned to the wall, but instead must be imagined, intuited, experienced. It is the same with conflict, which does not have an independent tangible existence, except in the ways it moves in our bodies, minds, emotions, and spirits; the ways it alters our attitudes and intentions; the ways it impacts the quality of our awareness, the depth of our relationships, the openness of our hearts, and the wisdom of our choices in responding to it. All of this can make conflicts appear confusing, intractable, and beyond our capacity to resolve, and the possibility of resolving it seem magical, mystical, and unimaginable. Yet this magic happens *often* in mediation, as a very real consequence of small, prosaic, ostensibly un-magical processes, techniques, methods, and interventions that, bit-by-bit, dismantle the invisible scaffolding, remove the nails, bolts, and screws that hold it together, and turn it, like a Rubik's cube, until it returns to a harmonious, un-conflicted state.

How, exactly, does this magic happen? What are the processes, techniques, methods, and interventions that enable us to find, feed, and foment it? How do all the apparently infinite forms of conflict fit together? And how might it be possible to translate what works magically on a small scale to successively larger and more consequential scales, and *vice versa*?

In seeking answers to these questions, and better ways of formulating them, it is helpful to think of conflict resolution *holistically*, rather than reductively, and from the point of view of metaphor and meaning, rather than facts and issues. This will help reveal the sacred *within* the profane, the beauty within the ordinary, the magic within the mundane. Ralph Waldo Emerson observed, "The invariable mark of wisdom is to see the miraculous in the common."

So how do most people respond most often to conflicts, regardless of their issues, personalities, proximities, or scales? Logically, there are just five fundamental options available to anyone who is interested in trying to mediate them:

1. Avoid the conflict, distance oneself from it, and resist getting involved in trying to fix it.
2. Side with A against B, affirm A's version of the facts as true, and reject, discount, or disregard B's.
3. Alternatively, side with B against A, affirm B's version of the facts as true, and reject, discount, or disregard A's version.
4. Remain neutral regarding A and B, refuse to affirm either version of the facts as exclusively true, and encourage compromise to settle the dispute by making concessions in incremental, win/lose, zero-sum, adversarial negotiations.
5. Invite A and B into open, honest dialogue and creative contention, affirm both their experiences as *subjectively* true and valid for each of them, and encourage collaboration to resolve the dispute by improving their communications, processes, and relationships through transformational, win/win, non-zero-sum mediations and negotiations between them.

Each of these options requires successively higher orders of skill. Each alters the course of the conflict, impacts it in deeper and more lasting ways, and brings us closer to its' *heart*, and the invisible, almost unimaginable magic that awaits there, patiently sending subtle signals that everything can be transformed and transcended, if we could only figure out how.

METAPHOR AND MEANING IN MEDIATION

We think of metaphors as symbols or figures of speech that allow us to discover unnoticed aspects of a thing by comparing it to something else. People in conflict often unknowingly use metaphors to describe themselves, their opponents, or the issue in dispute, or to point at some hidden truth or meaning. While the reasons we recite for engaging in conflict are often grounded in facts and logic, our *experience* of conflict is profoundly emotional. But rather than participate in direct, emotionally charged communications with people we dislike or no longer trust, we prefer to transmit our feelings indirectly through the *symbolic* language we use to characterize the facts, or animate our logic. For this reason, the *language* of conflict is often highly emotionally charged, and full of allusion, metaphor and symbolism. Here are three commonly cited examples:

1. Conflict as War:

- "Your position is indefensible."
- "I shot down that idea."
- "We've got a battle on our hands."
- "She dropped a bomb on me."
- "He won't negotiate."
- "I won."
- "My enemy ..."
- "We blew him out of the water."

2. Conflict as Opportunity:

- "This presents us with a real challenge."
- "Your feedback has given me some ways to improve."
- "We now have a chance to make things better."

- "What are all the possibilities for solving this problem?"
- "Let's work together to find a solution."
- "What could we learn from what happened?"
- "Let's find a solution that works for both of us."

3. Conflict as Journey:

- "Your idea points to a solution."
- "This isn't getting us anywhere."
- "Where do you want to go with that?"
- "Let's do it together."
- "I think we've arrived at an agreement!"
- "Let's search for common ground."
- "Now we are getting somewhere."
- "What if we ...?"
- "Let's try to find a way out of this."

George Lakoff, in *The Contemporary Theory of Metaphor,* [in *Metaphor and Thought*, 2nd Ed., edited by Andrew Ortony (1998)] has deepened our understanding of the complex role and importance of metaphor in mediation, especially in political conflicts. Among his most useful ideas, in my view, are these:

- Metaphors are the main mechanisms through which we comprehend abstract concepts and perform logic or reasoning.
- Much subject matter, from the most mundane to the most abstruse, can only be understood through metaphor.
- Metaphors *map*, as functions do in mathematics, from one idea, feeling, experience, or conceptual domain to another.
- Metaphors create a link, resonance, or correspondence between a "source domain" and a "target domain."
- Metaphors connect concepts and images.
- Metaphors are, for the most part, beneath the level of conscious attention, and mapped unconsciously.

- These mappings include interference patterns and culturally specific assumptions and experiences.
- Some metaphors may be universal.

These ideas suggest that metaphors can unexpectedly reveal sources of magic in mediation. They are, as Roland Barthes brilliantly suggested, *codes*, symbols, signifiers, myths, and semiotic "tools" for exposing and dismantling the mystifying, superficial language that is thrown up by people in conflict to divert attention from deeper and more painful truths.

These metaphors, myths, and symbols not only *hide* the true emotional and relational meaning of what is happening in the conflict, they also *point* to it. They are *requests* for the other person to care enough to dig beneath the surface, like a mother or father might do with a child, and translate or intuit from these false signs, what actually happened and what it felt like, in order to begin recovering from the trauma they seek to both hide and express.

The magic in mediation often begins with mediators asking questions, sometimes *in loco parentis*, that emerge not from a place of neutrality or professionalism, but of *caring*, kindness, and concern; that are not just about the issues in dispute, but the complex human beings who have been stereotyped and cast by each other as implacable enemies; who have mistaken their injured feelings and loss of trust for an evil intention, or desire to harm them for no reason.

Math and science also offer immensely useful metaphors for conflict resolution. Here, for example, are 15 successive metaphors representing paradigm shifts in the ways we describe matter, each of which offers a fundamentally different set of suggestions for thinking about conflict:

1. From "essences" (earth, air, fire, water) to substances
2. From substances to molecules

3. From molecules to knots of "luminiferous ether"
4. From knots of ether to atoms
5. From atoms to elementary particles with mass
6. From mass to equivalence with energy and the speed of light
7. From mass and energy to waves and wave functions
8. From waves to wave/particle duality and complementarity
9. From wave/particle duality to fields and quantum uncertainty
10. From fields and quantum uncertainty to entanglement
11. From entanglement to measurement and instantaneous collapse
12. From elementary particles to symmetries and the Standard Model
13. From symmetries and the Standard Model to strings, M theory, and loop quantum gravity
14. From a factual orientation to counter-factual theories of what can and can't happen

THE METAPHOR OF POLARITY

An example of how a scientific metaphor may be useful in dispute resolution is the metaphor of *polarity*, as it appears, for example, in electromagnetism. We know that anything that is magnetically charged, like the Earth, will have north and south poles. The entire earth is then "polarized," with a charge at one pole that *forces* the other pole into opposite alignment–except, that is, for two locations: the poles themselves, and the equator where they meet.

As metaphors, the equator translates into locating the midpoint of their polarity, which corresponds to compromise, while searching for the pole that connects them corresponds to topics both sides care about. The second suggests that opponents in *all* conflicts, no matter how polarized, are invisibly connected along a line of *caring* about the issues that matter to them.

As a result, mediation consists of at least two entirely different ways of responding to polarized ideas, personalities, proposals, or demands; and on a large-scale, to contradictory social, economic, political, and environmental forces that are *innately* impermanent and eternally evolving. These can be conciliated, compromised, and temporarily settled without ever reaching the *source* of the opposition, resulting in chronic, systemic clashes.

Alternatively, they can be resolved, transformed, and transcended, allowing them to evolve from less to more complex forms and interactions, each with deeper and more impactful consequences, and each requiring higher order skills, processes, relationships, structures, and systems that enable otherwise destructive conflicts to turn in the direction of growth, adaptation, learning, and evolution.

These divergent approaches to conflict respond to polarization and the seemingly unending disputes that emanate from it, either by ignoring or defending the *status quo ante* and preserving an unstable, lower order equilibrium; or by helping bring about a fundamental transformation in the attitudes and approaches to conflicts that encourage them to adapt and evolve to more stable, higher order states.

In fact, we can respond to polarization in conflict resolution in eight fundamental ways, each of which produces a different set of outcomes. These include:

1. *Cease-fire,* which freezes the polarization.
2. *De-escalation,* which reduces the stresses and tensions of polarization.
3. *Settlement* of the issues, which consists mostly of negotiated compromises that keep the fundamental polarization in place.
4. *Conciliation* of the emotions, which elicits empathy and eases emotional antagonism and polarization.

5. *Resolution* of the underlying reasons for the dispute, which addresses the reasons for chronic conflict by seeking consensus, and tries to transform and overcome the polarization at its source.
6. *Forgiveness*, which attempts to eliminate the polarization by apologizing for what happened and trying to repair the relationship.
7. *Reconciliation*, which rebuilds trust by telling their truth about what happened, acknowledging what was true for others, collaborating in solving shared problems, and ending the polarization.
8. *Systems Design*, which redesigns the systems that generated, ignored, or aggravated the conflict, and prevent future polarization by transitioning to higher order systems with fewer sources of conflict.

In these ways, we can transform polarization into a *positive* force, and shift from fueling destructive, adversarial conflicts to inviting collaboration, learning, evolution, system redesign, and similar higher order outcomes. It is not polarization, but *hyper*-polarization that is the more serious problem. As I wrote in *Mediation in a Time of Crisis:*

> Polarization, in every conflict, is a sign that we are approaching a crossroads, a definitive choice, a point of departure. It is a signal that something deep, fundamental, and systemic has *already* been born; that the past is over, yet the future is uncertain and insecure; and that confusion, nostalgia, resistance, and fear of loss are intensifying in an effort to reverse course and return to a world that no longer exists, and *can* no longer exist.

While the metaphor of polarization helps people in conflict contrast the old with the new in preparation for a higher order synthesis, *hyper*-polarization resists the new in an effort to preserve a lower order past, triggering a *reciprocal* polarization directed against those who seek a new, higher order. While both sides may be hyper-polarized, their opposition is not equal and does not lead to equal amounts of conflict. From a conflict *resolution* perspective, hyper-polarization leaves chronic conflicts in place, and often resists even the *idea* of mediation, leaving resort to violence, trauma, and destruction as the only option imaginable, while mandating a formal "neutrality" as the only possible non-polarized practice.

FROM NEUTRALITY TO OMNI-PARTIALITY IN MEDIATION

It is common for mediators to describe themselves, or be described, as neutral. What is usually meant by this is that mediators should not be beholden to either side, or have a stake in the outcome, or stand to benefit in any way from the result, and are not biased in favor of or against either side. What parties in mediation usually mean by neutrality is that the mediator is not biased *against* them—a bias *for* them is soon overlooked and regarded as fair and just.

Bernie Mayer has incisively analyzed this issue in two excellent books, and I will try not to repeat anything he has already said, except to note that we both came to a critique of neutrality through social activism—initially, for me, in the civil rights movement, where the impact of neutrality regarding lynching and the denial of Constitutional rights was both obvious and morally reprehensible. As Archbishop Desmond Tutu famously pronounced: "If you are neutral in situations of injustice, you have chosen the side of the oppressor." He also wrote, "If an elephant is standing on the tail of a mouse, the mouse will not appreciate your neutrality."

It is important to acknowledge that neutrality is a step *forward* from absolutism, monarchy, dictatorship, and autocracy, which are openly and unabashedly biased in favor of the "powers that be." Judges in dictatorships and autocracies who are *not* biased toward their rulers are quickly eliminated and replaced with those who are.

For this reason, neutrality is not an issue in *power*-based institutions or systems like dictatorships — even on a small-scale in couples, families, and workplaces. Neutrality is then seen as condescension, apathy, or lack of caring. Nor is it an issue in *interest*-based processes, like dialogue, mediation, and restorative justice, where diversity and dissent are not only acceptable, but actively encouraged.

The primary place where neutrality *is* an issue is in *rights*-based institutions like courts, where it is widely considered a *condition* for just adjudication. Why? Because rights are *limitations* on the exercise of power, and the exercise of rights in a *context* of unequal, hierarchical power makes them vulnerable to efforts by those with power to expand their power and manipulate the system in their favor.

Another reason goes back to a set of assumptions best expressed in Aristotle's three laws of logic, which make excellent sense as responses to the *illogic* of power-based dictatorships and tyrannies, but little or none as responses to interest-based practices like mediation. Here are Aristotle's three laws:

1. *The Law of Identity:* A statement is what it is. In other words, A is identical to A. Yet we know that there are times when A is not entirely A, as in quantum physics where position and momentum become uncertain, and particles are only *probably* at any fixed location. Or to use a more familiar example, someone may be cowardly and courageous at the same time.

2. *The Law of Non-contradiction:* A statement and its contradiction cannot both be true. If A is true and B is the opposite of A, then both A and B cannot be true. Yet we know that there are times when A and B are both true and opposite, as in relativistic physics where no single reference frame offers a truer version of reality than any other. Or more commonly, it is possible to love and hate another person at the same time.

3. *The Law of the Excluded Middle:* A statement is either true or false and cannot be both true and false. For example, A must either be true or false and cannot be both simultaneously. Yet we know that there are times when a statement is true and false at the same time. For example, light is both a wave and a particle. Or more simply, the stories we tell about our conflicts with others can be true and false at the same time.

The law of the excluded middle means there can be no *content* that is not right or wrong. Being neutral therefore means judges must at least wait to hear from both sides before deciding whether a claim will be denied or upheld, which is an enormous advance over tyranny, dictatorship, and autocracy.

Having been a judge, and having worked for over forty years as an arbitrator and mediator, I can *feel* the difference when I perform each of these distinct tasks. As a judge or arbitrator, I am equally distant from both sides, personally withdrawn, entirely logical, grounded in facts and the written word, emotionally affectless, neutral, and on neither party's side until the moment of decision, when I choose one side over the other, causing one to win and the other to lose.

As a mediator, I am *all* of these things simultaneously, and none of them. I am personally present and connected to both sides; appreciative of the hidden logic within what may *seem* illogical; grounded in subjective impressions and what is unspoken; emotionally present, empathetic, and available; and on both party's sides at the same time, because I am *not* the one who decides, but am focused instead on helping *them* search for solutions that satisfy both sides' interests.

In any zero-sum contest like litigation, or counting ballots, a minimal pretense of neutrality is important to avoid tipping the scales unfairly toward one side or the other. But even here, complete neutrality is impossible, simply because *everyone* is born

White or Black, male or female, rich or poor, with countless shades in-between, and each of these sets of life experiences and cultures produces subtle biases—*especially* in those who deny they are biased.

If, for example, bias consists of a judge being a close relative of one of the parties and therefore more likely to decide in their favor, are we not equally biased as a White, male, wealthy, urban, Protestant judge, and more likely to decide in favor of someone with similar backgrounds, as opposed to someone who is Black, female, poor, rural, Jew, Catholic, or Muslim?

In the last play in *The Orestia,* a trilogy written by Aeschylus over two millennia ago, Clytemnestra has killed her husband Agamemnon who just returned from the Trojan War. Their son Orestes kills his mother and her lover Aegisthus, and is pursued by the Furies, ancient female goddesses of revenge, to Athens where he begs Athena, goddess of Wisdom, for help. Athena sets up the first jury trial, and when the jury deadlocks, Athena—until now an accepted neutral—decides in favor of Orestes, arguing that she was born of man (Zeus), rather than woman, and her vote will always be with the man, showing how neutrality often masks bias.

More deeply, neutrality is a distanced response to polarized, zero-sum choices: for or against, victory or loss, and *digital,* adversarial, competitive, either/or attitudes toward justice: the desire to see our enemies *smited,* cast out, and punished for what they did. This enables us to reverse our feelings of powerlessness in the presence of conflict through the support of a superior, paternalistic, ostensibly neutral person, like a judge; or a dictatorial, authoritarian, autocratic leader who will not even *pretend* to be neutral, but will seek vengeance for us, even unjustly or immorally, and *call* it justice and morality.

In this way, neutrality serves as a cover, shield, and mask for domination; and with domination comes a subconscious fear of retribution, social disapproval, ostracism, punishment, and revenge;

and with these comes a desire to suppress disagreement, diversity, non-conformity, complexity, chaos, and conflict.

Even in rights-based organizations, neutrality creates a kind of hypocrisy, a sham, an alluring illusion that camouflages privilege, inequality, and systemic bias. This glaring hypocrisy led the novelist Anatole France to satirically describe "the majestic equality of the law, which forbids the rich as well the poor from sleeping under bridges or begging in the streets for bread."

The denial of bias is more profoundly a denial of *subjectivity*, humility, and the universality of human emotional experience; it is an effort to conceal the subtle, *innate* biases that are present in everyone. Scientists have identified over a hundred *cognitive* biases, many demonstrated by Daniel Kahneman and Amos Tversky, and cited by Kahneman in his outstanding book, *Thinking Fast and Slow*. Among these nearly universal biases can be found the following 24, in alphabetical order, with special relevance for conflict resolvers:

1. *Availability heuristic*: The tendency to overestimate the likelihood of events with greater "availability" in memory, which can be influenced by how recent the memories are, or how unusual or emotionally charged they may be.
2. *Anchoring*: The tendency to rely too heavily, or "anchor" on one trait or piece of information when making decisions (often the first piece of information acquired on that subject).
3. *Bandwagon effect*: The tendency to do or believe things because many other people do or believe the same.
4. *Bias blind spot*: The tendency to see oneself as less biased than others, or able to identify more biases in others than in oneself.
5. *Belief revision*: The tendency to revise one's beliefs insufficiently when presented with fresh evidence.

6. *Confirmation bias*: The tendency to search for, interpret, focus on, and remember facts in a way that confirms one's preconceptions.

7. *Continued influence effect:* The tendency to believe previously learned misinformation, even after it has been corrected.

8. *Declinism*: The belief that a society or institution is tending towards decline, and thus view the past favorably and future negatively.

9. *Empathy gap:* The tendency to underestimate the influence or strength of feelings, either in oneself or in others.

10. *Expectation bias*: The tendency to believe facts that agree with expectations, and to disbelieve those that conflict with expectations.

11. *Framing effect:* Drawing different conclusions from the same information, depending on how that information is presented.

12. *Hindsight bias:* Sometimes called the "I-knew-it-all-along" effect, the tendency to see past events as predictable before they happen.

13. *Illusion of control:* The tendency to overestimate one's degree of influence over external events.

14. *Illusory truth effect*: A tendency to believe that a statement is true if it is easier to process, or has been repeated several times.

15. *Loss Aversion:* It's harder to give something up than to acquire it.

16. *Negativity bias*: Greater ability to recall unpleasant memories.

17. *Normalcy bias:* The refusal to plan for, or react to, a disaster that hasn't happened before.

18. *Omission bias:* The tendency to judge harmful actions as worse, or less moral than equally harmful inactions.

19. *Post-purchase rationalization:* The tendency to persuade oneself through rational argument that a purchase was good, or for value.

20. *Pseudo-certainty effect:* The tendency to make risk-averse choices if the expected outcome is positive, but risk-seeking choices to avoid expected negative outcomes.
21. *Reaction devaluation:* Devaluing proposals only because they are believed to have originated with an adversary.
22. *Semmelweis* reflex: The tendency to reject new evidence that contradicts a prevailing paradigm.
23. *Subjective validation:* A perception that something is true if someone holds a belief that demands it be true.
24. *Zero-sum heuristic:* Intuitively judging a situation to be zero-sum, even when it is non-zero-sum.

In conflict resolution, we experience biases not only as preferences or distortions, but as *judgments* regarding those with whom we disagree, or are in conflict. In essence, biases are *boundary violations*, distancing us both from the facts, and the people we most need to listen to. Worse, they freeze people in attitudes and behaviors that do not allow them to grow or evolve or learn.

Neutrality in mediation doesn't guarantee authenticity or transparency, or seek to equalize power imbalances, or help people solve problems — except by blaming others and making it their responsibility to fix them. Neutrality isn't interested in finding out what really matters to people, or why. It doesn't want to hear about their suffering. It doesn't care about repairing or redesigning systems. It wants a quick fix that allows people to pretend that the conflict is over, even when it is chronic and preventable, and destined to return.

What is worse, neutrality is an attempt to erase the *self* — which is impossible because no one can stop being themselves; and to the extent they can, they become inauthentic, emotionally strangled, and as a result, capable of *far worse* injustices. Neutrality then becomes the high point, the culmination, the apex of subtle, uncaring, passive/aggressive behavior, because it *pretends* it is just and unbiased, while it is actually just cold, distanced, heartless, and pretentious.

Consider, for example, the role played by neutrality in couple, relational, and family conflicts, where it is nearly always *experienced* as not caring or being cared for. Neutrality then becomes a *defense* against trauma (including the vicarious trauma of the conflict resolver), an emotional retreat, a compartmentalization of pain, a shield made of apathy and avoidance. It can then fuel patriarchal biases that repress women's emotional skills, pressure men to deny difficult emotional experiences, and belittle mediative efforts to acknowledge and resolve them.

Neutrality saps the soul, weakens the spirit, strips us of joy, and confines us to an isolated little room far from the messy, complex, upsetting chaos of human pain and suffering—and *equally* far from intimacy, caring, emotional intelligence, moral responsibility, open dialogue, genuine reconciliation, and the magic of transformation and transcendence.

NEUTRALITY IN POLITICAL CONFLICTS

Every political conflict offers its' participants a Faustian bargain, allowing them to choose means and tactics that are power-, or rights-, or interest-based — each leading to fundamentally different ends. Every party, advocate, and partisan group must then decide how far it will go in pursuit of what it *knows* for a certainty to be true; what tactics it will be willing to use in order to win; how far it will go to defeat what it believes to be false, injurious, and destructive—even traitorous, heretical, and evil. Salman Rushdie expressed this idea quite simply:

> [A]ny idea is asked two questions. When it is weak: will it compromise? [And]: How do you behave when you win? When your enemies are at your mercy and your power has become absolute: what then?

When powerful opponents view each other as traitorous, evil, or immoral and become *hyper*-polarized, neutrality can be just a step away from the abyss. Yet neutrality can also become complicit and "co-dependent" on power, passing over its' brutal and amoral bullying in silence. In this way, when power-based factions try to undermine democracy and replace it with dictatorship or autocracy, they begin by projecting their *own* biases onto others, and presenting them as unfair attacks by the *other* side—as, for example, when "election deniers" accuse the winning side of stealing an election, in order to justify stealing it themselves.

To be neutral when inhumane acts occur is to embolden and empower dictators, autocrats, fascists, and tyrants; it is to surrender democracy, morality, and fairness to the biased, bullying, and brutish behavior of despotic power. What, for example, did neutrality *mean* during the holocaust? What were its consequences in relation to concentration camps, slave labor, and genocide? What did it consist of when confronted with rape, dehumanization, and cruelty to children? And how is it really any different in other, *far* less egregious conflicts?

Dante, in Canto 3 of the *Inferno* in the *Divine Comedy*, described how people and angels who were neutral in difficult times were to be stung eternally by wasps and gadflies. He concluded: "The darkest places in hell are reserved for those who maintain their neutrality in times of moral crisis." Hundreds of years later, Albert Camus, who served in the Resistance to Nazi occupation during World War II, wrote insightfully in *Reflections on the Guillotine*:

> I do not believe … that there is no responsibility in this world and that we must give way to that modern tendency to absolve everyone, victim and murderer, in the same confusion. Sentimental confusion is made up of cowardice rather than generosity and eventually justifies whatever is worst in this world. If you keep on excusing, you eventually give your blessing to the slave camp, to

cowardly force, to organized executions, to the cynicism of the great political monsters; you finally hand over your brothers.

Later still, Michel Foucault described the need to look beneath the appearance and claims of neutrality, especially in political conflicts, and publicly reveal the potential for violence that is poorly concealed beneath it:

> The real political task in a society such as ours is to criticize the working of institutions which appear to be both neutral and independent; to criticize them in such a manner that the political violence which has always exercised itself obscurely through them will be unmasked, so that one can fight them.

THE LIMITATIONS OF NEUTRALITY

What, then, are the most common limitations, impacts, and outcomes of neutrality in mediation? Here are a few, drawn from my experience resolving thousands of primarily small- and mid-scale disputes:

- An inability to be genuinely, personally, and completely present.
- An inability to experience real empathy for the parties; a kind of "emotional Botox" that turns intense, subjective, emotional experiences into watered-down, objective, factual issues.
- A view of "negative emotions" as dangerous, counter-productive, irrational, distractions, a sign of instability or insanity, and an inability to turn them in the direction of problem-solving.
- A patriarchal form of control based on emotional discounting, denial, suppression, and hostility to emotional intelligence.

- A lack of skill at being able to be in the presence, at the center, and in the midst of conflict, because it feels alien and uncontrollable.
- A difficulty appreciating the cultural lenses through which the parties and the mediator detect and assign meaning, and as a result, an inability to draw them into useful conversation or dialogue.

These are just a few out of many. What, then, is the alternative? They are several, and most are multi-dimensional. First, it is clear that mediators can readily agree not to benefit from the outcome of their mediations. Second, they can agree not to harbor grudges or biases. Third, they can be more aware of their biases. Fourth, they can suspend their judgments, and just be curious. Fifth, they can, as Fisher and Ury advise in *Getting to Yes*, separate the person from the problem, be soft on the person, and hard on the problem. Sixth, they can be what I call *omni-partial*, or equally biased in favor of both *people* at the same time, while not agreeing with their assertions or requests. In these ways, mediators can defuse people's defensiveness and hostility, and turn them in the direction of collaboration, consensus building, and problem-solving. In *Mediating Dangerously*, I wrote:

> In *dangerous* mediation, we are asked to surrender the illusion of separation between ourselves from others, to be "omni-partial" and speak, listen, and behave as though we actually were on both sides of the dispute. We are asked to be ourselves and become one with our opponents; to believe in the possibility of transformational change, and allow everyone to choose; to accept people as they are, and ask them to behave differently toward each other; to be ourselves, and revolutionize our way of being.

Omni-partiality represents a shift from the digital, zero-sum view that conflicts are *exclusively* binary, permitting only "either/or" choices—not just by creating a neutral "no man's land" between the parties, but offering a *third* option (what William Ury calls "the third side,") that is a step toward a more advanced *analog* view of conflict that identifies an *infinite* number of gradations between opposites, all of them in constant flux, allowing for creative, personalized, non-zero-sum, *"both/and"* options, greater subtlety, and increased likelihood of change.

Together, these methods enable us to discover what is deeper, more profound, and central in any conflict, what breathed life into it, what it *means* to each of the parties — and in this way, lead us to its *actual* source–not in the cupidity or evil of the other side, but in a one-sided understanding of the problem, or a lack of skill at being able to invite "opponents" into collaborative problem-solving conversations that acknowledge and seek to satisfy both sides human interests.

There are at least three hidden difficulties. First, to give up both neutrality *and* bias, it is necessary to give up all efforts to gain power over and against others; all desire to dominate, make decisions unilaterally or autocratically, and control the decisions and choices that belong to others; all wishes to enjoy the privileges that flow from unequal status, wealth, and power; all desire to find a superior place in the pecking order; all longing for triumph, revenge, and vindication.

Second, it is necessary to listen empathetically to *everyone*, to acknowledge their emotions, surface their interests, negotiate collaboratively, and reach consensus on what works best for each person, while not necessarily agreeing with what they say, do, request, or demand. None of these, of course, is easy, and neutrality seems far easier because it means less chaos, confusion, and conflict; little or no responsibility; greater safety; not having to give up our baser instincts, the possibility of acquiring more "perks," and climbing the pecking order over the backs of others. As Gore Vidal humorously quipped, "It is not enough that I succeed, others must fail."

Third, in doing so, it is helpful to try to understand and practice the Buddhist idea of "non-attachment," which can lead to a kind of neutral, uncaring isolation from others, yet it's true goal is to discover joy, loving-kindness, "skillful means," and an omni-partial-like capacity for openness, awareness, and caring for others.

Within Buddhism, the "Four Noble Truths" describe the source of suffering and its' solution through non-attachment, leading directly to the "Eight–fold Path." This asserts that the way out of attachment is not indifference, but the practice of "skillful means," or what conflict resolvers might describe as techniques for responding to conflict and the suffering it causes by neither resisting nor clinging to it, but seeking to transform and transcend it. [See discussion in Chapter 3.]

When we move in this direction, we *automatically* elicit the magic that lies hidden within each conflict, a magic that is waiting to be discovered and released; a magic that lies hidden in metaphor and the deeper meanings of conflict that are obscured by neutrality, distance, and attachment to outcomes. And as William Shakespeare rhetorically asked in *Macbeth:*

> *Who can be wise, amaz'd, temp'rate, and furious,*
> *Loyal, and neutral, in a moment? No man.*

TWO

The Magic in Mediation

HOW TO FIND, FEED, AND FOMENT IT

A layman will no doubt find it hard to understand how pathological disorders of the body can be eliminated by 'mere' words. He will feel that he is being asked to believe in magic. And he will not be so very wrong, for the words that we use in our everyday speech are nothing other than watered-down magic.

Sigmund Freud

The world is full of magic things, patiently waiting for our senses to grow sharper.

William Butler Yeats

There are only two ways to live your life: One is as though nothing is a miracle. The other is as though everything is a miracle. I believe in the latter.

Albert Einstein

ANYONE WHO HAS MEDIATED EVEN A FEW DISPUTES IS LIKELY TO HAVE experienced the magic in mediation, and would very much like to do so again. But if asked where this magic came from, how it happened, what it consisted of, and how they might replicate it, most would be hard pressed to answer.

These unanswered questions, of course, form part of what makes any experience feel magical. But they are also the beginning of all arts and sciences. If we want to explore the magic in mediation more deeply, or explain the "fuzzy logic" that turns conflict into resolution, or consciously replicate these moving experiences, we need to unfold, unpack, dissect, and demystify the "miracles" of resolution we experience in mediation, hopefully without cancelling, mangling, or eviscerating them in the process.

By magic, I do not mean illusion, trickery, sleight-of-hand, or superstition, but the very real, unpredictable metamorphosis of impasse into resolution. Nor do I mean fantasy, mysticism, or "spooky action at a distance," but real laws of motion that are subtle, camouflaged, largely unexamined, and *implicit* in the nature of conflict and the methodology of resolution.

By magic, I *do* mean something inexact, probabilistic, meaningful, and poetic; something with hidden variables, something so sensitively dependent on changing conditions that it can quickly turn chaotic, unpredictable, and irreplicable. In whatever ways we define magic, it requires a mixture of just the right ingredients, in just the right way, at just the right time, in just the right circumstances, with just the right people, in just the right mood, and it can disappear without warning when these are not in exactly the right ratio.

In mediation, these ingredients are often subtle, complex, hidden, camouflaged, ignored, multi-dimensional, intensely emotional, and constantly changing, so that the very same techniques that result in agreement at one moment may end in impasse just moments later. A single word or gesture, if handled correctly, can lead to a breakthrough, or if not, can trigger aggression, aggravate tensions, prompt distrust and denial, and end in intractability.

For this reason, *nothing* in conflict resolution works always, everywhere, or for everyone–and equally for this reason, *everything* in mediation is imbued with magical possibilities. What we therefore need to do, is work together to figure out what it consists of, where it comes from, how to release it, and gradually get better at finding, feeding, and fomenting it.

SOME SOURCES OF MAGIC IN MEDIATION

In reflecting on the sources of what we regard as magical, mystifying, or miraculous in mediation, we want to ask: "What is it *specifically* that gives rise to magic in mediation?" And as a follow-up question: "What can we *do* as mediators to invite this magic into ordinary conflict conversations?"

Based on my experience mediating many disputes over more than four decades, I believe it is possible for *all* mediators to identify the potential causes, explanations, and "sources" of magic that are *unique* to each dispute, each set of parties, and each *mediator*. As a consequence, there are *hundreds* if not thousands of potential sources of magic in every conflict. Here is my personal (somewhat overlapping) top 15 list, described in greater detail below:

1. A shift in awareness, attitude, emotion, thought, or intention.
2. A fresh insight, realization, unanswered question, or imaginative leap.
3. An added dimension, duality, or degree of freedom.
4. A profound improvement in process, relationship, shape, or form — a "transformation."
5. A new, innovative, or advanced technology.
6. A higher order technique, skill, aptitude, or capacity.
7. An emergent phenomenon, arising out of chaos or complexity.

8. A new symmetry, synthesis, or combination of existing ingredients.
9. A recognition of hidden sources, connections, or meanings.
10. An evolution or adaptation to new environmental conditions.
11. A revolution, paradigm shift, systemic change, or phase transition.
12. A re-discovery of integration, balance, poise, authenticity, integrity, or center.
13. A completion, transcendence, rising above, or deep learning.
14. An increase in love, caring, or kindness.
15. A metamorphosis of experience and heart-knowledge into wisdom.

Each of these sources can be considered *scientifically*, to identify more precisely how it operates; and *artistically*, to apply it creatively to an immense variety of conflicts between diverse individuals in unique circumstances, under rapidly changing conditions, in an effort to achieve something that is not only different, but *unimaginable* moments before it occurs. This can be done in many ordinary ways, even before considering these 15 methods.

If we define conflict as a state of being stuck, or at impasse, then by definition, it is nearly impossible for anyone *inside* a conflict to imagine how it might be possible to become unstuck, and outside it. To them, the conflict *feels* intractable, confining, immobile, and hopeless, leading those in its frozen grip to slip into frustration, aggravation, escalating hostility, and negative thinking–not just with regard to each other, but *themselves* for being stuck — leading them to surrender whatever hope they may have had of ever becoming unstuck.

The very first "ordinary miracle" or source of magic that takes place in many conflicts is the resurrection of hope that is triggered by mediation itself. Simply the *arrival* of the mediator—i.e., someone who is *outside* the conflict and therefore able to escape its hypnotic, circular, adversarial, hopeless assumptions; yet is also *inside* the conflict, and therefore able to use listening, empathy, reframing, and similar skills to unravel its deeper causes; and simultaneously *around* the conflict, and therefore able to see and consider the subtle effects of contexts, systems, cultures, histories, biases, environments, and other sources of conflict that might pass unnoticed because they are so pervasive, disguised, or taken for granted.

A second "ordinary" miracle in mediation can occur when the parties recognize that their conflict is just a place where they are stuck arguing over the same issues — perhaps because they were emotionally triggered by each other's defensive or adversarial actions; or lacked the skills they needed to respond successfully to each other's behaviors; or there were two or more truths and they each assumed there was only one, which was theirs.

A mediator may then evoke a third, deeper, more subtle, and simple yet profound "ordinary" miracle by helping each person calm their emotions, or modeling mediative skills, or drawing their disparate truths into conversation or dialogue with each other. A mediator can help them explore the nuances and subtleties of their respective experiences; surface their deeper interests; search for syntheses and creative combinations; validate and empower their diversity and dissent; ask them questions; or suggest novel approaches and collaborative solutions.

Even in the most intractable and emotionally intense conflicts, a mediator can sometimes deepen this miracle in a fourth way by revealing — perhaps through questions, facilitated dialogues, or practical proposals for resolution — how their conflict comes from caring, and might be transformed into opportunities for learning, growth, and improvement; openings into insight, awareness, and empathy; or pathways to wisdom, heart-knowledge, and transcendence.

Beyond these "ordinary" miracles in mediation, the 15 sources of magic identified above offer ways we can understand *how* magical outcomes occur; bring to the surface all the unspoken, unexplored, underlying elements, components, and characteristics that invisibly define the conflict; and shift the ways the parties think, feel, and respond to the issues, each other, and *themselves*, that keep them locked in conflict, orbiting around each other, and unable to escape. For example:

1. A shift in awareness, attitude, emotion, thought, or intention.

People in conflict often ascribe very different meanings to the same events, communications, and behaviors, based both on their conflict-driven perceptions and experiences, and the fluctuating state of their awareness, attitudes, emotions, thoughts, and intentions. Hence, any significant shift in either party's awareness, attitudes, emotions, thoughts, and intentions can fundamentally alter the *form* of their conflict — either by triggering, sustaining, or escalating it; or magically unlocking and transcending it at its hidden source.

While much of our focus as mediators is on the substantive *factual* issues that divide people, most of what transpires in conflict is a consequence of the parties' core *attitudes*, emotions, and intentions. If their attitudes, emotions, and intentions are negative and hostile, their intransigence and resistance will make the issues appear more important and less amenable to solution than they actually are; whereas if they are positive and constructive, the issues may cease being obstacles and instead become gateways to synergistic, higher order outcomes.

As mediators, we want to explore the means and methods we might use to reach conflicted parties–not merely at the relatively superficial level of the issues they are fighting over — but at the far deeper level of the *meanings* they attach to their issues; that is, at the level of their *choice* of a state of awareness, attitude, emotion, thought, or intention in relation to their conflict. These choices can be viewed as options leading to fundamentally different outcomes, allowing mediators to *design* interventions around what I describe as "pivot points," or locations where conversations and conflicts become "unstable," and can rapidly shift and turn.

There are countless places where conflicts can pivot, change direction, and assume fundamentally different forms. In ordinary mediations, it is possible to find pivot points that take the form of "dangerous" questions that can redirect a party's focus from the misdeeds of their opponent to *themselves*; to what they might have done better; or from what happened in the past to what they want to happen in the present or future; or from accusatory stories to underlying emotions; then from emotions to interests, from interests to creative problem-solving, and from problem-solving to collaborative negotiations.

The real difficulty lies, first, in identifying the "work" needed to complete each task in navigating our way through the conflict; second, in knowing when that work is done; and third, in designing *transitional* questions that help draw attention away from the past and the work that is now complete, and toward the next task that is waiting to be finished, and do so in the right order.

In the process, it is important to identify the stages, steps, phases, decision-gates, and boxes that need to be checked in order to move through each step in the process; and to recognize that if we try to move from one step to the next without completing the initial work, we are likely to be drawn back to these earlier tasks until we complete them.

For example, people in conflict commonly interlace their communications with negative, indirect, emotionally laden accusations, insults, exaggerations, and "power words;" or metaphors; or with gestures, body language, signs, and signals that indicate: first, that they are experiencing intense negative emotions; and second, that they do not feel entirely comfortable or skillful expressing them directly or constructively to the other person.

These uncommunicated, indirect, negative emotions are then sublimated, distilled, distorted, stifled, and repressed, yet each leaves tiny traces, even in the words and phrases, tones of voice, body language, subtle signs and semiotic indicators, that *indirectly* point to their hidden meanings. Anna Freud, in *The Ego and the Mechanisms of Defense,* identified several subconscious ways people defend themselves and their egos against unresolved conflicts, including, for example:

- *Repression,* which seeks to suppress conflict by hiding it under a rug
- *Denial,* which refuses to accept reality and blocks external events or experiences from becoming conscious
- *Projection,* which shifts our own unacceptable or conflicted thoughts, feelings, or motives onto others, and accusing them of doing what we were doing
- *Internalization,* which turns angry or humiliating feelings inward
- *Reaction-formation,* which uses exaggerated or compulsive behavior to oppose or conceal repressed feelings, sometimes by expressing the exact opposite of what we feel
- *Sublimation,* which channels aggressive impulses by acting them out in socially acceptable ways
- *Regression,* which leads us to move backwards in psychological time when faced with stress or conflict
- *Displacement,* which seeks to satisfy an emotion or impulse like aggression by re-directing it to a relatively powerless substitute person, symbol, or object
- *Rationalization,* which distorts facts or feelings to make them appear ordinary, justifiable, or less threatening
- *Divorcing ideas from feelings,* which uses logical arguments to divert attention from sensitive emotional issues and protect wounded feelings
- *Identification with the aggressor,* which leads victims to imitate their perpetrators and seek to overcome their feelings of

powerlessness or shame and avoid harm by acting
aggressively against others

Beneath these distrustful, stifled, distorted emotional defenses lie
repressed *desires* for open, trusting, wholehearted, honest
communications; unspoken requests for respect, recognition, and
acknowledgement; hopes for forgiveness; and cries for help in reorienting the conversation to constructive, collaborative efforts to
satisfy mutual interests. Together, these can be interpreted by
mediators as unspoken *invitations* and *implicit permissions* to
intervene, dig deeper, and get their communications and
relationships back on track. As mediators, we may, for instance, ask
questions that make the parties' emotional states explicit ("How
does this conversation feel to you?" "What could the other person
say or do to make it feel more constructive?"). Or we may invite
people to express their deeper desires ("What words would you use
to describe the kind of relationship or communication you *most*
want to have with each other?" "What is one thing you would like
him to acknowledge or thank you for?" "Are you willing to do that
right now?"). Or we may identify ways people can shift their conflict
dynamics ("Is this conversation working?" "What is one thing she
could do or say that would make it work better for you?" "Are you
willing to do that right now?"). Any of these interventions or
questions, and thousands like them, can create significant shifts in
the parties' awareness, attitudes, emotions, thoughts, and intentions,
and in doing so, fundamentally transform the dynamics between
them, resolve the issues that are invisibly driving their dispute, and
alter the course of the conflict, as though by magic. As Willa Cather
nicely put it, "Where there is great love there are always miracles."

2. A fresh insight, realization, unanswered question, or imaginative leap.

Mediators in every conflict can design and ask difficult, dangerous,
complex, *paradoxical* questions that may elicit fresh insights or
realizations in the minds of the parties; or surface and address

unasked or unanswered question; or trigger an imaginative leap in a brand-new direction, and unlock the conflict in unanticipated, unpredictable ways. There are two primary reasons for asking questions in mediation: first, to find answers; and second, to reveal deeper questions, which may themselves be partly answers, and lead to still deeper questions and answers–questions not merely about what the parties think and feel, but who they *are*, or want to be; questions that they answer with their *lives*, as described in the opening quotation to this chapter by the brilliant Hungarian novelist, Sandor Marai. In my experience, there are two deep, transformational goals in conflict resolution that can be advanced by asking deep, poignant, and profound questions:

1. Helping people gain *insight* into the sources of their conflict and the reasons they are stuck, thereby revealing a path, or multiple paths, forward; and

2. Aid people in gaining *perspective* on themselves, their opponents, and their issues, thereby strengthening their empathy and humility, recalibrating their attitudes and intentions, surfacing their unsatisfied interests, and redefining their problem–not as a "you," or a "them," but as an "it," an "I," or a "we."

In conflict resolution, insight and perspective are corollaries of awareness and mindfulness — in other words, we can narrow the parties' *forms* of attention, so they focus on a point, like a spotlight; or broaden them so they encompass a field, like a floodlight. These may lead to questions that illuminate unnoticed details and patterns; or suggest alternative ways of thinking and acting; or reveal hidden truths; or help the parties discover fresh ways forward. [For more detail and examples, see Chapter 4.]

3. An added dimension, duality, or degree of freedom

In mathematics and physics, there are two commonly recognized definitions of a dimension: first, how many pieces of information are required to identify where something is located; and second, how many *degrees of freedom*, or discrete, "orthogonal," right-angle directions are available for something to move in. With zero dimensions, no information is required, and no movement is possible. In one dimension, corresponding to a line, a single number describes location, and it is possible to move only back and forth, representing a single degree of freedom. In two dimensions, corresponding to a plane, two parameters are needed to describe a location, and it is now possible to move sideways as well, and so on.

If we can imagine, as novelist Edwin Abbott did in *Flatland*, beings living on a two-dimensional plane who are unable to detect depth, a three-dimensional coffee cup placed on the plane will appear simply as a circle, and no one will be able to say what is inside it. But for a three dimensional being, it will be easy to see inside the cup, and this ability will appear magical to anyone restricted to a lower dimension.

If we imagine conflicts as *at least* three dimensional, and the perspectives of the parties as confined to one- or two-dimensions on the "either/or" plane of their adversarial, zero-sum hostility, any mediator who introduces a three-dimensional perspective that allows them to see and explore the *depth* of their conflict will appear magical to someone who can only experience it in two dimensions.

How, then, can mediators increase the number of dimensions in dispute resolution? The physical or mathematical answer is by taking a one-dimensional line and *dragging* it 90 degrees in a brand-new direction to create a plane, then dragging a plane 90 degrees in a brand-new, right angle direction to create a cube. The same orthogonal operation will transform a cube into a hypercube, etc., mathematically *ad infinitum*, with significant consequences for mediation.

If we adopt dimensionality as a metaphor in dispute resolution, each time we drag a conflict conversation 90 degrees in a brand-new direction, we introduce an additional degree of freedom — i.e., a new set of insights, understandings, orientations, processes, interventions, forms of participation, outcomes, and limits or constraints on what it is possible to achieve — as in the following diagram:

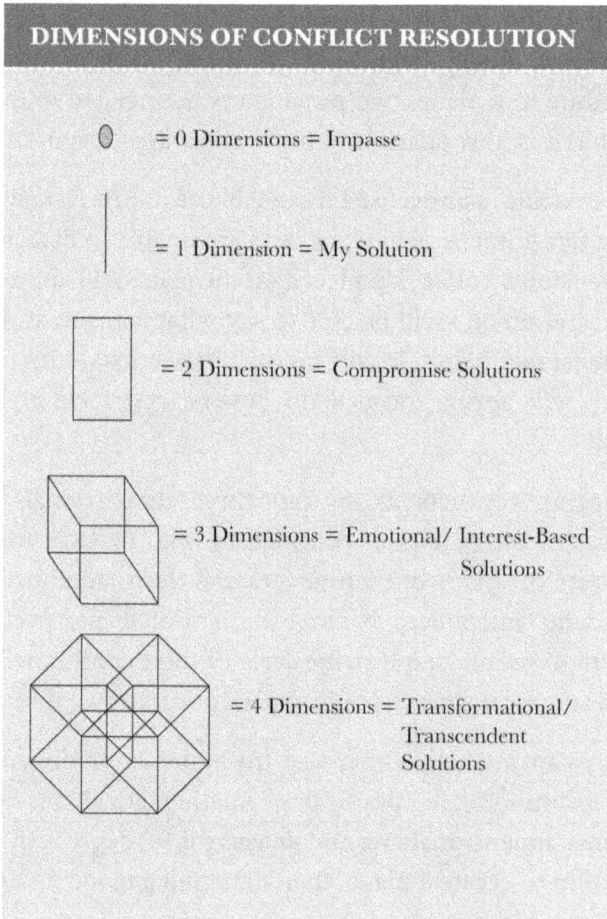

DIMENSIONS OF CONFLICT RESOLUTION

= 0 Dimensions = Impasse

= 1 Dimension = My Solution

= 2 Dimensions = Compromise Solutions

= 3 Dimensions = Emotional/ Interest-Based Solutions

= 4 Dimensions = Transformational/ Transcendent Solutions

Each additional dimension allows us to understand conflict in more complex and multi-faceted ways, yet for this reason, may also take us longer to address and require higher orders of skill to resolve, while revealing far more information and achieving deeper and more lasting outcomes than would be possible, describable, or even *imaginable* at lower dimensions.

Mediators can move the parties' conversations and interactions from lower to higher dimensions, for example, by asking deeper questions, designing exploratory dialogues, and initiating interest-based processes that *invite* them into conversations and relationships that drag them at a 90-degree angle *away* from the ones they are currently experiencing, in which they feel entirely stuck. If conflict is approached one-dimensionally, as though there were only a single solution, as where a dictator, autocrat, patriarch, or authoritarian figure decides, a mediator might introduce a two-dimensional element, as in litigated cases or judicial settlements where there are two claims, allowing a judge to suggest a compromise solution; or a mediator to elicit criteria for a successful outcome; or broaden the issues; or "expand the pie;" or search for "trade-offs." A mediator might then introduce a three-dimensional element, for example, by asking questions that elicit interests; or facilitating emotionally intelligent conversations; or acknowledging that there may be multiple truths; or supporting diversity in perspectives, inviting dissent, and searching for creative options. [For more on dimensionality in mediation, see Chapter 6.]

Each new dimension then introduces or encourages a new set of attitudes, questions, interventions, relations, and processes that allow conflicts to be experienced in fresh ways, processed with new techniques, and resolved at deeper and more fundamental levels. In computing, this has led to "hyper-dimensional vectors," or "hyper-vectors," that can closely *approximate* a right angle, with algorithms for expanding them. It may then perhaps be true for mediation, as the brilliant Bernard Riemann proved for mathematics, that the number of dimensions, and hence opportunities for magic, is *infinite*.

4. A profound improvement in process, relationship, shape, or form — i.e., a "transformation."

Without regard to the specific content, parties, or issues in dispute, mediators can improve the *processes* of communication, problem-solving, and decision-making by, for example, making them more inclusive, respectful, and collaborative. We can strengthen *relationships* by making them more open, trusting, and caring. We can alter the *shape* of organizational structures by making them less hierarchical, bureaucratic, and power-driven. We can modify the *form* of interactions by making them more transparent, egalitarian, and honest. Each of these can change the form, or "*transform*" conflicts, without directly resolving the factual or substantive issues over which people are arguing.

Conflicts successfully focus our energy and attention on what our opponents are saying or doing that might harm us, while leaving us less focused and aware of how we might instead move *laterally*, creatively, and strategically to alter the processes, relationships, shapes, and forms of our interactions. Yet each of these moves subtly encodes and recapitulates the *expression* of our conflicts, allowing us to shift the *ways* we argue by bringing our focus and attention to bear—not on *what* we are doing and saying, but *how* and *why* we are doing and saying it, and what we might do and say instead.

It is possible, for instance, for mediators to ask people to engage in a process I call "conflict mapping," in which they chart the history of their dispute, then identify opportunities they may have missed, or ways of reaching different outcomes. Conflict mapping is a process people can use to better understand *exactly* how and where and why they got stuck, and can be done in four distinct ways:

1. Jointly with their opponent(s) — especially in marital, family, and relational conflicts
2. Collaboratively with teams and groups — especially in workplace, organizational, social, political, and public policy conflicts
3. Separately with each party — especially in caucuses and internal emotional disputes

4. Jointly with a conflict coach-especially where individuals want to gain insight into the places where they got stuck, or acquire additional skills in handling them

The conflict mapping process begins with each person writing a timeline showing what s/he knows about how the conflict started, identifying each new event or experience moment by moment, then expanding, amending, and supplementing the map together, in increasing detail. A mediator might ask the parties, for example, to list, either separately or together:

- Each point where something was said or done that impacted the conflict, either positively or negatively
- Each point where something was *not* said or done, but could or should have been, that might have stopped the conflict or made it easier to handle
- What the response of the other party was, and what was added or changed in the conflict, process, or relationship as a result
- What it would have cost each person to say or not say it, do or not do it; how long it would have taken; and how important it would have been to say or not say, do or not do it
- What it would have meant to each person in the relationship, in personal satisfaction and morale, for it to have been said or not said, done or not done
- What each party might have said or done *instead* that could have resolved the dispute, or improved their process and relationship

On the following page is an example of an "initial" conflict map, followed by a jointly "modified" map with sample responses and reflections.

INITIAL CONFLICT MAP EXAMPLE

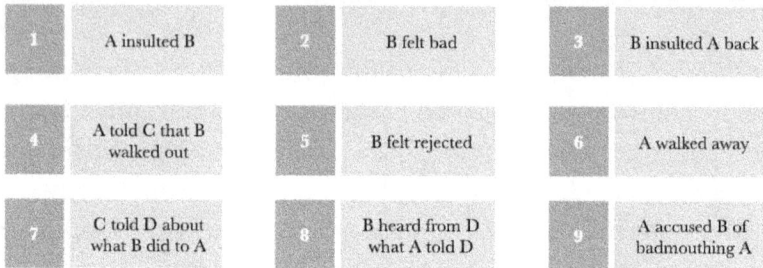

1	A insulted B	2	B felt bad	3	B insulted A back
4	A told C that B walked out	5	B felt rejected	6	A walked away
7	C told D about what B did to A	8	B heard from D what A told D	9	A accused B of badmouthing A

MODIFIED CONFLICT MAP EXAMPLE

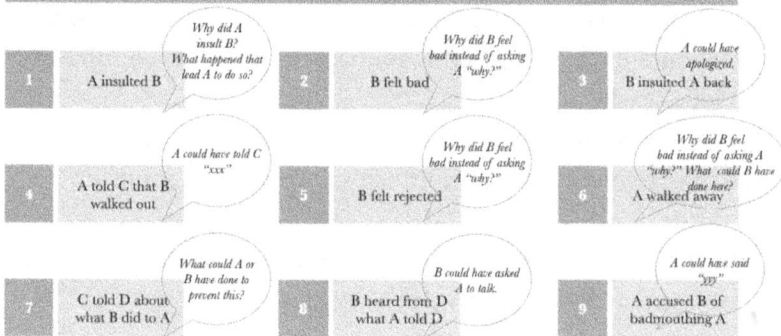

1	A insulted B *(Why did A insult B? What happened that lead A to do so?)*	2	B felt bad *(Why did B feel bad instead of asking A "why?")*	3	B insulted A back *(A could have apologized.)*
4	A told C that B walked out *(A could have told C "xxx")*	5	B felt rejected *(Why did B feel bad instead of asking A "why?")*	6	A walked away *(Why did B feel bad instead of asking A "why?" What could B have done here?)*
7	C told D about what B did to A *(What could A or B have done to prevent this?)*	8	B heard from D what A told D *(B could have asked A to talk.)*	9	A accused B of badmouthing A *(A could have said "yyy.")*

Mediators can map or dissect the conflict, then perform micro-surgery on each of its separate parts, then create fundamental shifts by drawing the attention of the parties to their overall relationship. We might ask each person, for example:

- "What words would you use to describe the kind of relationship or map you want to create?"
- "Do either of you disagree with any of those words?"

People rarely do, but if they do, try to find an acceptable substitute. Then, "What might you do to begin living up to those words?"

Alternatively, we can ask them to reverse roles, or brainstorm ways of improving their relationship, or sit next to (as opposed to across from) each other, or use "I" rather than "you" statements, or tell personal stories that might help the other person understand why this issue is so important to you, or other options to shift the antagonistic *form* of the conflict, while preserving the collaborative *content* of their communications and interactions.

5. A new, innovative, or advanced technology.

Science fiction writer Arthur C. Clarke observed that "Any sufficiently advanced technology is indistinguishable from magic." Each new, innovative, and advanced technology gives rise to fresh forms of conflict; and equally, though usually belatedly, to innovative approaches to resolution. Computers, the internet, artificial intelligence, and smart phones, like the telegraph, radio, and television before them, fundamentally transform the ways we communicate, relate, and interact with each other, exposing cracks and fault lines that give rise to unique forms of conflict requiring fresh new skills to resolve.

For many people, mediation simply *seems* magical simply because they have not examined it closely or deeply enough, or considered in detail how it actually works. Moreover, newer, innovative, and more advanced ways of experiencing, understanding, and responding to conflict are constantly being born, sometimes taking the form of generational conflicts that begin by taking for granted what previous generations struggled to create, understand, or implement.

Many of the conflicts we experience today, for example, over racism, sexual harassment, homophobia, and similar biases, reflect changes in the way we understand, communicate, interact, and relate to each other that have advanced unevenly, leaving those who grew up with more rigid or antiquated rules either unable or unwilling to adopt newer, more flexible ones. This underlying resistance to change often takes a political form, resulting in a learning or a control orientation, generating attitudes either of openness or hostility toward others, and spilling over into unrelated areas of change.

In promoting advanced, seemingly magical technologies, it is essential to consider potential underlying sources of resistance, which may include finding out what people fear will be lost through the change process that is important to them, and finding ways of recapturing it–perhaps by initiating more intimate conversations, or deeper dialogues that strengthen empathy, clarify intentions, reduce biases; and strengthen people's skills in improving them.

All new, innovative, and advanced technologies tend to divide people by their facility with recently acquired skills or capacities, increasing the success and competency of a few — and often their hubris and egotism as well — and decreasing the trust and self-confidence of others, generating chronic conflicts. The resulting "digital divide" aggravates the historical division of societies into "haves" and "have-nots," and increases social, economic, political, and ecological polarization.

In a similar way, conflict resolution technologies are also unevenly distributed, and unavailable to those most in need. Yet our global experience, for example, in prison mediation programs, training former child soldiers in refugee camps, inviting immigrants and citizens into dialogues, problem-solving conversations, and similar examples, can be profoundly transformational. And these higher order techniques, skills, and capacities are often regarded as magical by those who have yet to understand or develop them.

6. A higher order technique, skill, aptitude, or capacity.

Each new, higher order challenge or conflict we face in life requires a unique set of techniques, skills, aptitudes, and capacities to master or overcome it, and each higher order challenge requires higher order responses to reach resolution. The skills required to shift from crawling to walking to track and field competitions are not merely additive, but multiplicative, and at times, exponential.

Similarly, the transition from fighting and warfare to ceasefire and de-escalation, then adversarial negotiation, conciliation, and compromise; then collaborative negotiation, consensus building, emotional intelligence, and satisfaction of interests; then full resolution, forgiveness, and reconciliation; then restorative justice, prevention, and systems design, requires not just more of the same lower order skills, but innovative, complex, subtle, emergent, higher order skills and capacities, each resting on the shoulders of the ones beneath.

Thus, if we think of the orders of skill required for conflict resolution and social problem-solving as evolving from lowest to highest, we can define, group, and elaborate them in traditional conflict resolution terms, yielding 10 successive orders of magnitude in skill building, as follows:

1. *Skills in Amassing and Exercising Power*: These require proficiency in giving orders or obeying them without question. They encourage aggression, conformity, and deference. They are fear-based, directive, and oriented to action, and frequently result in win/lose outcomes, hierarchies of domination, suppression, and subordination, leading to apathy, cynicism, resistance, and revolt.

2. *Skills in Securing and Defending Rights*: These require proficiency in rhetoric, advocacy, and adversarial negotiation. They encourage competition, are anger-based, focused on rules, oriented to facts and issues, and often result in litigated outcomes that are win/lose or lose/lose, and negotiated agreements based on compromise, leading to lingering dissatisfaction, resentment, and repeated conflicts.

3. *Skills in Listening and Reframing Stories and Narratives*: These require proficiency in curiosity, openness, and

understanding the language of conflict and the narrative structure of conflict stories. They encourage people to listen to each other, release their hostile judgments and false expectations, and respect each other's' cultures and meanings, leading to de-escalation and conciliation.

4. *Skills in Facilitating Dialogues and Asking Questions*: These require proficiency in drawing adversaries into communication, building trust, supporting diversity, learning from dissent, designing questions, building consensus, and facilitating dialogues. They encourage people to agree to meet and talk in spite of their distrust, fear, grief, and anger, leading to empathy building, mutual understanding, problem-solving, and collaborative negotiation.

5. *Skills in Surfacing and Satisfying Interests:* These require proficiency in asking open-ended questions, separating people from problems, and eliciting appropriate criteria. They encourage surfacing and recognizing hidden issues, focusing on underlying needs and desires, interest-based bargaining, and improving relationships, leading to deeper satisfaction and resolutions that are often transformative and win/win.

6. *Skills in Acknowledging and Processing Emotions:* These require proficiency in emotional insight, intelligence, and communication. They encourage eliciting, acknowledging, and constructively expressing emotions, are feelings-based, focused on stories, experiences, and subjective truths, and frequently result in empathy and compassion. They are not about winning or losing, leading to emotional intelligence, deeper resolutions, and closure.

7. *Skills in Letting Go and Forgiveness:* These require proficiency in insight, mindfulness, and awareness. They encourage release from the past, and are energy-based, spiritual, and focused on non-attachment. They frequently result in release, completion, and closure, seek victory over

ourselves, rather than others, and lead to the end of continuing enmity and suffering.

8. *Skills in Open-Heartedness and Reconciliation:* These require proficiency in loving-kindness, integrity, recreating trust, and relationship building. They encourage caring and wisdom, are ethical, heart-based, focused on kindness and restorative justice, and oriented to being, enjoyment, and values. They frequently result in intimacy, heart connection, learning, and transcendence. They are beyond winning and losing, and lead to happiness and joy.

9. *Skills in Designing and Changing Systems:* These require proficiency in transforming diversity, dissent, ambiguity, and complexity into systemic change. They encourage systems thinking, identify the sources of chronic conflict, and design preventative solutions. They are systems-based, focused on problem-solving, oriented to culture and environment, and often result in innovation, revitalization, and renewal, leading to fewer chronic conflicts.

10. *Skills in Continuous Learning, Reflective Practice, and Openness to Transformation and Transcendence:* These require proficiency in discovery, invention, openness to feedback, self-reflection, honesty, and willingness to change. They encourage normalizing, analyzing, and thinking creatively about errors, mistakes, and failures, as well as successes, both alone and with others, leading to personal growth, evolution, improved skills, and wisdom.

Each of these rough descriptions of techniques, aptitudes, and capacities may, in the right circumstances, enable us to unlock conflicts at one level, yet become ineffective when we try to apply them to deeper or more complex conflicts, requiring us to discover higher order methods that cannot be fully imagined or predicted from a lower order perspective, where the *idea* that anything could release us from conflict seems magical.

While lower order skills are rarely successful in solving higher order problems, higher order skills can create transformational outcomes in addressing lower order issues without great difficulty. Once people become accomplished at higher order skills, they are able to graduate and evolve to confront higher order conflicts that do not arise until we are ready to start learning the higher order skills needed to solve them.

7. An emergent phenomenon, arising out of chaos or complexity.

We commonly think of conflicts as negative, complex, chaotic, and lacking any kind of logic or order, yet in nature, we routinely find what scientists call "deterministic" chaos, in which increasing complexity and crises suddenly give rise to some new, unexpected, "emergent" form of order.

There is nothing, for example, that can be described as "wet" in either hydrogen or oxygen, of even single molecules of H2O, yet when added in the right ratios, droplets of liquid water are formed. And these droplets, as they combine and interact, can take the unexpected, emergent form not only of wetness, but of waves, whirlpools, waterfalls, and rainbows, as if by magic.

Complexity and chaos are equally common in human conflicts, also giving rise to unexpected, emergent phenomena and higher forms of order. These higher forms of order may likewise seem mystical or magical to those trapped in conflict, or regarding it from a distance, or from a lower order perspective, yet it is possible for mediators to *elicit* these emergent forms of order, which are only later recognized as nascent paths to higher order resolutions.

An initial step in creating these outcomes is for conflict resolvers to simply follow the chaos and complexity back to their points of origin in the subterranean world that the parties subconsciously repressed, or ignored, or disguised, including their unacknowledged emotions, unspoken ideas, unarticulated wishes, repressed needs and desires, camouflaged requests, and hidden underlying interests.

A second step is to design, organize, and facilitate conversations over highly charged issues, in which mediators invite these separate subterranean worlds to arise and speak to each other, to listen empathetically, to respond not only to what is spoken, but what is unspoken, yet meant or felt; and to help the parties rephrase, reframe, and repurpose their communications so they can be heard at a deeper level, allowing them to discover nascent collaborative solutions that satisfy both sides needs and interests.

A third step is to assist each person to expand and strengthen the *quality* of their presence, skills, and caring; reopen and re-invigorate their *capacity* for communication and depth in their relationship, so that, like molecules of water in a wave, whirlpool, waterfall, or rainbow, they begin to move and act as one. This happens *naturally* in mediation as people start to see their differences as legitimate and rational, discover how to combine their perspectives, and experience the pleasure of collaborating and overcoming their problems together.

8. A new symmetry, synthesis, or combination of existing ingredients.

Symmetry, in common usage, refers to balance or equality, as in "mirror" or "reflection" symmetry, where the left and right sides of our bodies match. In mathematics and physics, there are multiple symmetries that refer to what is *invariant,* or does not change, when an object is rotated, flipped, relocated, rescaled, rescheduled, or reflected. As the brilliant mathematician Emmy Noether proved, every global symmetry represents a quality that is conserved, and therefore a law of conservation. [For more, see Chapters 6 and Chapter 7.]

In conflict, by analogy, the *issues* may be conserved and remain essentially the same, even when people reverse their roles or switch sides. An emotional symmetry may occur when *both* parties feel angry, sad, ignored, unloved, scared, or disrespected. Indeed, symmetries in conflict suggest the presence of deeper polarizing dynamics that conserve the quality of the parties' relationship and communications, *independent* of the substantive issues that divide them, as when people disagree even about petty issues, revealing a deeper, invariant hostility, and a higher, "second order" symmetry, as between symmetry and asymmetry.

Polarizing symmetries in conflict, as in physics, can also be broken, making many different outcomes possible. In the first place, they allow mediators to distinguish opposing forces, latent tendencies, and a variety of potential futures that may have been obscured, camouflaged, discounted, or intermingled, but are now revealed more clearly in their differences, meaning, and importance. Indeed, conflict is often a consequence of breaking old, outdated patterns or symmetries.

It then becomes possible to discover fresh ways of combining opposites that lead to higher forms of synthesis or order, or in math, to different symmetry groups. It is possible in mediation, for example, to combine opposites in two fundamentally different ways. First, at a lower level or order of combination, we can combine hot water with cold water to create lukewarm water. In conflict resolution, this represents the relatively trivial, commonplace, superficial method of compromise.

Second, at a higher level or order of combination, we can combine water with flour, yeast, and heat to make bread. The bread does not appear to have any connection with water, flour, yeast, or heat, but only *emerges* when these diverse ingredients are combined in the right ratios, in the right order, at the right temperature, for the right period of time. The emergence of a higher form of order in the form of bread is an unanticipated, profound, seemingly magical method of creative combination, or synthesis, that becomes possible in mediation.

According to ancient, classical, spiritual dialectical philosophies and their more modern forms, as articulated for example, by Kant, Fichte, Hegel, and Marx, everything starts as a *thesis*, which gives rise to an *antithesis*, or negation, which gives rise to a *synthesis*, or "negation of the negation," which represents a new, positive thesis that permits the process to start over again and continue evolving from lower to higher orders of being, complexity, skill, and capacity.

In mediation, it nearly always happens that one party asserts a personal truth or subjective impression that — *because* it is framed universally and adversarially — *automatically* invites those on the other side who experience different truths or impressions to contradict it in an *equally* adversarial manner that implicitly excludes the possibility of creatively combining them, or reorienting them from negative to positive, or turning them in a *collaborative* direction, or using them as a foundation for joint problem-solving.

These collaborative possibilities, while tacit and implicit in the nature of conflict, and the transformational capacity of dispute resolution, can be disregarded or merely tolerated, reinforcing the continued negative orientation of the process, and the distinctly *unmagical* short-term approach of compromise. Or, they can be encouraged and supported, leading to the conversion of these negative frameworks into positive ones by means of empathetic dialogue, collaborative negotiation, consensus building, creative problem-solving, and mediation. These, in turn, invite the parties to return to what lay beneath the surface of their dispute from the moment it began: its' *immanent*, and therefore *magical*, evolution to higher forms of order, process, and relationship.

9. A recognition of hidden sources, connections, or meanings.

The initial presentation, manifestation, expression, and appearance of nearly every conflict concerns some disagreement over relatively superficial, objective, hotly contested issues. These turn out to be driven by a set of deeper, subjective, intensely adversarial, amygdala-infused, zero-sum attitudes and assumptions that are grounded in cognitive biases, perceived hostilities, and defensiveness, and fueled by cycles of reciprocal negative emotions that oscillate between fear, anger, pain, grief, guilt, and shame in countless combinations and permutations.

These responses generate a sense of urgency, immediacy, and short-range focus of attention on the past, highlighting the *foreground*, and making whatever is long-range, or in the present or future, or in the *background*, seem less exigent, essential, and apparent. While disagreements are often relatively simple and superficial, conflicts can quickly become complex, deep, and confusing, requiring time to unravel. Conflicts can also be hypnotic, lulling people into defensiveness, denial, and a false sense of stability and stasis — or an equally false sense of panic, impending chaos, and catastrophe.

As a consequence, it is rare for either party to be able to hear what is subtle, hinted at, or *implied* in the other person's outbursts; to see what is beneath the surface of their falsely polarized, argumentative rhetoric and self-rationalizing logic. It also becomes difficult to gain perspective on their *own* deeper needs, wishes, and desires; to understand what *actually* led to their dispute; to expose their vulnerable, heartfelt intentions and desires; or to step back from the brink and jointly search for mutually satisfying solutions.

Part of what feels magical in mediation consists simply of stopping all the pointless exchanges of insults, accusations, and denials; disrupting the cycles of recrimination and resistance; and reorienting everyone's attention to the hidden sources, connections, and *meanings* of their conflict that can help explain not only what happened to them, but how and why, encourage them to ask questions that reinvigorate their curiosity, and help them restore their capacity for insight, perspective, collaboration, and caring.

While there are thousands of ways mediators routinely do this, the simplest are grounded in a combination of curiosity, humility, and caring. Humility without curiosity can appear egocentric; without caring, it can feel judgmental. Curiosity without humility can look like prying; without caring, it can seem distant and clinical. By combining these elements in the right ways, it is possible for mediators to create *openings,* or heart-spaces in which people feel welcomed, acknowledged, and accepted for who they are, in which the deeper, hidden meaning of their conflicts can begin to emerge.

Whatever we have hidden deepest creates the greatest resistance to exposure, produces the most persistent obstacles to resolution, and triggers the most intense feelings of fear and anger as they are approached, either directly or indirectly in mediation. At the same time, whatever we have denied or camouflaged *wants* to be released and revealed, and therefore *signals* its presence, along with the discomfort and emotional cost of keeping it hidden, through metaphors, distortions, gestures, over-reactions, and other indirect means that seek to hide it from view, yet point directly to the precise spot where we hid it.

Whatever we repress, reject, or refuse to acknowledge within ourselves, we resist noticing and become less able to see or appreciate in others, and *vice versa,* creating a kind of tragic blindness, like that experienced by Oedipus in Sophocles' play, who runs away from, and at the same time seeks out, fails to avoid, and paradoxically *invites* the tragic consequences he tries to avoid.

While *internal* blindness is often triggered by the arrogance and guilt that inevitably accompany aggression, or the loss of empathy for others that results from exercising power over and against them, *external* blindness is triggered by the bias and contempt people use to justify their aggression; or by the stereotypes and hostile, dismissive narratives they create about others to rationalize their own cruelty and greed, which inevitably leads them to misread their own intentions and capacities, and those of others. In both cases, blindness is *induced* by conflict, leading to alienation, loss of connection, failed communications, adversarial relationships, stress, trauma, delusion, and grief.

If internal and external blindness are connected in these ways, so is *seeing,* which brings forth the creative possibilities of combining the apparent opposites of self and other. We can easily recognize in mediation how self-understanding and self-acceptance increase our capacity for empathy and compassion; how our personal happiness bolsters our ability to care about and for others; and how our willingness to search for what is deeply hidden inside gives us the courage to be deeply honest and supportive in our relations and interactions with others.

10. An evolution or adaptation to new environmental conditions.

Conflicts often give rise to intractability and impasse in complex adaptive systems when changes in environmental conditions reward new skills and capacities and penalize old ones that evolved to take advantage of conditions that are now outmoded. To conserve energy, these evolving, internally conflicted systems seek stasis, giving rise to sub-systems designed to defend and sustain it, sometimes merely by ritual, repetition, or reiteration.

On the one hand, there is *pleasure* in ritual, continuity, habit, tradition, and the comfort of routine, which are reinforced by rules and regulations, systems and structures, organizations and institutions, scripts and cultural practices that circle and reiterate, reward and punish — all in an effort to faithfully and predictably return to whatever was done before.

On the other hand, everything is constantly changing, dissipating what only seconds before seemed solid, and introducing fresh elements that are unfamiliar and require fundamentally different responses. What is worse, the *rate* of change may also be changing, demanding quicker responses and adaptations, with less time to comprehend where they are heading, or decide whether we even *want* to go there. We then begin changing — not "at the speed of thought" — but far faster.

Conflict and resolution are *each* complex adaptive systems that periodically require new skills and capacities that were not necessary or useful before. Also, while the human brain appears to be hardwired both for aggression and altruism, competition and collaboration, these contrasting orientations are perceived as mutually exclusive, requiring fundamentally different, ostensibly fixed and unmovable approaches, so it often comes as a shock when people find themselves suddenly shifting from one set of approaches to the other.

Yet conflict and resolution are not *merely* equal and opposite responses, for the simple statistical reason, connected with the concept of "entropy" and the Second Law of Thermodynamics, that there are *vastly* more ways of destroying anything complex than there are ways of creating it. Therefore, it will *always* be easier to break trust and destroy relationships than to create them. Therefore, more complex, higher *orders* of skill are required for altruism to succeed than for aggression; for collaboration than for competition; for resolution than for conflict.

As our population, communications, and interactions expand exponentially and the problems we face grow more complex, urgent, and difficult to solve, we are increasingly aware that the changes we are making in our global environment demand more complex, higher order, equally *global* skills, especially in collaboration, altruism, and conflict resolution, simply to avoid extinction. And because these skills *are* more complex, urgent, difficult, global, and higher order, they take more time and effort to identify, acquire, diffuse, and perfect.

We can therefore predict that any individuals, groups, or societies that are able to develop and strengthen these higher order adaptive skills will exhibit a seemingly magical ability to weather internal conflicts and solve intractable problems that others are simply too polarized and divided to agree on, or face together. Two simple, clear, and consequential examples are our fractured responses to the Covid pandemic, and the threat of global warming, reflected in the conflicts we face in creating unified, global, collaborative responses to each.

Our inability to exercise these skills, respond in time, adapt, and evolve in response to these and other challenges has cost us *enormously* in lives, wealth, and resources; given rise to hyper-polarization, armed resistance, and myriad conflicts; crippled sensible scientifically obvious solutions, and made these costs seem political, inevitable, and unresolvable.

The ability of any person, organization, or society to evolve and adapt to changing environmental conditions can be measured in part by their ability to jointly address the problems and resolve the conflicts that are triggered by them. Yet, as Albert Einstein famously remarked, "The significant problems we face cannot be solved at the same level of thinking we were at when we created them." Thus, the ability to work innovatively and collaboratively makes every solution and resolution seem magical to those who are trapped in old ways of thinking.

11. A revolution, paradigm shift, systemic change, or phase transition.

If evolutionary adaptations feel magical, then revolutions, paradigm shifts, systemic changes, and phase transitions feel even more so, as they are large, sudden, *qualitative* leaps that are triggered by tiny, gradual, quantitative steps, each of which by itself seems trivial and unremarkable, yet at some point these small changes can combine to produce something entirely new.

Similarly, people can experience petty frustrations that go unheeded and result in huge, terrible, implacable conflicts; or alternatively, they can communicate and interact with each other in small ways that result in major, profound, and lasting resolutions. While any single, tiny, insignificant step along the way in either direction cannot be regarded as solely responsible for the larger ultimate outcome, *cumulatively* they can produce rapid, qualitative shifts and transitions from one "ground state" to another.

This allows us to regard the magic in mediation as a *paradigm shift*, similar to those described by Thomas S. Kuhn in *The Structure of Scientific Revolution*, and define "conflict paradigms" as perceived models or patterns of response to conflict, whether explicit or implicit, that limit or expand our perceptions; freeze or free up our ideas, expectations, processes, relationships; offer new definitions of success; and shrink or enlarge our awareness of possibilities.

Conflict paradigms, like scientific ones, ignore and filter out information that could lead to new or significantly different paradigms, creating circular systems that fuel self-fulfilling prophecies. For example, a common paradigm in conflict is that nothing is likely to change, which justifies the refusal to try anything new, confirms the success of the old paradigm in predicting negative outcomes, and makes it impossible to discover or invent fresh solutions.

Yet paradigms start to shift *precisely* because problems have arisen that cannot be solved under the old paradigm, *simultaneously* generating a search for new approaches to problem-solving, together with conflicts over whether to reform or completely abandon the old paradigm in order to solve them; or refuse to change the old paradigm, deny that it is a problem, blame and attack those who want to change it, and make problems chronic, and more destructive.

Conflicts are highly sensitive sources of information about the emergence of new paradigms, as they signal opportunities for change, suggest sources of energy and motivation to make it happen, and undermine efforts to prevent it from happening. We can then define conflicts as *evolutionary anomalies* that arise whenever prevailing paradigms begin to shift. As Thomas Kuhn pointed out,

> [A]nomaly appears only against the background provided by the paradigm. The more precise and far-reaching that paradigm is, the

more sensitive an indicator it provides of anomaly, and hence of an occasion for paradigm change.

Hence, conflicts arise along the cracks or *fault lines* in the old paradigm, while resolution consists either of accepting, exploring, shifting, and repairing those fault lines; or discovering, creating, and implementing newer, more successful paradigms, which make what seemed difficult, impossible, or unthinkable under the old paradigm magically feel simple, inevitable, and logical.

Every resolution is therefore not only a paradigm shift, but potentially a *revolution* — i.e., a deep, rapid, fundamental evolution; a transformation and transcendence; a systemic change; an entirely new *form* of order that arises by means of disorder; a more effective approach to the problem of how to solve problems. In *Conflict Revolution*, I described 15 *potential* revolutions that have the ability to transform social, economic, and political life, and perhaps clarify our understanding of how ideas shift in the move from conflict to transcendence. There are, for example:

1. Revolutions in *ideas*, marked by the emergence of dissent; marginalized voices now being heard and acknowledged; and the appearance of new paradigms that suddenly become thinkable
2. Revolutions in *vision*, marked by an implicit understanding that it is possible to change, and the articulation of a set of organizing principles and strategies for doing so
3. Revolutions in *power*, marked by institutional access, public acquiescence, and political permission to put new ideas into practice
4. Revolutions in *leadership*, marked by the succession to state and organizational power of a new generation of leaders representing a new constituency
5. Revolutions in *implementation*, marked by attempts to transform circumstances and behaviors in conformity with

the ideas that inspired the revolution, and efforts to translate them into action

6. Revolutions in *dominance*, marked by the subordination of old social, economic, and political hierarchies to the new majority, represented by a newly reformed state and bureaucracy

7. Revolutions in *governance*, marked by subordination of the state and bureaucracy to the will of the majority, represented by civil society

8. Revolutions in *pragmatism*, marked by continuing internal conflicts and discoveries through implementation that not all the problems attributed to the old paradigm can be solved by the new one

9. Revolutions in *participation*, marked by the transformation of civil society through popular involvement, self-managing teams, and democratic, collaborative, community participation

10. Revolutions in *integrity*, marked by personal and systemic integration of values, ethics, and principles, and their translation into practice

11. Revolutions in *process*, marked by a shift to interest-based methods, and increased reliance on consensus decision-making

12. Revolutions in *relationships*, marked by the encouragement of collaborative, heartfelt, supportive relationships

13. Revolutions in *responsibility*, marked by the integration of personal autonomy, systemic decentralization, and collective empowerment, with each responsible for the whole, and the whole responsible for each

14. Revolutions in *attitude*, marked by an orientation to personal growth, learning, self-actualization, and continuous systemic improvement

15. Revolutions in *being*, marked by a focus on spiritual development, improving hearts and minds, raising the quality of life, and leaving no one behind

It is possible to identify analogous possibilities in dispute resolution: to translate seemingly magical large-scale shifts into small-scale practical interventions; to "reverse-engineer" the mediation process by re-imagining the fundamental transformation and transcendence of conflicted relationships on all scales–internally inside ourselves, relationally between ourselves and others, and systemically, culturally, and environmentally in all the contexts in which we live.

12. A rediscovery of integration, balance, poise, authenticity, integrity, or center.

When we are immersed in conflict and engaged in this "dance of opposites," our sense of integration, balance, poise, authenticity, integrity, and centeredness become *contingent*, situational, conditional, and dependent — both on our internal emotional dynamics, and on the external behaviors, attitudes, and emotions of our opponents. Even in opposition, our options and *identities* appear to be shaped and controlled by *their* choices.

One of the more insightful, profound, and lesser-known secrets of conflict is that we *choose* our opponents *precisely* so they will help us discover our own authentic selves; that we *externalize* our own internal conflicts and attribute them to others, then do battle with *them* to discover what *we* think or feel, and in the process, seek a place of integration and balance.

I believe it works like this. Everything has an opposite. There is light and dark, up and down, positive and negative, self and other. We discover what is true and what is false by exploring each opposite pole separately, pitting them against one or the other, and searching amid the rubble for what is real. I think of this process as the "lowest" middle way, or "mediated" outcome.

If we define the middle in every conflict as a *field* with opposite poles (like a gravitational or electromagnetic field) that connects, separates, and lies between opposites, simultaneously attracting and repelling them, the "lowest" middle way is simply mutual trauma, destruction, and exhaustion. A somewhat higher "middle" middle way consists of compromise and settlement, in which the conflict reaches equilibrium or stasis, and each side wins some and loses some.

Only after considerable dialogue, creative problem-solving, collaborative negotiation, and mediative intervention, does a third, "higher" middle way emerge, in the form of consensus, collaboration, and genuine resolution of the conflict. Beyond this, it is possible to imagine a fourth "highest" middle way, in which both sides discover how to transcend the underlying reasons for the conflict within themselves, in their relationship, and in the systems, structures, and cultures that created the conflict and kept it alive. Each higher order of "middle ground" seems magical to those who are stuck at a lower level.

While *every* effort to locate possible settlements or resolutions is *mediative*, each level of mediation is merely a search for the *center* — that is, not only the place where opposites integrate and become whole; but where the conflict that takes place within us, between us, and around us gives rise to a renewed sense of integration, balance, poise, authenticity, integrity, and centeredness.

Many "lower order" mediative outcomes can appear tiny, trivial, and non-transformational, as is often the case with de-escalation, conciliation, compromise, and settlement; or they can appear huge, consequential, profound, transformational, revolutionary, and transcendent, as often occurs with dialogue, emotional closure, forgiveness, reconciliation, and restorative justice.

This process can also work in reverse: not only can these higher order outcomes create an enhanced sense of integration, balance, poise, authenticity, integrity, and centeredness; but cultivating an enhanced sense of integration, balance, poise, authenticity, integrity, and centeredness can make it far easier to reach resolution, forgiveness, and reconciliation.

For this reason, mediation *naturally* includes a range of internal "spiritual" practices, such as meditation, mindfulness, awareness, loving-kindness, equanimity, compassion, and similar exercises, each of which can have a magical impact on conflict, as they allow us to become more present and accepting of ourselves and our opponents, before we even face them. Eckhart Tolle described Zen as "walking along the razor's edge of Now," implying that mediators can be:

> ... so utterly, so completely present that no problem, no suffering, nothing that is not who you are in your essence, can survive in you. In the Now, in the absence of time, all your problems dissolve. Suffering needs time; it cannot survive in the Now.

There is thus a natural affinity between mediation and meditation, as both recognize the simultaneity of unity and opposition; the presence of diverse and multiple truths; the search for higher middle ways; and encourage people to have a *complete* experience of their conflicts, allowing them to learn, adapt, evolve, and leave their attachment to ego and outcomes behind them. [See Chapter 3.]

13. A completion, transcendence, rising above, or deep learning.

The process of resolving conflicts, in my experience, often involves helping people successfully pass through different stages or *levels of attachment* to conflict. These stages do not always occur in linear order, and some may happen simultaneously or not at all, yet they all represent increasingly complex stages, aspects, elements, or experiences, each of which requires higher order skills that are *exponentially* more challenging. In my view, they include the following 10:

1. Engagement, aggression, impasse, and revenge
2. Suppression, shaming, blaming, and punitive or *retributive* justice
3. Denial, disengagement, alienation, and avoidance

4. Stopping the fighting, cease fire, separation, and de-escalation
5. Settlement, adversarial negotiation, caucusing, and compromise
6. Conciliation, dialogue, accommodation, and civility
7. Resolution, collaborative negotiation, consensus building, and satisfaction of interests
8. Forgiveness, self-forgiveness, emotional completion, and letting go
9. Reconciliation, open heartedness, rebuilding trust, and relational or *restorative* justice
10. Prevention, conflict resolution systems design, closure, and renewal

To move from lower to higher stages, it is necessary first to complete the work of the lower stage. Unless we do, we are more likely to remain stuck, and unable to solve the "riddle" or paradox of how to get unstuck, except by transcending our *own* one-sidedness, discovering what is false in our polarization, overcoming hostility to our opponent, and learning how to solve problems collaboratively.

We can think of each of these stages as a *crossroads*, fork, or "decision-gate" that repeatedly bisects, blocking or opening our path forward, and presenting us with evolutionary, static, and devolutionary choices. As we try to navigate our way out of being stuck, the old skills that led us to this stage or level no longer suffice, and new ways of thinking and behaving have to be acquired so as to evolve.

For example, to complete the fourth stage and stop the fighting or de-escalate, we first need to recognize the unsustainability and destructiveness of continued fighting. We then need to figure out *how* to stop fighting; then decide we are going to act differently, and last, be willing to meet with our opponent to discuss and resolve the issues that could otherwise retrigger our willingness to fight.

A number of key crossroads appear at every stage in every conflict, representing on the one hand, problems we are now required to solve; and on the other hand, the fact that we do not yet have the skills we need in order to solve them. [For more on this topic, see my book, *The Crossroads of Conflict*.]. These crossroads present us with distinct choices and decision gates that *generically* include:

- Whether to engage in the conflict and behave badly, or calm down and try to discuss it
- Whether to acknowledge the other person's truth or deny it, remain rooted in our own story, and slip into biased or delusional thinking
- Whether to experience intense negative emotions and feelings, or to repress and sublimate them
- Whether to experience our opponent as a human being entitled to equal respect, or to demonize him or her and victimize ourselves
- Whether to aggressively assert and hold tight to our position, or to search for solutions that satisfy both our interests
- Whether to acknowledge and grieve our losses and let them go, or hold on to our pain as something precious and continue reliving it
- Whether to learn from our opponent and the conflict so as to transcend it, or hold on to our grievances and being right, and let them bottle up inside
- Whether to forgive our opponent and release ourselves from the burden of our own false expectations, or remain isolated and wounded deep inside
- Whether to reopen our hearts, reconcile and re-integrate with our opponent, or remain distant and closed-hearted
- Whether to ignore the systemic sources of chronic conflict, or redesign the systems that created them to prevent future disputes, so others will not have to experience what we experienced

As we acquire each new set of skills, we automatically evolve, and magically release ourselves from the places we are stuck. In this way, "magic" is always and continuously present in every conflict, at every crossroads, offering us a choice, a challenge, a task, and a higher order of skills to practice. These skills consist not simply of stopping or settling the conflict, or even transforming the reasons that gave rise to it, but magically completing, transcending, rising above, evolving, and learning at a deep level how to pass beyond it at every level, navigating each unique crossroads in unique ways and moving on to ever-higher orders of conflict and resolution.

Reaching these successively higher orders of conflict requires ever deeper understandings of the sources of conflict, broader skills in resolution, and a willingness to pass on to more advanced and complex crossroads for which older, lower order skills are suddenly inadequate. As we do so, we discover, often to our immense surprise, that we are now able to resolve not only the specific conflicts that kept us stuck, but more magically, *all similar conflicts* we will ever encounter that might keep us stuck at that level.

14. An increase in love, caring, or kindness.

Our first, nearly automatic, instinctual response to any conflict is to protect our most vulnerable spaces, the places where we can be hurt most deeply, especially our *hearts*, which we immediately close to those who have hurt us. The deeper we care, the greater our pain, the more tightly we close our hearts, and the less capable of kindness, caring, and loving we become. The poet Apollinaire wrote:

> *I know all sorts of people*
> *Who are not equal to their lives.*
> *Their hearts are poorly smothered fires*
> *Their hearts*
> *Open and close like their doors.*

Our difficulty is that we are unable to close our hearts in just one direction; we cannot isolate our defensive responses to a single person, and we cannot sustain our capacity for love, caring, and kindness when we shut them off because of conflict. Once trust has been broken, as it nearly always is in conflict, it takes considerable effort and a fresh set of skills to restore it. And when trust is gone, it is harder still even to *imagine* how it might be repaired, or believe anything the other person says or does, or trust that the mediator will be able to fix it for us.

There are countless ways of breaking trust, and only a few that can sometimes restore it. Some of the behaviors we can engage in, or ways we can relate to others that *might* help us "magically" rebuild trust, even after it has been shattered, in my experience, include:

- Honesty about ourselves
- Openness about problems
- Unconditional respect
- Clarity about boundaries
- Consistency over time
- Actions based on vision or values
- Collaboration and joint action
- Empowerment of others
- Teamwork and joint participation in decision-making
- Listening and empathizing
- Dependability in crises and hard times
- Authenticity, and congruency between words and actions
- Social interactions and dialogue
- Curiosity and asking open-ended questions
- Personal sharing, especially about mistakes
- Willingness to sacrifice something important
- Sincere apologies and reparations
- *Unconditional* acts of love, caring, and kindness

We can think of trust as a measurement of *predictability*, the degree to which we feel we can rely on someone, based on our past interactions and what we know of their behavior and character. We then calibrate our degree of trust; but we do so based partly on our *own* uncommunicated needs, desires, and false expectations; on the degree to which we feel dependent on other peoples' behaviors for our own self-esteem, security, and emotional well-being; and on the depth of our desire for them to *be* the ones we want or need them to be.

We rarely articulate, make explicit, or negotiate the satisfaction of our deepest, most heartfelt desires, but buttress and reinforce them with subtle signals based on the slimmest evidence, which is highly dependent on context and culture, and can easily be misinterpreted. As a result, our deepest desires for love, caring, and kindness can quickly and easily be converted into hope or despair, loyalty or betrayal, genuineness or duplicity–even into a *desire* for conflict that will allow us to discover which of these possibilities is true.

As a result, the introduction of love, caring, and kindness into any conflict or communication can have a magical impact, partly by allowing people to bypass the relatively superficial issues over which they are arguing, disarm their own distrust, reduce the automaticity of their adversarial responses, and simply *feel* better about themselves and others.

Mediators can assist conflicted parties in beginning to rebuild trust by asking questions that invite them into deeper, more heartfelt conversations. [For a list of these questions, see Chapter 4.]. Heart-based questions remind us that *no one* gets into conflict over things they *don't* care about. Therefore, every conflict can be regarded as a place of mutuality in caring that can lead to two very different conversations: one is about the sources and justifications for their antagonism; the other is about the things they both deeply care about. The first can produce settlements, the second can create magic.

15. A metamorphosis of experience and heart-knowledge into wisdom.

Each of these sources of magic in mediation can be regarded as a wellspring of method, process, and technique, or as leading us to unimagined openings and transformational outcomes. At a deeper level, far more important than method, process, or technique, each of these sources can also be seen as a way of turning painful experiences into learning, and profoundly, magically, into *wisdom*.

In this way, we can justly regard mediation as a *wisdom tradition*, one among many, that is concerned not just with physical, mental, and emotional perceptions and responses, or with distinct ways of understanding and changing the world, but equally with what we can describe as "spiritual," or "heart" knowledge, and the deeper, profound *entirety* of human experience that encompasses, links, and is somehow greater than the sum of its parts.

When we are in conflict, our deepest need is not merely to find useful methods and processes, or new behaviors and systems to help us resolve them, but to capture the profound, transformational, transcendent wisdom that silently and imperceptibly gave rise to them. This is the wisdom that comes to us in mediation when we occupy a space that is *simultaneously* inside, outside, and around the conflict; when we empathize deeply with both parties at the same time; when we strengthen our *capacity* for perspective, integrity, and caring; when we are completely open and available for whatever the parties may decide to say or do next. Nobel Prize winning novelist Octavio Paz observed that "Wisdom lies neither in fixity nor in change, but in the dialectic between the two. A constant coming and going: wisdom lies in the momentary."

The continually shifting combinations of stories and narratives, thoughts and feelings, empathy and honesty, stillness and motion, caring and equanimity, continuity and change, triviality and depth, opposition and unity, can reveal, as if by magic, not only what mediators and parties can *do* about their conflicts, but how we can *be* in the midst of it. For mediators, this includes our ability to:

- Show up and be as present and authentic as we can be
- Listen empathetically for what is hidden beneath words
- Tell the truth without blaming or judgment
- Engage in poignant, vulnerable, heart-felt communications
- Be open-minded, open-hearted, and unattached to outcomes
- Act collaboratively in all relationships
- Display unconditional integrity and respect
- Draw on our deepest intuition
- Work for completion and closure
- Be ready for anything at every moment
- Be willing to let go, but give up on no one

In conflict, where subjective truths regularly clash and compete for dominance, a mediator's wisdom consists not solely in listening to the ideas, feelings, beliefs, and experiences of one side or the other; nor does it lie in being neutral, standing to the side, and refusing to choose between them. Instead, it is *entirely,* and in its heart, in my view, *omni-partial,* and on *both* people's sides at the same time. [For more on neutrality and omni-partiality, see Chapter 1.]

Wisdom is not a zero-sum game with a single face or a single truth; nor is it the ability to alternate or compromise between them. What is *exponentially* better than alternation and compromise is the ability to elicit dialogue, collaboration, synthesis, and creative combination that seek to capture not only the trivial truth of adversarial, one-sided, self-serving assertions, rationalizations, defenses, demands, and biased narratives and stories–but the deeper, subtler, far more powerful truths that *gave rise* to them, to the poignant, profound truths of who each person actually *is,* what they most deeply *mean,* and why it *matters* to them.

Wisdom is an under-acknowledged, early casualty in every conflict, because it cannot coexist with hatred, cruelty, and the countless ways we dismiss and deny each other's truths in order to give greater credence to our own. Simple forms of wisdom therefore feel magical in mediation, partly because they do not distance themselves, or refuse to know, empathize, or acknowledge what the other person thinks and feels. Wisdom emerges, equally and paradoxically, from our *inability* to know; from our own incomplete and inadequate empathy; from our difficulty in acknowledging what really matters to others– i.e., from our humility, curiosity, and desire to learn who our opponents *are*, what matters to them, and why.

Of course, one can be knowledgeable, informed, and intelligent without being wise. Wisdom is an *activity* of the heart, which requires openness and humility. In a famous story, when Socrates was informed that the Oracle at Delphi had declared that he was the wisest man alive, he tried at first to prove the Oracle wrong, and only later realized it had done so because he did not believe he was wise at all. Wisdom therefore invites *self*-discovery. Marcel Proust wrote,

> We do not receive wisdom, we must discover it for ourselves, after a journey through the wilderness, which no one else can make for us, which no one can spare us, for our wisdom is the point of view from which we must come at last to regard the world.

To which the Nobel Prize winning Nigerian novelist Chinua Achebe added,

> The truth is not like the canons of orthodoxy or the irrationality of prejudice and superstition. It begins as an adventure in self-discovery and ends in wisdom and humane conscience.

One source of wisdom therefore lies hidden in our conflicts, and emerges with the realization that every conflict we experience is a place where wisdom has yet to be discovered, or take hold; where heart-knowledge is incomplete; where self and other remain isolated and remote; where our skills are simply too primitive; where the magic has not yet been discovered.

MORE SOURCES OF MAGIC IN MEDIATION

There are, of course, *far* more than fifteen sources of magic in mediation. And since magic is subtle and sensitively dependent on existing conditions, it will never happen always, everywhere, or for everyone. Magic is an *activity*, a process that inevitably begins with a search, which turns into a succession of failures and recoveries, until suddenly, somehow, something works, often for reasons we do not fully understand at the time, and therefore experience as magical.

Magic is a kind of *immediacy*, a quality of presence, intuition, and intention, which can be found in language – not in the sense of the external objects language usually describes, but in the music, artistry, poignancy, and *mediative* quality of language itself. As Walter Benjamin brilliantly described it

> Mediation, which is the immediacy of all mental communication, is the fundamental problem of linguistic theory, and if one chooses to call this immediacy magic, then the primary problem of language is its magic. At the same time, the notion of the magic of language points to something else: its infiniteness.... For precisely because nothing is communicated *through* language, what is communicated *in* language cannot be externally limited or measured, and therefore all language contains its own incommensurable, uniquely constituted infinity. Its linguistic being, not its verbal contents, defines its frontier. ...

Every mediation begins with the most magical assumption of all: that somehow, against all odds and expectations, we will be able bring people together who are *completely* stuck in their conflicts; who are experiencing intense feelings of hatred, fear, distrust, frustration, hopelessness, and desperation; who have been traumatized repeatedly and been unable to resolve their differences. Yet we believe we can somehow help them discover or invent a way out, without even the slightest inkling of where or how this will occur. The *idea* that this might even be possible is an *extraordinary* leap of faith, yet one that routinely results in mediation settlement rates of 85-98% in disputes that are 100% stuck.

The only way of explaining these results is to suggest that there is a science and an art that lie hidden beneath the surface, creating *impressions* of magic, simply because we do not fully understand them. Yet despite this lack of complete understanding, magic happens–and not primarily because of what we *do*, but who we *are*; and the strength and quality of our commitment.

Mediator Elizabeth Healy in County Mayo, Ireland, offered the following brilliant story on-line that, for me, perfectly describes the process of finding, feeding, and fomenting the magic that is latent in every conflict:

> Working in a psychiatric hospital at one point, an elderly man who lived alone was brought in for admission. He was roaring and shouting and physically resisting admission. I was called at one point, as staff could not restrain him. ... The wild noise greeted me as I arrived. I sat to try to talk with him. he was incessant in his roaring. But I listened to his almost unintelligible gibberish. Then I caught the word 'cat.' I managed to ask him, at a moment when he was taking a breath to let fly again, 'do you have a cat?" He stopped roaring and replied in panicky voice, 'Yes.' I asked what was the cat's name? More calmly, he told me. (I forget the name). I asked, 'Will X be OK while you're in hospital?' He then broke down and sobbed, 'there's no one to feed the cat if I'm not there.' 'If we arrange for

someone to feed X while you're in hospital, would that be OK? Would you be happy to come into hospital for a while?'. His whole body softened and relaxed, his speech became calm and quiet ... and he said, 'That would be mighty.'

This story suggests that magic happens *in spite* of everything the parties have said and done to each other; in spite of their belief and determination that it will not work; in spite of all their anguish and pain and trauma and loss, all their failed efforts and hopelessness. Why? Because we, their mediators, *believe*, in our minds and hearts and bodies and souls, that magic is possible, and are ready, in every mediation, to step away from light and certainty into darkness and chaos, and try to find it there.

In doing so, we allow ourselves, just for a moment, to *become* the magic the parties are seeking, simply because they do not yet understand that the magic is *already* present and waiting for them. The greatest magic of all is their discovery that the magic is not in the mediators, but within, between, and around them; that each of them can become a magician, an alchemist who discovers how to turn the lead of conflict into the gold of resolution.

THREE

Mediation, Meditation, and Mindfulness

CULTIVATING AWARENESS, INSIGHT, EMPATHY, AND INTUITION

Every conflict begins with thoughts of fear, animosity and aggression, which pass through some people's minds and spread like wildfire. The only antidote to these aberrations is to take on fully the suffering of others.

Matthieu Ricard

Conflict is the denial of what is or the running away from what is; there is no conflict other than that.

Jiddhu Krishnamurti

Hey you, expecting results without effort! So sensitive! So long-suffering! You, in the clutches of death, acting like an immortal! Hey sufferer, you are destroying yourself!

Santideva

IT IS DIFFICULT TO DESCRIBE IN WORDS WHAT IS, AT ITS DEEPEST LEVEL, a wordless experience. One approach would simply be to leave the pages in this chapter blank, inviting the reader to become curious, wonder which of the countless words that might have been written would have been chosen by them, and search inward for the poetic sensibility that comes closest to saying what ultimately cannot be said. This is the approach taken by Ludwig Wittgenstein in his famous injunction, "Whereof one cannot speak, thereof one must be silent."

Yet there is value in taking on the difficult Boddhisatva-like task of returning to the world of description and trying to illuminate, elucidate, and point in the direction of successful practices, techniques, steps, stages, methodologies, and approaches. Each of these may ultimately prove beside the point and finally need to be jettisoned as excess baggage, in the same way that *practicing* respect differs from *being* respectful.

What follows then, is itself a kind of meditation on the role of meditation, awareness, and mindfulness practices in conflict resolution, especially mediation and conflict coaching, where the quality of presence of the mediator or coach can have a profound, transformational impact on the conflict.

While meditation and mediation sound similar, and both refer to the "middle way," there are, as discussed in Chapter 2, *multiple* middle ways: a "lowest" middle way (fighting), a "lower" middle way (compromise), a "higher" middle way (resolution), and a "highest" middle way (transcendence). A similar distinction appears in meditation. The highest forms of both require awareness, concentration, presence, letting go, loving-kindness, and similar practices, and while mediation and coaching are mostly practiced externally and relationally, and meditation is mostly practiced internally and alone, these different practices intersect, and when combined can produce magical outcomes.

Yet in mediation, we can start by asking, "Where, exactly, are conflicts located?" and imagine them taking place in at least the three fundamental locations mentioned earlier: *internally*, or within us; *relationally*, or between us; and *environmentally*, or around us. Each of these can be divided into a set of *sub*-locations, so that internal conflicts, for example, may be experienced physically, mentally, emotionally, spiritually, and in something we can call a "heart space."

Each of these locations and sub-locations rests on our sensory awareness and perceptions, as well as our neurophysiology and "interoception" (internal physical awareness); our thoughts and ideas, feelings and emotions, contexts and memories, needs and expectations, energies and personalities, insights and understandings, empathy and intuition, and capacity for love and kindness.

We can initially define conflict as a state of being *stuck*; of being unable to move freely, adapt, synchronize, collaborate, or evolve in one or more of these locations — in other words, as a state of *attachment*; a knot, disorientation, or lack of skill in being able to escape the orbital trajectory, centripetal force, and gravitational tug of our conflicts. Conflict *resolution* can then be defined as a methodology for letting go of these attachments, getting unstuck in each location, and more profoundly, realizing that all these locations are one, with a single center.

We can then imagine conflicts as *resonating*, vibrating, and drawing our attention to the subtle locations where we are stuck, in ways that are accessible to our senses, yet limited by our capacity for awareness and mindfulness, our ability to use "skillful means" and engage in "right" behaviors, which in turn depend on our centeredness, flexibility, authenticity, and openness to experiencing the ebb and flow of everything, connecting what is inside us, between us, and around us.

In these ways, awareness and mindfulness practices have proven highly beneficial for mediators, and for anyone in conflict. [For more, see Leonard L. Riskin's excellent book, *Managing Conflict Mindfully*, or my chapter, "Mediation and Meditation," in *The Dance of Opposites*.]. Let's start with these questions:

1. How exactly do we become *aware* of conflict in each of these locations and sublocations?
2. How do conflicts arise and escalate at a *microscopic*, subconscious level in each location and sublocation? How do they fade and disappear?
3. What are some *generic* methods and practices mediators can use to encourage resolution in each location and sublocation, or holistically in all of them at once?
4. What are some *specific* methods and practices mediators can adapt from meditation to heighten our sensitivity and skills, and help hostile parties move their conflicts in the direction of resolution?
5. What can mediators do to assist the parties in understanding, resolving, transforming, and transcending their conflicts in each of these locations, or all at once?

WHAT LINKS MEDIATION AND MEDITATION?

Our centuries-old search for what is real has been obstructed, not only by our fears, desires, illusions, and attachments, but our responses to conflict, which have countless faces, facets, and forms. Yet each tiny insight and breakthrough in understanding can reveal unimaginable connections and synergies that can accelerate our search for deeper understanding.

The search for safety, security, eternal Truths, and escape from chronic conflicts — sometimes by repeating words over and over and accepting them as true when they are merely superficially satisfying illusions—can produce stalemates, impasses, and ingenious defenses against the discovery of still deeper truths, based on the idea that whatever worked before may work again.

This search for safety, security, eternal Truths, and escape from chronic conflicts, in the world of spirituality, has led to formalized dogmas, reified creeds, institutionalized churches, frozen religions, and a kind of "power-," or "rights-based" spirituality. In the secular world, the same process leads to the illusion of immutable laws, courts, bureaucracies, and governments.

Yet the Buddhist idea of "impermanence," when combined with "interest-based" approaches to conflict resolution, enable us to re-imagine the spiritual *and* secular worlds as undergoing a transition from power- and rights- to interest-based practices that seek to *dissolve* the desire for security, safety, and eternal Truths, and escape from chronic conflicts internally, relationally, and systemically.

Many of the core ideas in Buddhism offer fresh approaches to understanding conflict, creative avenues for mediators searching for resolution, and innovative transformational techniques. These ideas include, in addition to impermanence, seeing suffering as a consequence of attachment, the idea of "maya" or illusion, the emphasis on living in the "now," the doctrine of "no-self," and many others. While all of these have been written about in detail, they have not been adequately explored from the perspective of conflict resolution, in spite of the fact that conflict is a significant source of attachment, suffering, and illusion, and that these are, with different terminology, important elements in mediation practice.

TRUTH IN MEDITATION AND MEDIATION

In mediation, as well as meditation, there is a fundamental difference between Truth as an "it," and truth as a *process*, a *practice*, an attitude, an intention, a way of living, a *relationship* with what is. As philosopher Gianni Vattimo wrote,

> We don't reach agreement when we have discovered the truth, we say we have discovered the truth when we reach agreement. It is in this sense that when the word 'truth' is uttered, a shadow of violence is cast as well.

Perhaps for this reason, Stephen Batchelor, in *After Buddhism: Rethinking the Dharma for a Secular Age*, recast the "Four Noble Truths," in ways that offer fresh insights for mediators. These can be re-formulated as follows:

1. *Comprehend Suffering*: "Comprehend" here means not just awareness, but complete, total, all-round knowing. "Suffering" here is similar to the dissatisfaction or dis-ease that flows from not getting what we want, or getting what we do not want, and requires paying attention to the large and small, nearly unnoticeable ways that we become attached and reactive to everything that happens. Comprehending these ways, which include conflict, requires great concentration as well as equanimity.

2. *Let Go of Arising*: Arising here implies greed and desire, but also clinging, craving, and attachment to the sensations and stimuli that feed our "monkey mind" responses and "knee-jerk" reactivity, and distract us from the simple awareness that flows from being. Through clinging, the self-preoccupation and self-centeredness of "I am" arises.

3. *Behold Ceasing*: The fading away of reactivity leaves only calm, insight, and pleasure, which we "be/hold" or hold in our being, rather than in mind or ego. This gives rise to "nirvana," a state of bliss that is empty of thought yet full of awareness.

4. *Cultivate the Path*: Once we comprehend the source of suffering, let go of attachment to its arising, and behold its ceasing, we need to complete and integrate them by weaving them into everyday actions, which are known as "The Eightfold Path."

The Buddha explained this path as follows:

> By and large, ... this world relies on the duality of 'it is' and 'it is not.' But one who sees the arising of the world as it happens with

complete understanding has no sense of 'it is not' about the world. And one who sees the ceasing of the world with complete understanding has no sense of 'it is' about the world.

These ideas can be adapted and applied to the experience of conflict: the arising of intense negative emotions and ego defenses; the suffering caused by lost relationships, self-doubts, and attachment to false expectations; the fading of anger, fear, and reactivity; and the duality of "it is" and "it is not," or in the language of family conflicts, "you did" and "no I didn't."

In Bachelor's formulation, the "eight-fold path," instead of just being "right" practices, becomes "complete", "integral," or "right" paths to follow, which include the same eight practices:

1. Complete, Integral, or Right View
2. Complete, Integral, or Right Thought
3. Complete, Integral, or Right Speech
4. Complete, Integral, or Right Action
5. Complete, Integral, or Right Livelihood
6. Complete, Integral, or Right Effort
7. Complete, Integral, or Right Mindfulness
8. Complete, Integral, or Right Concentration

If we consider these paths from a conflict resolution perspective, we can describe them as *mediative* skills, approaches, and practices, allowing us to identify evolutionary patterns in which higher order outcomes require higher order skills. A "complete, integral, or right view," for example, might include seeing the parties and their stories, or versions of the conflict, as equally "true," or "right" from their unique perspectives; equally entitled to respectful, empathetic, and responsive listening; and equal elements in a search for "integral" solutions.

Within each of these skill sets, it is possible to identify sub-skills that enable mediators to respond fluidly to whatever emerges during conflict conversations. As a consequence, we can identify a set of "meta-skills" that draw mediators inexorably in the direction of meditation practices, including being mindful, concentrating awareness, observing impermanence, practicing loving-kindness, etc.–and doing so not only *internally* within themselves, as in meditation; but *relationally* between themselves and others, as in mediation; and *systemically* or environmentally around them, as in conflict resolution systems design.

The experience of being in conflict is nearly identical to that of people who simply lack awareness and equanimity, or have low-level skills in handling conflict, or are unable to release themselves from suffering and false expectations, and cannot let go of their desire for permanence in an impermanent world.

There are countless ways of defining conflict, and among the most useful, I find, are these, each of which has echoes in the world of meditation:

1. Conflicts arise when there is a lack of mindfulness about how our actions impact others; a lack of empathy for the suffering of our opponent; a lack of awareness of our essential inter-connectedness.
2. Conflicts represent a loss of self, a failure of perspective, an internal imbalance, misplaced priorities, a loss of center.
3. Conflicts reflect a lack of skill in being able to communicate what we want, and an inability or disinterest in finding out what others want.
4. Conflicts occur when we become attached to outcomes that are unrealistic or impossible; hold onto false expectations of others or ourselves; or deny the right of others to make different choices.
5. Conflicts arise because of a lack of acceptance of ourselves that we project onto others; or blame others for what we perceive as failures in our own lives, or to divert attention from our mistakes.

6. Conflicts are triggered by attitudes of defensiveness and hostility, selfishness and ego, aggressiveness and competition, disrespect and insensitivity, distancing and distrust, which are within our control.

Martin Buber offered a simpler, yet profound and useful way of connecting the Buddhist principle of "skillful means," with the primary sources of conflict:

> There are three principles in a man's being and life, the principle of thought, the principle of speech, and the principle of action. The origin of all conflict between me and my fellow-men is that I do not say what I mean and I do not do what I say.

Meditation teacher and author Ken McLeod has recommended a simple, practical, modern translation of the "eight-fold path" to skillful means, many of which are used by experienced mediators to guide conflict conversations:

1. Start from where you are.
2. Bring attention to what you are doing.
3. Bring attention to how you are doing it.
4. Experience what you are doing at all levels of your being.
5. Sense any imbalance.
6. Go empty.
7. Make a small movement in the direction of balance.
8. Repeat.

Impasse, Impermanence, and Flow

From the point of view of conflict resolution, it is possible to "reverse engineer" these practices, and start by describing conflict as a state of being stuck–for example, between opposing ideas, attitudes, intentions, personalities, beliefs, truths, energies, or courses of action. Indeed, drawing from meditative practices, we can define conflict as an *obstacle* to the movement of energy, whose natural state is to flow unimpeded, from which it follows that any obstruction to that flow, any knot or hindrance, any distortion or blockage, will divert our life energy from its "natural" path, causing it to create a new one, as the meander of a river flows around an obstacle.

Impermanence is a consequence of the flow of energy within, between, and around us, which helps mediators understand *why* suffering follows from attachment, and blocks the flow of conflicted emotions, like anger, fear, pain, etc. Unresolved conflicts are a potent source of attachment and suffering, and therefore our acceptance of impermanence, the unity of opposites, and non-interference with the flow of life energy, can help relieve that suffering.

What is worse, conflicts distort the *meaning* of life energy by giving it a personal, hostile, adversarial character, which automatically triggers resistance and suppression, causing it to intensify, or assume a passive-aggressive form, and pop up in locations where it doesn't belong — locations that make the parties seem crazy or irrational.

We can reduce or eliminate these sources of resistance to conflict by practicing meditation and developing awareness, mindfulness, insight, and higher orders of skill in the ways we respond to conflict, deepening the levels of resolution, and improving not only our *external* responses as mediators to conflicts between others, but our *internal* responses to the unresolved conflicts in our own lives, and end the duality and separation between them.

THE CARESS OF THE NOW

Conflicts possess enormous power, including the ability to shift our focus of attention from the present to the past. Part of what resolution therefore consists of is releasing ourselves from our attachment to what someone did to us in the past, together with our false expectations, disappointed hopes, and frustrated desires for the future, and realize how our conflict keeps us from being present. This means freeing ourselves from what happened to us. This, perhaps, led Jean-Paul Sartre to define freedom as "what we do with what was done to us."

The word "freedom" has hundreds of meanings, and can refer, for example, to the freedom to *have* (i.e., to own property or wealth), which can give rise to conflicts with "have-nots" over unequal distribution; the freedom to *do* (i.e., the right of independent action or movement), which can give rise to conflicts with those who are adversely impacted by our actions or movements; and the freedom to *be* (i.e., the freedom of self-actualization, including personality, thought, speech, religion, etc.), which can give rise to conflicts with those who wish to deprive others of the right to be, think, and speak in their own ways.

Being in the present in mediation, is not only being released from what happened in the past, or desires for an uncertain future, but from a *divided self*. For this reason, when experienced fully, being present initiates a return to authenticity. The "now" can feel like a caress, a sudden ecstasy, a moment of enlightenment. One approach to conflict resolution is therefore simply to shift people's attention from the past to the future, and then to the present and what is happening in their conversation, relationship, thoughts, and feelings, *right now*.

INVITATION TO A DANCE BETWEEN SELF AND OTHER

All conflicts, whether internal or external, concern the relationship with ourselves and with others, presenting mediators with a fundamentally *spiritual* question: How can hostile, closed-hearted, adversarial relationships be transformed into friendly, open-hearted, collaborative ones? Five answers automatically arise:

1. By changing the ways we think about and respond to them.
2. By changing the ways they think about and respond to us.
3. By changing the ways we communicate, negotiate, interact with, and relate to each other.
4. By changing the ways our systems, structures, institutions, and cultures model, encourage, and enforce responses to conflict.
5. By changing the ways we understand and respond to conflicts in general.

One contribution Buddhism has made to conflict resolution is to focus on the first, directing us to search for the sources of conflict within ourselves, rather than trying to change the way other people or systems act. Jiddu Krishnamurti wrote:

> The soil in which the meditative mind can begin is the soil of everyday life, the strife, the pain, and the fleeting joy. It must begin there, and bring order, and from there move endlessly. But if you are concerned only with making order, then that very order will bring about its own limitation, and the mind will be its prisoner. In all this movement you must somehow begin from the other end, from the other shore, and not always be concerned with this shore or how to cross the river. You must take a plunge into the water, not knowing how to swim. And the beauty of meditation is that you never know where you are, where you are going, what the end is.

The problem, according to the Buddha, as described in the *Aranavibhanga Sutta*, as described by Andrew Olendzki, can be seen in the ways we distinguish those we agree with, who are on the "right path," from those we oppose, who are on the "wrong" one. It is not, however, a matter of the path being either right or wrong. Indeed, Buddhism is filled with descriptions of right and wrong activities, including the "eight-fold path." Rather, the problem is one of failing, in the language of Fisher and Ury in *Getting to Yes*, to "separate the person from the problem," then being "soft on the person and hard on the problem."

When we agree with others, we praise them, and when we disagree, we criticize them, in hopes of changing their beliefs through reward and punishment. But both methods focus on the person, rather than on the problem or issue, leading to ego inflation, either through approval and self-importance, or disapproval and self-righteousness. Olendzki writes,

> At its worst, of course, the separation of persons from their views or behaviors does little good, for people often identify so strongly with these things that any criticism is taken as a personal attack. If you disparage my beliefs, I hold these so much as a part of who I am that you are essentially disparaging me. This is the insidious side of grasping, and of creating a self to which so many things belong.

Yet this separation is highly useful in mediation, in stopping the parties from engaging in "fight or flight" responses and focusing their attention on what they want, why it is important to them, what stands in *both* their ways, and what they might do together to overcome it. Then they will perhaps see that their mutual disparagement is simply a cover for their frustration and hurt feelings.

Initial separations can help mediators identify what gets people stuck in conflict, be it a loss of awareness or perspective, or simply being confused by hostile ideas, possibilities, or desires, and no sense of how to reconcile them. The Trappist monk Thomas Merton believed this confused state of mind itself can itself lead to conflict, even to violence:

> To allow ourselves to be carried away by a multitude of conflicting concerns, to surrender to too many demands, to commit oneself to too many projects, to want to help everyone in everything is to succumb to violence.

Alternatively, as suggested, we can define conflict as a quality of *energy* that arises between people, that both attracts and repels them, opens their eyes and blinds them, keeps them stuck and frees them. Four initial steps can then be taken to alter this energy, either by the mediators or the parties, for example:

1. Use empathy to find the *frequency* of the conflict inside themselves – the vibrational *quality* of their anger, fear, defensiveness, etc.
2. Search within themselves for the *opposite* frequency of respect, caring, openness to experience, etc., then flip or reverse these frequencies inside themselves.
3. *Amplify* positive energies to help reduce, calm, and cancel the negative vibrational energy the parties brought to their conflict.
4. *Occupy* or rest in that positive vibrational state, vibrate in sync with it, and turn it into an *unconditionally* positive quality of presence.

It is difficult to do *any* of this in the midst of conflict, not only because what our opponents say and do throws us off balance, but because one of the reasons we lose balance is that we are vulnerable to what they think of us, or get lost in the insecurities and self-doubts that emanate from our egos, and allow our integrity and sense of self to be influenced by what others think and how they treat us, and berate ourselves for not being who we should be. As Krishnamurti described it:

> We endlessly measure who we are with whom we think we should be. This habit of comparing ourselves with something or someone is one of the major causes of our conflicts. If we don't compare ourselves to anybody, we become who we are.

Conflict resolution turns integrity into a daily practice and connects it to the Buddhist idea of "no-self," in which the "self" is not a single, coherent, fixed, uniform, well-defined thing, but a collection of diverse aspects and processes, each of which is diverse, malleable, permeable, contingent, conflicted, and evolving moment-by-moment, based on the decisions we make, the voices we listen to, the ground on which we choose to stand.

MEDITATIVE PRACTICES IN MEDIATION

Before considering the specific ways mediators, coaches, and conflict resolvers can strengthen their meditative skills and capacities, it will be useful to consider what these skills and capacities fundamentally consist of. In my experience, an essential *initial* element in all awareness, mindfulness, insight, and similar spiritual practices is *stillness* or silence, even in the midst of chaos and conflict.

Being silent allows us, mediators and conflicted parties alike, to withdraw our attention from the *foreground* of conflict, consisting mostly of mutually reinforcing fight-or-flight reflexes, and amplify our awareness of the *background*, consisting of what the conflict *means*, how it feels, what matters about it, and why. These allow us to improve our ability to bring concentrated awareness to the moment-by-moment experience of the flow of life energy within, between, and around us, as we experience the parties' responses to their conflict.

In this sense, meditation is not about *doing*, but about *undoing*, in ways that allow us to return to *being*. Doing includes language, which carves the world up into separate, sometimes competitive pieces. It includes ego and the sense of a single, indivisible self, and all the ways we react and respond to conflict — especially how we try to push it away, without realizing that pushing away is the same as holding on. We can consider silence a first step in the translation of meditative ideas into mediative techniques and practices. [For more on these and a full range of meditation topics, see *The Mind Illuminated* by Culadasa (John Yates), a neuroscientist with a profound knowledge of meditation practices.]

A second step is to fine-tune our awareness, notice the ebb and flow of the fight-or-flight reflex with equanimity and acceptance. As we experience anger, fear, grief, or guilt, we can notice that the part of us that is *aware* of these emotions is not itself angry, frightened, grieving, or guilty, but instead stands *outside* them and looks in. In this way, awareness helps us diminish the blindness, compulsion, paralysis, and hypnosis that keep us stuck.

A third step is to allow, accept, and acknowledge each emotion, and notice how it appears, rises, wanes, and disappears. As Culadasa writes,

> Acknowledging, allowing, and accepting are the antidotes to avoiding, resisting, and rejecting. Acknowledge the validity of whatever comes up, even if you don't know its' origins. Allow it to be there without analyzing or judging it … Last, accept it as a manifestation of some hidden part of yourself.

Many meditators stop here, while mediators who want to defuse their own and the parties' intense emotions may want to go further. Culadasa again, writes,

> The strategy [in meditation] for dealing with emotions, thoughts, or images is simply to ignore them. … It's important not to get bogged down in examining the content of unconscious material. That's time-consuming and can interrupt your progress.

While this may be true for meditators who want to avoid distractions and practice concentration, these moments offer mediators unique opportunities to gain insight into the underpinnings of emotional experience in conflict, and dig deeper to discover its' laws of motion, and how to assuage and shift them.

A fourth step in mediation is to use empathy and compassion to notice that everyone in conflict experiences essentially the same intransigent emotions, ego defenses, moral rationalizations, and alienations, causing them to feel equally stuck. They can feel how emotions and the practice of empathy and compassion deeply connect us. As Tibetan monk Yongey Mingyur Rinpoche observed:

> Every technique of Buddhist meditation, ultimately, generates compassion. Whenever you look at your mind, you can't help but recognize your similarity to those around you. When you … look clearly at your own fear, anger, and aversion, you can't help but see that everyone around you feels the same fear, anger, and aversion. That is wisdom.

A fifth step is to gain insight into the deeper sources and underlying reasons that give rise to each emotion and conflict response, and use them to dismantle the fight-or-flight reflex from the inside out. Consider anger as an example. Imagine for a moment that you have a small child, and your child has run out into the middle of a busy street. You are likely to immediately run into the street and drag your child back to the sidewalk. Afterwards, you are likely to want to say something to your child, and will infuse your tone of voice with anger so your child, who was not hurt, will experience a bit of pain, and remember in the future not to do that again. If you dig deeper into your anger, you may discover that:

1. Your anger was an expression of your own feeling of powerlessness, together with a need to protect and warn your child.
2. Directly beneath your anger was a fear that something bad could have happened to your child.
3. Beneath your fear was a perception of the possibility that you might experience pain, loss, grief, and guilt.
4. Beneath the possibility of your pain, loss, grief, and guilt was *love*, caring, and kindness for the child who could have been harmed.
5. Each of these will take the form of different conversations, leading you deeper into the *ground* of your emotions.

6. The ground of anger is therefore not simply fear, or the possibility of loss, but *caring*.
7. We can then see that *no one* gets angry over things they *don't* care about.
8. It is therefore possible, in *any* angry exchange, to simply ask: "What are you afraid might happen?" Or: "How would you feel if it did?" Or: "Why do you care so deeply about this?" Each response will come from a place that is deeper than anger.

It is, of course, possible to be mindful and aware of our thoughts and emotions, yet stuck in them, without gaining insight into their deeper layers or meanings. What, then, can mediators and conflicted parties *do* with their highly emotional experiences? The simplest answer is: *nothing*, other than be present with them. But sometimes it feels more useful to do *something*, in order to arrive at a place where it is *possible* to do nothing.

What we can then do, not only in response to conflicts and other intense emotional experiences, but *all* impermanent, moment-by-moment experiences, is:

- Zero in on it, fine-tune it, and purify it.
- Distill it, concentrate it, and simplify it.
- Magnify it, expand it, and enlarge it.
- Diffuse it, suffuse it, and saturate oneself in it.
- Stop doing anything to it, rest in it, and watch it come and go.
- Figure out how to learn from it, discover what lies beneath it, and transform it into technique.
- Laugh at it, even enjoy it.

Some of these actions correspond to a set of ancient meditation practices called *"jhanas,"* or meditative absorptions. In a generic and implicit way, our capacity for insight can be found hidden, in miniature, and deeply embedded in a number of common meditation practices. We can, for example:

- Observe the breath.
- Scan the body and bring attention to sensory experiences as they arise, ebb, and flow.
- Concentrate attention on an object of concentration.
- Repeat a mantra.
- Chant or sing.
- Focus awareness on letting go of bodily sensations, thoughts, and emotions.
- Maximize feelings of pleasure, contentment, and well-being.
- Experience pain or pleasure moment-by-moment and concentrate on watching and letting them go.
- Breath in the pain and suffering of others, and breath out your health and happiness for the benefit of others.
- Practice mindfulness by paying attention to whatever is happening.
- Use imaging practices, like imagining that you are a bowl of delicious soup, or made of honey, and can taste it.

If we compare consciousness to a liquid or fluid, awareness in the midst of conflict is analogous to white-water rapids, and in resolution to slow, meandering rivers, or near-bottomless lakes, in which activity slows and stops. Each energy state gives rise to a different form of consciousness and quality of attention, ranging from the rapid, laser-like focus it takes to navigate rapids, to the slower, deeper, broader sensibilities that surface when the pace of events slows down.

A similar analogy can be used to describe conflict, and part of what many mediation, coaching, and conflict resolution practices consist of is slowing the pace of events, calming the fight-or-flight reflex, and allowing people time to reflect, so that simple acts, such as self-observation and listening to others; or more complex interactions, like appreciative inquiry, non-violent communication, emotional acknowledgement, empathetic dialogue, joint problem-solving, and collaborative negotiation, have sufficient time to succeed.

Another, subtler part of what mediation, coaching, and conflict resolution consist of is the evocation of a *mood*, attitude, mindset, perspective, orientation, or disposition toward the experience of conflict that allows mediators, coaches, and parties to gain insight into what triggered it, drop their attachment to demonizing and victimizing others, and shift their approach from one of antagonism and hostility to one of discovery and collaboration. This allows us to see, as Emily Dickenson described it, with "the unfurnished eye." Or as the eminent philosopher William James insightfully observed:

> Whenever you're in conflict with someone, there is one factor that can make the difference between damaging your relationship and deepening it. That factor is attitude.

Our ability as mediators to transform the attitudes of conflicted parties is significantly strengthened by meditation practices, especially those that improve our ability to identify and complete the various *stages* of letting go of attachment to false expectations of permanence, solidity, continuity, and successful outcomes. These stages are remarkably similar to the stages of grief in response to death and dying, initially identified by Elisabeth Kübler-Ross. [See Chapter 14.]

We may, for example, assume that everything in our lives and relationships will remain the same and have no reason to notice our attachments. But when we realize that what we hoped for and counted on to remain the same is fluid and changing, we may experience a desire to hold on, resist, or defend ourselves, and enter denial. Subsequent stages, characterized by anger, bargaining, depression, and acceptance, are also common responses to conflict, which causes traumas and losses that are exceeded only by death and dying.

MIRRORING, RESONANCE, AND SYNCHRONICITY IN MEDIATION

A central element in many meditative practices is the cultivation of a radical *openness* to experience that receives and reflects without denying, distorting, or disturbing; that does not intend, strive for, or try to be someone or something we are not. A famous Zen poem expresses this nicely: "The flying geese do not intend to cast a shadow. The lake has no desire to receive it."

In conflict, there is striving and suffering, and an effort to deny, distort, diminish, and *intentionally* disturb the qualities of conflict experience that might lead us to a deeper understanding–not only of where it came from and why it happened, but who we *become* when we are in it, what it *means* to us, what it can teach us as life lessons, how we can free ourselves from its' grip, how we can use it as a source of insight and wisdom, and a means of transformation and transcendence. This can be done, to begin with, by being *mindful* of our conflict-driven communications and behaviors, and those of others. Sometimes, simply taking a deep breath, slowing our breath, adopting a relaxed posture, or forming a friendly intention, will relax the fight-or-flight reflex, be recognized by others, and lead them to reciprocate, slow *their* breath, relax their posture, become less stressed, and disarm their fight or flight reflex. These "mirroring" responses can dramatically alter the quality of our presence; our degree of openness to empathy and compassion; our capacity for loving-kindness, our "radical acceptance," as Tara Brach labels it; our commitment to working through the conflict; the quality of our presence; and our availability for connection and problem-solving, at every moment.

A recent study by Associate Professor Maria Kozhevnikov from the Department of Psychology at the National University of Singapore, researched a group of *non*-mindfulness meditation practices that sought to regulate the stress individuals experienced, rather than trying to reduce it, using "arousal-based" meditations. These included Vajrayana (Tantric Buddhism), practiced by Sufis and others, such as Hindu Tantra and East Asian martial arts. Kozhevnikov showed that it is possible to stimulate the brain, rather than relax it, achieve a level of voluntary control over stress and the "fight or flight" response, and thereby maximize physical and cognitive performance:

> These practices push practitioners to their limits, so they can stay focused on the task, being free from any distracting thoughts, even in the most threatening situations. The findings open up a wide range of potential medical and behavioral interventions that not only allow meditation practitioners to regulate stress but also boost physical and attentional capacities upon demand, and even access latent brain resources to prevent cognitive decline.

A 2022 meta-analysis that examined numerous brain-scanning studies showed how meditation alters brain activity and connectivity. The authors reported that meditation reorganizes the brain's connectivity and spatial topography, leading meditators to experience a "dissolution of the boundaries between the self and the environment," and "a state of unity with the world." For meditators, rather than being separate, "inner and outer world exist in an undivided continuum," and "self, body, and environment are strongly aligned."

These and similar meditative practices enable mediators to not just watch and take note of what conflicted parties do, but to *enter* the conflict, with all its negativity and intensity, and discover *from the inside* how to find a way — not out, but *through*. One way of doing so is to transition from mindfulness to awareness and insight practices, for example, by asking some deceptively simple questions:

- What *is* the mind that is mindful?
- How do we learn what to be mindful of?
- What activates the mind?
- What are its' deeper sources?
- How does the mind move and react when it is in conflict?
- Why does it move and react in those ways, as opposed to others?
- How might the mind move and react to conflict more "mindfully"?
- How does the mind construct the self?
- How does it perceive the minds of others?
- What happens when we become mindful of mindfulness?
- What does the mind consist of when it is silent and at rest?

We do not yet know the scientific answers to these questions, yet mediators may intuitively recognize many of the answers using meditation and other Buddhist practices. Sōtō Zen monk Katagiri Roshi brilliantly described something similar when he wrote, regarding Western philosophy:

> I have been reading your Descartes. Very interesting. 'I think, therefore I am.' He forgot to mention the other part. I'm sure he knew, he just forgot: "I don't think, therefore I'm not."

MEDITATION PRACTICES FOR MEDIATORS

Many mediators want to improve *both* their mediation and meditation practices, yet see them as separate activities, whereas they are deeply interconnected. We can therefore hypothesize: *Every* mediation *is* a meditation, and every meditation is a mediation. This allows us to ask: How might these practices be combined in ways that are not merely additive, but multiplicative, and exponential?

To begin, here is a simple 10-step meditative practice mediators, coaches, and conflict resolvers can use before, after, and even *during* their next session:

1. Balance your posture.
2. Withdraw a part of your attention from your senses, the parties, and the world around you, and focus it inward.
3. In your mind, take a backward step, as Dōgen suggested, rotate your attention, and focus it inward.
4. Find the place inside that is silent, and deeper than words or thoughts.
5. Concentrate your awareness, then let it go and rest there.
6. If you are in a mediation session, use empathy to discover both parties inside yourself, without ever losing touch with yourself.
7. When you are ready, rotate your attention, and bring the *feeling* of that connection back to the session.
8. Increase awareness of your basic senses: sight, hearing, smell, taste, and touch, plus mind, emotion, interoception and proprioception (the state of your body and changes that take place inside it).
9. Add an extra "spiritual" sense, and try to experience, moment by moment, the flow of life energy within, between, and around you.
10. Center yourself in that energy, become clear in your *intention*, values, and integrity, and let the rest flow naturally.

Meditation practices sometimes begin by focusing or concentrating attention on an *object* of concentration, like the breath. That is: there is a *subject* (us), a *verb* (concentrating), and an *object* (the breath). We can then move to concentrating attention *without* an object of concentration, leaving only a subject (us), and a verb (concentrating), without a *thing* or object to concentrate on. We can move further to simply *being* concentrated, or being, without the presence of a verb or object—or even a subject. As meditation teacher and writer Ken McLeod observed:

When you let the practice work on you, what you think about what is happening—whether practice is going well, whether you are going to achieve anything, whether you have what it takes, and so on—becomes irrelevant. The only thing that matters is that you do the practice. When you take this approach to practice, practice slips beneath the cognitive mind and you feel its impact emotionally and physically. At first, you may not notice anything, but over time, as you give yourself over and over again to the practice, you find that changes take place in how you sit and move, how you speak and listen, how you experience the world, and how you respond to what you experience — in ways that you did not anticipate or expect.

For mediators and conflict resolvers, here are a few additional *implicit* meditative practices you might try using, even during highly emotional mediation sessions:

1. From your center, expand your full attention and spatial awareness to include the parties, and the world around you.
2. Mirror the postures, thoughts, emotions, energies, and "heart spaces" of the people you are listening to.
3. Construct an inner space that seeks ways of combining these inputs with empathy and compassion, without ever losing your sense of yourself in the process.
4. Slow ... the pace ... of your speech, lengthen the silences ... *soften* your tone of voice, and take a moment in silence to reflect calmly on what was just said.
5. Use gentle gestures to communicate, via mirror neurons, your empathy and compassion — for example, through body movements, tone of voice, emotional openness, and small acts of kindness.
6. Ask questions about what is happening right now in the session, or what just happened, and what they would *like* to happen when they resume their conversation.
7. Ask questions about what emotions the parties are feeling, where in their bodies they are feeling them, whether the one

who is aware of these feelings is inside or outside the
feelings, and what happens to these feelings as they become
more aware of them.

8. Ask them if they would be willing to take a moment in
   silence to reflect on how they are feeling, where they are in
   the conversation, and what they might do to move it in a
   more positive direction.

9. Ask them, "If this were the last conversation you were going
   to have with each other, what is the very last thing you
   would want to say?"

10. Ask whether either of them has become more mindful or
    aware, or gained any insight into what went wrong as a
    result of their conflict, what they would like to do better,
    and what *you* might do better as their mediator.

None of these suggestions requires the parties to participate in a
"typical" meditation practice, yet each indirectly replicates some
common aspects of those practices. In cases where the parties are
practicing meditators, or belong to a spiritual community or
religious organization, you can ask if they would like to begin the
session with a guided meditation, or offer a prayer for the session,
or sit in silence a moment and think about what they want to
achieve today, or tell each other what they hope the mediation will
achieve, and why.

We can decide to go still deeper, and ask them if there is anything
either of them would like to apologize for, or thank, or appreciate,
or acknowledge the other person for; or one thing they are grateful
for, or that they learned as a result of this conflict; or one thing they
now wish they had done differently.

In my experience, the deeper *I* am willing to go in exploring and
gaining insight into myself, the deeper they will allow me to go in
exploring theirs. From my center, I can often touch theirs, but from
my periphery I am rarely able to move beyond theirs. Meditation
enables me to *calibrate* and fine tune my intuition about what *might*

be true for them, allowing me to then formulate a more empathetic, dangerous, and targeted question to find out what *is* true for them.

In an effort to describe the inner journey of meditation more obliquely, I opted to try to express it as a parable, which became "The Parable of the Mountain Top:"

> Imagine for a moment that you live in a city and would like to climb to the top of a mountain. You can't see the mountain from the city and don't know how to get there, but are determined to try. You climb inside your car, pack everything you think you might need, and begin to drive. At first, you have lots of errands to run and are not even sure how to get out of the city, so you spend a lot of time stopping and starting, getting lost, and driving around in circles.

> At last, you reach the outskirts of the city and start to relax. The further you get from the city the more relaxed you become. Off in the distance, through the smog and haze, you can just make out the presence of a mountain and begin to drive in its direction. You may stop along the way to rest or picnic and pick the flowers, and may think that this is as far as you really want to go.

> After a while you decide to keep going anyway, and the mountain becomes clearer and closer as you drive. At last you reach the base of the mountain and discover that as long as you continue driving you will circle the mountain without getting any higher or closer to the top. The mountain is quite beautiful, and you may again think that this is all you really want, and besides, leaving the security, comfort, and familiarity of your car feels risky.

> You are now in the spell of the mountain, however, so you grab your backpack, leave your car, and begin hiking along a trail. You are now on the mountain and amazed at its beauty. You notice things you could not have seen from a distance, and your relaxation becomes deeper the further you go into the forest. Still, you find

yourself circling the mountain at the same modest altitude, and could easily continue wandering amidst its beauty, but decide to keep on climbing.

Sooner or later, the trail begins to peter out and the climbing becomes more difficult. The trees grow fewer and the rocks more numerous, and you again stop and could decide not to go any further. Nonetheless, you reluctantly leave your backpack, put on your daypack, and begin scrambling over the rocks, relying on your awareness and instincts, with no trail to guide you. You feel yourself becoming more fit, and taking pleasure in the challenge of the climb.

Inevitably, you come to a sheer precipice that offers no clear way forward. Even so, you ditch your daypack, keeping only your pickaxe and rope, and start to scale the precipice hand-over-hand. There is now no room for idle thoughts. Every inch is a struggle, exhausting, and at the same time exhilarating. Every moment is ecstasy. You are completely alive, awake, focused, and relaxed. Once again, you might easily remain, but decide instead to keep on climbing.

Ultimately, you reach a point where you discover that you are circling the pinnacle and can go no higher by climbing. The peak is now in clear view, and you discover that the only way you can reach it is by dropping everything, shedding your clothes, letting go — even of your desire to reach the top, and floating upwards. Nothing in your journey until now has prepared you for such a move, but you let go, discovering as you do that the mountain is actually inside you, and that you can reach the top any time you want, even within the confines of the city, simply by being who you already are.

One of the consequences of impermanence is that *nothing* works always, everywhere, or with everyone. What we are looking for is *not* the universal, but the generic, the essential, the core. From there, we hypothesize the strategic, and develop specific, tactical ways of applying our insights; and from there, we can evaluate, learn, evolve, and self-correct. This is what makes anything a practice.

A final insight: research in neurophysiology has revealed that the neurons responsible for smiling also produce happiness, and *vice versa*. For this reason, happiness makes us smile, and smiling makes us happy, letting us consciously decide to smile and produce happy feelings. In similar ways, dismantling our fight-or-flight reflex makes us calmer when we are in conflict and better able to solve the underlying problems that gave rise to it; and calming ourselves through meditation practices teaches our minds and bodies how to dismantle the fight-or-flight reflex and develop more skillful, collaborative approaches to solving problems, even in the midst of immense chaos, bitterness, and confusion.

If we wanted to learn new skills in meditation or conflict resolution using only language, it would be like trying to tell our bodies, synapse by synapse, how to execute an intricate dance step, or ride a bicycle – it would take forever. But through continual practice, trial and error, and quieting the frightened mind, our bodies easily, quickly, and naturally learn how to dance and ride bicycles.

Meditation teaches us how to listen with *rapt* attention, not only to the words people use in conflicts, but to their bodies' responses, to our own and others' wishes and desires, interests and intentions, hopes and fears, that are rarely, if ever, spoken to those our conflicts have taught us to distrust. Nonetheless, they are all implicit in our tone of voice, body language, facial movements, gestures, and inflections – even in our heart rate and style of breathing.

In a fascinating study, people who felt deeply connected or attracted to each other during a speed dating exercise not only began to breathe in sync, but their hearts also began beating together. This raises the question: How did their bodies figure out how to do this? And a follow-up question: Can our goal as mediators be to connect so deeply and profoundly with *both* parties that our hearts beat in sync? As meditation teacher Tara Brach advised, "Whatever you most care about, let this tenderness of heart energize your meditation. The sincerity of your longing will carry you home." It is no different in mediation.

FOUR

The Art of Asking Questions

CURIOSITY AS A SOURCE OF TRANSFORMATION AND TRANSCENDENCE

We are all partners in a quest. The essential questions have no answers. You are my question, and I am yours – and then there is dialogue. The moment we have answers, there is no dialogue. Questions unite people, answers divide them. So why have answers when you can live without them?

Elie Wiesel

If the solution to a problem of absolute disagreement extends to a call for bloodshed, then neither party has demonstrated the intelligence to formulate the question properly.

John Steinbeck

One's life, viewed as a whole, is always the answer to the most important questions. Along the way, what does it matter what one says, what words and principles one chooses to justify oneself? At the very end, one's answers to the questions the world has posed with such relentlessness are to be found in the facts of one's life. Questions such as: Who are you? What did you actually want? What could you actually achieve?

At what points were you loyal or disloyal or brave or a coward? And one answers as best one can, honestly or dishonestly, that's not so important. What's important is that finally one answers with one's life.

Sandor Marai

THERE ARE TWO PRIMARY REASONS FOR ASKING QUESTIONS. THE FIRST, of course, is to find answers. The second is to find deeper questions, which are themselves partly answers, and may lead to still deeper questions and answers. The primary reason for asking questions in mediation is to reveal the deeper, disguised, repressed sources of conflict that are hidden *beneath* the issues people are arguing about, and surface the complex wishes, desires, and interests that inform and give rise to each party's positions. Alternatively, we can describe the reasons for asking questions in conflict resolution as:

- Helping people gain *insight* into the sources of their conflicts, the reasons why they are stuck, and reveal a path forward.
- Helping people gain *perspective* on themselves, their opponents, and the issues, strengthen their capacity for empathy and humility, recalibrate their attitudes and intentions, surface their interests, and seek ways of jointly satisfying them.

WHAT ARE QUESTIONS?

To begin, what exactly *are* questions? What do they *do*? What makes them useful or effective in achieving these goals? We can think of questions in mediation as:

- Methods for stimulating and strengthening curiosity
- Means of pointing awareness toward hidden meanings
- Ways of looking together in the same direction
- Invitations to a journey or adventure, of discovery

- Explorations of the unknown and unknowable
- Dialogues with the truth
- Paths to insight, awareness, and self-discovery
- Sources of permission to change, adapt, and evolve
- Searches for buried treasure
- Scalpels to excise what is diseased or harmful
- Meetings with mystery and surprise
- Expressions of love and caring

Each of these can help guide the question asking process, by shaping, fine-tuning, and sharpening the question, transforming it from a blunt instrument into a precision crafted probe that can disarm the natural defenses people in conflict throw up to protect themselves from their own vulnerability, and the pain of rejection and loss.

THREE CATEGORIES OF QUESTIONS

It is important for mediators to recognize that, like all dispute resolution processes, asking questions is an *intervention* that can be categorized according to conflict resolution principles. As a result, the kinds of questions we ask can be grouped into three distinct categories:

1. **Questions based on *power*,** resulting in answers that directly and indirectly reinforce:

- Obedience
- Loyalty, or acceptance of ranking
- Dominance in hierarchies and status

A simple example might be: "Who is the oldest or tallest person in the group?", which will result in a single correct answer for everyone, as there can only be one oldest or tallest. Also, every answer will be located on a line, generating a hierarchy or ranking system from best to worst, and reinforcing other hierarchies.

2. Questions based on *rights*, resulting in answers that directly and *indirectly* reinforce:

- Compliance with abstract rules and regulations
- Bureaucratic forms and processes
- Single, uniform, objective facts

A simple example might be: "How old or tall are you?", which will result in a single correct answer for each person, as we can only be one age or height. Also, every answer will be located on a plane, creating hierarchies or ranking systems as before, and "breadth," or diversity.

3. Questions based on *interests*, resulting in answers that directly or *indirectly* reinforce:

- Unique personal wishes and desires
- Complex emotions
- Multiple, diverse, subjective truths

A simple example might be:

"What issues are you facing at whatever age you are at?"

"What does your height *mean* to you?"

"What did it mean to you growing up?"

These questions will result in multiple correct answers for each person that *cannot* be ranked hierarchically, and are far more complex, diverse, and interesting. Also, every answer will be located in a cube that now has "depth. While "magic," in the sense of unexpected answers or fresh insights, is unlikely to occur in response to questions in categories 1 and 2, it is far more likely to arise in response to questions in category 3, as these evoke reflection, resist simplification, and invite deeper insights.

There are *countless* questions like this that can fundamentally transform what happens in conflict conversations. Consider, for example, what people might feel and say in response to these questions:

- What question, if it were answered, would mean the most to you right now?
- What does the other person's response mean to you? What is important about it? Why does it matter to you?
- What *draws* you to this issue? What is your history with it?
- What is your intention or deeper purpose regarding this issue?
- What hidden opportunities do you see in this conversation?
- What dilemmas or dangers do you see in it?
- What assumptions do you need to test or challenge in addressing it?
- What do you know about it so far? What do you *not* know, or still need to learn?
- What do you think may lie *beneath* the opinions you've formed about it, or about each other?
- What is at the center of this issue for you?
- What has surprised you in what you've heard so far? What has challenged you?
- What is absent or missing from the picture so far? What is it either of you is *not* seeing? What do you need more clarity about?
- What has been your greatest learning, insight, or discovery so far?
- What is the next level of thinking you need to get to in order to solve this problem?
- If there is one thing that hasn't been said, but *needs* to be said in order to reach a solution, what would it be?
- What would it take to improve the way you are communicating with each other, or addressing this issue?

- What would enable you to feel more engaged, energized, or effective in solving it?
- What do you imagine *you* might be able to do to solve it?
- What most needs your attention right now, or going forward?
- If your success were completely guaranteed, what creative ideas might you be willing to try?
- What support do you need to move forward?
- What conversation, if you started it today, could create new possibilities for your future?
- What seed could you plant together that would make the greatest difference to your future?
- What questions might you ask each other that could change everything?
- What question would you most like to be asked right now? What question have you been waiting for? What question do you yearn or pine for?
- What question have you always wanted to ask him/her, but were afraid to ask?
- What question do you, or they, most hope you will *not* be asked?
- What question, if it were asked right now, could take your breath away, or drop you to your knees?
- What question could either of you ask that, if answered, might convince you that you are *completely wrong* about what you've been thinking about each other, or about the issue?
- What question have you been withholding or hoarding? Why?
- What question, when you are going home afterwards, will you wish you had asked today, or be disappointed that you didn't ask?
- What kind of person would you most like to be in this conflict? What values or higher qualities would you most

like to bring to this conversation? What questions might you ask that would allow you to be and do that?

[Some questions based on work by Eric E. Vogt, Juanita Brown and David Isaacs in *The Art of Powerful Questions*]

These "category 3" questions encourage people to reflect on how their conflicts have trapped or confined them in ways of thinking, feeling, acting, and being that have kept them stuck and blocked their capacity for dialogue, learning, and growth; and this realization, *by itself*, has magic in it.

Clearly, the most useful and effective questions in mediation are those that mirror the interest-based nature of the process, allow conflict resolvers to elicit the deeper meanings of the conflict to each person; and point to multiple, diverse, non-zero-sum answers, or to alternate paths that might be taken to resolve, transform, and transcend it.

QUESTIONS ABOUT ASKING QUESTIONS

We may also find it useful in conflict resolution to consider asking some foundational questions regarding the deeper nature, process, and meaning of asking questions. We may, for example, want to start by asking *ourselves*, and perhaps the parties, if it feels appropriate, questions like:

- Who is it who wants to know the answer? Who, *exactly*, is asking?
- Why do you want to know? What is driving your curiosity?
- Why do you care what the answer is?
- Is the question *dangerous* enough? Is it courageous, and willing to go to the heart of the problem?
- What question do you, as the mediator or the parties, most or least want to answer?
- What, in your life or theirs, could change based on the answer?

- What is the significance of the question, to you and to them?
- What is the type and quality of *energy* contained in the question?
- How much *audacity* and *kindness* are represented in the question?
- How willing are you to ask the same question of yourself?
- How prepared are you to be shocked, or touched deeply by the answer?
- How might you turn the answer into a deeper question?

What to Listen *For* in the Answer

Mediators are routinely taught active, responsive, and empathetic listening techniques, which are highly useful, but we are rarely taught what to listen *for* as the parties respond to our questions, or their questions to each other, or their stories and narratives.

The following page includes a few things we can all listen *for* in the parties' statements and responses, each of which suggests additional questions. These responses are present *microscopically* in all conflict conversations. Each one increases in strength and importance with the depth of the question and the profundity, poignancy, and vulnerability of the response.

By learning to listen for these qualities in ordinary conflict conversations, we get better at designing questions that give people permission to answer with honesty, caring, and authenticity. By doing so, we strengthen their ability to tell each other what is real and true for them, and convince them that their interests are more likely to be satisfied through collaborative, than by adversarial methods. See the following page for a comparison for "what to listen for in the answer."

- Facts
- Subjective Experiences
- Emotions
- Intentions
- Interests and Positions
- Dreams and Visions
- Humiliations
- Family Patterns
- Defensiveness
- Denials
- Insults
- Metaphors
- Stereotypes
- Openings to Dialogue
- Need for Support
- Universality
- Conflict Styles
- Cries for Help

- Interpretations
- Modes of perception
- Roles
- Expectations
- Wishes and Desires
- Fears
- Ego Defenses
- Self-Esteem
- Resistance
- Confessions
- Self-Doubts
- Subconscious Meaning
- Prejudices
- Offers to Negotiation
- Need for Validation
- Uniqueness
- Vulnerabilities
- Desire for Forgiveness

WHAT IS *BETTER* THAN PERSUASION?

For the most part, people engage in conflict conversations to persuade the other side that they are right, or at least not wrong, hoping thereby to increase the likelihood that *their* needs, desires, expectations, hopes, and interests will be met. Unfortunately, their approach to persuasion is nearly always adversarial and defensive, which triggers the other person's "fight-or-flight (or-freeze-or-fawn-or-flock)" reflex, resulting in cycles of defensiveness, counterattack, withdrawal, and similar adversarial responses. These adversarial approaches to persuasion often take the form of factual assertions that are denied, ignored, minimized, or countered with alternative facts by the other side, or by self-serving references to logic, character, or emotion. These arguments roughly follow Aristotle's classic description of the elements of rhetoric, which he argued were grounded in:

1. *Logos:* Arguments based on logic or reason, or on evidence such as facts or figures
2. *Ethos:* Arguments based on character or ethics, or on credibility or expertise
3. *Pathos:* Arguments based on emotion or feelings, or on trauma and suffering

As mediators, we recognize that these are nearly always ineffective in convincing the other side. We may therefore want to ask different, deeper questions, which are answers to a practical philosophical question: what is *better* than persuasion? One answer is a finely-honed question that could lead the parties to a place of:

1. Self-discovery
2. Profound realization
3. Fresh insight
4. Heightened awareness
5. New ways of thinking
6. Increased ownership of the problem
7. Discovery of complex, multi-sided truths
8. Improved capacity for communication
9. Creative problem-solving
10. Better and more satisfying relationships
11. Learning and wisdom
12. Greater humility and increased skills
13. Transcendence of the problem
14. Personal, relational, and systemic change

We can therefore "reverse engineer" the conflict resolution process by asking: What kinds of questions might be able to achieve these outcomes?

Before beginning this process, it is important to first question our own attitudes and approaches to conflict resolution, and our motivation for asking questions.

SOME INITIAL QUESTIONS FOR MEDIATORS AND PROBLEM SOLVERS

Mediation is a form of joint problem-solving, and it is important at the outset to ask some foundational questions about how and why we want to solve problems.

Here are five sets of questions I have asked myself, and now ask others, regarding our orientation and bias toward *answers*, which can sometimes result in imposing solutions prematurely that do not adequately address the root causes or underlying reasons for the problem. These are:

1. You have solved thousands of problems and learned a great deal in your life. How open are you to the possibility that what you have learned is now irrelevant or completely wrong? How do you manage to stay in touch with your ignorance? How good are you at unlearning? How able are you to live in the present without focusing on the past or the future?

2. You have learned countless ways to solve problems. Have you also learned how to *not* solve them? How willing are you to live with paradox, riddle, polarity, and enigma? Do you understand that by solving your problems too quickly, you could cheat yourself out of learning from them?

3. You know how to make things happen. Do you know how to let them happen naturally and fluidly on their own? Do you know how to *not* intervene? Can you let things happen to you, and simply watch them as they happen? Are you addicted to controlling the outcome or the process?

4. You understand a great deal about what is. Do you also understand what is not, and what could be? Do you see not only what, but *who* is in front of you? Do you understand that what you understand includes the nature of your own understanding?

5. You have developed a number of strengths and achieved successes. Do you recognize that for every strength there is

a corresponding weakness? Do you understand that continued success leads to complacency, while failure leads to learning and change? Which, then, is the success and which the failure?

12 Questions for Anyone in Conflict

After we dismantle our biases, predilections, compulsions, and addictions to solving problems, together with our need to help others who are confused or conflicted or feel unable to help themselves, it is possible to ask people in conflict an initial set of very simple questions to reveal some of the ways we get stuck.

Here are 12 questions, originally designed to be asked by elementary school children, their parents, teachers, staff, and school administrators, in a coordinated effort to create a *culture* of conflict resolution that would be basic, simple, and accessible to children as well as adults, yet grounded in a complex understanding of the reasons for their conflict. Each question is a threshold, or starting place, leading to additional questions that flow from the answers:

1. What happened?
2. How did it feel?
3. What do you want?
4. Why do you want it?
5. What does the other person want?
6. Why do they want it?
7. What are each of you doing in order to get it?
8. Is that working?
9. What do you think you might do instead?
10. What could you each do to help solve the problem? Are you willing to try that?
11. What have you learned that you want to do differently next time?
12. Is there anything else you want to say to each other before we end?

These questions can be laminated, pinned to clothing or kept in a wallet, and revised or expanded as circumstances shift and people become more skillful. Many school mediation programs practice more elaborate techniques, but I find simpler ones more useful for nursery school and kindergarten students, and there are significant advantages to adopting a single "lowest common denominator" approach that envelops everyone, and strengthens skills everywhere.

PRE-SESSION EVALUATION QUESTIONS

Sometimes, in workplaces and organizations, people are ordered or coerced into attending mediations or conflict resolution trainings to get them to fix their dysfunctional behaviors, without specifying what they are.

Here are some questions to ask people who are resistant from the outset, several suggested by Peter Block, in the form of a written survey or poll:

Please rate your expectations regarding the session we are about to have and how you expect to participate on a scale of 1 to 10, 10 being highest.

1. *How valuable an experience do you plan to have today?* (1 = terrible, 10 = fantastic)
2. *How participative and engaged do you plan to be?* (1 = asleep, 10 = extremely excited)
3. *How much risk do you plan to take?* (1 = none, 10 = serious adventure)
4. *How open, honest and constructive do you plan to be?* (1 = silent, 10 = painfully honest)
5. *How willing are you to listen non-defensively and non-judgmentally to others?* (1 = doing email, 10 = completely open)
6. *How responsible do you feel for your own learning?* (1 = not at all, 10 = entirely)

7. *How responsible do you feel for the learning of others?* (1 = not at all, 10 = totally)

8. *How committed are you to implementing what you learn?* (1 = amnesia, 10 = complete commitment)

After answering, people meet in small groups to discuss their answers and what they mean, and it rapidly becomes apparent that their answers are self-fulfilling prophecies that will generate the results they anticipate.

When the small groups report on their insights, we can ask: which result do you want, why, what do you expect will happen as a consequence, and what are your intentions now?

QUESTIONS ON ASSESSING CONFLICT

In many conflicts, especially in groups and organizations, it is helpful to begin the resolution process by interviewing people on both sides of the issue, as well as in the middle, and do so both vertically and horizontally across the organization, in order to assess the issues that need to be resolved in the conflict by asking a few simple, initial, fact-gathering questions about it, such as:

- How and when did it begin?
- Who is involved? Who is impacted by it?
- What are the presenting issues?
- Is it one-of-a-kind or chronic and repeating?
- Is it superficial or deep?
- Is there a more fundamental problem beneath the surface?
- Is it connected to a system or to other problems?
- What emotions are people are experiencing?
- What metaphors are being used by different people to describe it?
- Is the conflict specific or general, localized or widespread, controlled or chaotic?
- *Why* does it exist? What caused it?

- What has been done to resolve it? What hasn't been done?
- What is reinforcing the conflict, or rewarding negative behaviors?
- How urgent is it to each person?
- What is the potential damage or cost of not resolving it?
- What is causing it to turn in a circle?
- How does it impact the vision, mission, objectives, values or goals of the organization, team, or group?
- How does it impact each participant?
- What is the level of distrust?
- What are the sources of resistance?
- How much desire is there for change?
- What *kind* of resolution is required? Why?

Conflicts quickly evolve, mutate, and shift focus, so whatever initial answers people may give, the assessment process *itself* will alter them, as will every other intervention. This means the focus should not be on the answers, but on creating a culture of curiosity and investigation around the conflict, using questions to find answers that lead to better questions, encouraging people to dig deeper, and demonstrating that the assessment process is continuous and never complete.

SOME CONFLICT COACHING QUESTIONS

A next step in the resolution process may be one-on-one coaching sessions with key people who have participated in, or been impacted by the conflict. This may take the form of a "conflict coaching" session, in which there is greater permission to ask difficult and dangerous questions.

If the mediator has been successful in empathizing and building trust, and can do so without judgment, bias, or blame, it may be helpful to ask some of the following "edgy" questions:

- What have you contributed, by action or inaction, to allowing or making this conflict happen?
- With hindsight, how might you have handled it better?
- How would you evaluate your responses so far? What have you done that has been effective? What hasn't been effective?
- How have you suffered as a result of your own actions or inactions?
- How have other suffered?
- What does this conflict ask you to let go of or learn to accept?
- What is the most important lesson you've learned from this conflict?
- Is it possible for both versions of what happened to be correct? How?
- In what way could this conflict improve your life, or make it worse?
- Is there anything that feels funny or ridiculous about this conflict? Anything that feels apt or profound? Pointless? Meaningful? Etc.
- What would you most like to say to your opponent? Why?
- What would it take for you to let go of this conflict completely?
- What would happen in your life if you did?
- Have your communications been effective in creating understanding in the other person? What could you do to improve them?
- What skills might you develop in handling this conflict? In responding to negative behavior?
- What values would you most like to live up to in the future?

The goal of conflict coaching questions is to encourage reflection, which can lead to insight and elicit a realization that the attitudes and behaviors we experience, and responsibility for the difficulties we face, are our own; and we can improve our lives by looking more carefully and accurately at what isn't working, and strengthening the ways we respond to it.

INTERNALIZING QUESTIONS

Most people in conflict are focused *externally* on their opponents, on what they are saying and doing, the quality of their intentions, and what is wrong with their personalities or positions or proposals. As mediators, we can shift this pattern and preoccupation by asking questions that turn their focus inward. For example, depending on the circumstances, we may want to ask:

- Have you ever experienced this kind of conflict before? When? With whom? What did you do then? Did that work? Why not?
- What kinds of conflicts have you experienced in your life? What do they have in common?
- Can you imagine letting it go and releasing it forever? If not, why not?
- What are some things you *haven't* done in this conflict but should have? What kept you from doing them?
- What are some things you *have* done but shouldn't have? What compelled you to do them?
- What part of your past controls your present? What would change or be different if you decided to let it go?
- How much of what you have done in this conflict was *chosen* by you? How much was chosen by others?
- Who wrote the script for what you did or did not do or say in this conflict? When was it written? Why? What purpose does it serve?
- What myths and assumptions do you think shaped this script?
- What is this conflict asking you to learn, or let go of?
- Is there any difference between what you thought or felt and what you said? What is the difference? How does that

feel? What would you like to do or say instead? What's keeping you from doing it?

- What are the most important lessons you've learned in your life? How could you apply them to this conflict?
- What judgments do you have about yourself, or your opponent, based on your life choices? How have they impacted this conflict?
- What have been the peak experiences in your life? Your greatest failures? How have they each impacted this conflict?
- What do you never, *ever* want to hear or experience again? What do you think you might do to prevent that from happening?
- What do you imagine your life will be like in 5 years? Your relationships? How might you start moving toward the future you want, *today*, in this conflict?

QUESTIONS FOR CLOSE RELATIONSHIPS

Much of what takes place in couples, families, friendships, and other close relationships lies buried beneath *layers* of unspoken desire, expectation, anxiety, hope, fear, anger, shame, guilt, jealousy, and similar emotions, each of which can be stirred up by a combination of uncaring, uncertainty, absence of attachment to outcomes, dysfunctional responses to conflict, and lack of skill, which lead to an accumulation of unasked and unanswered questions that diminish our *capacity* for intimacy, connection, and authentic, loving relationships.

Here are a few questions couples, families, friends, and others in close or intimate relationships can ask one another to cut through these layers and surface unspoken concerns, with the goal of strengthening their communications and relationships, or that mediators can ask in joint sessions or in caucus:

- What qualities initially attracted you to each other?

- What did you first love or appreciate about each other? Have those changed, now that you know each other better?
- Why are you interested in being in a relationship with each other?
- What words or phrases would you use to describe the kind of relationship you *most* want to have with each other?
- Do either of you disagree with any of those words? If so, you have reached consensus. Now how can you make them happen?
- Do any of us have permission to stop the conversation if we begin moving away from those words?
- What do you hope to achieve through this conversation that could strengthen your relationship?
- Do you have any fears, anxieties, or concerns about talking about your relationship? What are they?
- What is one thing the other person could say or do that could help you reduce your fears, anxieties, or concerns? Would you like to know one thing you could say or do to reduce their fears, anxieties, or concerns?
- What is one thing about you, your history, or your wishes that you haven't yet communicated to each other, but would like to?
- What is one argument or conflict you have had in your relationship? How often have you had it? What triggers it for you?
- What happens when you argue that you wish would not happen, or happen differently?
- What is one thing the other person could say or do that could help you communicate better when you have a disagreement? Would you like to know one thing you could do or say that would help the other person communicate better with you?
- What is one thing you would like the other person *not* to do or say the next time you have an argument or conflict? What

does it mean when the other person does that? Why does that matter to you?

- How did people in your family of origin argue or behave when they disagreed or had conflicts?
- What issues did your parents argue about? Were those the *real* issues? If not, what were they?
- How did they finally *stop* arguing, overcome their differences, or resolve their conflicts?
- Would you like to do the same as your parents? If not, what would you want to do differently?
- What are some of the patterns you slip into when you argue that you would like to break? How can you help each other break them?
- Are there any ground rules or protocols you would like to propose to help resolve future conflicts and disagreements with each other?
- Were there patterns to the conflicts in your family of origin regarding money? Physical intimacy? Emotional issues? Illness? Time or space? Eating? (etc.). What were they?
- Which of these patterns would you like to change? Why?
- What do these patterns mean to you?
- What do you want from each other? *Why* do you want it? What are you afraid will happen if you don't get it, or can't agree about it?
- What does the word "relationship" mean to you? The word "love"? The word "conflict"?
- What other issues would you like to discuss that we haven't talked about, but you feel are important to your relationship?
- If you were to write a "Constitution" for your relationship, what would you want to include? What would the Preamble say? The Bill of Rights? Etc.
- What do you most want for your future?
- How would you like to make decisions regarding divisive issues that arise in the future?

- How might you sabotage your own happiness? What can you do to make sure that doesn't happen?
- What issues, concerns, or fears have you been holding on to that you haven't mentioned? Why have you been holding on to them?
- What would you like to say to each other right now, as a reassurance that, in spite of talking about these difficult issues, you still want to be in a caring relationship with each other?

QUESTIONS FOR DIALOGUE AND POLITICAL POLARIZATION

Conflict resolvers, coaches, and facilitators may try to design questions that will deepen the dialogue between people who disagree with each other, especially ethically, morally, religiously, or politically, and assist them in discovering how to turn their adversarial, hyper-polarized responses in the direction of deeper understanding, empathy, communication, problem-solving, collaborative negotiation, and consensus building. We can do so by asking questions, such as:

- What life experiences have led you to feel so passionately about this issue?
- What is at the heart of this issue for you as a person? Why?
- Do you see any gray areas in the issue we are discussing, or ideas it's difficult to define?
- Do you have any mixed feelings, uncertainties, or discomforts regarding this issue that you would be willing to share?
- Is there any part of this issue that you're not 100% certain of, or would be willing to discuss and talk about?
- Even though you hold widely differing views, are there any concerns or ideas you may have in common?
- What underlying values or ethical beliefs have led you to your current views?

- What values or ethical beliefs do you think you might have in common?
- Do the differences between your positions reveal any riddles, paradoxes, contradictions, or enigmas regarding this issue?
- Is it possible to view your differences as two sides of the same coin? If so, what unites them? What is the coin?
- What is *beneath* that idea for you? Why does it matter to you?
- Can you separate the issues from the people you disagree with? What might you do if you can't?
- Is there anything positive or acknowledging you would be willing to say about the people on the other side of this issue?
- What processes or ground rules might help you disagree more constructively?
- Instead of focusing on the past, what would you like to see happen in the future? Why?
- Are you disagreeing about fundamental values, or about how to achieve them?
- Is there a way that both of you might be right? How?
- What criteria could you use to decide what works best?
- Would it be possible to test your ideas in practice and see which work best? How might you do that?
- Would you be willing to jointly investigate your conflicting factual assertions? How could you do that?
- How is everyone in the group feeling right now about the tone of this discussion? What could we do to improve it?
- What could be done to make each side's ideas more appealing?
- Could any of the other side's ideas be incorporated into yours? Which? How?
- Is there any aspect of this issue either of you may have left out? Are there any other perspectives you haven't described?
- Are there any other ways you can think of to say what you just said?

- Do you think it would be useful to continue this conversation to learn more about each other, and what you each believe to be true?
- How might we make this conversation more ongoing or effective?
- What could each of you do to improve the ways you disagree with each other in the future?
- Would you be willing to do that together?
- What did each of you learn from this conversation?
- What would you like to do differently in the future if you disagree?
- How might you make your future conversations more effective?

QUESTIONS TO INITIATE DEEPER, HEART-TO-HEART CONVERSATIONS

It often happens that people in conflict get emotionally triggered by their interactions and find themselves engaged in angry, destructive, superficial, disrespectful diatribes or shouting matches when they would rather have deeper, more caring, constructive, heart-to-heart conversations with each other, but don't know how to switch from one to the other. When this happens, they will often drop subtle, subconscious clues to indicate their preferences, but because these clues are subtle and subconscious, they are often missed or misinterpreted, both by their opponent and by the mediator.

Here are a few examples of such clues, with a rough translation or guess about what they may actually mean, followed by an initial question to find out whether this is what they are asking for, and help them transition to a deeper discussion:

1. Declaration: "He doesn't think I'm a very good person."

- *Possible Translation:* "I'm not entirely confident that I am a good person, I feel vulnerable to what he thinks of me, and

am exaggerating what he thinks because I need some reassurance that he doesn't hate me."
- *Opening Questions:* [to him] "Is that right? Do you think she is not a very good person?" "If not, can you give an example?" [to her] "Why does it matter to you what he thinks?"

2. Declaration: "She did it for no reason."

- *Possible Translation:* "I really don't know why she did it but am afraid to ask, because she could have done it because of something I did that I don't want to admit, or for some reason that will force me to stop playing the victim."
- *Opening Questions:* "Would you like to know why she did it?" "Why don't you ask her right now?"

3. Declaration: "He's lying."

- *Possible Translation:* "What he said does not match my experience, I feel defensive about what he said, and I need him to hear my experience before I can hear his."
- *Opening Questions:* "What truth do you know that is not reflected in his statement?" "What do you think is the *underlying* truth he is trying to communicate?"

4. Declaration: "I don't trust him."

- *Possible Translation:* "I am feeling insecure about what is going to happen, distrustful about his intentions regarding me, and need to hear that he is really committed to making our relationship work."
- *Opening Questions:* "What are you afraid he will do?" [To the other person:] "Is that what you are going to do? If not, why not? Do you want this relationship to work? Why?"

SOME HEART-BASED QUESTIONS

Every sincere question in conflict resolution conveys a heart message, if only in the form of "I care enough about you to want to know what you think and how you feel." Heart messages can be very large or very small, and the goal in asking heart-based questions is to try to open a heart space, sometimes simply by asking a caring question, then moving into the space created by the answer, and asking follow-up questions to see whether it's possible to expand it. The goal is not to "get" the parties to care, but to give them permission to express what they *actually* care about *directly* to each other, and begin dismantling the elaborate, counter-productive defenses they have created to hide and protect their most vulnerable feelings. It is easy to slip into manipulation, so it is important for mediators to adopt an attitude and *intention* that give full permission to *reject* the question. We can then start with questions that are not so large, obvious, or easy to hear as biased, but simple, tiny, and straight-forward, such as:

- Before we begin, can you tell me a little about yourselves?
- What do you hope will happen as a result of this conversation? Why is that important to you?
- Why are you here? Why do you care? What did it take for you to come here today?
- What kind of relationship would you *like* to have with each other? Why?
- What is one thing you like or respect about each other? Can you give an example? Another? How does it feel to hear each other say these things? What would happen if you said them more often?
- Is there anything you have in common? Any values you share?
- What role have you played in this conflict, either through action or inaction?
- If you had 20/20 hindsight, what would you do differently?
- Is there anything you would like to apologize for?

- On a scale of 1 to 10, how would each of you rank that apology? What could you do to make it a 10? Are you willing to try right now?
- What is one thing you would like him to acknowledge you for? What is one thing you are willing to acknowledge him for?
- What do you think she was trying to say in that apology/ acknowledgment? [To her] Is that accurate? [If not] Would you like to know what is accurate for her? Why don't you ask her?
- How would you evaluate the effectiveness of what you just said in reaching him? How could you make it more effective? Would you like some feedback or coaching? Why don't you ask him?
- Is this conversation working? Would you like it to work? *Why* would you like it to work? What is one thing she could do that would make it to work for you? [To her] Are you willing to do that? Would you be willing to start the conversation over and do those things now?
- What is the crossroads you are at right now in your conflict?
- Are you ever going to convince him you are right? If not, when will you stop trying?
- What would you most like to hear him say to you right now?
- What would you have wanted him to have said instead?
- What does that mean to you? What other meanings might it have? What do you think it meant to her? Would you like to find out? Why don't you ask her?
- Can you imagine what happened to him also happening to you? What do you think it would feel like? Would you like to know what it felt like to him? Why don't you ask him?
- Would you be willing to take a moment of silence right now to think about that?
- Has anything like this ever happened to you before? Who? When?

- What issues are you holding on to that the other person still doesn't even know about?
- What price have you paid for this conflict? What has it cost you? How much longer are you going to continue paying that price?
- What would it take for you to give this conflict up, let go of what happened, and move on with your life?
- Do you really want this in your life? What would it take to let it go?
- What would change in your life if the conflict ended?
- If this were the last conversation you were going to have with each other, what would you want to say?

QUESTIONS ON DIFFICULT BEHAVIORS

Many conflicts are caused less by difficult people and personalities, which are far less amenable to change, than by difficult *behaviors*; or rather, by behaviors *we* lack the skills to handle. Framing the problem as one of behaviors or skills allows us to focus less on what other people should be, or do differently, and more on what *we* can do to dismantle our own emotional triggers and reactiveness, and learn ways of being more effective in our responses. We can start, whether we are mediators, facilitators, conflict coaches, or one of the parties, by asking questions that try to tease apart and clarify what *specifically* is making the behavior difficult for us. We can ask questions like:

- What is the specific behavior they engaged in that you find most disturbing? Why is that disturbing to you? Why do you think they engaged in it? [To the other person:] Is that right?
- Did anyone in your family of origin engage in similar behaviors? How did you respond then? Was that successful? Why not? What might you have done instead?

- How are you responding to their difficult behavior right now? What might you do instead? Would you like to hear their ideas?
- Is the other person benefiting in any way from your responses to their behavior?
- What benefits do you think they are deriving from their behavior?
- Have your responses been successful in stopping their behavior?
- How could you change your responses to stop rewarding them for behaviors you find unacceptable?
- How are others responding to their behavior? Is there anyone who handles their behavior skillfully? What are they doing differently?
- Have you *actually* given them honest, detailed, *skillful* feedback about their behavior? If so, how did they receive it?
- Has anyone *ever* given them such feedback?
- What feedback have you *not* given them? Why not?
- What would it take for you to give them fully honest and empathetic feedback?
- What do you think might motivate them to change their behavior? What would motivate you, if it were you?
- How could you reward them for behaviors you find more constructive? How could you support them in changing?

Questions on Bullying

A frequently cited example of difficult behaviors is bullying, which occurs in many couples, families, schools, neighborhoods, and workplaces, and often takes social, economic, political–even environmental forms.

Here are a few questions a mediator, facilitator, conflict coach, or either of the parties *might* consider asking when someone (let's say "A") makes an accusation of bullying (by"B"). In doing so, it is important to be "omni-partial," and not "blame the victim."

- "What specifically did B *do* that you consider to be bullying?"
- "What made that *feel* like bullying to you?"
- "What would you have *liked* B to have done instead?"
- "How did you respond?" "Was that successful?"
- [In some cases] "Why did you *allow* yourself to be bullied by B?"
- "How could B have made the same point, but in a way that would not have been *experienced* by you as bullying?"
- "What do each of you think are the reasons people bully others?"
- "What are some of the rationalizations people offer for allowing themselves to be bullied?"
- "What do you think B wants to *get* through what you call bullying?"
- "If you talk about those issues, do you think B will still feel the need to push so hard for what s/he wants?"
- "Was there anything A *did* that encouraged you to engage in what s/ he called "bullying"?
- "What could A do that would encourage you (B) to act differently in the future?"
- "Would you be willing to try that approach right now and see if it works?"
- "Why do you (B) think A felt afraid, or intimidated by you?"
- "Was there anything you (A) did that encouraged B to think his/her behavior was acceptable?" "Why did you do that?"
- "Did A do anything that encouraged you (B) to feel s/he accepted your behavior?"
- "Can you both agree that you would have a better relationship if you did not engage in or accept bullying behavior?"
- "What are some of the ways your relationship could improve if you moved away from these behaviors?"
- "Was there anyone who was a bully, or was bullied, in the neighborhood or school where you grew up, or in your

family of origin?" "How did you respond to it then?" "Would you respond to it the same way now?" "Why?"

- "Can you agree, as a ground rule for your communication in the future, that neither of you will act in ways that lead the other person to feel bullied or intimidated?" "Can you agree that it is OK for both of you to refuse to engage in or accept bullying behavior?"
- "Can you agree that you will both listen to what each other is saying and not engage in or tolerate bullying behavior?"
- "B, is it acceptable to you if A lets you know in the future if s/he feels intimidated by you?" "If s/he does, can s/he raise it with you as a topic for discussion and negotiation?" "How would you like her/him to do that?" Etc.

SOME DIFFICULT AND DANGEROUS QUESTIONS

There are a few questions that are so difficult or dangerous that they can stop us in our tracks, take our breath away, or drop us to our knees, questions that openly and directly disrupt the unexamined patterns of thinking and feeling, or responses to conflict that have gotten us nowhere, and it's time to give them up. Yet these questions can also break the empathetic bond that gave us permission to ask them in the first place, and result in people feeling judged, hurt, misunderstood, or ganged up on. If we are going to ask them, we need to find the right moment, soften our tone of voice, redouble our empathy, be willing to ask the same questions of ourselves, and be ready to handle whatever happens in response.

Here are a few examples, several suggested by Peter Block:

1. What have you done to bring about the very problem you're most troubled by?
2. What have you been clinging to or holding onto that it's now time for you to release and let go of?

3. What are you responsible for in your conflict that you have not yet acknowledged to the other person?

4. What do you most want to hear the other person say to you that you still haven't mentioned?

5. What do you *long* for in your relationship with the other person?

6. What is the refusal, or "no," that you have not yet communicated?

7. What is the permission, or "yes," you gave in the past that you now want to retract?

8. What is the resentment you're still holding on to that the other person doesn't even know about?

9. What is the promise you gave in the past that you're now betraying?

10. What is it s/he or you did that you're still unwilling to forgive?

11. What price have you paid for your refusal to forgive?

12. How much longer are you prepared to continue paying that price?

13. What promise are you willing to make to the other person with no acknowledgement or expectation of return?

14. What lessons have you learned from the other person? What have they taught you? What if you had never learned them?

15. What gift could you give the other person that you continue to withhold? What would happen if you stopped withholding it?

16. Who would you become if you let go of your anger, fear, or grief?

17. What are you prepared to do *unconditionally*, without any expectation of gratitude or reciprocity?

18. Why did you *choose* this conflict, and this opponent?

19. What are you grateful to this conflict for teaching you?

20. How has this horrible experience made you a better person?

21. Have you ever *thanked* the other person for opening your eyes, setting you free, or releasing you from your own false expectations?

THE QUESTIONING CURE

The questions I have listed are only a few of the countless ones we can ask; questions we can tailor to conflicts in marriages, neighborhoods, and workplaces. [For example, see my book with Joan Goldsmith, *Resolving Conflicts at Work*, 3rd Ed.]. We can always design questions to match specific issues in conflict, or explore the subtle biases, stereotypes, and political polarizations, [for example, see those in my book *Politics, Dialogue, and the Evolution of Democracy*], or *invent* them for specific circumstances, or generically for everyone. My favorite question of this type is: "What question would you most like me to ask you right now?"

The art of asking questions is simply a search for truths that are deeper and more meaningful and consequential than the ones we ordinarily ask in response to our conflicts. The questions that matter most are not the simple, superficial, rhetorical ones about who's to blame or what happened, but the more profound and poignant ones about what it means, and why, and what we might do instead. If we want to stimulate transformational and transcendent outcomes, we need to ask transformational and transcendent questions. As Susan Sontag insightfully observed, "The only interesting answers are those that destroy the question." In mediation, the opposite is also true–the most interesting questions are those that destroy the narrow, self-serving, defensive, adversarial answers we are holding on to and weaponizing — answers that change *nothing*.

As Joseph Joubert pointed out, "It is better to debate a question without settling it than to settle a question without debating it." We can add that it is more important to be open and honest in our communications with one another and confront whatever is not working for either of us, than to insist on the validity of our *exclusive* ideas about whose fault it is.

If, as Sigmund Freud wrote, psychoanalysis is "the talking cure," mediation can be considered "the questioning cure." Indeed, the *attitude* of questioning is already, automatically, *inherently* respectful, and if done correctly, can *instantly* give rise to a shift in the orientation of both sides in a conflict, helping them transition from a competitive, hostile, punitive focus on "me vs. you," to a collaborative, restorative, problem-solving approach of "us vs. it."

Questions are the axes, the hubs, the pivot points around which conflicts rotate. They are catalysts, not only of knowledge, but insight, and wisdom. They are the yeast that invisibly prompts empathy to rise, the light that reveals the pathway to openhearted, authentic relationships.

It is fitting to close with the well-known advice offered by Rainer Maria Rilke to a young poet:

> I want to beg you as much as you can, to be patient toward all that is unsolved in your heart and to try because to love the questions themselves like locked rooms and like books that are written in a very foreign tongue. Do not now seek answers, which cannot be given you as you would not be able to live them. And the point is, to live everything. Live the questions now. Perhaps you will then gradually, without noticing it, live along some distant day into the answer.

FIVE

Literature, Drama, and Poetry in Conflict Resolution

Does creativity like loud or soft voices? The loud, the passionate voice seems to please most. The voice upraised in conflict, the comparison of opposites. Sit at your typewriter, pick characters of various sorts, let them fly together in a great clang. In no time at all, your secret self is roused. We all like decision, declaration: anyone loudly for, anyone loudly against.

Ray Bradbury

Borders make us feel stable. At the first hint of a conflict, at the least threat, we close them. The border serves to gather us into a unit, to diminish the hidden centrifugal thrusts that undermine our identity. But it's purely an appearance. A story begins when, one after another, our borders collapse.

Elena Ferrante

... the books we need are the kind that act upon us like a misfortune, that make us suffer like the death of someone we love more than ourselves, that make us feel as though we were on the verge of suicide, or lost in a forest remote from all human habitation – a book should be an axe to break the frozen sea within.

Franz Kafka

EVEN AS A VERY SMALL CHILD, STORIES TRANSPORTED ME, INVITING ME into worlds unlike my own. I later discovered that each story had left a *permanent* imprint, shaping my awareness, casting shadows, echoing for years; and by osmosis, became manifest in my own life, in my sense of self and appreciation of others. Simply by reading, listening, and vividly imagining these made-up, non-existent worlds, they vibrated, resonated, and became real inside me, like a kind of invisible scaffolding; a sensitivity to subtlety and nuance; a map of my internal terrain. Even today, each novel, each poem, each play and story I read *lives* inside me–not simply in the distinctive words with which they were sculpted, or the intricate plots and story lines their authors gave or discovered in them — but in the complex characters, ethical dilemmas, and lived experiences; the heart-rending tragedies, hilarious comedies, and cunning farces; the paralyzing fears, self-consuming wraths, bottomless griefs, profound insights, deep intuitions, and startling possibilities they convey and elicit. What is most remarkable is that these frozen, unreal, imaginary scribblings have made me — and perhaps you — a better person, a more empathetic listener, a more creative problem solver, a more loving partner, a more supportive parent, a more successful mediator, coach, and dialogue facilitator. But *how?* What exactly does literature *do* that makes these outcomes possible?

LITERATURE AND CONFLICT

Literature, whatever its form, is an *imagination practice*, an exercise in empathy and compassion, an invitation into alternative realities — which is why writers get persecuted or shot, and books get banned. Literature is *dangerous* — to dogma and hypocrisy, rigidity and pretense, to tyrants and dictators everywhere—*especially* within. It is a window into the deepest recesses of conflict, an unlikely guide to mediators who want to explore, understand, resolve, transform, and transcend it.

Most literature is an exploration of the sources, manifestations, and meanings of conflict — not by means of scientific analysis, but description, dramatization, metaphor, and plot. It evokes these meanings by inviting us to *resonate* with the sound, symbolism, and subtle nuance of carefully chosen words and phrases used to describe people, places, and events; actions, ideas, and emotions; conversations, reflections, and relationships—all as ways of permitting the reader to *experience* the vibrations, qualities, and meanings that fill and invisibly influence the lives of imagined others, and in the process, ours as well.

To illustrate, track your bodily sensations, emotions, thoughts, and flow of energy inside as you read each of the following words and phrases:

> *Once upon a time, long ago/far off in the future,*
> *in a forest/cottage/mansion/hovel ...,*
> *there lived a boy/girl/horse/dragon ...*
> *who was very happy/sad/ angry/frightened ...*

In just a few words, we can begin to imagine not only a time, place, person, or being, but what it looked and felt like, how people dressed, how they behaved, and begin to relax and feel our way into the story. What happens next in nearly every story is conflict or dissonance, without which the story would become less gripping and evocative.

But if conflict is central to literature, what can mediators learn from reading it? Can a familiarity with literature enable conflict resolvers to recognize the poetry of their own process, the drama in its countless acts and scenes, the truths squirreled away and buried within its' fictions? An ancient Jewish proverb asks, "What is truer than the truth?" It answers, "The story." Why? Because within the story lies a deeper truth, revealing not only what happened, but how it *felt*, what it meant, and did — not only to those *within* the story — but to the *storyteller*, and more subtly, to the reader.

In conflicts, people make things up. And they do so in ways that suggest a dramatic *logic*, a narrative consistency; in ways that have a *storied*, poetic feel to them. Indeed, fiction has been described as "a lie in search of a deeper truth." We can all figure out through experience which stories sway our audiences and which do not, then edit them in the telling to create the effects we desire. These tweaks make up what I call the "narrative structure of conflict stories," described in two earlier books, *The Crossroads of Conflict*, and *The Dance of Opposites*. What I intend to focus on here are some of the ways novels, plays, and poetry helped me, and I think others, become better mediators.

THE *SCRIPTING* OF CONFLICT

People in conflict often seem to be reading lines from an invisible script, slipping into rigid, pre-defined roles, using catch phrases, and adopting dramatic poses. They do so, in part, to convey by means of a relatively constrained, superficial, and inadequate language the *vastly* deeper emotions, thoughts, and meanings of what happened to them and how it felt, in hopes of finding some release from the plot. They do so by adopting and adapting common literary conventions, forms, and techniques, and using them to analogize and suggest to their audience–often indirectly and inauthentically — the direct and authentic elements of their experience that embarrass or frighten them, or might otherwise escape notice.

Scripts and stories are techniques for describing what happened to us, but words are always poor a substitute for experiencing it ourselves. The parties therefore communicate through *form*, tone of voice, posture, analogy, metaphor, gesture, and similar dramatic devices, what was left *unsaid*, and cannot, or *dare* not, be spoken. Tobias Dantzig wrote: "Fiction is a form in search of an interpretation."

Conflict stories are therefore a kind of *camouflage*, revealing a fear of authenticity, an escape from honesty. Why? Because of the deeper meaning and vulnerability of what they have carefully hidden; because of its' intense, precarious, frightening emotionality, and the perceived or imagined consequences of revealing it.

At a deeper level, scripts are ego defenses, labyrinths, and symbols that allow us to discover *within* the story a little trail of breadcrumbs leading deeper into the subconscious mind of the person who created it. A simple example is: "It's your fault." Like all conflict stories, beneath this accusation lies a confession ("I'm afraid of being blamed for it."), and beneath the confession lies a request ("Can we work together to solve the problem, rather than blaming each other for it?").

It's easy to see the impact of conflict scripts in couples and families, a bit more difficult in communities and organizations; and far more so in social, economic, and political conflicts. Yet all of these conflicts run along hidden, ignored, and concealed, tracks. The simplest way of revealing them is to ask a question that cannot be answered *within* the script, as shown in the last chapter. For example, "What are your goals for this conversation we are having right now?" "How well do you think you are doing in achieving those goals?" "What is one thing each of us might do better?"

SEARCHING FOR THE STORY CONCEALED WITHIN THE SCRIPT

If we feel stuck in a script that is not of our own making, it is possible to bypass it entirely, refuse to be stereotyped or typecast, and step outside it. It may also be possible to dig deeper, *complicate* the script by asking questions, and search for its unstated, hidden sources. We may then be able to transform it into its' opposite—a script that is *anti*-stereotypical, non-adversarial, unconflicted, non-superficial, and not at all boring. We can do this by making *our* characters or theirs more complex, nuanced, layered, and subtle than the script permits.

Someone, I can't recall who, observed that "We know more about Anna Karenina than we do about our own mothers." Our knowledge of each other *without* literature is often superficial, partially because we are bound by codes of privacy and politeness, and literature is not. As a result, our communications rarely probe beneath the surface, and a great deal of what we regard as insight into other people's ideas, feelings, intentions, etc. is mere guesswork based on a smattering of clues — mostly superficial, circumstantial, ill-informed, or projected on to others based on what *we* might think, feel, or intend. Literature does not *substitute* for what we think, feel, and perceive, it adds to it, allowing our minds to connect with the minds of writers in profound, additive, and insightful ways. Novelist Kurt Vonnegut connected reading literature with deep learning and the practice of meditation, stating:

> I believe that reading and writing are the most nourishing forms of meditation anyone has so far found. By reading the writings of the most interesting minds in history, we meditate with our own minds and theirs as well. This to me is a miracle.

These are useful beginnings, because novelists, dramatists, and poets invite us to look inside and use their works to imagine our own lives or those of others in detail, in ways that are often far more subtle, truthful, and convincing than the things they say — especially when we are immersed in conflicts that shape and distort our perceptions. This makes it useful for mediators to reflect on how the best writers achieve this miracle. Let's consider a few randomly selected examples, drawn from a field of millions, portraying conflicts in different ways. Here, for example, is Leo Tolstoy's classic description of a husband's view of marital arguments with his wife as they become increasingly estranged, in language that helps us understand the origin and meaning of many couple, family, relational, and workplace arguments:

> Our relations to one another grew more and more hostile and at last reached a stage where it was not disagreement that caused hostility but hostility that caused disagreement. Whatever she might say I disagreed with beforehand, and it was just the same with her. ... We no longer tried to bring any dispute to a conclusion. We invariably kept to our own opinions even about the most trivial questions. ... As I now recall them the views I maintained were not at all so dear to me that I could not have given them up; but she was of the opposite opinion and to yield meant yielding to her, and that I could not do.

Literature can teach us by stimulating our empathy and imagination, allowing us to feel within ourselves some of what others have suffered. Here, we learn about morality, human values, personal responsibility, and the pitfalls of hypocrisy. An example with contemporary significance is Thomas More's soliloquy rebuking Londoners for their violent attacks on immigrants in the 16th century play, *Sir Thomas More*, now widely attributed to William Shakespeare:

> *Imagine that you see the wretched strangers,*
> *Their babies at their backs and their poor luggage,*
> *Plodding to th' ports and costs for transportation,*
> *And that you sit as kings in your desires,*
> *... What had you got? I'll tell you. You had taught*
> *How insolence and strong hand should prevail,*
> *How order should be quelled; and by this pattern*
> *Not one of you should live an aged man,*
> *For other ruffians, as their fancies wrought,*
> *With self same hand, self reasons and self right,*
> *Would shark on you, and men like ravenous fishes*

Would feed on one another.
... whither would you go?
What country, by the nature of your error,
Should give you harbor? ...
Why, you must needs be strangers. Would you be pleased
To find a nation of such barbarous temper,
That, breaking out in hideous violence,
Would not afford you an abode on earth,
Whet their detested knives against your throats,
Spurn you like dogs, and like as if that God
Owed not nor made not you, nor that the claimants
Were not all appropriate to your comforts,
But chartered unto them, what would you think
To be thus used? This is the strangers' case;
And this your mountainish inhumanity.

Or consider how even the deepest misery can wane, dissipate, collapse, and give way to unimagined joy, as in the following poem by the brilliant Russian poet, Anna Akhmatova, writing in the deadly, chaotic, famine filled early 1920s during the Russian civil war:

Everything is plundered, betrayed, sold,
Death's great black wing scrapes the air,
Misery gnaws to the bone.
Why then do we not despair?
By day, from the surrounding woods,
cherries blow summer into town;
at night the deep transparent skies
glitter with new galaxies.
And the miraculous comes so close
to the ruined, dirty houses—
something not known to anyone at all,
but wild in our breast for centuries.

Even nonfiction and simple prose can capture a mood, a feeling, or an idea and express it in poignant ways that stir us, inspire us, elevate us, and incite us to action. Here is a beautiful prose passage by the poet Mary Oliver, with special meaning for mediators, expressing her belief that "Attention is the beginning of devotion."

> I learned: that the world's *otherness* is an antidote to confusion, that standing *within* this otherness—the beauty and the mystery of the world, out in the fields or deep inside books—can re-dignify the worst-stung heart.

Literature can exaggerate, as most people do in conflict conversations, in order to emphasize a point, clarify an underlying idea, or express an intense, powerful emotion. Here, for example, is environmental author and essayist Edward Abbey, commenting on the public response to his book, *Desert Solitaire*:

> Do not jump into your automobile next June and rush out to the canyon country hoping to see some of that which I have attempted to evoke in these [poetic reflections]. In the first place you can't see anything from a car; you've got to get out of the goddamned contraption and walk, better yet crawl, on hands and knees, over the sandstone and through the thornbush and cactus. When traces of blood begin to mark your trail you'll see something, maybe. Probably not. In the second place most of what I write about in this book is already gone or going under fast. This is not a travel guide but an elegy. A memorial. You're holding a tombstone in your hands. A bloody rock. Don't drop it on your foot — throw it at something big and glassy. What do you have to lose?

There are countless other gorgeous examples, each pointing in unique ways to issues that are critically important to all of us, yet so difficult to capture, so inexact, complex, subtle, obscure, and ineffable that only *art* can express it. The reader is then presented with two tasks: first, to grasp the meaning that arises from and is revealed through art; and second, to grasp the art itself–to see not only the *thing* being pointed at, but the process of pointing, and how it operates.

SAVING THE FIRE

This idea reminds me of an interesting story. A reporter, on a whim, asked the French writer Jean Cocteau: "If there was a fire in your house, what would you save?" He immediately and unexpectedly responded: "Why the fire, of course." In a similar vein, within every conflict there are issues being fought over, and at the same time, there are passions, caring, anger, fear of loss, which fuel the "fire" that alone explains the intensity of the conflict — an intensity that should be *preserved*, rather than repressed, moderated, squelched, side-lined, compromised, or diminished — and redirected from attacking the *person* to solving the *problem*. Literature and conflict stories are compelling because they convey not only the facts and issues people care about, but who they *are*, how they communicate their caring, and why they care about them. They do not always do so directly and literally, but often indirectly and metaphorically, in ways that are designed to be *felt*, rather than simply heard, and not just with words, but gestures, symbols, metaphors, and similes that require subtle interpretation. There is a wonderful well-known Zen saying: "The sound of the rain needs no translation." This suggests a tripartite separation between:

1. *Directly experiencing* the sound of the rain, perhaps by hearing, feeling, smelling, touching, or tasting it
2. *Indirectly defining* it, perhaps by using descriptive words, known facts, or scientific principles to explain it to someone who may have been born deaf and has no idea what it sounds like
3. *Empathetically describing* it, perhaps by using art, simile, metaphor, or related experiences to convey the feelings and senses associated with it

In dispute resolution, a similar distinction can be found in the parties' efforts to describe their personal experience of being in conflict, as opposed to their factual assertions, contested rationales, and adversarial analyses of the issues over which they are fighting. These are both distinct from the mediators' efforts to encourage empathy, understanding, acknowledgement, recognition of what they may have meant and felt, clarification of what they want from their opponents and why; and opening channels of empathy and communication between them, while encouraging and empowering them to collaboratively negotiate solutions that satisfy both their diverse sets of interests. Mediators can then, if they have the requisite awareness and skills, bring science *and* art, objectivity and subjectivity, ideas and feelings, facts and meanings, data and metaphor, analysis and empathy into the story telling process, and use both to search for unique, creative ways of *combining* equally valid perceptions, needs, desires, and interests, revealing complex and subtle meanings, areas of potential consensus, higher dimensional solutions, fresh skills, and hidden paths forward. Just as plot and character in literature are forged in conflicts between people, the life challenge they face, and the need to discover or invent ways of overcoming them, everyone in conflict faces similar issues, and their characters and *dénouements* similarly hang in the balance. If literature is partly an effort to imagine and explore the meanings and ramifications of conflict through character, plot, language, emotion, and storyline, then mediation and similar efforts to resolve it in the "real world" can learn from literature how to dissect the parties' stories and narratives to reveal their hidden truths.

THE LISTENER CREATES THE STORY

If I read the same book, but in a different time or place, or in a different mood, or after some meaningful life experience, the words will be differently imagined, accentuated, ignored, and felt, and as a result, assume altered meanings. Because I am now a different reader, I will be reading a different book. In this way, I am a participant, a co-creator, a *writer* of what I read.

In similar ways, as mediators, we listen to people tell stories about their conflicts and help them re-contextualize, re-imagine, and *re-experience* what happened—not as one who is under attack, or being insulted, or ignored, and responding in kind. Instead, as *listeners*, we help them re-interpret and re-live what took place as one who is now safe, respected, acknowledged, and no longer feels a need to fight or flee (or freeze, fawn, or flock), and can therefore rewrite their story of what happened in language that is more likely to end in resolution, forgiveness, and reconciliation—even with the words, "they lived happily ever after."

In mediation, people rarely reach this stereotypical literary ending, yet all conflict stories are subconsciously structured in ways that mirror, mimic, or imitate the emotionally satisfying dramatic arcs of fairy tales, which perfectly portray the clash between good and evil. Fairy tales and conflict stories are both, from their beginning, searches for resolution, invitations to heartfelt discoveries and satisfying dénouements.

They are even, at times, requests for assistance, for someone to co-author, ghost write, edit, or re-plot the story—not to cancel, gloss over, or omit what happened — but to reveal its deeper *meanings*, accentuate different tones, and reach happier endings — ones they cannot imagine, and ones that can give them closure. In the fairy tale, this role might be played by a wise counselor, a magician, a riddle that needs to be solved, a frog or princess waiting to be kissed. In conflict resolution, it is often played by a mediator, conflict coach, facilitator, or any active, empathetic, and responsive listener.

What all these roles have in common is the ability to shift peoples' perceptions by describing the world and the parties in ways that transform them from alien, adversarial, fixed, or intractable, into friendly, collaborative, malleable, and changeable. Elif Batuman, in her novel, *Either/Or*, has a fictional student comment on Edith Wharton's novel, *Age of Innocence*:

> To describe the world more fully is to change it. To let the world go undescribed is, in some way, not to know it, at one's own peril... This is a novelistic insight, the kind that comes with living through historical change. It isn't particular to the 1870's, or the 1920's, ... because every age has its own unsaid, half-known truths, ... because novels are about change and realizations, and we never stop changing and realizing things.

Batuman then has her student ask, "Was that what a novel *was*, a plane where you could finally juxtapose all the different people, mediating between them and weighing their views?" If it is possible to recognize that there is mediation in literature, we can equally see that there is *literature* in the dramatic encounters between hostile parties in mediation. If conflicts are places where people get stuck, feel traumatized, abandoned, and unable to evolve, then mediation can rightfully be regarded as a *plot rewriting* process, a final edit to remove what doesn't belong. What most requires description in conflict resolution are not the facts and issues in dispute, but the *characters* and emotions of the parties, their unspoken histories and life experiences, their secret wishes and desires, their unacknowledged motivations and intentions, their heartfelt thoughts and feelings, and the ways these interact, change, set off in new directions, and do unexpected things — all of which belong as much to literature and art as to law and science. Henry Miller wrote,

> Life, as we all know, is conflict, and man, being part of life, is himself an expression of conflict. If he recognizes the fact and accepts it, he is apt, despite the conflict, to know peace and to enjoy it.

From a conflict resolution perspective, what is required to know peace and learn life lessons from our disputes include not only the recognition and acceptance Miller describes, but higher order skills and attitudes of *curiosity* toward the sources and origins of our conflicts. Literature feeds this curiosity, in part by:

1. Presenting complex characters who are not fixed and eternal, but change in response to events and circumstances, just as we would
2. Offering a glimpse of the inner lives of people as they navigate their ways through conflict, often stumbling or taking wrong turns, just as we do
3. Preserving a sense of surprise and wonderment, as though even the author did not know what they would do or feel or think next, just as we might feel confused and uncertain in conflict

By intimately imagining and exploring the inner life of a character, or setting, or circumstance, a capable writer can breathe *life* into it, and from the writer's mind to ours, something new is brought into the world that would not exist otherwise, but lives now, in and through us. In the beginning, there is only the writer's imagination, but when we add the readers' empathy, suspension of disbelief, and ability to re-imagine what was written from the perspective and context of our own unique circumstances, we create something new, together with what the brilliant novelist Elena Ferrante describes as "the third book:"

> Between the book that is published and the book that readers buy there is always a *third book*, a book where beside the written sentences are those which we imagined writing, beside the sentences that readers read are the sentences they have imagined reading. This third book, elusive, changing, is nevertheless a real book. I didn't actually write it, my readers haven't actually read it,

but it's there. It's the book that is created in the relationship between life, writing and reading.

Ferrante beautifully describes *how* she writes in ways that create the characters, settings, and circumstances that enable readers to experience them *directly*, as though they were there:

> Certainly in my experience the word is always flesh. ... [I]t's there, I see it and feel it, it's a world made up entirely of living material, of breath, of heat and cold. I who am writing sit with fingers on the keys of the computer and, at the same time, in the middle of that world, and I let myself be carried along by its vortex, which drags in everything, without before or after. Over the years, I have to admit, I've come closer and closer to the idea that real writing is what emerges by itself, from an ecstatic condition. ...The ecstasy of writing is feeling not the breath of the word that is liberated from the flesh, but the flesh that becomes one with the breath of words.

We can think of this description as a goal for mediators in the process of listening–not only to one party or character, but to both; to find in their bodies, emotions, and spirits, as well as their minds, what it might have felt like to have gone through their experience, and from there to imagine what each conflicted party most wants to hear and experience; what they deeply have in common; and what they subconsciously hope the mediator will do next. How do we do this? Here is some centuries old advice from the Sufi poet, Jelaladin Rumi:

> *Keep your intelligence white-hot*
> *and your grief glistening,*
> *so your life will stay fresh.*
> *Cry easily like a little child.*
> *Do not seek any rules for worship.*
> *Say whatever your pained heart chooses.*

The depth of empathy required to do this is not without risk, as it requires mediators to discover both parties' stories within themselves, then connect them, re-imagine them, and encourage them to mix, as *three* distinct, yet-to-be-united voices: those of the storyteller, the opponent whose harmful actions the story is about, and the mediator who is listening, searching for ways of merging each story with its' opponent's, while remaining entirely separate from both stories, and not subsumed, or conflicted, or lost in empathy and compassion.

The mediator needs to be *simultaneous* inside and outside, before and after, around and beyond the story; and so *intimate* with it that it becomes possible to discover its' hidden meaning, what it represents and was created to point at. No ordinary, distant, safe, professional listening can do this. Many mediators shy away from it, for reasons Elena Ferrante points out:

> [T]o throw into disorder one's cultivated 'I' is a dangerous undertaking. You can't change your form for one that seems truer without the risk of not finding yourself anymore.

THE SCIENCE OF STORYTELLING AND NARRATIVES

Ursula K. Le Guin described it very nicely: "Science describes accurately from the outside, poetry describes accurately from the inside. Science explicates, poetry implicates." By weaving these two together and finding the places where they meet or intersect, amplify and cancel, we discover deeper truths about each.

In *The Science of Storytelling*, Will Storr argues that our identities are built around stories the brain tells itself, with ourselves as hero or victim, and rarely as wrongdoer. These stories are mostly fictional and self-serving, as studies show that we frequently create false stories to support the identities we want to have and project, and conveniently forget the times when we behaved badly.

Storr suggests that all compelling characters have a flaw—not only in their idea or model of the world, but in their confidence that they can control it. Circumstances inevitably arise in which it is revealed that their understanding is inaccurate on both counts. In stories that end happily, the person recognizes their flaws and changes who they are to overcome their challenges. In tragedies, they refuse to learn or change or evolve, leading to their downfall.

Storr argues that stories also inform political beliefs, which become part of our identity. In one study, when volunteers were presented with arguments contradicting their political views, brain scans showed neural responses similar to what would be provoked by a predator, while another study showed that simply watching sitcoms or music videos with Muslims or Arabs was enough to reduce Israeli viewers' prejudices towards them. In another study, personal storytelling by itself was sufficient to significantly reduce hyper-polarization in political foes.

In *The Hero with a Thousand Faces*, Joseph Campbell described the narrative and archetypal structure of mythic stories, or from a mediation perspective, the journey from conflict to transparency, transformation, and transcendence. Campbell, building on work by Carl Jung, revealed some of the hidden meanings of conflict stories, which are often disguised as metaphors that subtly point beyond themselves to the possibility of discovery — i.e., to an evolution that allows the protagonist to move beyond the limitations of the story.

At the same time, Campbell's idea of the "monomyth" that unifies all stories is, I find, only partly accurate as a description of conflict stories, whose subtlety, diversity, openness, complexity, sensitivity to culture, and emotional nuance resist compression into a single coherent, overarching framework. Instead of a static monomyth, conflict stories reflect *evolving*, complex, multi-dimensional archetypes, stereotypes, and mythologies regarding the opponent, "enemy," or Other; the problem, issue, or "quest;" and the storyteller, "hero," or Self.

This can be seen in the evolving stories people construct to explain to *themselves* what happened in the conflict, the role they played, and the reach of what they might do to handle the conflict and overcome it. Research has shown that the stories we tell ourselves about our lives powerfully shape our capacity for resilience, ability to recover from stress and trauma, and willingness to participate constructively in mediated conversations about what happened.

People who create stories of struggle and redemption about the issues in their own lives have been shown to have much better mental health. Dan McAdams at Northwestern University calls this "the life story model of identity."

> An identity is supposed to integrate your life in time. It's something in your mind that puts together the different roles in your life and situates you in the world. And like every story, it has characters, it's got a plot and it's got themes that run through it.

Yet people differ dramatically in their capacity to create coherent personal narratives and sense of *"agency"*–i.e., whether they describe themselves as having some control over events in their lives. Agency is an important predictor of mental health, yet a common feature of conflict stories is the powerlessness of the storyteller to positively impact their opponent or end the conflict.

McAdams also explores the idea of *redemption*, which he defines as finding positive meaning in the aftermath of stressful events. What he actually describes is a kind of *self*-redemption, which is separate from redemption of others, and can happen without confliction, or resolution. Other researchers have shown that people can be trained to improve these outcomes through narrative therapy, but few, to my knowledge, have considered these issues from the perspective of conflict resolution. [For more on "narrative mediation," see the writings of John Winslade, Gerald Monk, Sara Cobb, and others; or my chapters on "Transforming Conflict Stories" in *The Crossroads of Conflict*, and

"The Narrative Structure of Conflict Stories" in *The Dance of Opposites*.]

EMOTIONAL ARCS IN CONFLICT STORIES

Another largely unexplored connection between literature and conflict resolution can be found by comparing the nature, movement, and narrative structure of conflict stories with those in popular fiction. In both, we can discern patterns, for example, in the ways emotions are described and how they fluctuate.

In 1995, novelist Kurt Vonnegut gave a lecture in which he described the shapes of stories, and plotted several examples on a blackboard. "There is no reason why the simple shapes of stories can't be fed into computers," he said. "They are beautiful shapes." [Click here to watch on YouTube.]. Vonnegut showed through graphing that stories follow "emotional arcs," which have many different shapes, and some are better for storytelling than others.

Based on this idea, Andrew Reagan's team at the Computational Story Lab at the University of Vermont in Burlington used "sentiment analysis" to map the emotional arcs of over 1,700 stories, and data-mining techniques to reveal the most common arcs. [See, e.g.: arxiv.org/abs/1606.07772]. Here is a quote from the abstract describing their research:

> Advances in computing power, natural language processing, and digitization of text now make it possible to study a culture's evolution through its texts using a 'big data' lens. Our ability to communicate relies in part upon a shared emotional experience, with stories often following distinct emotional trajectories and forming patterns that are meaningful to us. Here, by classifying the emotional arcs for a filtered subset of ... stories from Project Gutenberg's fiction collection, we find a set of six core emotional arcs which form the essential building blocks of complex emotional trajectories [and that] particular emotional arcs enjoy greater success, as measured by downloads.

They assert that the six basic emotional arcs of stories follow these patterns:

1. A steady, ongoing rise in emotional valence, as in a rags-to-riches story such as *Alice's Adventures Underground* by Lewis Carroll.
2. A steady, ongoing fall in emotional valence, as in a tragic story such as *Romeo and Juliet* by William Shakespeare.
3. A fall then a rise, as in a "man falling in a hole and getting out story," as discussed by Vonnegut in the video.
4. A rise then a fall, as in the Greek myth of *Icarus*.
5. A rise-fall-rise, as in the romantic story of *Cinderella*.
6. A fall-rise-fall, as in the tragedy of *Oedipus*.

Here are diagrams for the first three arcs taken from popular literature. The second three have the opposite shapes.

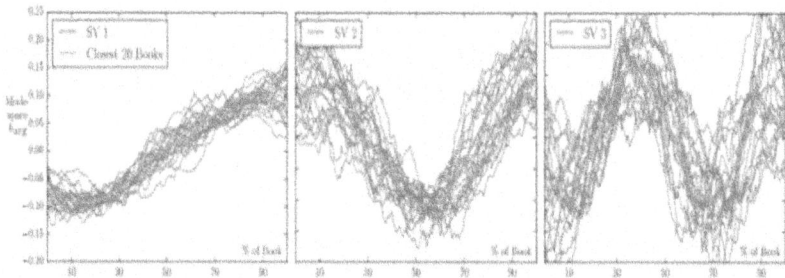

This suggests the presence of hidden patterns or "laws of motion" in conflict stories that follow subconscious emotional paths that have their own timing, and can change when events, attitudes, or circumstances shift. The parties may even share a deep subconscious awareness of these patterns, perhaps understand *intuitively* where the storyteller would like the story to go next, and what sort of shift in their communication or behavior could encourage that to happen.

The most common conflict stories describe a downward arc, and forget or fail to mention a previous upward arc, then resist or deny the possibility that a subsequent upward arc is even possible. Yet the subconscious expectation of movement *within* the arc, or what we can think of as the *sine wave* of conflict stories, may be enough to initiate the start of an upward movement.

Darkness, at its' worst, *automatically* suggests light, as they are opposites that cannot exist without each other, and are interdependent, co-existent — and in the language of Buddhism, "mutually arising." The downward, unremittingly negative stories told by people in conflict can therefore be heard not merely as *accusations* or self-accusations; but more deeply, as *confessions* of being stuck and unable to escape the downward spiral they just described; and far more profoundly, as *requests* for an upswing — for acknowledgement or assistance in turning the arc of their stories in more positive and satisfying directions.

How Mediation Transforms Conflict Stories

The turn of the story arc toward a satisfying dénouement, finale, or climax in literature closely corresponds to the movement towards settlement, resolution, transformation, and transcendence in mediation. These start with the mediator *complicating* the conflict story, perhaps by drawing forth its forgotten origins. clarifying its hidden meanings, acknowledging the unexpressed emotions that fueled it or kept it stuck, listening empathetically until people feel heard, and searching for "the third story" that removes demonization and victimization, and combines the parties' seemingly contradictory stories in new, creative, and synergistic ways.

This "third story" in mediation is the precursor to what "they lived happily ever after" represents in literature: it is a reminder of what really matters, a realization that the goal is not to suffer or inflict suffering, but to overcome and transcend suffering, and live happily ever after. If we imagine *every* part of the story as a metaphor for what is happening inside the storyteller, it is clear that the opponent's perfidy and baseness are simply stand-ins for the pain and frustrated *desire* of the storyteller. The conflict then becomes *internal*, and so does the resolution. What is required then is not a victory over our opponents, but learning the skills that enable us to act toward them with unconditional integrity.

In *The Dance of Opposites*, I described the two most common outcomes that are implied by the adversarial structure of conflict stories:

1. Victory over one's external enemies, vanquishing one's foes, triumphing over evil, plus a *retributive* form of justice that punishes the evil doer
2. Victory over oneself, vanquishing one's own weaknesses and temptations, triumphing over selfishness, anger, and willingness to be taken advantage of, plus a *restorative* form of justice that returns the parties to a more equal, fair and non-adversarial relationship

Most conflict stories take the superficial form of an attempt to bring about the first, while simultaneously disguising, even denying, the far deeper, unexpressed wish to bring about the second. The subconscious goal of the conflict story is to reveal to the listener what it would take for the storyteller to reach this outcome. For example, if a storyteller describes feeling disrespected, a mediator might ask:

- "What specifically did the other person say or do that led you to feel disrespected?"
- "How does it feel to be treated that way?"
- "Why is respect important to you?"
- "What does respect mean to you?"
- "Do you believe you have been respectful to the other person?" "If so, how did you express it?" "If not, why not?"

- "What could you do or say to be perceived as more respectful?"
- "What could the other person do or say that would lead you to feel more respected?"
- [To the other person] "Are you willing to try that?" "If not, what might help you get to a place where you would be willing to try it?"
- "Do you both agree that it is important for people to be respectful toward each other?" "Why?" [Or "Why not?"]
- "Can you both agree that, regardless of what happened in the past, you will do your best to be respectful to each other in the future?
- "Would you each be willing to make a list of respectful behaviors you will do your best to implement?"
- "Would you both be willing to *jointly* make a list of *disrespectful* behaviors you will do your best to avoid?"
- "What would you like to happen if either of you slips in the future?"
- Has this conversation felt respectful to you? Why?

TIMING IN LITERATURE AND CONFLICT RESOLUTION

Conflicts, like literature, alter our sense of time — not only by suspending, extending, manipulating, or collapsing it, but by *biasing* it, turning it in a frustratingly endless circle, dragging it out, speeding it up, using it to connect disparate events; and if the parties have the skills to do so, by *transcending* it and turning it into a spiral. Again, Elena Ferrante describes the issue beautifully:

> The eruption of suffering cancels out linear time, breaks it, makes it into whirling squiggles. The night of time crouches at the edges of the dawn of today and tomorrow. Suffering casts us down among our single-celled ancestors, among the quarrelsome or terrorized muttering in the caves, among the female divinities expelled into the darkness of the earth, even as we keep ourselves anchored – let's say

– to the computer we're writing on. Strong feelings are like that: they explode chronology. An emotion is a somersault, a tumble, a dizzying pirouette.

In conflict stories, events are often described as happening "always," or "never," rather than "too often for me" or "not often enough for me;" or they are presented as though they are eternal and will never end. This is simply the translation into words of a feeling of frustration at being stuck, or at impasse, feeling confused at not knowing what to do to get unstuck, and wanting to blame the other person for a *mutual* lack of skill at being able to handle each other's difficult behaviors.

Conflicts are often resolved, transformed, and transcended in mediation by tracing their past trajectory, revealing their chronic or systemic sources, and collaboratively charting or negotiating a mutually agreeable path to a different future — even if the parties are as yet unaware that they are *already* on it.

More powerfully, it is possible in conflict conversations to alter the timing by bringing the narrative to a complete halt, thereby drawing people into a heightened state of awareness of how they are behaving, revealing where exactly they are stuck, and what they might say or do to get unstuck. A mediator might ask, for example:

- "Is this conversation working for you? Why? Why not?"
- "Would you like it to work? Why? Why not?"
- "What is one thing the other person could do to make it work better for you?"
- "How are you feeling right now in this conversation?
- "What happened in the conversation that led you to feel that way?"
- What could either of you do to help you feel better about it?"
- "On a scale of 1-10, 10 being highest, how would you rank the conversation you were having before I interrupted you?"
- "Would you like to hear how the other person ranks it?"

- "How would you rank the conversation we are having right now?"
- "What would it take to make it a 10?"
- "Would you be willing to start over again and see if you can reach a higher score?"
- "What would you most like to hear her/him say to you right now?"
- "What do you wish he/she had said instead?"
- "What question would you most like her/him to ask you?"
- "What do you think is underneath, or hidden, in all the things s/he has been saying?" "You've been saying?"
- "What haven't you said that you will later wish you had?"
- "What are you not talking about that needs to be discussed?"
- "If you were an outside observer, how would you describe yourself, or your role in the conversation you were just having?
- "Would you like some feedback on how the other person sees you?" "Is that who you want to be, or the role you want to play?"
- "How am I doing as a mediator so far? What would you like me to do or say differently to help move the conversation forward?"
- "If we were to start this conversation over again, what would you want to say or do differently?" [For more, see Chapter 3.]

The first reason for these questions is to disrupt the communication/storytelling process, allowing the parties to step back, look at it from the outside, and gain perspective on where and how they got stuck. A second purpose is to restart the conversation by initiating an honest assessment of what isn't working on a micro-level, jointly fixing it, and enlarging it to address larger issues. A third purpose is to subtly, indirectly, nearly unnoticeably rewrite the stories they have been telling or narratives they have constructed about each other, themselves, and the conflict, by opening conversations they have resisted or deemed impossible.

In these moments, people may begin to see themselves, both individually and jointly, as the *writers* of their conflict stories — which are not fixed or predetermined, but like all good literature, emerge, adapt, and evolve as the veils are lifted, and darkness recedes. When this happens, conflicts are not exactly "resolved," but *disappear,* or are left behind as a new path appears, and what seemed mountainous and frozen suddenly shrinks and becomes passable.

CONFLICT AND CHARACTER

Novels are created by combining elements like character, plot, setting, theme, point of view, conflict, and tone. At their heart are characters who respond to stresses, traumas, and conflicts in ways that resonate with the reader, who is able to recognize, empathize, and experience them inside, and so vividly imagine each of these elements as to make them seem *real*, and in this way, bring fiction, imagination, and alternate realities to life.

Whether it is Alice's adventures in Wonderland, or Gregor Samsa waking to find he has turned into a giant insect, or Colonel Buendia facing a firing squad in *One Hundred Years of Solitude*, or the rage of Achilles, the travels of Odysseus, the adventures of Harry Potter, or contact with an alien civilization in *The Three Body Problem*, countless worlds invented by fiction writers touch us deeply, shape our characters, and alter our attitudes and expectations, including the ways we think about, feel, and act when we are in conflict, and who we *become* as a result.

If "we are what we eat," we are also what we read, and perhaps more consequentially, we are the stories and narratives we construct in response to conflict. There are three fundamental *sets* of stories we tell about our conflicts: the *internal* stories we tell ourselves, the *external* stories we tell others, and the *core* stories, which are the reasons why we made up the other two stories. [For more, see my book with Joan Goldsmith, *Resolving Personal and Organizational Conflicts: Stories of Transformation and Forgiveness*]

If we ask, "Which of these stories is true?" there are three correct answers: none of them, all of them, and it depends. None of these stories contains the sole and exclusive truth; all of them reveal different aspects or parts of the truth; and it depends on the kind and *level* of truth we are looking for. Yet it is nearly always the third story that is the deepest, most profound, offers the greatest insight into the meaning of what happened, and is potentially the most transformational — yet is also the least likely to be expressed, discussed, or examined in detail.

Storytelling can be seen as an effort to make sense of the chaos and confusion of conflict, as a search for some way out. As I wrote in *The Crossroads of Conflict,*

> People tell stories about their conflicts principally to alleviate the shock and pain of their experiences, reweave the fabric of perceived reality and tell themselves everything will be all right. But there is more to conflict stories than a desire for emotional comfort. Every conflict story identifies, for anyone willing to listen, what the storyteller most needs to learn, understand, do and become.

Beneath the surface of literature are not only entertaining stories, but the reasons we get so captivated and swept up by them, why every re-reading reveals something new. These are not just stories about Jean Valjean fleeing through the sewers of Paris, or Ahab's fanatical pursuit of Moby Dick, or the forbidden love of Romeo and Juliet, or Anna Karenina and Prince Vronsky–they are each and all about *us*, describing *our* flights and pursuits and forbidden loves.

It is the same with conflict stories, each of which somehow also happens to us. As the Zen monk Thich Naht Hahn wrote in this excerpt from his moving poem, *"Call Me By My True Names,"*

I am a mayfly metamorphosing
on the surface of the river.
And I am the bird
that swoops down to swallow the mayfly.
I am a frog swimming happily
in the clear water of a pond.
And I am the grass-snake
that silently feeds itself on the frog.
I am the child in Uganda, all skin and bones,
my legs as thin as bamboo sticks.
And I am the arms merchant,
selling deadly weapons to Uganda.
I am the twelve-year-old girl,
refugee on a small boat,
who throws herself into the ocean
after being raped by a sea pirate.
And I am also the pirate,
my heart not yet capable
of seeing and loving.
I am a member of the politburo,
with plenty of power in my hands.
And I am the man who has to pay
his "debt of blood" to my people
dying slowly in a forced-labor camp.

Novels, plays, and poetry teach us how to find *all* stories inside ourselves; how to open ourselves to other possibilities; how to learn from lives not our own; how to become larger, more tolerant, more caring, and wiser. And we can learn the same lessons by listening closely to the stories told by people in conflict — listening as though it were *us*, as though we were stuck — but also as though we were *not*, and can imagine a way out. As the novelist Russell Banks concluded in the last lines of *Continental Drift*:

Good cheer and mournfulness over lives other than our own, even wholly invented lives – no, especially wholly invented lives – deprive the world as it is of some of the greed it needs to continue being itself. Sabotage and subversion then are this book's objectives. Go, my book, and help destroy the world as it is.

SIX

Mediation and the Metaphor of Mathematics

A SEARCH FOR METHOD AND MEANING

The universe cannot be read until we have learned the language and become familiar with the characters in which it is written. It is written in mathematical language and the letters are triangles, circles and other geometrical figures, without which means it is humanly impossible to comprehend a single word. Without these, one is wandering around in a dark labyrinth.

Galileo Galilei

Our mistake is not that we take our [mathematical] theories too seriously, but that we do not take them seriously enough.

Steven Weinberg

All truth is comprised in music and mathematics.

Margaret Fuller

WHAT CONNECTION COULD POSSIBLY LINK MEDIATION WITH mathematics, two disciplines that, on the surface, seem so dissimilar, untranslatable, and irrelevant to one another? Mathematics feels precise, logical, unemotional, and objective, while conflict feels imprecise, illogical, highly emotional, and invariably subjective. Math consists of numbers, shapes, and symbols, while conflicts consist of feelings, experiences, and stories — and as novelist Pat Conroy reminds us, "No story is a straight line. The geometry of a human life is too imperfect and complex, too distorted by the laughter of time and the bewildering intricacies of fate to admit the straight line into its system of laws."

Nonetheless, three intriguing, potentially useful answers to the question of what connects mediation and mathematics suggest themselves:

1. Nothing links them, yet mathematics may offer illuminating metaphors, similes, and analogies that can aid us in imagining creative approaches to problem-solving, collaborative negotiation, and conflict resolution.
2. They are linked indirectly, because both are concerned with *forms* of equality and inequality, unity and opposition, integration and differentiation; with symmetry, complexity, chaos, fractal self-similarity, and other mathematical topics that offer insights into what is taking place at a deep, abstract, structural, or systemic level in conflict. Both are puzzles in which there are unknowns, leading us to search for solutions that are subtly encoded in basic principles, yet discoverable through theory, logic, technique, and proof.
3. There is a deep, profound, and fundamental connection *everything* has to mathematics, and conflict is no exception. The forms and patterns we observe in conflict can be teased out and more deeply understood by considering how mathematics might treat them, leading us perhaps to a set of logical formalisms, like those in Bayesian logic; or to hidden mathematical patterns, like Lie algebras; or symmetry groups that, as mathematician Emmy Noether proved,

reveal deep, universal, far-reaching laws of conservation,
that may also impact mediation.

It will be useful for us to keep all three of these possibilities in mind as we begin this exploration of the relevance of mathematics to mediation, and not decide at this phase which is more accurate or useful. First, however, an important disclaimer: I am <u>not</u> a mathematician, and possess neither great skill nor deep insight into it, but have enormous respect and profound admiration for those who do, and for the extraordinary insights and incomparable predictive power of mathematics. The ideas that follow are *entirely* the product of eclectic reading over the course of many years. They are intended merely to raise the issue, in humble hopes that others who are more skilled and intuitive will jump in.

It is *not* my goal to fully present or explain mathematical ideas, and I may do so in ways that professional mathematicians will find simplistic or misleading, for which I apologize in advance. Instead, I want to open a conversation among mediators about how mathematical concepts, methods, and ways of thinking might be applied to the nature and characteristics of conflict; and to conflict resolution, as complex, multi-dimensional *operations* we perform on conflicts in an effort to settle, resolve, transform, and transcend them. And as the brilliant French mathematician Évariste Galois reminds us, for both math and mediation,

> [T]he most worthwhile scientific books are those in which the author clearly indicates what he does not know; for an author most hurts his readers by concealing difficulties.

SOME INITIAL CONCERNS

At the outset, it's important to acknowledge that the precision and predictability we ordinarily associate with mathematics are quite different from the imprecision and unpredictability we commonly experience in conflict. To insist on too great a similarity between them would undermine the usefulness of mathematical ideas in revealing, as metaphor, analogy, and simile, some of the elements and features of conflict and resolution that we might otherwise miss. At the same time, it is helpful for us to keep in mind, as Johann Wolfgang von Goethe suggested:

> Mathematics has the completely false reputation of yielding infallible conclusions. Its infallibility is nothing but identity. Two times two is not four, but is just two times two, and that is what we call four for short. But four is nothing new at all. And thus it goes on and on in its conclusions, except that in the higher formulas the identity fades out of sight.

Indeed, mathematicians have struggled for centuries to create rigorous foundations for simple arithmetic, and used axioms, assumptions, set theory, one-to-one matching (which Georg Cantor used to distinguish different types of infinity), and similar methods to prove even the simplest propositions, like one plus one equals two, or two times two equals four.

Even in mathematics, there are well defined fields like probability, catastrophe theory, and the theory of games, where there is ample room for unpredictability and uncertainty. There are also areas like transcendental numbers, the precise distribution of primes, deterministic chaos, and non-linear equations, where it is common to come across patterns that are non-repetitive and unpredictable. There are even specific equations, like the square root of 16, that have more than a single correct answer (4 and -4), so that square roots routinely generate two or more correct answers, cubic roots three, quartic roots four, quintic roots five, etc.

In similar ways, if we define conflicts as places where there are *at least* two or more truths, and regard each party as analogous to an exponent, then the more parties who participate in a conflict the greater the number of truths that need to be acknowledged, examined, and integrated into a final resolution, the more "just" or "fair" outcomes become possible, and the more important dialogue and mediation become, simply because of the number of truths, and the factorial ways in which they can be combined.

Indeed, even mathematics can quickly lose its' precision, as in trying to calculate the gravitational orbits of three or more planets (the "three body problem"), or mapping random movements, in what is called "the drunkard's walk," where solutions may fluctuate so wildly or become so random that they can hardly be said to be answers at all. Even transcendental numbers like *pi* or *e* are *infinite* in length and cannot be precisely predicted. We therefore need to begin with the question, what exactly *is* mathematics?

What Is Mathematics?

Mathematicians have offered many interesting reflections on the nature of their craft. The brilliant French mathematician Henri Poincaré quipped that "Mathematics is the art of giving the same name to different things." Albert Einstein, on the other hand, believed that "Pure mathematics is, in its way, the poetry of logical ideas." And the great Russian mathematician A. N. Kolmogorov insightfully wrote, "At any given moment there is only a fine layer between the 'trivial' and the impossible. Mathematical discoveries are made in this layer."

Each of these useful ideas can be translated into metaphors for describing what mediators routinely experience in seeking to resolve conflicts. The idea, for example, that we might use different words to describe the same issues; or that emotions in conflict display a kind of logic and have a poetic quality; or that there is a fine layer between the trivial and the impossible where mediators make discoveries–all these seem apt in conflict resolution, where differences sit next to one another, and can combine in diverse ways to make resolutions either impossible, or trivial, or profound and transformational.

In considering mathematics as a metaphor in mediation, it is helpful, as British mathematician and science writer Marcus du Sautoy suggests, to distinguish not only pure from applied mathematics, but both from other scientific endeavors. "Science," he writes, "does the actual, mathematics does the possible. Science charts a single pathway through a tree of possible universes, mathematics maps every possible journey."

By analogy, it is common for mediators to focus on finding a single pathway to settlement, but it is equally important for us to think about how we might map *every possible* path to resolution, helping us realize that each path is one of many. We can regard potential paths in mediation as alternative approaches, or *styles* of mediation, and realize that there is an enormous difference between focusing on specific points of agreement, and the deep, transformative, and transcendent possibilities that search for the meaning and nature of conflicts, and consider the full range of what is possible in our efforts to overcome and synthesize them.

Math can also be distinguished from science by the ancient question of whether, in Gertrude Stein's words, there is a "there there;" that is, whether mathematics can be said to *exist* somewhere. Plato believed that "The highest form of pure thought is in mathematics," and together with Paul Erdős, Kurt Gödel, and perhaps most mathematicians, thought that math is not only real, but in some ways *more* real than the world we live in. The marvelous, eccentric mathematician John Horton Conway described it this way:

> There is no doubt that [mathematical things] do exist but you can't poke or prod them except by thinking about them. It's quite astonishing and I still don't understand it, despite my having been a mathematician all my life. How can things be there without actually being there?

In a similar way, conflicts do not have a direct physical existence that can be pointed to, but instead occupy some ephemeral, abstract space that does not make them feel any less real. It is through the parties' body language, words, stories, and narratives that we try to describe their shadows or outlines, and through empathy and logic that we struggle to discern their meaning.

As mathematician Edward Frenkel described it, "Mathematics allows you to see the invisible," but only in a language that is abstract, difficult to grasp, and nearly impossible to put into words. Even the incredibly brilliant mathematician John von Neumann believed that "In mathematics you don't understand things. You just get used to them." Quantum "weirdness" is a prime example, predicting with extraordinary mathematical accuracy to 10 or more decimal places events that seem absurd or impossible, like entanglement, tunneling, wave/particle duality, superposition, decoherence or wave function collapse, quantum leaps, Heisenberg uncertainty, and others.

Similarly, much of what happens to people in conflict takes place internally, emotionally, and invisibly, making it difficult for anyone who has experienced it to communicate to anyone who hasn't what it actually *feels* like. Emotions can lead people to behave not only irrationally, but *non*-rationally, and engage in behaviors that may feel weird or absurd to others, yet possess their own internal logic or rationale.

Mathematics, which often ignores or dismisses reality, has nonetheless proven "unreasonably effective," as mathematical physicist Eugene Wigner described it, in accounting for a vast range of seemingly unconnected real-world physical phenomena, especially in cosmology and physics, leading Albert Einstein to ask, "How can it be that mathematics, being after all a product of human thought independent of experience, is so admirably appropriate to the objects of reality?"

Indeed, the celebrated mathematical formulas attributed to Einstein and Erwin Schrodinger made unexpected predictions even their discoverers did not initially accept, but were later confirmed by observation and experiment. In response, as Heinrich Hertz observed,

> One cannot escape the feeling that these mathematical formulae have an independent existence and an intelligence of their own, that they are wiser than we are, wiser even than their discoverers, that we get more out of them than we put into them.

Some mathematicians attribute this uncanny accuracy, power, and effectiveness of mathematical ideas and equations to their "beauty." The British mathematician G. H. Hardy was outspoken about the value and importance of beauty:

> The mathematician's patterns, like the painter's or the poet's, must be beautiful; the ideas, like the colors or the words, must fit together in a harmonious way. Beauty is the first test; there is no permanent place in this world for ugly mathematics.

Bertrand Russell also described the beauty of math, but in different terms:

> Mathematics possesses not only truth, but supreme beauty—a beauty cold and austere, like that of sculpture, without appeal to any part of our weaker nature, yet sublimely pure, and capable of a stern perfection such as only the greatest art can show.

Other mathematicians have argued that while beauty, harmony, symmetry, and simplicity may be potent indicators of the presence of a deep, underlying truth, not all beautiful equations are necessarily true. Nonetheless, the beauty we encounter throughout nature makes sense, for example, as a consequence of the law of conservation of energy, or the simplicity and symmetry of complex forms, prompting Edna St. Vincent Millay's famous observation that "Euclid alone has looked on Beauty bare." Many mathematicians, for example, believe that the most beautiful equation is this one, discovered by Leonhard Euler: $e^{i\pi} + 1 = 0$, where e = 2.71828, i = -1, and π = 3.14159. [For more, see, e.g., David Stipp, *A Most Elegant Equation*.]

At a deep level, conflicts can also be said to possess a kind of beauty, though it is sometimes difficult to see it in the presence of all the suffering, heartbreak, cruelty, and ugliness that surround even the silliest and most trivial of disputes. This "cold and austere" beauty resides not at the surface, but in the deeper, more abstract, complex level of its core meaning, which can be said to be "conserved," together with the possibility of its resolution. Nonetheless, we can go a step further, as Henry David Thoreau suggested, and conclude:

> The most distinct and beautiful statement of any truth must take at last the mathematical form. We might so simplify the rules of moral philosophy, as well as of arithmetic, that one formula would express them both.

In conflict resolution, this simplification consists of gradually stripping away the superficialities and distractions, accusations and defenses, anger and hurt feelings, and discovering beneath their deeper profound and poignant sources, which point to *why* people have fallen short, and the simple, subtle beauty of what their conflict took place in order to teach them.

How Mathematics Works: Abstraction and Simplification

To understand how mathematics works and why it is regarded by those who study and practice it as beautiful, profound, and compelling, we need to begin at the beginning, and see it as a series of ever deeper abstractions and simplifications, all of which follow agreed upon rules, definitions, operational laws, and proofs; each of which peels away what is trivial and unnecessary, allowing us to generalize the *specific* descriptions, characteristics, and results that draw our attention to underlying similarities, unities, and hidden truths.

At the simplest possible level, we can start with three chickens, three cats, and three cows. We can easily see that abstracting and simplifying these objects by generalizing and collapsing them into the number 3 will allow us to work solely with *quantities*, irrespective of the *qualities* of whatever is being counted. It is then a short step to adding, subtracting, multiplying, and dividing these abstractions, and performing other operations on them without being confused by their specific nature as chickens, cats, and cows.

We can then further abstract the number 3 by using the letter n, which can represent any number. It is then possible to recognize, for example, that $(n + 1) + (n - 1) = 2 \times n$, or $2n$ for all numbers. Or we may discover deeper patterns we might otherwise miss, like:

$1 + 3 = 4 = 2^2$; $1 + 3 + 5 = 9 = 3^2$; $1 + 3 + 5 + 7 = 16 = 4^2$; ... (where "..." means the pattern continues forever).

Thus, adding successive odd numbers is the same as multiplying the next number times itself. Or we can dig deeper into *series* of numbers and find similar patterns:

$1/2 + 1/4 + 1/8 + 1/16 + 1/32 \ldots = 1$

$1/1 + 1/2 + 1/4 + 1/8 + 1/16 + 1/32 \ldots = 2$,

which can also be written as: $1/2^0 + 1/2^1 + 1/2^2 + 1/2^3 \ldots = 2$

We can abstract these even further, in a somewhat scarier step for non-mathematicians, by simplifying and reducing them to algorithms or instructions, using symbols that call for *repeated* operations, allowing these series to become:

$$\sum_{n=1}^{\infty} 2^{-n} = 1 \quad \text{and} \quad \sum_{0}^{\infty} \frac{1}{2^n} = 2$$

The Greek letter sigma stands for sum and simply tells us to add all the numbers that follow, for example, from 0 to infinity.

Each of these levels of abstraction reveals hidden characteristics, relationships, and laws that govern quantities without concern for their qualities, just as using geometric symbols like triangles or circles allows us to understand the spatial characteristics of shapes and forms without considering what they are made of; or topological rules let us transform triangles into circles and doughnuts into coffee cups, just by stretching or compressing them.

In advanced mathematics, we encounter even more abstract objects like manifolds, rings, knots, maps, categories, etc., often in higher dimensions that are difficult to imagine, and make useful metaphors harder to construct. Still, many of these highly complex and abstract ideas are powerful simplifications with practical consequences that have proven useful throughout the sciences.

In similar ways, mediators can abstract and genericize the issues people are arguing over to reveal deeper, hidden patterns. We can, for example, simplify their hostile, adversarial responses by temporarily ignoring everything related to the *content* of their dispute, and focus instead on the *form* of their communications, processes, interactions, or relationships. This may reveal patterns of behavior that keep them stuck and suggest interventions that might result in their getting unstuck.

We might, for example, decide to *map* their conflict, or diagram and chart the options that are possible in their conflicts with one another, using arrows or vectors to display the actions they might take, or thickness to indicate the magnitude of an issue, or rotation to indicate the directions they are moving, or dotted lines to show alternative actions they might take instead.

At a simpler level, we can diagram the parties' *adversarial* responses to their conflicts, and the things they might do to move their communications and interactions in a more *collaborative* direction, as in the following two diagrams.

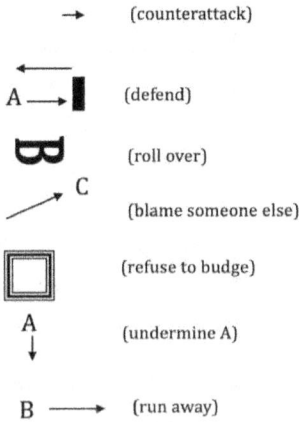

AGGRESSIVE RESPONSES TO CONFLICT

If A attacks B (A   B), B can respond in several ways:

→ (counterattack)

A→ ▌ (defend)

B (roll over)

↗ C (blame someone else)

□ (refuse to budge)

A ↓ (undermine A)

B ⟶ (run away)

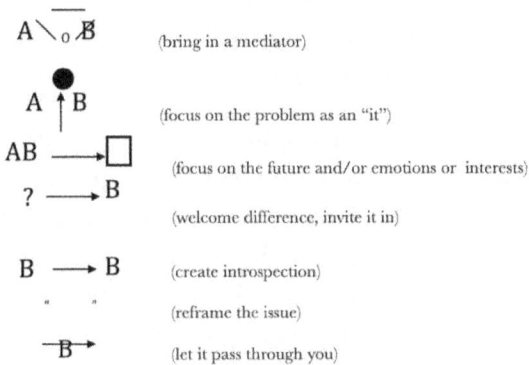

COLLABORATIVE RESPONSES TO CONFLICT

A↘₀ B (bring in a mediator)

A ↑ B (focus on the problem as an "it")

AB ⟶ □ (focus on the future and/or emotions or interests)

? ⟶ B (welcome difference, invite it in)

B ⟶ B (create introspection)

(reframe the issue)

B (let it pass through you)

Somewhat more imaginatively, we might define the most intractable conflicts as fractals that reach their limit at -1, while the most thorough resolutions do so at +1, allowing us to categorize any particular conflict or resolution by a set of (yet to be defined) numerical criteria as, for example, +.0386, or -.5211, and select more appropriate interventions accordingly. Alternately, we could consider these numbers on an exponential or logarithmic scale, permitting multiplication and division through addition and subtraction.

It would also be possible to imagine using topology as a metaphor, allowing the "shape" of a conflict to be seamlessly transformed without altering its content or meaning directly, and ignoring both the hostile behaviors and substantive issues over which people are arguing. This might be done, for example, by shifting the pronouns they have been using to describe the problem from "you" or "them" or "s/he" to less accusative and adversarial pronouns, such as "it" or "I" or "we."

Or we might think of conflicts as analogous to circles, with balanced centripetal and centrifugal forces that simultaneously draw us toward their centers, where resolution lies, while at the same time encouraging us to run away, where impasse lies. We may then more easily understand, at an abstract level, why chronic conflicts trigger "fight, flight, or freeze" responses; why people both resist and welcome mediation; and why the "circles" generated by chronic, *systemic* conflicts rekindle disputes in seemingly infinite ways.

We may also be able to imagine how circles of conflict might be altered by turning them into spirals; how elliptical curves might reveal hidden orbital patterns in conflict conversations; or how "fields" of conflict are created by opposing forces, similar to electromagnetic and gravitational fields, revealing a common center or hidden pole that invisibly unites opposing charges or rotating masses, and an equator or Lagrange point where they cancel each other out.

We may additionally understand why people who are "poles apart" in their conflicts can nonetheless be united, not only at their "equator," where their opposition ends, but at the pole itself, i.e., at the point of *intrinsic* commonality in their caring or concern for the same issues or problems. While the equator represents the possibility of compromise, the pole represents collaboration or "complementarity," and the transformational potential of far deeper, more heartfelt, constructive conversations that are grounded not in opposition and animosity, but in commonality and caring.

THE SYMMETRIES OF CONFLICT

One of the most fruitful sources of mathematical metaphor and understanding is the notion of symmetry, which can be described as what remains the same, or "invariant," when other things change. There are several kinds of mathematical symmetry, including mirror or reflectional symmetry, radial or rotational symmetry, "glide" or translational symmetry, and scale or "dilational" symmetry.

Using symmetry as a metaphor, conflicts can be said to exhibit characteristics that remain invariant under transformation, as when opposing parties switch roles, or contested issues are looked at from different angles, or reframed using different words, or scaled up or down in magnitude or importance. Symmetries can take a *positive* form, as with empathy, acknowledgement, reciprocity, altruism, relational intimacy, and mutual affection — or a *negative* form, as with exchanges of insults, self-centeredness, emotional distancing, relational distrust, and cycles of revenge.

Conflicts can therefore be regarded as having mirror or reflectional symmetry, as revealed in the mirroring of hostile attitudes and behaviors; radial or rotational symmetry, as expressed in the circular nature of arguments; glide or translational symmetry, as indicated in the similarity of conflicts over completely different issues or topics; and scale or dilational symmetry, as conveyed in the commonality of clashes over issues that are miniscule and momentous.

Conflicts may also possess symmetries that extend across time and space; symmetries of emotional experience, intelligence, and logic; symmetries of culture, bias, stereotyping, and rituals that convey and preserve meaning; symmetries of systems that are circular or reversable; and symmetries of approaches to settling and resolving conflicts.

These symmetries are analogous to mathematical forms of invariance, as they consist of things that may be said or done that do not alter the fundamental shape or nature of the conflict, and can aid mediators in identifying what is *conserved* by the conflict, as Emmy Noether proved — i.e., what keeps it going, and is most important to the parties to address before it will be possible to resolve it.

We can go further, and describe every conflict as a *search* for symmetry, in which people instigate, trigger, and *create* conflicts as a means of balancing perceived inequalities in power; or acquiring and consolidate rights as a hedge against abuses that flow from broken symmetries of status, wealth, and power; or of rectifying these imbalances by introducing *inherently* symmetric, egalitarian, non-zero-sum elements, such as interests, desires, and emotional connection.

Mathematical symmetries can be organized into "symmetry groups," with finite "simple" groups as constituents or building blocks for larger groups, just as prime numbers form building blocks for larger numbers. These symmetry groups are able to predict many of the properties of elementary particles and forces, and could perhaps lead to a "grand unified theory" that unites general relativity (a smooth, continuous theory of the very large) with quantum mechanics (a discrete, discontinuous theory of the very small). [See discussion in Chapter 7.]

By analogy, it may be possible to group conflicts by type, and identify the symmetries that connect, for example, the very small, seemingly discrete conflicts that upset siblings or spouses with the very large, continuous, and more consequential conflicts that generate prejudice or hatred between neighbors, and wars between competing nation states. Identifying these symmetries can help us link conflicts across issues and parties, identify missing elements, and suggest questions, interventions, and techniques that might bring them to resolution.

IMAGINARY AND COMPLEX NUMBERS

"Imaginary numbers," offer additional opportunities for insight. Represented by the letter i, imaginary numbers are based on multiples of the square root of -1, and have been proven profoundly useful in mathematics, engineering, and physics. The square root of -1 does not exist within the real number system, because the square of any negative number is always positive, so there is no "real" number that, multiplied by itself, equals -1.

Yet the mathematics of imaginary numbers makes it possible to regard each new multiplication as a *rotation* in two-dimensional space, and identify imaginary numbers by their distribution along the y axis. These axes form a two-dimensional Cartesian grid that helps us explain how they intersect, and calculate complex numbers lying between them, as shown in the following diagram:

REAL, IMAGINARY, AND COMPLEX NUMBERS

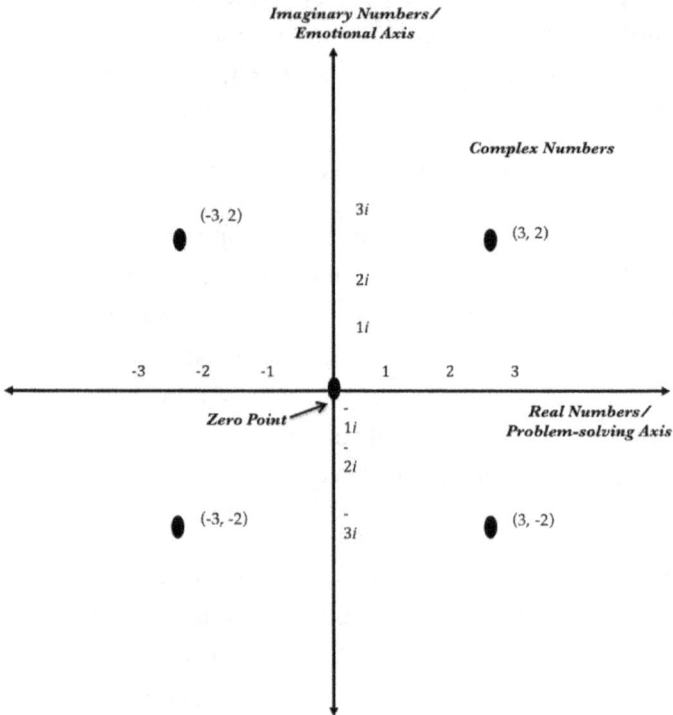

Imaginary Numbers/
Emotional Axis

Complex Numbers

(-3, 2)   3*i*   (3, 2)

2*i*

1*i*

-3   -2   -1   1   2   3

Zero Point   -   *Real Numbers/*
                   1*i*   *Problem-solving Axis*
                    -
                   2*i*

(-3, -2)   -   (3, -2)
                   3*i*

By analogy, we can think of conflict as also having at least two dimensions: one that ranges along a practical *problem-solving* axis and addresses "real," objective or systemic issues between the parties (similar to real numbers); and a second dimension that is distributed along an "imaginary" *emotional* or "interest-based" axis that addresses subjective or personal ones.

We can think of each imaginary operation as producing a rotation, with every multiplication, for example, shifting the outcome to a different quadrant. Thus, if an imaginary number $I = \sqrt{-1}$, then $i^2 = -1$, $i^3 = -I$, and $i^4 = 1$. In this way, a multi-dimensional object may be said to rotate as it revolves around a common center. These outcomes can be understood more clearly when they are diagrammed for two dimensional objects, as in the chart that follows:

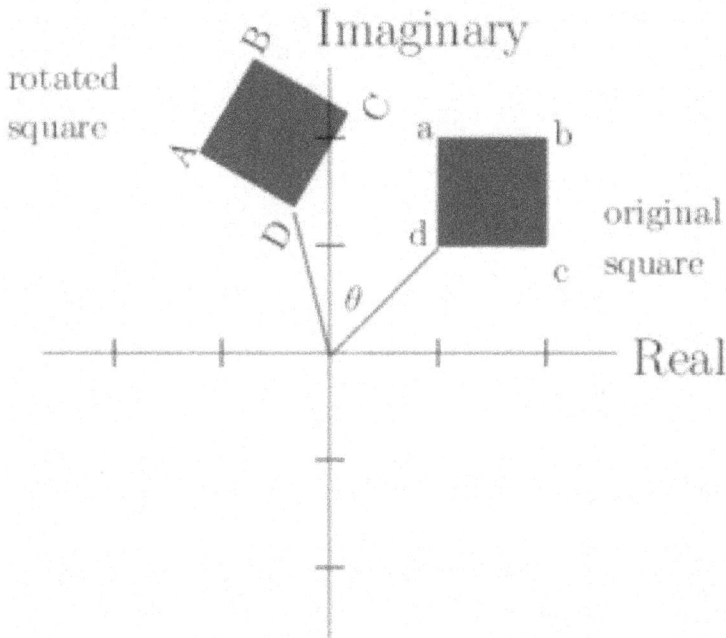

This mathematical metaphor allows us to think of conflicts as also rotating around a center, and the product of multiple, complex inputs that may *literally* be both real and imaginary. It has recently been demonstrated experimentally that the laws of quantum mechanics actually *require* imaginary numbers, and that any version of quantum mechanics that is devoid of imaginary numbers will lead to a faulty description of nature.

The same may be true for its' metaphoric significance in conflict resolution. Instead of thinking of conflicts, for example, as described by a single negative number representing one party's outlook or position on an issue, we can imagine both parties occupying a higher-dimensional rotating space defined by two or more parameters. We can then consider the *complex* outcomes that result from the combination of a real component representing a practical problem or position, with an imaginary component representing a single parties' emotions, intentions, wishes, or underlying interests. These may be added together to create higher order combinations, as can be achieved in mathematics by using "quaternions" in four dimensions, or "octonions" in eight, representing additional elements.

THE DIMENSIONS OF CONFLICT

It has been helpful for me to imagine conflicts as existing in more dimensions than one or two, and to regard dimensionality, not merely as the number of directions in which we can move in physical space, but as "degrees of freedom" that represent what we can think of as *conflict space*. In mathematics, as I wrote in *The Crossroads of Conflict*:

> It is possible to shift from lower dimensions to higher ones by dragging a lower dimension 90 degrees in a brand-new direction. Thus, a plane dragged 90 degrees in a new direction turns into a cube. Each new dimension can be described as a transformation, which in conflict resolution can be understood as asking questions that shift the parties' pointless and unproductive conversations 90 degrees in a brand-new direction.

> For example, if we are operating in zero dimensions, represented by a point, no information is required to define where an object is located, and there is no freedom of movement. This is analogous to impasse in conflict resolution, where either or both parties are stuck or unwilling to change, and no solutions or movements are seen as possible.

> One dimension, which is created by dragging a point 90 degrees in a new direction to form a line, allows us to create a single degree of

freedom. This is analogous in conflict resolution to stopping the fighting or deescalating the confrontation, which can be achieved simply by separating the parties and asking them singly to identify what they want, or by an authority figure imposing a solution on them, which requires only a single piece of information – what a parent or boss or dictator wants — to define a single outcome "solution-space."

A second degree of freedom can be created by dragging a line 90 degrees in a new direction, producing a plane that possesses both length and breadth. In conflict resolution, this can be analogized to settling a dispute, which can be achieved by both parties identifying their positions, or what they want, and negotiating a result. Every outcome in a two-dimensional space represents a compromise, as it consists of some combination of two parameters on a positional plane, with vertical and horizontal axes or vectors representing the limits or boundaries of what each person wants.

A third degree of freedom can be symbolized by a cube, which is created by dragging a plane 90 degrees in a new direction, creating depth in addition to length and breadth. Depth can be analogized to resolving the underlying emotional issues in a dispute, or to identifying the parties' interests, allowing them to move beyond adversarial, positional bargaining and solutions based on compromise, to create emotionally satisfying, interest-based solutions that invite people to move beyond compromise and invent creative outcomes that could not have been imagined in two dimensions.

We can also imagine a fourth physical dimension represented by a hypercube created by dragging a cube 90 degrees in a nearly unimaginable new direction. In conflict resolution, this can be analogized to forgiveness. This fourth dimension is more difficult to envision or define, and represents the spirit, intention, energy, life force, attachment or *chi* of people in conflict. Adding a fourth dimension allows forgiveness to emerge in ways that would appear magical to anyone operating in only three dimensions, just as three-dimensional solutions will appear magical to anyone who is unable to perceive depth.

Similar, yet even more difficult to visualize, is a fifth dimension represented by a geometrical figure that cannot be drawn adequately on a two-dimensional page, but can be analogized to reconciliation, based on an attitude that is now heartfelt, positive, open and compassionate. Including a fifth dimension allows intangible elements such as heart-to-heart communications and expressions of apology and compassion to be imagined, along with the interventions and techniques that trigger transcendence.

We can use this mathematical technique as a metaphor to help us finally imagine a sixth dimension that represents the *space* within which all these lower dimensions become manifest and constantly change, along with the systems, contexts, cultures and environments in which they occur. This dimension expresses the *holographic* nature of spacetime; or what physicist David Bohm called the "enfolded" element that contains a hidden "implicate order;" or what happens when elementary particles are "entangled," invisibly correlating their directions of "spin." Without this dimension, we might forget that there is always a field, stage, structure or backdrop on and against which each of the lower dimensions in conflict is revealed, played out, transformed and transcended.

If we consider any dimension — for example, a single dimension consisting of a line — we need to ask: a line in, or on *what*? Each of the first five dimensions describes a direction *in* space, which represents the background or context in which conflict occurs. Without identifying a sixth dimension, these implicate elements might pass unnoticed and unexamined.

Finally, we can imagine a seventh dimension representing the unidirectional flow, or "arrow" of time. This dimension expresses the impermanence of even the most hardened conflicts, the ability of people to become stuck in the past and unstuck in the future, and the enduring possibility of change, resolution, transformation and transcendence—not only in a specific conflict, but in the system, context, culture and environment within and against which it occurs, *all* of which are constantly changing. For practical purposes, following Einstein, we can combine the sixth and seventh dimensions into a single entity representing the *field* of space-time, or the changing environment and context of conflict.

The first four of these dimensions are illustrated on the following page. The fifth and sixth are left to your imagination, while the seventh can be thought of as any movement, evolution or transformation in the first six. While additional dimensions are possible, perhaps even an infinity of them, as imagined in higher mathematics, they are not especially helpful in analyzing conflict.

The chart on the following page [see also Chapter 2] maps the first four of these dimensions in relation to conflict resolution and roughly describes the most common options and outcomes that seem to me to be available to mediators and parties at each successive level or dimension.

Again, as I wrote in *The Crossroads of Conflict*, using dimensionality as a metaphor suggests a rational explanation for the role played by emotions and interests, as well as by intentions, attitudes, spirit, and heart in dispute resolution, as sources of transformational techniques and transcendence:

It also helps us explain the magic that so often happens in mediation, and how people are able to resolve, transform and transcend their conflicts in ways that seem to defy rational explanation. Finally, it suggests that for conflicts to disappear completely we need to transform and transcend not only the issues and emotions that divide people, but their personal attitudes and intentions, and the entire "conflict space," which includes the systems, contexts, cultures and environments that create the field in which it evolves.

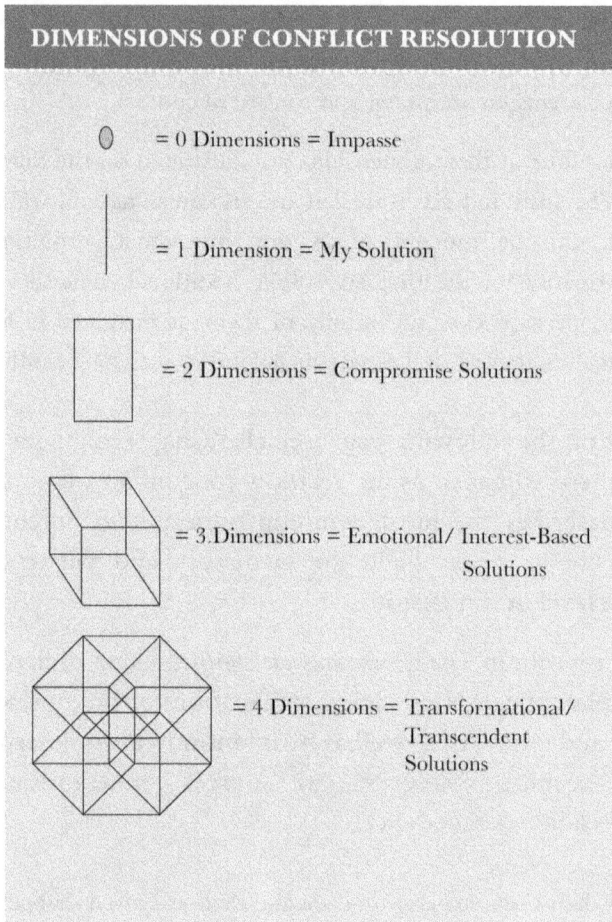

DIMENSIONS OF CONFLICT RESOLUTION

= 0 Dimensions = Impasse

= 1 Dimension = My Solution

= 2 Dimensions = Compromise Solutions

= 3.Dimensions = Emotional/ Interest-Based Solutions

= 4 Dimensions = Transformational/ Transcendent Solutions

IT IS IMPORTANT, IN CONSIDERING MATHEMATICAL IDEAS, THAT WE DO not confuse metaphor with reality and recall, as Lenin satirically commented regarding similar efforts to use mathematics as a metaphor for revolutionary political change, "Mathematics may explore the fourth dimension and the world of what is possible, but the Czar can be overthrown only in the third dimension."

CALCULUS AND CONFLICT

Calculus describes the mathematics of change, and as everything is impermanent and constantly changing, it provides a useful set of ideas, tools, and metaphors that might be applied to mediation, which is also concerned with change. [See Chapter 9.]

These topics, however, are so immense, complex, and abstract that only a tiny fraction can be considered here, and only in a basic, rudimentary way.

In my view, the most useful and important ideas mediators can draw from calculus are these:

1. Infinitesimals and Limits:

In calculus, any continuous change can be broken down into an infinite number of arbitrarily small, discontinuous or discrete pieces, each a tiny, infinitesimal amount larger than zero. This gives rise to the famous paradoxes described by Zeno, in which a hare never overtakes a tortoise, an arrow never reaches its target, and change seems impossible. Yet it also reduces the rate of change to such a tiny number that its overall behavior becomes clear, allowing us, for all practical purposes, to ignore the infinitesimal amount we just created. To make this operation more logical and rigorous, infinitesimals were replaced by the idea of *limits*–that is, while infinitely small additions can never end or reach their goal, they nonetheless continuously approach it as a *limit*. Thus, the number 0.999999… reaches its limit at infinity, allowing us to realize that it is, at that point, exactly equal to 1. Similarly, it is commonplace in mediation to take large, seemingly intractable conflicts and break them down into smaller, less emotionally charged pieces, or "bite-sized" bits, then perform what I call "micro-surgery" on each tiny part, and afterwards combine these small-scale resolutions on successively larger scales, based on the fractal self-similarity of conflicts across multiple scales.

It is common for people in conflict to focus on achieving small gains and successes, while failing to recognize that they are approaching a limit on what they can *possibly* achieve using rights- or power-based adversarial methods, which make it difficult to creatively and synergistically *combine* both sides needs, interests, ideas, emotions, expectations, and desires. Yet doing so, along with their sense of what constitutes a fair or just outcome, allows them to acknowledge and overcome their limits openly, honestly, collaboratively, and in detail.

2. Functions and Mapping:

A function in mathematics is simply an algorithm or instruction to perform a given operation on a set of numbers, "domains," or inputs. It "maps" the changes from one domain to another, describing a relationship between them, along with an instruction, process, or method for getting from one to the other that generates an output or result. A function might be, for example, to turn a set of numbers into letters, or divide each number by two, or find the difference between them.

A "multivariate function" is one that depends on several variables, inputs, or "arguments," as the position of a car traveling on a highway, for example, depends on its starting location, the time it has traveled, and its average speed. These variables can be complex and require imaginary or complex numbers, or be expressed as vectors that have size or magnitude, and orientation or direction.

In conflict resolution, we can consider the parties' behaviors as a function, output, or consequence of their adversarial, biased, disrespectful communications. It is then possible for mediators to use the mathematical idea of a function, sometimes described as a "machine" or "black box," to clarify and map how their conflicts arose over time. I call this method "conflict mapping" [described in Chapter 2, and in my book with Joan Goldsmith, *Resolving Organizational Conflicts*].

If we take a function like $f(z) = z^2 + 1$, and substitute a complex number with a real and an imaginary part for z, then take the answer and plug it back into the function and repeat, the outcome will be a series of points that form incredibly elaborate and beautiful "fractal" paths through the complex plane, as can be seen with the Mandelbrot or Julia sets, which are self-similar on all scales. Here is one view of the Mandelbrot set [Source: Wolfgang Beyer]

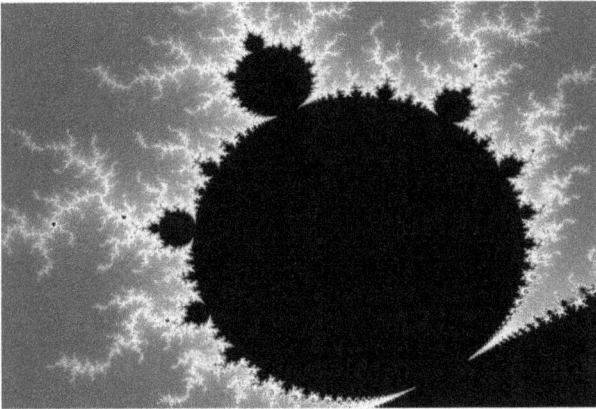

Conflicts can similarly be seen as fractally organized, self-similar on all scales, and having fractional dimensions which create elaborate paths that duplicate or link the core dynamics and instinctual responses of conflicted parties, whether they involve petty fights between children on a playground, or political battles between the heads of nation states.

3. Integration and Differentiation:

Roughly speaking, it is possible to use tiny, infinitesimal quantities in two ways. If we want to know how fast things are changing or growing, we can differentiate, subtract, separate, or divide them from a larger body of information, producing a "derivative;" and if we want to know how those small changes are accumulating or accreting, we can add, integrate, or multiply them, producing an "integral."

In these ways, even something that is moving very rapidly, like a bullet, can be described statically as though it were still; and something that is not moving at all, like the area of object, can be described dynamically as though it were growing. We can then *reverse* these processes and derive the velocity of a bullet from tiny changes in its' position, or its position from tiny changes in its' velocity.

As addition and multiplication are the reverse of subtraction and division, differentiation and integration are also mathematically opposite, or "dual" to each other, so that if one becomes too difficult to calculate, it is possible to use the other to reach the same result. This is known as the "fundamental theorem of calculus."

In a similar way, we can describe mediators as working in two opposite yet connected ways: on the one hand, *differentiating*—that is, taking large issues and dividing them into smaller pieces that may be easier and more manageable; and on the other hand, *integrating*—that is, taking small issues and connecting them into larger wholes to explain aspects of their meaning or significance that might otherwise be overlooked. We can think of these as missing the trees for the forest, or the forest for the trees. Leo Tolstoy described it this way in *War and Peace*:

> Only by taking infinitesimally small units for observation (the differential of history, that is, the individual tendencies of men) and attaining the art of integrating them (that is, finding the sum of these infinitesimals) can we hope to arrive at the laws of history.

Toward a "Fundamental Theorem of Mediation"

In mathematics, there is a "fundamental theorem of *arithmetic*," stating that all numbers other than one are either prime numbers or the sums of primes. There is a "fundamental theorem of *algebra*," which is that all polynomials of any degree (or "n degree") with real or complex coefficients have the same number of real or complex roots, as the square root of 25 is 5 and -5. And there is a "fundamental theorem of *calculus*," which is that integrals and derivatives are reverse functions.

These theorems represent a deep understanding of the ways seemingly opposite phenomena are united, or "dual" to one another. I would like to propose three elements that could constitute a "fundamental theorem of mediation." Here are three possibilities, modeled on the three listed above, but in opposite order:

1. Conflict and resolution are reverse functions.
2. All n-degree simple and complex conflicts possess n-degree simple and complex *truths*.
3. All conflicts consist of unsatisfied interests and unacknowledged emotions, or some combination of interests and emotions.

The first element expresses the idea that resolution is the inverse of conflict, suggesting that mediation is an operation we perform on conflict in an effort to reverse it, and that what gets us stuck can be reversed, allowing us to get unstuck. The second describes how complexity and dimensionality are *identical* in conflict and resolution, suggesting that mediation is a scale-free effort to shift from single, "either/or" to multiple, "both/and" truths. The third seeks to identify the "atoms" of conflict, suggesting that mediation is an effort to surface and address the unsatisfied interests and unacknowledged emotions that are driving it.

Each of these fundamental ideas or theorems suggests that the methodology and characteristics of mediation are defined by the nature of the conflicts it seeks to resolve; and that conflicts are complex, multi-dimensional, scale-free, and constantly changing, requiring us to continually adapt and reinvent mediation as each dispute evolves and assumes new forms.

MEDIATION AND THE THEORY OF GAMES

The modern theory of games was set in motion when the brilliant mathematician John von Neumann developed the idea of "mixed strategy zero-sum games" between two players leading to a fixed point, or equilibrium. In 1944, von Neumann and economist Oskar Morgenstern wrote *The Theory of Games and Economic Behavior*, which explored cooperative, non-zero-sum games, and suggested that society, economics, and politics might be analyzed mathematically by viewing them as games in which players can anticipate each other's moves.

Doing so allowed game theorists to distinguish "games of perfect information," such as chess, in which each player can theoretically know everything about the game at all times, from "games of imperfect information," such as poker, in which no player can know which cards the other players have received.

Zero-sum or constant-sum games are always and necessarily competitive; if one player wins the others must lose. Thus, if one player gets seven out of a total of 10, the other must get three. In non-zero-sum games, everyone can win or lose, and both can receive 10s. Mixed games, such as the Prisoner's Dilemma, allow separated players to choose whether they will both confess, or compete by being the first to snitch, or adopt a cooperative strategy and remain silent.

In cooperative games, players can communicate and reach agreements in advance, while in competitive or non-cooperative games they cannot. Games can also be "extensive," in which players follow a decision tree, or "normal," in which they develop a matrix, with each column representing one player's strategy and each row representing another's.

Finite two-person zero-sum games of perfect information such as chess are strictly determined, meaning that rational players make use of all the information available to develop an optimal strategy, and outcomes are preordained. Games of imperfect information, on the other hand, allow each player to select an optimal strategy no matter what the other player does.

A different outcome occurs if players have *multiple* interests, values, or goals. Building on work by mathematician and Nobel Prize winner John F. Nash, described in Sylvia Nasar's book, *A Beautiful Mind*, a utility function can be created, and a number assigned to each separate interest to convey its relative importance or attractiveness to each player. These interests need not be entirely "rational," and can have emotional or subjective components, such as a desire to help someone in need or punish a wrongdoer. Software lets mediators use these principles to generate interest-based options in divorce and other mediations.

Nash won the Nobel Prize in economics for a two-page paper describing how any competitive game has a place of equilibrium, which consists of a set of strategies for each player, and a place where no player can win more by unilaterally switching to a different strategy, thereby ending the competition. Nothing indicates, however, how players arrive at a place of equilibrium. Indeed, it has been proven that no method of adapting strategies in response to previous games will converge efficiently to a Nash equilibrium for every possible game, unless the players tell each other virtually everything about their respective preferences, which is increasingly time consuming and complex as more players are added.

In response, Robert Aumann, who also won a Nobel Prize, suggested that when each player receives advice from a "trusted mediator" about which strategy to play, they create a "correlated equilibrium" in which no player has an incentive to deviate from the advice, if they believe other players are also following the advice. Moreover, the mediator can withhold information regarding which advice has been given to other players, encouraging cooperation and more positive outcomes than the Nash equilibrium predicts.

Based on these results, Ivar Ekeland suggested that "An equilibrium is not always an optimum; it may not even be good. This may be the most important discovery of game theory."

It has been shown, for example, that players can increase the probability of all players using a given strategy if they use "regret minimization" strategies, in which, before each round, they indicate that they regret not having used a cooperative approach in the past. This can trigger the trusted mediator outcome of correlated equilibrium, which increases over time with repeated rounds.

In non-zero-sum cooperative games, these mediative methods allow players to gain, even if some of their interests cannot be met. Players will therefore want their opponents to be well-informed so they can collaborate more effectively. In these cases, the depth of communication and the order in which it occurs can have a profound influence on the outcome. Thus, two pilots attempting to avoid a midair collision clearly benefit by communicating quickly and honestly, and pursuing a cooperative strategy.

The more the players' interests overlap, the more advantageous communication and cooperation become. Harvard professor Martin Novak has shown that when people belong to a network, community, or integrated group, cooperation quickly becomes dominant over competition, especially when the benefit-to-cost ratio exceeds the average number of their neighbors, and when individual reputations for cooperation are taken into account. The lessons for mediators are clear, and require no explanation.

COMPLEXITY, CHAOS, AND SYSTEMS DESIGN

Simple things, when added or multiplied, or repeated in rapid succession, can become increasingly complex, giving rise to new or "emergent phenomena," "adaptive systems," "self-organization," and "nonlinear," chaotic behaviors. An example of emergence is fusing atoms of hydrogen and oxygen gas to create liquid water; or slowing water molecules until they freeze into solid ice, or amassing them until they become a river; or sending them over a cliff to form a waterfall, or refracting light through them at the right angle to create a rainbow.

Complexity can also give rise to adaptive systems that respond to feedback, change course, become stable, or evolve dynamically with their environment. These adaptations can produce "phase transitions" that result in self-organization, or "spontaneous ordering," in which disorder, in moments of "criticality," combines with feedback to produce random changes, some of which create "islands of stability" and predictability in a sea of chaos and uncertainty, allowing them to spread across the entire system, as when water turns to ice.

The non-linear dynamics and chaos that arise in complex systems reflect the fact that ordinary linear processes no longer result in predictable outcomes. Simple quantitative laws of addition cannot fully explain the *qualitative* changes that are triggered, for example, in water by a drop in temperature of just a single degree below freezing; or predict how a diverse set of complex components will interact; or describe what happens when chaos, with its sensitive dependence on initial conditions, makes outcomes non-linear, imprecise, and uncertain.

In a similar way, conflicts are often complex and chaotic, giving rise to emergent communications and behaviors, and resulting in *relational* phase transitions like estrangement, ostracism, and divorce, or their opposites. And, through feedback, conflict resolution, and higher order communications, mediative behaviors can emerge that stabilize and spread throughout the system, transforming the conflict within, between, and around people who, only moments before, felt trapped by it.

The mathematics of complexity is also concerned with the number of steps required to reproduce a given pattern or configuration, i.e., the amount of *information,* or number of bits or operations needed to fully describe or duplicate it. Information, in this sense, is the elimination of randomness and uncertainty created by disorder, chaos, conflict, and entropy, and thus a measure of diversity and complexity.

Emergence can also be described as the moment when information becomes qualitatively more complex, or is *integrated*, giving rise to some new, higher order of simplicity, reducing the number of steps needed to describe or duplicate it — as when a complex, disordered whole enters a phase transition and suddenly becomes simpler, more ordered, and greater than the sum of its parts.

In conflict resolution, emergence can take the form of empathy and active listening; acknowledgement and apology; a question that reveals hidden interests; an emotionally intelligent and heartfelt exchange; a letting go of anger, fear, grief, and guilt; or a deeper understanding of the underlying meaning of the conflict.

In these cases, the amount of information needed to describe the conflict is dramatically reduced, which can lead to a higher order of awareness and the possibility of a phase transition ending in settlement, resolution, forgiveness, and reconciliation; or in the design of *preventative*, emergent, adaptive, mediative systems that dismantle conflicts at their chronic, repetitive, underlying source.

By analogy, in seeking to explain what is called the "hard problem" of consciousness, neuroscientist Giulio Tononi, with Gerald Edelman, Anil Seth, and Kristof Koch, have proposed an "Integrated Information Theory," which regards consciousness as an emergent phenomenon resulting from increasing complexity and a combination of information and integration. They assert that it is not merely information, which computers can gather, but the ability to *integrate* it, simplifying complexity and reducing uncertainty, that results in consciousness.

The relationship between disorder, order, and the evolution of complexity can be roughly described in the following diagram, based on one presented by Anil Seth in *Becoming You*, which shows how complexity, individuation, and information can produce successively higher levels of order by interacting with regularity, integration, and symmetry along an uncharted three-dimensional time axis:

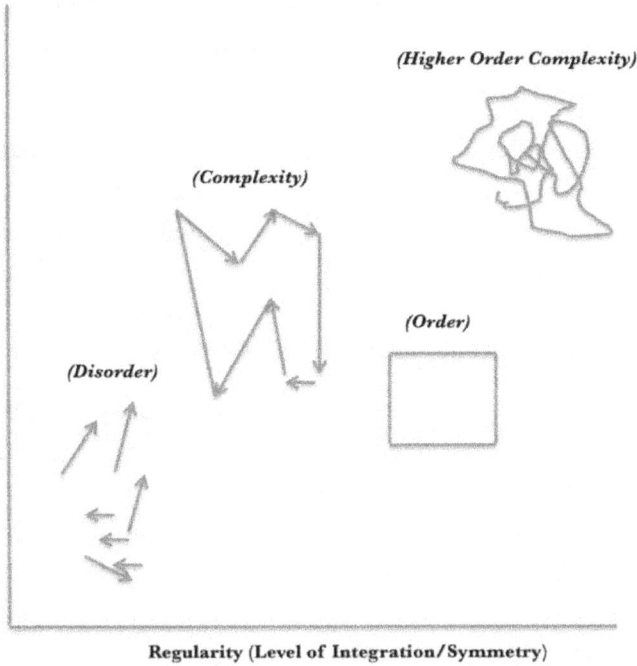

ORDER, DISORDER, AND THE EVOLUTION OF COMPLEXITY

Complexity (Level of Individuation/Information)

(Higher Order Complexity)

(Complexity)

(Order)

(Disorder)

Regularity (Level of Integration/Symmetry)

In a similar way, mediators can be seen to occupy a complex space that is neither completely disordered nor rigidly structured, but is able to adapt and evolve in order to explores the natural complexity of conflict, and thereby discover a higher order set of operations, techniques, and methods that could lead to higher order resolutions, and the creation of more adaptive and preventative systems.

Through a kind of "Bayesian" logic, mediators can use generic information about conflicts in general to estimate the conditional probability of a particular method or technique succeeding, then observe how the parties actually respond, revise their approach, and gradually narrow in on substantively fair, emotionally acknowledging, interest-based solutions that are acceptable to all.

Bayesian logic is useful in addressing social and behavioral issues that frequently arise in conflict resolution, because it is able to capture the flow of information over time and address the complexity, uncertainty, reactivity, and chaos that characterize the responses people commonly have when they are in conflict.

Bayesian calculation consists of a series of rough approximations that are updated periodically by measurement or assessment, and this accurately captures what mediators do while listening, which is to revise their approach moment by moment as the parties' moods and responses evolve during the mediation process. I think of this as "calibrating my intuition," or subtle knowledge, as they shift.

By asking difficult and "dangerous" questions that dig deep into the complex places where people get stuck, mediators can increase the amount of information about the underlying nature of conflict, integrate contradictory positions, surface higher order interests, correct misunderstandings and miscommunications, restore empathy and trust, renegotiate expectations, shift attitudes, and transform problems that seemed immense, impossible, and intractable into ones that are smaller, malleable, and can be collaboratively repaired.

Hidden Links, the Langlands Program, and Grand Unification

Most areas, operations, and topics in mathematics appear discrete, distinct, and self-contained, yet beneath the surface, hidden links, connections, symmetries, dualities, and correspondences are being discovered that surprisingly unify them, revealing concealed two-way streets that allow one set of operations to be translated seamlessly into another.

Many centuries ago, Rene Descartes discovered that *algebraic* equations could be graphed and transformed into *geometric* shapes, and *vice versa*, connecting these vastly different methods and ideas. Later, the brilliant Évariste Galois, shortly before his death at the age of 20, developed the idea of linking mathematical operations through symmetry groups with unique predictive characteristics.

Beginning in the 1960's, Robert Langlands proposed a far grander project of unification, seeking to connect key concepts in algebraic number theory, geometry, calculus or analysis, elliptic curves, and other highly specialized, seemingly disconnected areas through a series of conjectures that have revealed surprising links between them, with profound implications for many areas of mathematics, and for grand unification efforts in physics, like string theory, M theory, and loop quantum gravity. [See Chapter 7.]

While this work is highly technical and well beyond my understanding and skill, the Langlands program's search for hidden links between seemingly disparate ideas and approaches has great metaphoric significance for mediators. For example, while people in families, schools, prisons, workplaces, and political institutions often behave differently and present dissimilar problems, the conflicts experienced within these groups exhibit hidden common features that allow us to adapt approaches that succeed in one area and apply them in another.

More importantly, our extraordinary diversity, as genders, races, cultures, religions, languages, ages, nationalities, political affiliations, personalities, attitudes, beliefs, values, etc. — each of which impacts and shapes the conflicts that arise within, between, and around us — can easily camouflage or conceal the underlying unities, and universality of conflict as a *human* experience.

To succeed in solving complex problems and resolving conflicts, whether personal or political, we need not only diversity and dissent, but advanced skills in designing, organizing, and facilitating dialogues, building empathy, promoting consensus; in accepting ambiguity and leaving issues open for continuous improvement; and in turning complexity in the direction of collaboration and non-linear, evolving, multi-faceted, dynamical, paradoxical problem-solving.

While diversity makes us different, unity makes us the same. At a deep level, we all know what it feels like to be different, and be disrespected, insulted, maligned, and misunderstood as a result. We have all felt anger, fear, jealousy, shame, grief, and guilt. Our trust has been broken, our wishes ignored, our interests disregarded. We have all gotten stuck in conflicts with others and not known what to do. We have all, at some time, wanted it to have happened differently, or wished it hadn't happened at all, or hoped it would simply go away.

And we have all also (I hope) experienced what it feels like to be united, and be accepted, trusted, understood, and connected as a result. We have all felt love, trust, happiness, joy, empathy, and synchronicity. We have all experienced the camaraderie and pleasure of unity and friendship, intimacy and bonding. Our trust has been reciprocated, our wishes met, and our interests satisfied. We have all, at some time, resolved our conflicts, figured out what went wrong, and learned what to do to prevent and avoid them.

What connects these two disparate sets of experiences is our ability to understand the Langlands-like sources of our conflicts, and discover there how to transform the negative, destructive aspects of conflict into opportunities for learning, higher order skills and techniques, and solutions that do not require winners and losers.

In these ways, all of our methodologies, techniques, and skills; all our approaches, styles, and processes; all our mediations, dialogues, collaborative negotiations, system designs, restorative justice facilitations, and similar conflict resolution practices, however distinct and specialized, can be seen at a deeper level to be linked, connected, and united with one another.

These concealed links, connections, dualities, and correspondences can assist us in translating from one group or individual, gender or race, organization or institution, community or nation, to another, and allow us to adapt techniques and processes from one person or issue or variety of conflict to another, moving back and forth between them on multiple scales.

Most profoundly, mathematicians and physicists are actively searching for a "grand unified theory" or "theory of everything" that can connect quantum mechanics with general relativity. Significant progress has already been made, for example, in string or "M" theory, whose 10 or 11 dimensions include quantum gravity; or the "holographic principle," which reduces the three dimensions of information inside a black hole to the *two* dimensional surface of its event horizon; or "AdS/CFT correspondence," which makes a negatively curved five-dimensional space *with* gravity dual to a four-dimensional "conformal" field theory *without* gravity; or theories in which spacetime is not fundamental or given, but emergent; or in the duality of tiny wrapped up dimensions and large extended ones; and similar ideas that suggest ways of connecting, integrating, and unifying aspects of conflict resolution that seem unconnected.

While we are a long way from discovering a grand unified theory of mediation, we have made significant progress in understanding the nature of conflict and what successfully resolves it across diverse parties, cultures, issues, scales, histories, and settings. We are also increasingly able to connect conflict resolution ideas and practices with those in seemingly disconnected fields, starting with law and psychology and extending outward—not just to mathematics and physics, but literature, anthropology, sociology, politics, philosophy, spiritual practices, organizational theory, systems design, and many others. [See discussion below in Chapter 7 and in *The Crossroads of Conflict*.]

A CAUTION

As in algebra, mediators solve unknowns by finding ways of *equating* or equalizing people who are in conflict; by adding, subtracting, multiplying, and dividing both sides by the same quantity (or quality); by simplifying complex formulations; by making simplistic assumptions more complex, and *vice versa*, and similar operations. The same can be said of geometry, calculus, algebraic topology, and other areas of mathematics.

I think this is possible because each separate area of mathematics represents a fundamentally different, potentially unified approach to understanding the world by means of abstraction; that is, by differentiating its *essence* as pure, empty form, from its *appearance*, or manifestation, and its' specific, overflowing content.

The archetypal act of mathematical abstraction allows us to genericize commonalities, and thereby reveal hidden structures and systems, expose invisible scaffolding, uncover symmetries, and discover laws of motion, regardless of the specific field or topic or set of problems to which it is applied. This makes it extraordinarily useful as an instrument of understanding conflict.

Yet it is *vital* for us to always keep in mind that by doing so, we may end up ignoring, devaluing, or *stripping* it of everything personal and human, kind and compassionate, poignant and wise, heartfelt and spiritual. Without these human elements, Einstein's famous, simple, elegant formula for the conversion of matter into energy can be turned into a bomb, causing a "terrible beauty" to be born.

These intensely meaningful, deeply desired, *socially* emergent qualities form an essential part of every mediation, and are critical elements in any collaborative endeavor or restorative outcome. Yet they require a fundamentally different, more multi-sided, multi-dimensional process that has as much or more to do with poetry, subjective feelings, and emotional logic as with the manipulation of numbers, objective equations, and abstract shapes.

What is most successful in dispute resolution is the creative *combination* of these separate, diverse, sometimes opposing methodologies, and the integrated application of diverse problem-solving approaches in a collective effort to explore and unlock the places where people get stuck. Together, they enable us not only to analyze highly complex issues, but acknowledge emotions, brainstorm solutions, negotiate collaborative agreements, resolve underlying issues, elicit apologies, encourage forgiveness, reach reconciliations, restore justice, and design preventative systems.

Learning from mathematics can therefore be seen as a search for the discovery or invention of a larger, grander, more powerful duality that I believe lies at the heart of conflict resolution; a hidden *yin* that partners with some unarticulated *yang*; a whole that is vastly greater than the sum of its parts.

Mediation, at its best, invites us to become more skillful in both; to be analytical, and at the same time empathetic; abstract, yet fully present; practical, while generously acknowledging; critical, as well as unconditionally caring. As G. K. Chesterton perceptively observed:

> The real trouble with this world of ours, is not that it is an unreasonable world, nor even that it is a reasonable one. The commonest kind of trouble is that it is nearly reasonable, but not quite. ... It looks just a little more mathematical and regular than it is; its exactitude is obvious, but its inexactitude is hidden; its wildness lies in wait. ... It seems a sort of secret treason in the universe. ... Everywhere in things there is this element of the quiet and incalculable.

Over a century ago, Georg Cantor, whose stunning mathematical explorations of infinity reshaped mathematical thought, interestingly wrote that "The essence of mathematics is its freedom." It is a freedom, to be sure, that is tightly constrained by axioms, theorems, and the rigors of peer-reviewed proof — yet within these limits, it is possible to find truths about the universe that are genuinely freeing.

Perhaps the same will be true of the application of mathematics to mediation–not just as metaphor, but as a description of deeper, more profound, and fruitful realities, as sources of insight into the ways we think about and seek to resolve conflicts. The Austrian writer Hermann Broch expressed it nicely:

> For the world of mathematics, ... with all its algebraic symbols, its theoretical interrelation of sets of numbers, its infinitesimal infinitude in small things as in great, found only the crudest expression in the world of concrete fact; and even the delicate constructions of physical science, evolved from intricate and ingenious experiments, even the calculability of these physical phenomena, formed in sum only a small, inadequate, pale reflection of the manifold thought-complexity of mathematics, which was embedded in the concrete visible world as an original principle, far beyond the concrete, spanning the whole universe and yet immanent in the reality of the universe as in its own reality.

If mathematics, as Einstein believed, is "the poetry of logical ideas," or as Plato thought, the distilled essence of reality; if it spans the entire universe, or perhaps multiverse, reducing it to mere metaphor risks masking the deeper truths it alone can reveal, just as reducing conflicts to petty practical issues can conceal its' deeper truths, and the learning and wisdom it is uniquely able to impart.

By combining these truths in creative, evolving, complex, unpredictable ways, we may succeed, as we seek to do in every mediation, in connecting the abstract with the specific, the metaphor with the meaning, the simple with the complex, the quantity with the quality, the very large with the very small, the sacred with the profane, the head with the heart. It is here that the deepest beauty appears, often in the guise of poetry, or mathematics.

In spite of its' sweep and amazing explanatory capacity, there are profound truths that cannot be captured by mathematical formalisms, and times when $1 + 1$ does not equal 2, but 3–as when an egg and sperm combine to form an embryo; or two people fall in love and become a couple; or two ideas combine to create a third that is not simply additive, but new, unexpected, and greater than the sum of its parts. To express these truths, poetry is required, in math and mediation as well.

SEVEN

The Metaphor of Physics

THE VERY LARGE, THE VERY SMALL, AND THE VERY COMPLEX

[T]he task [of physics] is not so much to see what no one has yet seen; but to think what no one has yet thought about that which everybody sees.

Erwin Schrodinger

What is commonly called 'disorder' is merely an inappropriate name for what is actually a certain rather complex kind of order that is difficult to describe in full detail. Our real task can, therefore, never be to judge whether something is ordered or disordered, because everything is ordered, because disorder in the sense of the absence of every conceivable kind of order is an impossibility. Rather, what one really has to do is to observe and describe the kind of order that each thing actually has.

David Bohm

[The theory of relativity] occurred to me by intuition, and music was the driving force behind that intuition. My discovery was the result of musical perception.

Albert Einstein

THE LAWS OF PHYSICS, LIKE THOSE OF MATHEMATICS, ARE DEEP, profound, and universal, touching every aspect of our existence. Carl Sagan famously quipped, "If you want to make an apple pie from scratch, you must first invent the universe." And if making an apple pie is governed by the laws of physics, so are the less obvious ways conflicts arise and manifest themselves, dissipate and disappear.

I am not a physicist, although I have read widely in the subject over many decades–not only in popular books and magazines, but textbooks, scientific journals, physics arXiv articles, websites, and preprints. My purpose here is not to explore the awe-inspiring beauty, symmetry, and subtlety of physical phenomena, as tempting as that would be. Instead, it is to consider the ways conflict resolution theories and practices might be improved by considering them from the point of view of physics–not directly, but as metaphors, analogies, abstractions, principles, and generic understandings of how the universe works.

Physics is rich with metaphors that offer potential insights into conflict resolution, including many widely recognized ideas and phenomena, including:

- Frames of reference (Einstein's theory of special relativity)
- Gravity as the bending of spacetime (Einstein's theory of general relativity)
- Symmetry and symmetry breaking (group theory)
- Chirality (handedness)
- Parity/complementarity/duality (hidden unity or commonality)
- Entanglement and non-locality (quantum theory)
- Chaos (non-linearity)
- Fractals (scale-free self-similarity or fractions of a dimension)
- Counterfactuals (what is possible and what isn't)
- Bose-Einstein condensates (separate particles acting as one)

- Phase transitions/criticality (transition from one state to another)
- Emergence, entropy, and complexity (self-organization)

The eminent astrophysicist and cosmologist Martin Rees, the "Astronomer Royal" for Great Britain, wrote: "There are three great frontiers in science: the very big, the very small and the very complex." The same can be said of issues in conflict resolution. In both fields, especially in physics, significant efforts are being directed at linking these phenomena in what, from a mediation perspective, can be regarded as a search for scale-free understandings and practices.

My aim here is to explore a few key physical phenomena representing the very small, the very large, and the very complex, to determine whether, as metaphors, it may be possible for conflict resolvers to similarly peel back the layers of dispute resolution and reveal laws, dualities, similarities, and useful frameworks for illuminating what is unknown, poorly understood, or ineffectively practiced, in hopes that further and deeper analyses may then be undertaken.

THE VERY SMALL: THE METAPHOR OF QUANTUM MECHANICS

According to quantum theory, there is a smallest piece of length, energy, mass, time, temperature, and similar measures, all of which occur at what is called the Planck scale. The Planck length, for example, is $1.6 \times 10^{\wedge}\text{-}35$ meters; the Planck energy is 1.22×10^{19} GeV; the Planck mass is 2.17645×10^{-8} kg; the Planck time is 10^{-44} seconds (the time it would take a photon moving at the speed of light to travel one Planck length), etc. These are places where the known laws of physics break down and cease making sense. They are all based on Planck's constant (6.626176×10^{-34} Joule-second), symbolized by the letter h (or its "reduced" form, $h/2\pi$), which gives the relationship between the energy of a photon and its frequency, and is used to calculate nearly all quantum phenomena.

In conflict resolution, we may now be inspired to ask: "Is there a smallest unit of conflict?" I believe there is, and that it can be defined by three parameters or elements, without any of which there can be no conflict:

1. *Diversity*, or the presence of two or more persons (or parts of the same person), as without two or more, conflict is impossible.
2. *Disagreement*, or the presence of some significant unresolved difference or incongruity, as without disagreement over something important, diversity alone will not create a conflict.
3. *Negative Emotions*, or the presence of a hostile, "negative" emotional response, either to the issues or to each other, as without negative emotions, disagreement alone will not rise to the level of conflict.

All three are required to generate a genuine conflict, and each may be said metaphorically to have a minimum size, energy, mass, time, temperature, etc. If so, we can predict that breaking these parameters down into smaller pieces will make the conflict also begin to break down and cease making sense. This idea invites mediators to, for example, ask questions that minimize, transform, or cancel the ways the parties view their differences; or divide disagreements into smaller pieces and turn seemingly gigantic, implacable differences into bite-sized "atoms," of conflict, each of which may be solvable. Similarly, breaking emotions down into tinier pieces and sub-pieces might make it easier to label and acknowledge them, find out what gave rise to them, search for what lies beneath them, and describe what it might take for them to go away.

We can also imagine intense interpersonal spats and international wars as analogous to particle accelerators that smash elementary particles into one another at immense speeds to reveal tiny sub-particles in the rubble that expose the forces that hold them together. Conflicted parties on all scales also perhaps argue about petty issues to probe beneath superficial politeness and reveal, for example, whether they are *really* accepted, respected, loved, and safe; or whether the relationship will survive higher levels of stress, like illness or childbirth.

By studying the outcomes of quantum mechanical experiments and refining their understanding of how elementary particles and forces behave, physicists have discovered a bizarre set of "non-classical" phenomena, which even the brilliant physicist Richard Feynman asserted *no one* understood. These include complementarity, quantum entanglement, the "uncertainty principle," superposition, tunneling, decoherence, and many others.

Each of these has strong resonances in conflict resolution, and while each is mathematically complex and difficult to describe in a few words, as *metaphors*, analogies, and scale-free principles, they offer deep insights into conflict resolution problems, theories, and practices.

Consider, for example, the idea of "complementarity," articulated by Danish Nobel prize winning physicist Neils Bohr. For centuries, physicists debated whether light was a wave or a particle, and in 1905, Albert Einstein proved that Max Planck's idea of a "quantum" or minimal size could be applied to electromagnetic radiation, whose energy (E) is equal to Planck's constant (h) multiplied by its' frequency (v), or $E = hv$; as indeed are all elementary particles.

Bohr could then describe the photon in terms of what came to be known as "wave/particle duality"–that is, the idea that these seemingly opposite yet complementary properties cannot be separated until they are measured or observed, at which time their duality collapses, or is broken. Nobel prize winning Physicist Wolfgang Pauli wrote:

What has impressed me most in the development [of quantum mechanics], which in 1927 eventually led to the development of present wave mechanics, is the fact that real pairs of opposites, like particle versus wave, or position versus momentum, or energy versus time, exists in physics. Their contrast can only be overcome in a symmetrical way. This means that one member of the pair is never eliminated in favor of the other, but both are taken over into a new kind of physical law which expresses properly [the] complementary character of the contrast.

A precise mathematical expression of this idea was given by Werner Heisenberg in "the uncertainty principle," which simply states that the more precisely the position of an elementary particle is measured, the less certain its' momentum or "conjugate quality" becomes. The basic formula is quite simple–it says that a change in position multiplied by a change in momentum must be equal to or greater than Planck's constant divided by 2, or in a later version, $pq - qp \geq h/2\pi i$.

In other words, it is impossible to measure either position or momentum with 100% accuracy, as there will always be a tiny uncertainty at the Planck scale. As a result, there is what we can call a "conservation of duality" in the relationship between them, as 100% certainty in the measurement of one *cancels* certainty in the other. We can also regard this outcome as a "conservation of *ambiguity*" in their "opposition" or hostility; a minimal overlap, or "degree of connection" between them, which increases in one as it decreases in the other.

This "complementarity" has been applied not only to position and momentum, but energy and time, angular position and angular momentum, voltage and free electric charge, electric field and electric polarization density; so that, for example, the shorter the time period, the greater the uncertainty in the amount of inherent energy in that region, and the greater the potential energy fluctuation. This implies that, for extremely short periods of time, enormous amounts of energy can arise, and because of Einstein's $E=MC^2$, these can result in the appearance of "virtual" particle/anti-particle pairs that briefly pop in and out of existence.

While these quantum effects largely disappear in the macro world of classical physics — except, it seems, for entanglement — as *metaphors*, complementarity and the uncertainty principle offer a number of potentially fruitful insights for mediators and conflicted parties. Key among these are the dualities we observe in conflicts– for example, between positions and interests, objective facts and subjective emotions, or the parties' stories about what happened, in which the more we know about one, the less we know about the other.

A mediative approach that conserves duality, preserves ambiguity, and seeks to combine opposites rather than choose between them, may more accurately reflect the underlying nature of the conflict and maximize the perceived fairness and justice of the outcome. Indeed, Neils Bohr defined complementarity as "a great truth, whose opposite is also a great truth." Therefore, rather than forcing the parties, as power- and rights-based processes typically do, to choose between opposing truths, mediation and other interest-based processes allow mediators to acknowledge, affirm, and accept both, even when they are flatly contradictory, by paying attention to the hidden forces (such as meaning) that connect them.

ENTANGLEMENT

A related, profoundly useful metaphor in quantum physics is that of *entanglement*. According to quantum theory, if a particle, such as an electron, has a spin that is either clockwise or counterclockwise, it exists in a "superposition" of both until it is measured, at which time it must become one or the other. If two particles are entangled and sent in opposite directions at the speed of light, measuring the spin of one *immediately* "collapses" the wave function and superposition, requiring the other particle to spin in the opposite direction. This strange result has been demonstrated many times, even for different particles and opposite charges.

Yet this seems completely counter-intuitive since, as Einstein proved, particles and information cannot travel faster than the speed of light. Indeed, in 1935, Einstein, with Boris Podolsky and Nathan Rosen, argued, in what is known as the EPR paradox, that entanglement requires faster than light communication, resulting in a violation of relativity and what Einstein called "spooky action at a distance." Nonetheless, as numerous researchers have demonstrated over decades with different particles, entanglement is real and does not require super-luminal speed, and as the Big Bang and inflationary cosmology have shown, space can travel faster than light without contradicting relativity.

In 2013, Leonard Susskind and Juan Maldacena proposed, in what is known as "ER = EPR," that an earlier collaboration between Einstein and Rosen (ER), which proposed the existence of "wormholes" in space that could causally connect widely separated regions of space-time, is mathematically *dual* or equivalent to entanglement, allowing distant particles to be holographically connected.

As a metaphor, it is easy to imagine people in conflict being entangled, their conflicts as wormholes that causally connect them, and mediation as a kind of measurement that results in decoherence, or collapses their need to "spin" in opposite directions. More profoundly, we can think of couples, families, teams, communities, and social relationships as creating an "affective entanglement," in which opposing spins attract, connect, and reinforce one another, keeping the relationship vital and alive. Conflict might then represent a *loss* of entanglement, a symmetry breaking, a waning of "us," and a retreat to smaller, internally divided, less collaborative, less diverse, less balanced, less capable selves.

Physicist Carlo Rovelli cited similar ideas in support of what he calls "relational quantum mechanics," the principle that seemingly separate physical objects do not exist independent of one another. In his book *Helgoland,* describing Werner Heisenberg's discovery of the uncertainty principle, Rovelli asserted that physical objects are defined and understood by the ways they interact with other objects. If an object *is* simply the sum of these interactions, it cannot be said to exist at all in the absence of some interaction or relationship. [A brilliantly written, gripping account is given by Benjamin Lapatut in *When We Cease to Understand the World.*] In a similar way, people and conflicts are defined by their interactions and relationships. Conflict can then be seen as a kind of *friction* in these interactions and relationships that is felt and *interpreted* as personal, while merely representing some element between them that isn't working effectively. This suggests that mediators might pay more attention to the *ways* people communicate, interact, and relate to each other, than to the substantive issues over which they disagree. We can go further and recognize, as Mary Parker Follett did, that "all polishing is done by friction," encouraging us to see that *every* conflict represents an opportunity to improve our interactions and relationships, develop our skills and capacities, and deepen our insights and understandings, thereby contributing to fine-tuning our interactions and relationships so they can work better for all. There are physical interpretations of entanglement and quantum phenomena that regard them as descriptions — not merely of the very small — but also as integrally related to the very large, and a logical consequence of applying them to the universe as a whole (which we are "in," cannot be measured, and whose wave function cannot therefore collapse or decohere), deriving large-scale classical ideas from them, as Hugh Everett, Dieter Zeh, and others attempted to do.

The Very Large: The Metaphor of General Relativity

The very large world of "classical" physics operates differently, yet also suggests metaphors that are useful in thinking about conflict resolution. Again, there are many rich and fascinating topics from which to choose, ranging from Einstein's theories of special and general relativity; to the search for a theory of quantum gravity; string theory, loop quantum gravity, and other proposals for a grand unified "theory of everything;" to "AdS/CFT correspondence," the nature and emergence of spacetime, the holographic principle, entropy, black holes, dark matter and dark energy, amplituhedrons, and other rich topics.

One of the most helpful metaphors for mediators drives from the theory of special relativity. This is Einstein's idea, originating with Galileo and Lorentz, that there is no fixed, absolute, or universally correct frame of reference which privileges one observer over others. Instead, conflicting, even contradictory observations can *all* be true for different observers, each within its' own frame of reference.

Another immensely useful metaphor, drawn from general relativity, is the idea that gravity is a consequence of the curvature of spacetime due to the concentration of mass; or as physicist John Wheeler articulately explained it, "Spacetime tells matter how to move; matter tells spacetime how to curve." In like manner, conflicts can be regarded as a kind of curvature of emotional and perceptual space, which can become so great as to create a "black hole" from which the parties and their views are unable to escape.

From a mathematical perspective, here is a simple version of Einstein's equation for general relativity: $R\mu v - \frac{1}{2} Rg\mu v = - 8\pi GT\mu v$. In this formula, $R\mu v$ is the "Ricci tensor," or "Einstein tensor," which describes the curvature of spacetime; μv is Riemann's metric tensor, which gives the measure of distance in curved space; G is Newton's gravitational constant; and $T\mu v$ is the "stress-energy" or "momentum-energy"/matter tensor. This formula describes a "gravitational field," in which curvature is equivalent to acceleration, causing light to bend around massive objects, distorting their perceived locations and paths through spacetime, and creating gravitational rings, lenses, waves, and time delays.

In conflict resolution, this metaphor offers us a far better understanding of the distortions that commonly occur in the communications, emotions, perceptions, intentions, and positions of the parties in the presence of a "massive" conflict, plus ways of correcting these distortions through dialogue, in which the other party's reference frame appears equally valid. Or we can work backwards and discover the true meaning of conflict by measuring the amount of distortion created by it, then searching for whatever could "cause" that degree of deviation.

One difficulty in applying these metaphors is that relativity and quantum mechanics are regarded as incompatible, prompting physicists from Einstein forward to search for a "grand unified theory" that links them, in the form of a theory of "quantum gravity." One of the earliest and most promising of these ideas is "string theory," which includes both gravity and the "Standard Model" describing all observable particles and forces, but only in 10 or 26 dimensions, or 11 and 27 in a version called "M Theory."

While none of these extra dimensions has been discovered in particle collisions, other possibilities for their existence have been suggested. Most famously, after Einstein published his theory of general relativity, Theodor Kaluza proposed extending spacetime in a fifth direction, which *automatically* gives rise to Maxwell's equations describing electromagnetism. Oscar Klein later offered a quantum interpretation in which the fifth dimension is curled up in a circle with a tiny radius that is "compactified" down to the Planck length.

In addition to being shrunk to an unimaginably tiny size, extra dimensions might also be extremely large and still escape notice, extending even to the size of the universe as a whole. From my naïve, lay perspective, there would seem to be a third possibility. If we define the number of physical dimensions as the number of points in space needed to define where something is *located*, a consequence of Heisenberg's uncertainty principle might be that the location of an elementary particle *cannot* be described using only three dimensions. Instead, its' location is *inherently* fuzzy, smeared out, and probabilistically uncertain by an amount defined by Planck's constant. It's location would therefore seem to require at least a fourth spatial dimension, supporting Kaluza-Klein/string theory's suggestion that extra physical dimensions are possible.

As a metaphor in mediation, the addition of extra dimensions, or "degrees of freedom," permits conflict resolvers to expose hidden sources of conflict, resolve incompatibilities, and unify fundamentally opposite approaches, methods, and techniques across multiple scales, *intrinsically* connecting the very small with the very large. [See Chapter 2 and Chapter 6.]. The idea of an extra dimension describing a location that is *inherently* uncertain, fuzzy, smeared out, and probabilistic, makes great sense in conflict resolution, and is useful for describing emotions, attitudes, intentions, etc., suggesting the possibility that we might also benefit from a "grand unified theory" of dispute resolution (see discussion below).

In 1997, Juan Maldacena of the Institute for Advanced Studies came up with an idea called "AdS/CFT correspondence," which (roughly speaking) conjectured that there is an equivalence or duality between large-scale, negatively curved ("Anti-de Sitter") five dimensional spacetime *with* gravity (based on string theory or M theory), and four dimensional "conformal field theory" describing small-scale particle fields *without* gravity, allowing one to be transformed into the other based on the "holographic principle" which, like any hologram, allows a higher dimensional object to be captured on a lower dimensional surface.

Using this idea, Maldacena linked theories with and without gravity, and used string theory to bridge small-scale quantum field theory describing particles and forces with large scale general relativity describing gravity, showing that higher dimensional descriptions can be reduced holographically to lower dimensions, not only for a negatively curved, non-Euclidian universe very different from our own, but for the widely accepted idea that *all* the information contained in a *three*-dimensional black hole is entirely contained on the *two*-dimensional surface of its' event horizon.

In conflict resolution, the holographic principle is especially useful in revealing how the three-dimensional content of a disputed issue can be reduced to the two-dimensional plane of adversarial, zero-sum contests, and how this limited two-dimensional understanding can be responded to successfully by *raising it* to a three-dimensional level or higher, as by bringing in a mediator, acknowledging emotions, or satisfying interests.

While the physics of the very small is driven by a reductionist approach that seeks to break things down to their essential, unbreakable components, which quantum principles tell us is impossible without losing some of its' information, the holographic principle adopts a holistic approach to physical phenomena and views the universe as a whole. It is even possible that the entire universe is a broken symmetry, the non-decoherence of a "universal wave function," or large-scale quantum entanglement.

Analogously, mediators can break issues down into tinier bits that are easier to resolve, and regard conflicts holistically or holographically, and seek insight into their deeper, more profound, poignant, and systemic sources. Or what is better, they can do *both* at the same time. Doing so, however, is complex, and requires an understanding and approach to conflict resolution that acknowledges and analyzes its' complex character, leading us to still more effective techniques.

The Very Complex: The Metaphor of Emergence

The science of complexity has made significant contributions to our understanding of non-linear, chaotic, highly sensitive, intricate, unpredictable phenomena, ranging from the weather to the turbulent flow of fluids, to cellular automata and others. Complex systems can undergo "tipping point" transitions in which they suddenly alter their behavior dramatically, sometimes irreversibly, with little warning and potentially catastrophic consequences.

There are two fundamental varieties of complexity. There are complex *physical systems,* where our focus is on the relationship between intricately connected parts, or fixed arrays of elements, as with living beings or cellular automata. There are also complex *adaptive systems,* where our focus is on how the system as a whole learns and adapts in response to interactions with others and with its' environment, as with ecological adaptation, evolution, changing weather patterns like global warming, predator/prey fluctuations, and the complex behaviors of sentient beings. Complex adaptive systems are often described as possessing the following five characteristics:

1. *Self-organization over time,* where complex patterns are formed (like flocks of birds or schools of fish)
2. *Chaotic behavior,* where small changes in initial conditions later result in large, unpredictable changes (like the "butterfly effect")
3. *"Fat-tailed" behavior,* where rare events occur far more often than predicted by a bell curve distribution (like market crashes and mass extinctions)
4. *Adaptive interactions,* where interacting agents modify their strategies in diverse ways as experience accumulates (like markets, or games such as "the Prisoner's Dilemma")
5. *Emergent behavior over scale,* where new forms of organization arise that did not exist before (like waterfalls, rainbows, or ocean waves)

These complex systems are generally diverse, networked (or interconnected), collaborative (or interdependent), non-linear, rapidly changing, emergent, and adaptive. By means of these mechanisms, they are able to evolve through a combination of internal conflicts, variations, an ability to learn from changes in the environment, and natural selection. Variation, of course, like mutation, is not always beneficial, so the ability to detect and correct conflicts and errors is critical.

The beneficial results of complexity include not only improved adaptability and learning, but new, emergent, higher order skills and capacities that are often transformational. The brilliant mathematician John von Neumann, in his *Theory of Self-reproducing Automata,* observed that in the behavior of cellular automata:

> There exists a critical size below which the process of synthesis is degenerative, but above which the phenomenon of synthesis, if properly arranged, can become explosive, in other words, where synthesis of automata can proceed in such a manner that each automaton will produce other automata which are more complex and of higher potentialities than itself.

This is equally true in conflict resolution, and not only regarding size, but the ability to generate syntheses that creatively combine opposites in ways that make disputing parties — be they couples, families, organizations, communities, or societies — stronger, freer, more collaborative, and successful in their responses to environmental stresses and evolutionary opportunities.

On the one hand, conflicts and rapid changes in the environment can increase complexity, but they can also lead to chaos, which is defined scientifically as "sensitive dependence on initial conditions." On the other hand, these conflicts and changes may prompt the emergence of higher order skills and relationships. Complexity can, for example, encourage individuals and systems to learn from feedback or memory and adapt and evolve in response. Here, for example, are some characteristics of complex systems that can lead them in either direction:

- *Openness:* Complex systems are almost always open to changes in their environment, causing them to dissipate energy, move far from equilibrium, and fluctuate wildly between periods of stability.
- *Change:* Complex systems are "dynamical," change over time, and often exhibit what appear to be spontaneous failures and recoveries.
- *Cascading Failures:* Due to the strong connection between elements of the system, failure in one or more elements can lead to *cascading* failures, which can have catastrophic consequences on the system.
- *Memory:* Complex systems can possess memory, allowing prior states to influence present states.
- *Nesting:* The components of complex systems may *themselves* be complex systems. For example, an economic system may consist of corporations with departments made up of teams of employees, all of which are complex systems.
- *Networks:* Complex systems are often networked and interconnected, inviting synergy between their diverse parts
- *Emergence:* Complex systems are sometimes emergent, giving rise to new features with properties that can only be recognized or understood at a higher level.
- *Non-Linearity:* Relationships in complex systems are often non-linear, so that small changes in initial conditions can cause larger effects that are not proportional to causation. In linear systems, on the other hand, effects are always directly proportional to causes.
- *Feedback:* Feedback loops are nearly always present in complex systems, though they may possess different features that make them more or less effective in adapting to environmental changes.

It's easy to notice the similarity between these features and the ways conflicts manifest themselves within social relationships, systems, and environments, including the methods by which they are resolved, transformed, and transcended. Whether on a small-scale between couples, families, co-workers, and neighbors; or a mid-scale within schools, communities, workplaces, and organizations; or a large-scale within cultures, societies, and nation-states, conflicts may exhibit these same complex characteristics.

It's also easy to notice the places where each of these features, *because* they are complex, generate conflicts whose very complexity makes them difficult to resolve. If we consider marital conflicts, for example, we can identify the following features that are similar to those of complex, non-linear systems:

- *Openness:* Marriages are highly responsive to changes in their environments, dissipate energy through conflict, and can be far from equilibrium, or fluctuate wildly between periods of stability.
- *Change:* Marriages are often "dynamical," change over time, and exhibit spontaneous failures and recoveries.
- *Cascading Failures:* Failures in one or more aspects of a marriage often leads to cascading failures, which may result in divorce.
- *Memory:* Marital partners remember their past conflicts, which can influence their present states.
- *Nesting:* The issues in complex marriages are also often complex.
- *Networks:* Marital systems are networked and interconnected with friends and families, with synergies between their diverse parts.
- *Emergence:* Marriages often give rise to new, emergent, higher order relationships with features that can only be recognized or understood afterwards.
- *Non-Linearity:* Marital relationships are often non-linear, so that small change can trigger larger emotional effects that are not directly proportional to what caused them.

- *Feedback:* Feedback loops are always present in marriages, with aspects that are more or less effective in helping couples adapt to environmental changes.

Traumatic experiences, repeated dysfunctions, chronic unresolved conflicts, and systemic failures in any of these areas can impact each of the others, leading to emotional withdrawal, loss of trust, systemic crises, and if unaddressed, end the marriage. On the other hand, if they are acknowledged and addressed in skillful and loving ways, the relationship can grow deeper and more resilient, increasing intimacy, repairing trust, improving systems, and strengthening the marriage.

COMPLEXITY, SYNERGY, AND EMERGENCE

Jacob Burkhardt insightfully observed that "The essence of tyranny is the denial of complexity." On all scales, tyrannical behaviors arise when complexity is ignored, denied, feared, or repressed, giving rise to classical, eternal, or "Ur-conflicts," for example, between the new and the old, the adventurous and the cautious, the open and the guarded, the empathetic and the distant, the generous and the selfish, the anarchic and the ordered, the Dionysian and the Apollonian.

These conflicts occur because traumatic experiences naturally lead some people to be more cautious and prudent and others to be more adventurous and profligate. They may also occur because people lack the skills they need to resolve their disputes, as well as the ambiguity, complexity, differences, diversity, and dissent complex relationships require, resulting in crises and catastrophes.

We can then work backwards, and recognize that before *catastrophes* occur, there are unaddressed *crises*; before crises, there are unresolved *conflicts*; before conflicts, there are poorly handled *disagreements*; before disagreements, there are *differences*, divisions, diversities, and dissents; and before these, there are *complexities* in the issues people face, and the problems they're required to solve.

As a result, autocratic, fascistic, dictatorial, tyrannical, reactionary regimes on all scales often begin by attacking complexity in the form of racial and gender differences, religious and cultural diversities, petty disagreements, and seemingly inconsequential social and political dissents, which are viewed as dangerous, or seditious, or uncontrollable sources of conflict and anarchy that are hostile to domination, or harbingers of trauma and loss, and repressed in ways that paradoxically bring about the very things that are feared. Adolf Hitler, for example, wrote:

> I will tell you what has carried me to the position I have reached. Our political problems appeared complicated. The German people could make nothing of them. ... I, on the other hand, reduced them to the simplest terms. The masses realized this and followed me.

The two simplest responses to any problem are *denial*, as in: "there is no problem"; and *blaming*, as in: "it's someone else's fault," neither of which helps solve the problem. When problems are multiple or complex, this attitude leads to a rejection of science, facts, ethics, values, and morality — and more ominously, to the repression of diversity, individuality, empathy, and kindness; and the domination of one race, gender, religion, sexual orientation, nationality, political belief, culture, mode of artistic expression, physical condition over others, whose mere *presence* suggests complexity, and must therefore be eliminated.

The difficulty for all repressive, autocratic, zero-sum approaches to complexity is that while differences, diversity, and dissent are complex and conflicted, they are also essential elements in creativity, learning, synergy, emergence, individuality, authenticity, collaboration, adaptation, and evolution, all of which are required for science and art to flourish, problems to be solved, conflicts to be ended, and innovation, improvement, and higher stages of order to be successful.

These outcomes emerge out of the complex, creative integration and *synergy* of differences, diversity, and dissent–i.e., out of *success* in turning differences, diversity, and dissent in the direction of dialogue, creative problem-solving, collaborative negotiation, conflict resolution, and the evolution of higher order skills and techniques.

In science, as in art, the aim of *mediation* between complex differences, diversities, anomalies, and dissents is not primarily to bring about a ceasefire or superficial compromise, but to search for deeper resolutions, fundamental transformations, synergies, and profound transcendences–i.e., for the emergence of new, higher order simplicities and complexities.

In his book *Order Out of Chaos*, Nobel prize winning chemist Ilya Prigogine described how feedback in "dissipative structures" can "export entropy," *spontaneously* generating "phase transitions," in which "criticality" gives rise to "islands of order" and "self-organizing systems" that drive evolution and the emergence of higher forms of order. Cybernetician Heinz von Foerster described this as "order out of noise," which also takes place in the "chaos" of conflict.

Edward Ott, a leading chaos researcher at the University of Maryland and his team found that a type of machine learning algorithm called a "recurrent neural network" could predict the evolution of chaotic systems far into the future. It was able to predict the appearance of "tipping points," and a probability distribution of post-tipping-point behaviors while knowing nothing about the underlying parameters responsible for driving tipping-point transitions, even when it was trained on "noisy" and imprecise data. [See: https://arxiv.org/abs/2207.00521.]

These results suggest that it may be possible to use computer algorithms, neural nets, and artificial intelligence programs to model conflict systems. These might assist in predicting potential mediation tipping points leading to resolution, and assist us in defining unified, scale-free approaches to conflict resolution that directly link the very small with the very large and the very complex.

Toward a Grand Unified Theory of Conflict Resolution

Albert Einstein wrote, regarding relativity, that "[I]t is the theory which decides what we can observe." In conflict resolution as well, theory can reveal what is taking place beneath the surface of conflict behaviors and communications, guide us to innovative techniques and practices, point us in the direction of powerful, unimagined questions, and suggest counter-intuitive approaches to resolution, transformation, and transcendence.

Theories enable us to discover, as in mathematics and physics, metaphors and maps that point us to where insights may be found. The same is true in conflict resolution. If our theory of mediation, for example, is that it is an operation we perform on conflict to bring it to a state of resolution, then it is the nature of the *conflict* that defines which operations will likely succeed in reaching resolution.

And since conflicts are *inherently* complex, multi-dimensional, multi-determined, subtle, paradoxical, and chaotic, a "grand unified theory" of conflict resolution will be helpful in integrating our understanding of the very small, the very large, and the very complex into a scale-free description that allows us to translate our insights, intuitions, experiences, and techniques seamlessly from one scale, issue, and party to another.

Three of the most powerful theoretical approaches to unification in physics have been the discovery of fields, the application of symmetry groups, and the hypothesis of extra dimensions, each of which has revealed an underlying unity, as for example, between electricity and magnetism, or the weak and strong nuclear forces, and all of these, it is hoped someday, with gravity.

If we consider fields as a metaphor and regard *every* form of energy as a field, it is obvious that these fields extend everywhere, even to conflict, and include mediation and the ways of resolving them, that may be significantly impacted by every interaction, however subtle, down even perhaps to the Planck scale.

Energy, as Einstein's famously demonstrated, is mass moving at the speed of light squared, or maybe moving slower, colliding with other masses, generating friction and heat, congealing, and giving rise to gravitational attraction. If we regard energy as a wave, it will radiate outward like ripples in a pond, creating peaks and troughs and frequencies that can be separated or combined, amplified or canceled. If we see energy as a field, it will extend everywhere as a *probability* whose square indicates the likelihood of finding a particle there.

We can also imagine conflicts as not only particle-like (i.e., focused on issues) or wave-like (i.e., focused on emotions), but *field*-like, where the probability of an issue being mediate-able might be determined by the amplitude of the parties' emotions, the frequency of their collisions, and the "gravity" of their meanings, improving our insight and ability to successfully move them toward resolution.

We can also imagine theories that unify conflict resolution using the metaphor of symmetry and the mathematics of symmetry groups, or "Lie algebras," which inspired the "Standard Model" of physics that connects all elementary particles and forces. By analogy, as discussed, conflicts can be seen to possess a kind of *mirror* symmetry, as the issues parties are arguing over can be flipped without altering their meaning. They may have a 90-degree *rotational* symmetry, since they are invariant under role reversal; and *translation* symmetry, since they may seem the same, even when the issues are different or arise in different locations.

We might therefore consider developing a "unified theory of conflict resolution," based on these metaphors. From a conflict resolution perspective, enormous amounts of information about the *meaning* of any conflict and innovative approaches to resolution can be revealed by expanding the number of elements, or characteristics, or dimensions required to locate and define them.

For example, as discussed earlier, we can consider conflicts to be located in three physical spaces and one of time – that is, internally, or within us; relationally, or between us; and environmentally, or around us. We can then see the internal "dimension," by analogy with string theory, as "compactified" inside each party, and not immediately apparent to anyone viewing it from the outside.

If we look closely at what the *internal* location of conflict consists of, we will find that wrapped up inside each of us are several distinct compactified "dimensions," including not only physical, mental, and emotional, but "spiritual," consisting of our "quality of awareness," "chi," or "life energy;" plus another dimension for "heart," consisting of caring, love, or desire; and a final dimension we can call "contextual," "environmental," consisting of systems, structures, and processes. These added dimensions allow us to locate conflicts more precisely in a multi-dimensional field, or "conflict space," that offers mediators and parties additional degrees of freedom to resolve, transform, and transcend them in each location.

Without these added dimensions, people using lower-dimensional approaches will predictably get stuck because they will be unable to recognize, understand, acknowledge, or respond to complex conflicts in their higher-dimensional locations. Lower dimensional approaches may create an *appearance* of differences, distinctions, divisions, and disagreements, when hidden beneath the surface is an underlying unity that has not been recognized, accepted, or put into practice, because it does not reveal itself in lower-dimensional approaches or methods.

We can move closer to developing a unified theory of conflict resolution not only by modifying metaphors for fields, symmetry groups, and dimensions, but by adopting diverse ways of thinking, approaching, and exploring the topic. As I wrote earlier in *The*

Crossroads of Conflict, in a chapter called "Toward a Unified Theory of Conflict Resolution:"

> The first step in developing a unified theory of conflict resolution is to consider the methods by which we intend to craft it. There are dozens of ways of trying to understand conflict resolution, or any subject, many of which *appear* contradictory, but actually complement each other. We can, for example, try to understand a problem using either reductionism or holism, analysis or imagination, history or fantasy, abstraction or experience, intellect or emotion, logic or intuition. We can apply science or art, objectivity or subjectivity, divergence or convergence, contrast or commonality. We can look digitally or analogically, sequentially or summatively, in isolation or relationship to context and environment. Each approach will provide different answers, and when combined, reveal hidden symmetries that deepen our understanding.

Physicist Heinrich Päs, in *The One: How an Ancient Idea Holds the Future of Physics*, argued against the exclusive use of reductionism as a way of explaining the universe, and offered instead a holistic approach based on monism, inspired by the following statement by Heraclitus: "From all things One and from One all things." Päs argued that physics should begin by describing not the smallest units, but the largest – that is, the universe as a whole, citing David Bohm:

> [I]t seems necessary ... to give up the idea that the world can be correctly analyzed into distinct parts, and to replace it with the assumption that the entire universe is basically a single indivisible unit.

Päs wrote that, in principle, two kinds of quantum systems are possible. First, there are isolated microscopic systems that do not get measured or interact with their environment without decohering or collapsing; and second,

> ... there is the entire quantum universe: global, encompassing, with no external environment and thus not subject to decoherence. ... The experienced world, then, emerges from this foundational 'One' through decoherence.

The second approach, combined with the holographic principle that led to the AdS/CFT correspondence described earlier, suggests that space-time is not fundamental, but emerges as a direct consequence of entanglement. [See, e.g., discussion in Anil Ananthaswamy, *Scientific American*, March 2023.]. Metaphorically, conflicts can be thought of on two fundamental levels: either isolated, distinct, and microscopic; or global, entangled, and holistic. Mediators can divide them into isolated little bits, or treat them as integrated and connected. The second, as suggested earlier, leads in the direction of a possible "grand unified theory" of conflict resolution that may allow us to connect the very small with the very large and the very complex.

Holism in Conflict Resolution

Albert Einstein wrote,

> If I had an hour to solve a problem and my life depended on the solution, I would spend the first 55 minutes determining the proper question to ask, for once I know the proper question, I would solve the problem in less than five minutes.

We can begin with the three *categories* of questions described in Chapter 4: first, simplistic, blame-oriented, power-based questions, like "Who started it?" "Whose fault is it?" and "Who should win?" Second, specific, reductionist, rights-based questions about parts of the conflict, like "What happened?" "Who are the parties?" and "What are the issues?" Third, general, holistic, interest-based questions concerning the conflict as a whole, like "What does it mean?" "How does it feel?" "Why does it matter?" "What do you want?" "Why is that important to you?" and "What would you like to have happen?"

While the first set of questions lead to answers that are particle-like rejecting, punitive, elemental, and fault-based; the second lead to answers that are wave-like, narrow, practical, and distinguishing; and the third lead to answers that are *field-like*, broad, abstract, and unifying. Each can result in ending the conflict, but the second, where many mediators tend to focus, produce only settlements, while the third result in resolutions, transformations, and transcendences, which have little chance of emerging with the first or second approaches.

A unified theory of conflict resolution would need to include all three, and the reasons for choosing one over the other. It would explain why there are different "styles" of mediation, levels and sources of conflict, diverse fields of practice, and the full range of methodologies, outcomes, and what determines them, revealing the connections between these features, their subtle and systemic causes, the rationale or criteria for selecting between them, and a range of techniques that invite transition from lower to higher order approaches. While a "grand unified theory" of conflict resolution seems quite distant, the metaphor of physics suggests not only that it exists, but that it is essential to all fields of practice, especially if we want to link the very small with the very large and the very complex and create scale-free methods and approaches.

Conflict resolution is still in its' infancy, yet it possesses immense untapped powers and faces profound challenges that require innovative approaches and deep insights that *automatically* lead us toward unification. The metaphor of physics helps us by offering a multitude of potentially fruitful ways. And, as David Bohm reminds us, in *Wholeness and the Implicate Order,* the loss of unification is directly connected to global conflicts on many levels:

The notion that all these fragments are separately existent is evidently an illusion, and this illusion cannot do other than lead to endless conflict and confusion. Indeed, the attempt to live according to the notion that the fragments are really separate is, in essence, what has led to the growing series of extremely urgent crises that is confronting us today. Thus, as is now well known, this way of life has brought about pollution, destruction of the balance of nature, over-population, world-wide economic and political disorder and the creation of an overall environment that is neither physically nor mentally healthy for most of the people who live in it. Individually there has developed a widespread feeling of helplessness and despair, in the face of what seems to be an overwhelming mass of disparate social forces, going beyond the control and even the comprehension of the human beings who are caught up in it.

Finally, we can take inspiration from Henry David Thoreau, who was said to have kept two notebooks, one for facts and one for poems, and to have hoped one day to have only a single notebook in which every fact was a poem, and every poem was a fact. Mediation, for me and many others, is a search for that notebook.

EIGHT

Designing, Mediating, and Facilitating Large Group, Multi-Stakeholder, Consensus-Building Processes

Unity, not uniformity, must be our aim. Differences must be integrated, not annihilated, not absorbed. Anarchy means unorganized, unrelated differences; coordinated, unified difference belongs to our ideal of a perfect social order. We don't want to avoid our adversary but to 'agree with him quickly'; we must, however, learn the technique of agreeing. As long as we think of difference as that which divides us, we shall dislike it; when we think of it as that which unites us, we shall cherish it.

Mary Parker Follett

You can rule with a firm hand, or you can rule through consensus. Those with neither the strength for firmness nor the courage for consensus take refuge in the belief that they can remain somewhere in between. But that is an illusion.

Ivan Klíma

I do not determine what is right and wrong by looking at the budget of my organization or by taking a Gallup poll of the majority opinion. Ultimately a genuine leader is not a searcher for consensus but a molder of consensus.

Martin Luther King, Jr

MEDIATION IS GENERALLY THOUGHT OF AS A PROCESS FOR RESOLVING *small-scale* interpersonal conflicts, in which mediators meet with two opposing parties to assist them in reaching agreements that will settle or resolve it. Yet mediation has also been useful as a method for addressing *mid-scale* disputes involving teams, groups, neighborhoods, communities, organizations, and institutions, in which mediators convene small to mid-sized groups of people for the purpose of improving their relationships, strengthening empathy, reducing friction, repairing distrust, solving complex or intractable problems, and achieving common goals.

Mediation has only rarely been used to resolve chronic *large-scale* disputes — for example, between highly polarized political parties, advocacy groups, and factions; or resolving differences between large groups of diverse stakeholders, as in highly contested, multi-party social, economic, political, and environmental disputes; or in cross-cultural conflicts involving biases, prejudices, and systemic forms of discrimination; or in struggles for supremacy between competing races, religions, genders, classes, ethnicities, and other minorities; or in addressing large-scale public policy disputes; or in reducing tensions and reaching peace accords in civil wars and military contests between nation-states.

Yet if we regard conflicts as "scale-free;" that is, as *fractally* organized and self-similar on all scales, then it ought to be possible to treat mediation, facilitation, and similar conflict resolution processes as *scalable*, and adaptable not only to small- and mid-, but large- scale disputes. Indeed, mediation and facilitation have already been scaled- up and proven highly successful in addressing mid-scale conflicts, or reaching consensus-based agreements in a wide range of environmental, labor/management, and public policy disputes, ranging from community concerns over zoning ordinances to conflicts over water rights, mining, political polarization, police/community relations, and similar issues.

Over the last several decades, a number of critical lessons have been learned by many mediators who have worked with these disputes and helped design, mediate, and facilitate what are sometimes referred to as "large-group, multi-stakeholder, consensus building processes." While these lessons have emerged primarily from small- and mid-scale endeavors, many of these methods can be modified, adapted, and applied to large-scale conflicts between political factions, national economies, nation states, and entire populations.

In conducting these consensus building processes, it has helped me to start, not with what the parties are likely to accept and able to afford — that will come later — but from trying to design a *perfect* proposal, one that will *actually* solve the problem; one that is daring, transformational, and *beautiful* in its conception and construction; one that starts from first principles and goes straight to the heart.

SCALES IN CONSENSUS BUILDING

One of the core competencies in conflict resolution on every scale is the ability to break large, complex problems and mass communications down into smaller, simpler, interpersonal problem-solving conversations that occur one-on-one, or in teams and small groups; that *invite* participation, empathy, and creativity, and make it far easier to reach consensus. Similarly, many small-scale conflicts can be successfully resolved by linking them to larger, systemic improvements that address the broader contexts in which they occur, analyzing them, and adapting small- and-mid-scale techniques to the facilitation of large-group disputes.

Nonetheless, there are clear differences between these scales that will be useful to explore, as they can contribute to a deeper understanding of the *sources* of large-scale social, economic, political, environmental, and cross-cultural conflicts. To do so, it will be important to examine the impact of scale, size, and numbers of parties on the complexity of conflicts, and the skills needed to resolve them.

WHY SIZE MATTERS

Even small, purely quantitative shifts can produce *enormous* differences in processes, communications, and relationships. We have all experienced the changes that occur when we go from one person to two, two to three, three to four, and so on. The same shifts often create added complexity, greater confusion, more opportunities for misunderstanding, divisiveness, and conflict, and increased difficulty solving problems as each additional person is added.

Yet it also happens that adding an extra person or topic or complexity to the mix produces *better* solutions. As an illustration, William Ury, author of several classic texts on mediation and negotiation, including *Getting to Yes*, with Roger Fisher; *Getting Disputes Resolved*, with Steve Goldberg and Jeanne Brett; *The Third Side*, *The Power of a Positive No*, and others, tells the following story:

> There once was a man who had three children. In his will, he bequeathed to the first child one half of all the camels he owned when he died, the second child would receive one third, and the third child would receive one ninth.
>
> When he died, the man owned 17 camels, which cannot be divided by 2, 3, or 9. What were they to do? Since they were stuck, they decided to consult the Wise Old Woman. She told them she did not know how to solve the problem either, but she had a camel, and they were welcome to it.
>
> The three children took the Wise Old Woman's camel. Now, they had 18 camels. One half of 18 is 9. One third of 18 is 6 And one ninth of 18 is 2. That equals 17, so the first child received 9 camels,

the second received 6, the third received two, and they had one camel left over, which they gave back to the Wise Old Woman.

The point of the story should be clear to anyone who has been caught up in circular, "no exit," seemingly intractable, unimaginative forms of adversarial thinking that nearly always result in impasse, and the difficulty conflicted parties have in imagining how apparently minor changes in size or scale can produce profound shifts in the ability to solve what were seen as unsolvable problems.

Similarly, by counter-intuitively *complicating* the parties' overly simplistic approaches to problem-solving, or adding *more* diversity to the mix, or jointly exploring the subtlety, complexity, and enigmatic, paradoxical, self-contradictory nature of the problem, it is sometimes possible to make the solution simpler to imagine. What we are *actually* doing, however, is trying to make the problem-solving process *at least* as subtle, complex, enigmatic, paradoxical, and self-contradictory as the problem we are trying to solve.

If we imagine conflicts as physical objects that exist within a "conflict space" that can have an arbitrary number of dimensions, it will be immediately apparent that a two-dimensional problem will be far more difficult to solve if we approach it using one-dimensional techniques, and will be resolved far easier, and even appear trivial, if we approach it using three-dimensional techniques.

In mathematics and physics, as discussed in Chapter 2, Chapter 6, and Chapter 7, a dimension is defined either as the amount of information needed to describe where something is located, or more interestingly for mediators, as a "degree of freedom." The degrees of freedom in dispute resolution are increased by the parties' willingness to listen openly and communicate honestly with each other; their ability to acknowledge, empathize, and respond constructively to the deeper emotional meaning of the conflict; their skill in being able to surface and explore each side's deeper interests, needs, wishes, and desires, and search together for ways of satisfying them; and similar methods. Each new understanding of the nature, sources, and reasons for their conflict represents a potential new degree of freedom in helping them resolve it.

More subtly, we can identify *fractions* of dimensions, or "fractals" that are "self-similar on all scales." Fractal dimensions reflect the *complexity* of a pattern, as in the ratio of a change in *detail* to a change in *scale*. For example, a line is one-dimensional, while a curve is more complex, yet still only one-dimensional. Yet there are curves that possess higher dimensionality and degrees of complexity. A classic example is the "Koch snowflake," illustrated below, in which complexity and fractal dimensionality continue increasing to infinity without reaching a limit, or ever becoming a two-dimensional surface.

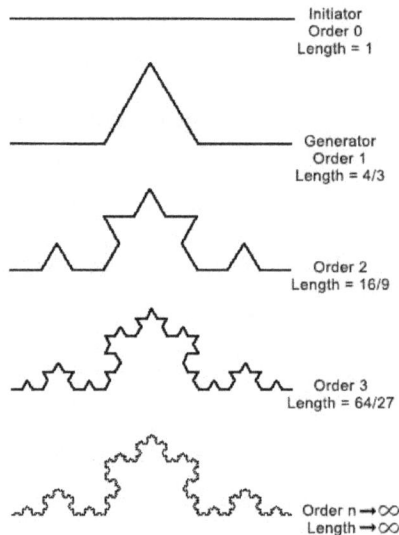

Initiator
Order 0
Length = 1

Generator
Order 1
Length = 4/3

Order 2
Length = 16/9

Order 3
Length = 64/27

Order $n \to \infty$
Length $\to \infty$

We can imagine conflicts as fractally self-similar on all scales; as activities whose dimensionality, complexity, and key characteristics increase with their scale. We can search for scale-free factors in *every* conflict, regardless of size, and optimize problem-solving techniques for each scale. Higher-dimensional skills, methods, and approaches to conflict resolution become *essential* if we are to successfully resolve, transform, and transcend problems at higher levels of complexity.

In large groups with multiple parties and diverse stakeholders, the levels of complexity rise sharply with each additional party, each new source of diversity, and each fresh set of interests, requiring mediators and facilitators to invent ways of simplifying their communications and interactions — for example, by putting people into small groups and asking them to perform simple, unifying tasks like introductions, storytelling, brainstorming, and prioritization.

Mid- and large-scale conflicts especially require innovative, higher dimensional approaches to problem-solving, collaboration, negotiation, consensus building, mediation, and facilitation, as for example, by elaborating and fine-tuning the convening process, designing large group dialogues, using expanded Samoan or restorative justice circles, conducting participatory root-cause analyses, and designing preventative conflict resolution systems.

More profoundly, as the French philosopher and sociologist Lucien Goldmann brilliantly observed, every group at every stage in its development, reaches a limit in its ability to solve problems or resolve conflicts, which points it in the *exact* direction it needs to move in order to evolve:

> [T]here can be information whose transmission is incompatible with the fundamental characteristics of some social group. Such information transcends the group's maximum potential consciousness ... Beyond this horizon, information can be received only if the group's structure is transformed, exactly as in the case of individual obstacles where information can be received only if the individual's psychic structure is transformed.

The idea that all groups have a "maximum potential consciousness" that is built into each successive level of its' structures and systems; that prevent it from evolving; and that can be transformed in ways that allow groups to evolve, is a potent element in explaining how and why some large group, multi-stakeholder, consensus building processes are magically successful, while others routinely fail.

More intriguingly, it suggests that the *experience* of collaborative problem-solving and conflict resolution may reveal not only the *general* nature of a group's structural and systemic limitations, but *specific* ways these might be transformed and transcended as groups evolve to newer, higher order dimensional skills and problem-solving capacities, and abandons its' former, lower order limits.

WHAT IS FACILITATION?

The word "facilitation" comes from the word "facile," which means to make easy or simple. Yet, as Einstein famously advised, "Make everything as simple as possible, but no simpler." Facilitators are often presented with problems that are multi-faceted, complex, and confusing, and require approaches, processes, and solutions that reduce the degree of difficulty in addressing them jointly, without becoming overly simplistic, suppressing diversity or complexity, and reducing them to levels of uniformity or triviality that only *pretend* to solve them. The purposes of facilitation are many, and frequently include a set of assumptions or expectations, for example, that a facilitator should work with the parties to:

- Design and lead a process, without regard to content, by means of which a group may reach a higher level of self-actualization and effectiveness.
- Assist others in building skills or capacity by participating in, taking responsibility for, and jointly leading the process themselves.

- Provide direction to group activity and dialogue without dominating it, while leaving substantive choices to the participants.
- Surface and overcome obstacles, problems, conflicts, and resistance.
- Strengthen and unify the group, and increase its synergy, skills, and capacity.
- Acknowledge, normalize, and validate all participants.
- Listen, collaborate, and model listening and collaboration for others.
- Design the process, adapt, improve it, and move it toward closure.
- Keep people on task, while stopping for profound, poignant, and transformational moments.
- Help the group become more aware of its process, energy, culture, communication patterns, and relationships.
- Evaluate results and improve so the next session will work better.
- Be as invisible, supportive, caring, and empowering as possible.

There are a number of additional core assumptions and expectations regarding the facilitator's role in group meetings, many of which are either unspoken or seemingly fixed, yet underlie the facilitation process and may need to be surfaced, discussed, modified, and agreed to by consensus. These often include:

- The facilitator has no vested interest in the issues or subject matter of the discussion, or stake in any particular point of view.
- Everyone will have an opportunity to say what she or he wants, and have important concerns discussed and addressed by the group.

- For most of the issues addressed in facilitation, there are no *exclusive* right or wrong answers, only diverse points of view.
- Individuals are encouraged to speak out and disagree, *especially* when they represent or hold a minority view.
- The comments of individual participants should not be for attribution, and individual contributions or identities should not be revealed by the facilitators to anyone outside the group.
- Group members should agree in advance to respect each other's privacy; or to repeat what was discussed without attribution; or that the discussion will be entirely off-the-record and confidential, etc.
- The participants should agree in advance on whether the sessions are open and can be recorded and notes taken.
- The facilitator is responsible for probing for what is underneath the presenting issues, problems, or conflicts; for clarifying answers, summarizing points of view, keeping the discussion on track, and protecting the rights of everyone in the group to participate, be treated respectfully, and have their ideas heard and addressed.
- Recommendations for future action will be by consensus, or unanimously agreed to by everyone.
- Copies of all written reports or summaries will be made available to all participants.

The purpose of these ideas, processes, and methodologies is to forge out of a multitude of diverse and conflicted parts a common sense of purpose, direction, strategy, understanding, and language; to create a fleeting ambiance of shared effort, a group "micro-culture" that mixes and creatively combines everyone's experiences, ideas, emotions, wishes, and hopes to produce something that is not only new, but *synergistic*; that could not have happened otherwise, and is felt by each participant to be *theirs*.

WHAT DO FACILITATORS ACTUALLY DO?

Facilitators are *catalysts* of consensus, agents of change, and alchemists who seek to transmute the lead of disparate, solitary, divided, incremental, conflicted efforts into the gold of synergy, collaboration, teamwork, transformation, consensus, and community. On a seemingly simple, banal, and superficial level, facilitators help organize and guide group dialogues and meetings, and:

- Lead participants through unpredictable, sometimes chaotic, and conflicted processes, and encourage open, useful, constructive, and respectful engagement.
- Provide guidance and judgment regarding every part of the process.
- Help keep the group focused, collaborative, and open to diversity, dissent, and change.
- Foster positive communications and relationships across differences.
- Promote constructive conflict engagement leading to resolution, transformation, and restorative solutions.
- Suggest alternate approaches, methods, or procedures when appropriate.
- Model and support collaborative, non-zero-sum, "win-win" attitudes and techniques.
- Encourage learning, growth, and meaningful closure.
- Assist in the creative design and development of mediative systems, cross-cultural communications, relationships, and activities.

FACILITATING TEAMS AND SMALL- TO MID-SIZED MEETINGS

It is common for facilitators, myself included, to work on a small-scale with leadership groups and work teams, and on a mid-scale to assist organizations with strategic planning projects and retreats; chair meetings between competing or conflicted departments;

moderate assemblies of local neighborhoods and city departments; conduct bias awareness and violence prevention meetings in diverse communities; reduce tensions among staff in schools, medical facilities, non-profits, and family-owned businesses; and design dialogues between citizens, competing factions in labor unions, and social justice organizations.

In general, the smaller and more homogeneous the group, the simpler and less formal the processes, relationships, and resulting facilitations; while the larger and more diverse the group, the more complex, multi-faceted, and skillful mediators and facilitators need to be. Yet group activities on *all* scales reveal important elements that are fractally self-similar, and can be articulated, tweaked, and modified, then scaled-up or -down and translated back and forth between small, mid, and large group sessions.

For example, a typical generic small- to mid-sized group session might be organized and broken down into the following activities, many of which have analogues in large group processes. These often consist of the following:

- Welcome participants, invite the groups' leaders to do the same, and introduce yourselves; then describe the context, goals for the session, ground-rules, logistics, and overview of the agenda; invite participants to ask questions, propose changes to the agenda, and introduce themselves, or each other.
- Divide the group into small teams of about 4 or 5 people by counting off, (or on Zoom by creating break-out groups) making certain each team is diverse and representative.
- Ask each team to select a volunteer facilitator, recorder, presenter, timekeeper, process observer, mediator, etc., (see list of roles below).
- Ask each person to write down the top 3-5 problems facing the group; collect them (or on Zoom, ask the group to send

them to you as a chat or email), and send each list to a different team.

- Ask each team member to read aloud the problems you gave them, as listed by someone on a different team, then discuss them and reach consensus on the top 3-5 problems facing the whole group.
- Then ask the team to debrief and the process observer to offer the team feedback on its' process.
- Alternatively, ask each team to identify the group's main problems and brainstorm what stands in the way of their communications or relationships; or to analyze a topic or issue, reach consensus and prioritize the top 5-7 issues to discuss, and write them on flip chart paper or whiteboard to present to the other teams.
- Each team presents their summary to the group, is thanked and applauded, and invites the other teams to ask questions and offer additions or suggestions for improvement, which are recorded.
- Ask the large group to identify commonalities in the teams, key ideas, and agree on the top (perhaps) 4 or 5 issues to work on, such as respectful communications, rebuilding trust, improving finances, protocols for decision-making, conflict resolution procedures, etc.
- Ask everyone to pick a topic or "solution team," to work on, with a maximum of 5-7 people on each team, and sub-divide into duplicate teams if more than 7 people want to work on the same topic.
- Each solution team picks new facilitators, recorders, presenters, timekeepers, process observers, presenters, etc., then discusses, brainstorms, prioritizes, and reaches consensus on the top 5-7 recommended solutions for each problem.
- The team debriefs and the process observers again give feedback.

- Each team reports to the group, which discusses each recommended solution, invites suggestions for improvement, reaches consensus, and creates a communicate plan for describing what they achieved to others. They agree on an action plan with next steps, a timetable, and a date to meet again to assess their progress and correct course.
- If the group is unable to reach consensus, everyone agrees to mediate, conduct further study, research, or dialogue, and to meet again to revise, synthesize their ideas, and come up with a new consensus-based set of recommendations; or joint research plans; or to conduct interviews to find out what others want; or create pilot projects to find out what works best in practice.
- If the group lacks adequate authority to implement solutions, ask each team to select an "ambassador" to meet with those who do, advocate for their recommendations, and find out what can be done to improve them, and agree to ease or expedite implementation.
- Ask each participant to say one thing they learned from the process, or will do differently going forward to improve communications and relationships, or to support or implement the proposed solutions.
- Thank everyone, acknowledge their contributions, identify useful learnings, remind them of future meetings and next steps, wish them future successes, and close the session.

Many of the most useful and effective roles played by participants who volunteer, or are selected by the teams in a small group session, include these:

- Facilitator
- Presenter
- Process Observer
- Consensus Builder
- Devil's Advocate
- Strategist
- Coach
- Advocate for Those Not Present
- Implementer
- Change Driver

- Recorder
- Timekeeper
- Ambassador
- Mediator/Conflict Resolver
- Subject Matter Expert
- Negotiator
- Advocate for the Group
- System Designer
- Consultant
- Culture Advisor

Of these, the most common are the first five or six, but others can be added based on the size and composition of the group, or the nature of the problem that needs to be addressed. The number of roles can be expanded to fit the size of the group or team so everyone can participate and take responsibility for part of the process. These roles can be altered and redefined to fit the circumstances. I have, for example, facilitated "charettes," adapted from architectural design review processes, in which community leaders are invited to offer feedback to the group based on their experiences working with diverse constituencies; or members of the public are asked to offer critiques and suggestions on proposals that were brainstormed by small groups; or teams may select "values champions" to make sure they are acting according to the groups' agreed upon shared values, etc.

PROTOCOLS FOR CONSTRUCTIVE ENGAGEMENT

From the outset, it's important to make the entire process transparent, owned by everyone, negotiable, and always open for improvement. This may initially take the form of ground rules, shared values, core principles, or (especially with groups of adversaries) what I call "protocols for constructive engagement." Here are a few examples of process agreements that may prove useful. These can be discussed and modified by participants, to which others may be added during the session if the group encounters a problem:

- *Voluntary Participation*: We agree that everyone is present voluntarily and no one should feel coerced into attending or speaking.
- *Attitude*: We agree to participate, and to engage in dialogue in a spirit of learning, collaboration, and open communication.
- *Honesty:* We agree to be honest, address real issues, and not withhold differences or disagreements.
- *Respectful Communication*: We agree to communicate respectfully, focus on the issues, and not engage in personal insults or attacks.
- *Courtesy*: We agree to act with courtesy and not participate in disruptive, bullying, or violent behavior.
- *Collaboration*: We agree to work collaboratively and build on each other's ideas.
- *Listening*: We agree to listen objectively, openly, empathetically, and non-judgmentally.
- *Suspension of Judgment*: We agree to ask questions, clarify interests, and discover what is behind an idea or proposal, instead of operating on the basis of unspoken assumptions.
- *Non-Interruption*: We agree, if requested, that one person will speak at a time without interruption. If that does not succeed, anyone who wishes to speak will summarize what the previous speaker said and ask if that is correct before speaking themselves.
- *Consensus Decision-Making*: We agree that no group decisions will be made during the dialogue except by consensus.
- *Ability to Change*: We agree that everyone can change their minds, and tell the group when they do.
- *Focus on Issues:* We agree to focus on issues, interests and behaviors when we have conflicts, rather than on people or personalities.
- *Transparency:* We agree that everything we do together will be transparent and open.

- *Public Support:* We agree to publicly support the group consensus once it is reached.
- *Retaliation*: We agree that we will not retaliate for anything anyone says or does during the dialogue.
- *Non-Attribution*: We agree that statements made during the dialogue will not be attributed to any individual.
- *Confidentiality:* We agree that anyone can ask that whatever they say be confidential, and not repeated to others, unless they expressly agree otherwise, and that everyone will respect their request.
- *Feedback*: We agree to evaluate the process, offer feedback about what worked, what didn't, and indicate what we want to do better.
- *Mediation*: We agree that any disputes during the dialogue will be discussed and mediated by a mutually agreeable mediator.

Once people begin to participate in genuine dialogue, their lives are momentarily transformed. They enter an interactive, mutually defined space that invites them to surrender their biases, assumptions, preconceptions — even their sense of a divided self. In so doing, they often discover truths that are surprising and may feel foreign, yet resonate and reverberate deeply inside them. They nearly always reach collaborative understandings and discover profound meanings that *synchronize* the interests even of former combatants, unifying and transforming their antagonistic, divided views of themselves, each other, and the world.

OVERVIEW OF LARGE GROUP PROCESSES

Whenever large groups with multiple diverse stakeholders come together, their vastly different needs and expectations, wishes and desires, goals and timetables, histories and prognostications, cultures and understandings, strategies and tactics, methods and processes that have been associated with, are appropriate to, and historically accepted by each party, may trigger intense conflicts, making it difficult to know even where to begin.

Before a useful conversation can occur, it may be necessary to initiate a collaborative "process design" process, in which prospective participants, or their representatives, are invited to help design the way they will work together. This may begin with each person saying what *kind* of process would enable them to successfully discuss the issues, draw them a little closer, incrementally increase their trust, begin building consensus, reduce resistance, and make the process feel like it was jointly designed, and owned by them.

More broadly, I find it useful to break large group, multi-stakeholder, consensus building processes down into the following 10 generic steps:

1. Contracting and Needs Assessment
2. Collaborative Process Design
3. Convening the Parties
4. Empathy and Trust Building
5. Exploration and Problem-solving
6. Consensus Building
7. Collaborative Negotiation
8. Mediation and Impasse Resolution
9. Communication Planning, Action Planning, and Implementation
10. Feedback, Evaluation, Systems Design, and Nonstop Improvement

A somewhat more detailed, elaborate, practical description, and overview of the *large* group consensus building process might include the following 25 steps, which I routinely redesign for each new set of parties, issues, and circumstances:

1. Initiate a discussion about *whether* to convene a large group process, consider which participants need to be present, select facilitators and mediators, and clarify the parties' needs, interests, and goals.

2. Prepare a draft proposal with a summary of the design, strategy, and plan for the process with a suggested budget to circulate, revise, and submit for approval.

3. Once a decision has been made to proceed, ask each of the main constituencies to identify their representatives, and a list of alternates or substitutes in case of scheduling conflicts.

4. Agree on who else should be included–not only to help the process succeed, but to draw into dialogue those who could block or prevent it from succeeding.

5. Identify a core team of volunteers, one from each key stakeholder group, to act as a "steering committee" throughout the process, and assist in preparing a "conflict assessment;" "root cause analysis," "conflict audit," list of recommendations for action, etc.

6. Identify "surrogate advocates" or proxies, who will try to represent important stakeholders who refuse to participate, or groups and perspectives that are unavailable, or difficult to represent accurately.

7. Draft a timeline and overview for participants to agree on, with proposed ground rules, shared values, or protocols for constructive engagement, including agreements on how publicity will be handled during the process.

8. Identify a first circle of key individuals to interview regarding background, history, insight into problems, psychological assessment, and ideas regarding possible solutions.

9. Identify a second circle of individuals who might also be interviewed, perhaps by co-facilitators or members of the steering committee, depending on how the process unfolds.

10. Identify missing actors who might impact the success of the process and decide whether to interview or include them as well.

11. Complete initial interviews and/or a written survey, edit minimally for readability and anonymity, and distribute to all participants.

12. Prepare a summary of the interviews and/or survey, with a draft conflict assessment, root cause analysis, conflict audit questions, systems design proposal, and/or recommendations for action.

13. Ask participating organizations to select volunteers to be trained as small group facilitators, recorders, process observers, mediators, etc.

14. Train as many volunteer facilitators, recorders, and similar process leaders as are willing to volunteer, partly to strengthen the on-going capacity of stakeholder groups to facilitate or mediate future issues.

15. Bring everyone together for an orientation and overview of the process, and reach consensus on the draft agenda and proposed ground rules, shared values, or protocols for constructive engagement.

16. Ask introductory, empathy building questions, periodically evaluate the process, and correct course as needed.

17. Use facilitated caucusing, sidebar discussions, and separate, *ad hoc* mediations where necessary.

18. Ask teams or small groups to identify the top 3-5 problems that need to be addressed, prioritize them, and present them to the group as a whole.

19. After each team or small group discussion, process observers offer feedback on what their team did well and could do better next time.

20. The whole group engages in dialogue regarding the small group reports, then critiques, improves, and reaches consensus on 3-5 key problems that need to be addressed.

21. Participants meet in different teams or small groups, select new facilitators, recorders, etc., and discuss in detail one of the key problems.

22. Each team then brainstorms and prioritizes 3-5 recommended solutions to report back to the large group, gets feedback from the process observer, and discusses ways of improving their process.

23. Alternatively, small groups amend the draft conflict assessment, root cause analysis, conflict audit questions, systems design proposal, and/or recommendations for action, and present to the large group.

24. The large group discusses, revises, synthesizes, and reaches consensus on the small group conflict assessments, conflict audits, root cause analyses, recommendations, proposals for action, etc.

25. The large group prepares an action plan for implementation, agrees on a communication plan and action plan, evaluates the facilitators and the process as a whole, and celebrates its accomplishments.

If the recommendations need to be referred to a separate decision-making group with final authority to implement them, a small team of volunteer "ambassadors" can be selected to present the recommendations and a draft action plan, explain the interests and thinking behind them, advocate for them, and ask the decision-making group to assign each recommendation to one of only three categories:

1. *Low Hanging Fruit:* These are proposals that can be implemented immediately, and are approved for implementation.

2. *Need A Little Tweaking:* These are proposals that are agreeable, but require fine-tuning before implementation, which is immediately begun in partnership with the ambassadors representing the group.

3. *Can't Be Done and Need Revision:* These are proposals where there is a significant obstacle to implementation, or there is no consensus. The decision makers identify the underlying *interests* that led them to reject the proposal, and the ambassadors help brainstorm alternatives that satisfy those interests, report back to the teams for discussion, and seek consensus until the new recommendation fits into one of the first two categories.

This twenty-five-step process reflects my approach, and is only one of many ways of facilitating large group, multi-stakeholder, consensus building processes, each with its own steps and processes, advantages and disadvantages. For example, *The Consensus Building Handbook*, prepared by the highly experienced Consensus Building Institute at MIT, founded by Lawrence Susskind, recommends the following steps for designing and organizing large group, multi-stakeholder, consensus building processes (with some minor edits and modifications):

1. Clarifying Roles and Responsibilities:

- Clarify the roles of facilitators, mediators, and recorders.
- Select and specify responsibilities of facilitators or mediators.
- Select and specify the responsibilities of recorders.
- Form an executive committee or leadership team.
- Consider the value of a chair.
- Set rules regarding the participation of observers.
- Set an agenda and ground rules.
- Get agreement on the range of issues to be discussed.
- Specify a timetable.
- Finalize procedural ground rules.
- Require all participants to sign the ground rules.
- Clarify the extent to which precedents are or are not being set.

- Assess computer-based communication options.
- Establish a mailing list.
- Accept an advisory role if that is all that is allowed.
- Clarify the presumed liability of the participants.
- Clarify confidentiality arrangements.
- Clarify legal obligations if the participants are simultaneously involved in pending litigation.
- Clarify the extent to which precedents are or are not being set.
- Create a dispute resolution procedure.

2. Investigating and Deliberating:

- Deliberate and express concerns in an unconditionally constructive manner.
- Don't trade interests for relationships.
- Engage in active listening.
- Disagree without being disagreeable.
- Strive for the greatest degree of transparency possible.
- Separate inventing from committing.
- Identify interests and invent options for mutual gain.
- Emphasize packaging.
- Test options by playing the game of "what if?"
- Create sub committees and seek expert advice.
- Formulate joint fact-finding procedures and identify expert advisors.
- Organize drafting or joint fact-finding subcommittees.
- Incorporate the work of subcommittees or expert advisors.
- Draft preliminary proposals and use A single text procedure.
- Brainstorm and withhold criticism.
- Avoid attribution and individual authorship.
- Consolidate improvements in the text.
- Search for contingent options.
- Modify the agenda and ground rules (if necessary).

- Consider responsibilities, obligations and powers of sponsoring agencies and organizations.

3. Mediating and Deciding:

- Welcome dissent and expression of differences.
- Search for synergies.
- Respond openly, honestly and collaboratively to disruptive behavior.
- Clarify confidentiality arrangements.
- Clarify legal obligations if the participants are simultaneously involved in pending litigation.
- Clarify the extent to which precedents are or are not being set.
- Try to maximize joint gains.
- Test the scope and depth of any agreement.
- Use straw polls.
- Seek unanimity.
- Accept an advisory role if that is all that is allowed.
- Clarify the presumed liability of the participants.
- Settle for an overwhelming level of support.
- Make every effort to satisfy the concerns of holdouts.
- Keep a record.
- Maintain a visual summary of key points of agreement and disagreement.
- Review written versions of all decisions before.
- Maintain a written summary of every discussion.

4. Implementing and Improving:

- Seek ratification by constituent representatives.
- Ask representatives to canvass constituents to obtain revisions and responses to a penultimate draft.
- Ask representatives to sign and commit to a final agreement in their own names.

- Include necessary steps to ensure that informal agreements are incorporated or adopted by whatever formal mechanisms are appropriate.
- Incorporate appropriate monitoring procedures.
- Set dates for check-ins.
- Include re-openers for issues that are changing.
- Identify dispute resolution procedures for future disagreements.
- Encourage organizational learning.
- Support organizational development.
- Ask for feedback for the facilitators and mediators and thank those who give it, especially when the feedback is critical.
- Evaluate the process as a whole.
- Identify areas for improvement in content, process and relationships.
- Acknowledge and appreciate everyone for their contributions.
- Celebrate!

Peter Adler, on the other hand, who also has extensive experience facilitating large group dialogues, mediating multi-stakeholder public policy disputes, and designing consensus building processes, with Kristi Parker Celico, recommends the following 16 step process (again with some minor edits and modifications):

1. *Exploratory Contacts.* Preliminary calls or letters to knowledgeable individuals in the public, private, and civic sectors to examine the viability and timing of a dialogic approach to a specific issue.
2. *Issue Framing.* The development of a key policy, planning, or regulatory question, or set of questions, to which the dialogue will then seek to develop consensus answers.
3. *Product Framing.* An initial conceptualization of possible products, i.e., joint policy recommendations, delineation of

issues and options, guidance to government, etc., and possible linkages to formal decision-making.

4. *Concept Paper.* The creation of a brief proposal and call for participation that is circulated to prospective participants and funders.

5. *Financial Commitments.* Multilateral pledges to help underwrite a dialogue and its associated costs.

6. *Co-Conveners.* For some projects, it is useful to identify and invite two respected and leading authorities to serve as "Co-Conveners." Conveners often come to the issue at hand with different histories and viewpoints but are committed to a search for common ground and the exploration of break-through solutions. They lend their name and intellectual leadership.

7. *Representation.* Ensuring that a broad spectrum of voices and viewpoints are invited to participate and that those invited are, as a condition of participation, committed to disciplined give-and-take discussions.

8. *Work Plan.* A detailed but flexible work plan that corresponds to the needs of the project and that outlines budget and timelines.

9. *Venue.* A meeting setting that is comfortable and business-like, usually with state-of-the-art audio-visual capabilities if such is available. For some projects, it is useful to organize brief field trips to examine first-hand a relevant on-the-ground example of the topic under discussion, i.e., an industrial plant, an eco-system, a meeting with regulators, etc.

10. *Briefing Book.* A notebook of background materials is compiled and given to participants in advance of the first meeting. Usually, the briefing book contains issue summaries, a multi-disciplinary history of the issue, position papers, summaries of pertinent research, and other materials that help ground and prepare participants for discussions.

11. *Protocols.* An initial set of ground rules which are negotiated at the first meeting (or prior), and which create common rules of engagement regarding project organization, group decision-making, participation by others, ground rules for media contacts and the use of data and technical information, and table manners.

12. *Working Groups.* Many dialogues often require smaller working groups and cross-sector teams that meet between plenary sessions. This allows more in-depth examination of specific sub-issues, contacts with wider audiences, and the development of proposals for the full group.

13. *Use of Experts.* Certain issues – climate change, chemical weapons destruction, and watershed restoration – may need a great deal of fact- finding and technical information and, in some cases, new modeling or research roundups. It is useful to work with all participants to define and secure the level of information that is needed to work on the issue at hand, to identify acceptable independent experts when those are appropriate, and to help secure state-of-the-art information.

14. *Individual Meetings.* Policy dialogues typically span a number of months and, in a few cases, more than a year. Facilitators and co-conveners may need to spend a considerable amount of time talking with participants between meetings to ensure that information is being exchanged, commitments to do between-meeting work are being honored, and to help solve procedural, substantive, or relationship problems that may arise.

15. *Reporting and Roll Out.* Typically, most dialogues produce a set of recommendations, guidance to government, or a report on future directions. It is important that leaders play an active role in distributing such reports and ensuring the widest possible logical policy relevance and use. For example, diverse Dialogue representatives may testify in front of Congress regarding consensus recommendations.

16. *Feedback and Continuous Excellence.* All dialogues are participant-driven, that is, the deliberation group sets the agenda, charts course corrections, and makes key decisions regarding the substance and process of the issue under discussion. However, it is crucial that co- conveners and/or facilitators solicit ongoing evaluation of the work, both during and after the life of a specific dialogue.

Each of these distinct, often overlapping processes and frameworks can be highly useful in thinking about designing group processes, facilitating them, and breaking them down into smaller, practical steps. Rather than regard them as fixed, comprehensive, or universal, I find it more useful to approach them: first, as *possibilities* that may or may not be successful in working with specific parties under unique and changing circumstance; second, as *design criteria,* each of which can be tweaked or modified to achieve the goals of the participants; and third, as indicators of underlying process and relational *interests,* or as strategies, wishes, and desires that can be satisfied in multiple and diverse ways.

The critical element, in my experience, is to *always* design the process from scratch, and only resort to these models as a prompt, inspiration, or first approximation that requires imagination, tinkering, and iterative improvement based on feedback from the parties and an assessment of their changing circumstances. This requires us, as mediators and facilitators, to be willing to change *everything,* and throw out every one of these ideas the moment it feels clunky, heavy-handed, or counter-productive.

This attitude or approach to process design is grounded in a collaborative, consensus-based understanding of the nature of facilitation, mediation, collaboration, consensus building, and conflict resolution generally — one that is worth examining in some detail, including directly, openly, honestly, and transparently *with* the parties before, during, and after the facilitated session.

BUILDING CONSENSUS

There are six fundamental varieties or *types* of group decision-making, each with unique advantages and that make it appropriate or inappropriate for use by different people in solving different problems on different scales at different moments and circumstances, of which consensus is merely one. These six, with an illustrative statement representing each, are:

1. *Notification:* "I will make the decision."
2. *Consultation:* "I would like your ideas before I decide."
3. *Delegation:* "You decide."
4. *Voting:* "Let the majority decide."
5. *Consensus:* "I am willing to accept the wisdom of the group."
6. *Unanimity:* "We are in complete agreement."

Each of these forms of decision-making requires clarity to distinguish it from the others, and reduce mixed messages and false expectations, and *none* is appropriate always, everywhere, or with everyone. For example, I may unilaterally call a meeting, announce the date, consult on the time, delegate the choice of a location, vote on the agenda, reach consensus on a proposal, and unanimously agree on a date for implementation. But if I announce what other people are going to say, or vote on how they feel, or try to reach consensus on what they think, I would be misusing the process and undermining its' purposes.

Each form of decision-making gives rise to *vastly* different perceptions, communication styles, and relational consequences; each leading to significantly different results, and each requiring radically different skill sets, social attitudes, and organizational capacities. This can be seen more clearly if we consider different forms of government decision-making and the political ramifications, and social or behavioral consequences *likely* to flow from each. See the following page for examples of different forms of government decision-making and the political ramifications.

This diagram is not meant to be precise or universal, but a prompt for dialogue regarding the forms, responses, and skill sets required for different forms of decision-making. A higher goal is for groups to become *conscious* of the ways they make decisions and pick the forms that best address the problems they want to solve, recognizing that the time required to make each type of decision increases with each extra person who decides, as does the level of collaboration, unity, and ownership that emerges as the decision is being made.

Type of Decision	Form of Government	Public Response	Skill Set
Announcement	Absolutist Monarchy	Obedience	Conformity
	Dictatorship	Silence	Total Loyalty
Consultation	Limited Monarchy	Observation	Diplomacy
	Oligarchy	Loyal Opposition	Deference
Delegation	Bureaucracy	Compliance	Rule Making
	Meritocracy	Competition	Expertise
Voting	Representative Gov't	Involvement	Debate
	Procedural Democracy	Minority Rights	Advocacy
Consensus	Popular Gov't	Participation	Dialogue
	Substantive Democracy	Problem-solving	Negotiation
Unanimity	Self-Government	Collaboration	Mediation
	Heterarchy or Holarchy	Ownership	Teamwork

On the other hand, the level of conflict concerning the correctness of the decision, and the number of people asserting their desire or right to be heard before making it, or their need to be consulted so they feel their interests have been acknowledged and satisfied, drop significantly with each successive form, and become quicker and easier with experience.

What is most useful is for groups to meet, discuss, and decide by consensus or unanimity *which* decisions should be made in which way. In doing so, it may be helpful for those involved to consider and discuss the following initial questions:

- What are the different kinds of decision that need to be made?
- *Why* does each decision need to be made?
- How quickly does it need to be made?
- How much unity is desirable after the decision has been made?
- Who should be able to participate in making which decisions, and why?
- Who should be consulted before deciding, and why?
- Who does *not* need to be involved in deciding, or whose time would be wasted by participating?
- What type of decision-making process is best for each issue?
- Who should be consulted or involved before making each type of decision? Why?
- What kind of communications and dialogues should be conducted before deciding?
- What outcomes and relationships should result from the process?
- What skills or capacities need to be strengthened to help ensure the decision is made correctly?
- Who should be notified or asked for support after the decision has been made and before it is implemented?
- What should happen if there is no consensus?
- How will the decision be measured, evaluated, and improved?
- How often should the decision be revised, revisited, or reevaluated?

Each form of decision-making expresses, symbolizes, and has serious consequences for the kind of relationship and communication that will emerge between the people who are impacted by it. While notification, for example, both implies and actively *creates* hierarchical relationships, which may include domination; consensus decision-making implies and actively creates egalitarian relationships that can reduce, eliminate, and even prevent domination.

How Does Consensus Building Work?

Consensus building is a scale-free, collaborative, decision-making process individuals and groups of all sizes can use to reach agreements and make decisions everyone in the group can support. It is a way of bringing unity to diverse populations, synthesizing dissenting opinions, and connecting diverging paths by revealing, discovering, or inventing common ground. It is a way of transforming the assumption that differences merely divide people, into the realization that they are also frames of reference or angles of perception that expose unique, subjectively valid aspects of a shared reality.

Consensus building begins by reaching agreement on almost anything, even relatively trivial agreements about whether, when, where, and how to meet, which can then be multiplied so they seep inwards and spread outwards, creating a context, momentum, and *energy* of collaboration and commonality. Differences that arise within a *positive* context do not easily overwhelm it; but when the context is negative, conflicted, and antagonistic, it is far more difficult to return to friendly, collaborative, trusting interactions.

A common, simple definition of consensus is that it is a decision-making process designed to assist diverse individuals and groups with multiple perspectives, options, or points of view, by allowing them to:

- Choose among several options
- Ensure that everyone has an equal voice
- Invite differences of opinion and dissent to surface

- Reveal hidden sources of resistance
- Promote empathy, understanding, and ownership
- Build unity and agreement on a common direction
- Support win/win thinking
- Reach a decision that is final
- Encourage ownership of the decision
- Minimize the likelihood of doubt, remorse, and sabotage after the decision has been made

The typical statements people make that indicate consensus commonly range from high- to low-levels of agreement, as in the following examples:

- "I can say an unqualified "yes" to the decision."
- "I find the decision perfectly acceptable."
- "I can live with the decision."
- "I'm satisfied that the decision reflects the wisdom of the group."
- "I'm not especially enthusiastic about it, but it's okay for now."
- "I do not fully agree with the decision and need to register my views about it, but do not choose to block the decision."
- "I don't agree but am willing to support the decision because I think it's the best we can do."

On the other hand, there are many statements people make that typically signal a lack of consensus, and consequent need for deeper conversation, exploration of differences, brainstorming, collaborative negotiation, or mediation before genuine agreement can become possible, for example:

- "This is a real deal-breaker for me."
- "If this is the decision, I will leave the group."
- "I strongly (or repeatedly) disagree."

- "I feel I need to stand in the way of this decision being accepted."
- "I do not agree with the decision."
- "I feel I haven't been heard."
- "I feel there is no clear sense of unity in the group."
- "We need to do more work before consensus can be reached."

What allows the second set of statements to metamorphose and turn into the first is the process of consensus *building*, which consists of a set of empathetic, informal problem-solving stories and conversations that can take many forms, including non-violent communication, appreciative inquiry, restorative circles, open space meetings, dialogues, collaborative negotiations, brainstorming, criteria setting, mediations, impasse resolution, and similar techniques that do not suppress dissent or deny differences, but seek to learn from, reframe, build on, synthesize, and creatively integrate them, as aspects of a larger, synergistic whole.

Ordinary conversations, especially between hostile parties, and unfacilitated, "business-as-usual" meetings between competing personalities, groups and factions can easily create misunderstandings that block consensus, as by:

- Excluding key participants or restricting participation
- Constricting the flow of information and lack of transparency
- Accepting adversarial "Us vs. Them" attitudes
- Tolerating hostile and aggressive behaviors
- Disregarding biased or disrespectful communications
- Permitting or ignoring shaming and blaming
- Supporting cynicism and apathy
- Not responding to impatience and intolerance
- Not probing the reasons behind unwillingness to change
- Rewarding defensiveness and making excuses

- Ignoring power plays and trust breaking actions
- Failing to discuss manipulation, dishonesty, bias or prejudice
- Creating cultures of "public compliance and private defiance"
- Accommodating or avoiding conflicts, and ignoring "conflict hoarding"

For *authentic* consensus to occur, rather than the superficial appearance of agreement that flows from acquiescence, it is important to create a space in which people can resist the tendency to conform to group opinions, or willingness to give in to overt and subtle forms of group pressure, or agree to "go with the flow," not "rock the boat," "be a team player," or "ignore" bullying, and domination, or settle for "majority rule." To do so, at a minimum, participants should be able to say, regarding the process, that:

- Everyone felt free to speak up and dissent, and had ample opportunity to influence the decision.
- Everyone felt they were treated with respect and listened to, even when others disagreed with them.
- Everyone was willing to live with the decision, although it may not have been their first choice.
- Everyone felt comfortable supporting and standing by the decision.
- Everyone felt committed to the decision as though it were theirs.
- The group felt cohesive, unified, comfortable with its' diversity, and ready to act together.

For genuine consensus to occur, participants need to be actively encouraged to object, disagree, and dissent, and be *complimented* and acknowledged for doing so–not falsely or cursorily, but out of a sincere interest-based recognition that *every* disagreement represents something that isn't working for someone, and as a result, raises the possibility that it could be redesigned, re-imagined, improved, and turned into something that works better for everyone.

WHY CONSENSUS AND COLLABORATION FAIL

Consensus and collaboration sometimes fail, often because people have genuine, deep disagreements over principles, goals, values, or substantive ideas about which direction the group ought to be taking. Yet there are other times when consensus and collaboration fail, or are rejected or resisted, for reasons that originate in process errors, factual mistakes, simple oversights, ineffective communications, or relationship issues that are foreseeable, preventable, and easily corrected if addressed jointly, sincerely, skillfully, and in time. Consensus can fail, for example, for any of the following reasons:

- Neglecting to invite and involve those who are most immediately and directly impacted by the problem
- Excluding critics and dissenters with useful ideas from the process
- Approaching consensus building and collaboration as single, isolated *events*, rather than as a continuing process that happens, sometimes in small, unnoticed ways, every day
- Being too timid or avoidant, and not exploring differences over values, visions, strategies, and systems
- Allowing ancillary internal or external conflicts to continue unaddressed or unresolved
- Not improving skills in communication, bias and prejudice reduction, teamwork, and conflict resolution
- Not making improvements in the design of existing systems, processes, relationships, communications, cultures, and technologies
- Not reducing or eliminating bureaucratic requirements that take time and energy away from collaborative efforts

- Not defaulting to other options when emergencies or uncertainties arise
- Using the language of consensus and collaboration without meaning it, or doing anything to implement it
- Thinking only tactically, traditionally, and incrementally about how problems should be addressed, or decisions should be made
- Beliefs by leaders or managers that they will not benefit from consensus and collaboration
- Failing to flatten hierarchies and institutionalize teamwork
- Not helping stakeholders understand the need for consensus and collaboration, and the costs of *not* doing so
- Not making consensus an objective of each member of the group
- Not aligning collateral systems, structures, and processes to reinforce and reward consensus building and collaboration
- Not implementing collaboration and consensus building at all levels in the team, group, or organization
- Not changing *cultures* of avoidance, aggression, bias, and competition to ones of engagement, collaboration, acceptance, and consensus
- Inability of participants to visualize what collaboration and consensus are meant to achieve, or using it only to pursue selfish priorities, or linking it only to vague objectives, or using it to manipulate and exercise power over others
- Inadequate financial resources to support the extra time, resources, and skill sets needed for consensus and collaboration to work
- Lack of clarity about how to put these skills into practice
- Seeing consensus and collaboration as simple, or a cure-all
- Using "one size fits all," clichéd words and phrases, or "flavor of the month" approaches, then giving up
- Using consensus and collaboration to address complex, holistic, and systemic problems only partially, piecemeal, or episodically

- Not addressing or fixing the underlying systems that created the problems and focusing instead on superficial or isolated issues
- Failing to transform deep-seated cultures, processes, relationships, systems, and environments, or improve day-to-day behaviors
- Incomplete efforts to transform power- and rights-based attitudes, cultures, and approaches into interest-based ones

OVERCOMING OBSTACLES TO CONSENSUS

Perhaps the single greatest obstacle to consensus is the presence of chronic, unresolved, *systemic* conflicts that have been personalized, broken trust, and made it impossible for people to agree, even on the time of day. Mediation is therefore a highly useful skill in consensus building, and it may be necessary, *before* facilitating meetings or seeking group unity, to try to resolve the deeper problems that have unnecessarily polarized people and the issues they care about.

False, or *hyper*-polarization often results from the prioritization of *one* aspect of a complex truth, in opposition to others that are equally valid; or assuming that solutions are "either/or" rather than "both/and"; or minimizing or denying important differences. Yet these can also represent a first, clumsy, halting step toward dialogue, which can still lead to the discovery of higher order syntheses.

This can be done by defusing emotions, probing the parties' conflicting positions to reveal their underlying interests, and combining them to create better solutions, or agreements that are greater than the sum of their parts. False, counter-productive, hyper, unnecessary polarizations dismiss, diminish, or deny the presence and importance of diversity, dissent, and the deeper, interest-based truths that lie hidden in their opposition, especially the truth that opposites *can* be synthesized, catalyzed, and combined to create higher order outcomes.

To figure out how to find these higher order outcomes, it is initially important to separate, distinguish, polarize, and pull apart aspects of the problem that have been confused with one another; or mistakenly, falsely, or superficially combined. It is helpful to think of these as "separations" in search of a deeper or higher unity. Here are several separations I find useful as steps in mediating group conflicts and overcoming obstacles to consensus, with some examples showing how mediators or facilitators might think about and apply them:

- *Separate people from problems*: by being, as Roger Fisher and William Ury advise in *Getting to Yes*, simultaneously "soft on the person and hard on the problem."
- *Separate problems from solutions*: by staying with the problem to understand it better, rather than rushing to decide whose solution is best.
- *Separate positions from interests*: by asking why each person took that position, what it means, and why it is important to them.
- *Separate emotions from analysis:* by acknowledging emotions, not analyzing them, then analyzing data without emotions distorting it.
- *Separate commonalities from differences*: by asking what people have in common, and normalizing having differences.
- *Separate the future from the past:* by inviting people to indicate what they want for the future, then whether it is likely that their past behaviors or unresolved conflicts will help them get there.
- *Separate process from content*: by temporarily setting content aside and looking only at the process people are using to achieve it, then returning to content and reintegrating them.

- *Separate behaviors from personalities:* by focusing less on personalities, which are difficult to change, and more on behaviors and how to modify and improve them.
- *Separate yourself from others:* by avoiding telling others what to do, and not claiming any more than what actually belongs to you.
- *Separate criteria from selection:* by postponing deciding which option is best, and instead ask each side to first identify their criteria for a successful outcome.
- *Separate feedback from evaluation:* by offering feedback in the moment, afterwards evaluating the process and what happened, and doing both honestly, non-judgmentally, and collaboratively.
- *Separate ending from closure:* by not simply terminating the process, or doing so prematurely, but looking for release, completion, and closure, through shared reflections, sincere affirmations, expressions of gratitude, mutual acknowledgements, and group learning.

If these separations are unsuccessful in removing the obstacles to consensus, the next step is to assume there is a deeper conflict or unrecognized source of impasse that may require mediation. In truth, *every* conflict is at impasse until either the mediator or the parties figure out how to unlock it–often by digging deeper into the substantive issues, or shifting the process, or revealing what lies beneath the surface. Here are a few process techniques for overcoming impasse in intractable mediations, facilitations, or negotiations that may help conflicted parties identify and resolve the deeper sources of their conflict, and move closer to consensus:

- Break the issue down into smaller parts, isolating the most difficult issues and reserving them for later.
- Ask the parties why an alternative is unacceptable, then look for narrow solutions tailored to the reasons that are given.

- Go on to other issues and circle back later after other, simpler agreements have been reached.
- Take a break and ask the parties to think about the alternatives and suggest options they think might be acceptable to the other side.
- Review each parties' priorities and common interests.
- Suggest consulting an expert to supply needed facts or advice.
- Caucus with each person separately to explore hidden agendas and willingness to compromise.
- Split the difference.
- Try to obtain agreement on what people originally expected the solution would be.
- Look for possible trade-offs or exchange of services.
- Encourage the parties to recognize and acknowledge each other's points of view.
- Tell them you're stuck and ask for their ideas on how to get unstuck.
- Ask people what they think would change or happen if they reached a solution.
- Make certain people prefer problem-solving, mediation, or negotiation, as opposed to appealing to some external source of authority, or letting the problem continue, and if not, ask why.
- Consider the likely impact of various solutions on third parties.
- Test for emotional investment by asking what it would take to give it up.
- Compliment people on reaching earlier points of agreement, being willing to listen and compromise, and encourage them to reach a complete agreement that will put the problem behind them.
- Remind them what will happen if they don't agree, and what they each stand to lose.

- Ask for a minute of silence to think about the problem, where we are in the process, how they could improve their conversation, and what might do to resolve it.
- Ask more questions about the problem, about feelings, priorities, alternative solutions, flexibility, hidden agendas, reluctance to compromise, anger at one another, etc., or return to agenda setting.
- Return to vision, goals, shared values, principles, interests, or criteria, then develop procedures or guidelines that flow from them.
- Serve food or drinks to encourage people to relax.
- Adjourn and assign homework to present and discuss at the next session, with written alternatives, or reasons, or facts and data, etc.
- Generate options by brainstorming, without regard to practicality.
- Tell them which alternative *you* think is fair and why, trying not to break trust or appear biased.
- Suggest paradoxically that they may want to continue fighting, as a way of revealing the pointlessness of their conflict.
- Suggest that they pick a different mediator or facilitator, or take the issue to arbitration.

If these methods prove unsuccessful and group consensus still seems unreachable, there are a few "last ditch," less mediative interventions that may be far less damaging than continuing to engage in chronic, destructive conflicts that break trust, raise costs, traumatize everyone, and never end. When this happens, mediators or facilitators might, for example, decide to:

- Consult with external authorities or the group's primary decision- maker, or say what you think might happen if consensus fails.

- Examine each objection separately to see if partial or interim solutions could be agreed to, or if the issue can be reframed using different words.
- Create a team, or "sidebar," composed of representatives from each side to brainstorm, prioritize, and recommend *possible* solutions.
- Refer the issue to a completely uninvolved group to suggest new or compromise solutions.
- Search together for hidden issues, and identify what would need to be known, said, or done for consensus to become possible.
- Bring in a different mediator or facilitator to help reach consensus.
- Separate into factions and engage in open dialogue or debate over the issues, summarizing or capturing the key points, then discussing them in detail to see whether consensus might yet be possible.
- Ask each side to meet separately and list 3-5 suggestions for consensus they think the other side might accept.
- Table the decision until some specified date to discuss again, while moving ahead in areas where consensus has been reached.
- Decide *not* to decide until some event (such as an election or change in leadership) happens, or fails to happen, that may impact the reasons for withholding consensus.
- Take a straw vote, then discuss again.
- Prepare majority and minority reports, then try to find ways of synthesizing them.
- Vote and follow majority rule.
- Invite the minority group to continue to convince the majority to change its' mind.
- Allow the group's leader or primary decision-maker to decide.

None of these is optimal, of course, and timing is critical, as the conditions for consensus may not yet have arisen, or matured, or been acknowledged or accepted by the parties. It is also possible, as was the case in nearly every country that decided to abolish slavery — and is arguably the case today with prejudice, global warming, and the transition to renewable energy — that powerful individuals and entrenched interests *outside* the mediation or facilitation process have a strong incentive to deny, obstruct, or delay necessary changes.

When this occurs, one or more of the parties may feel it necessary to create "facts on the ground" by using violence, coercion, or other power-based processes to coerce the other side into surrendering, accommodating, or giving in; or failing that, simply imposing their will on others either through extra-legal, violent, authoritarian means; or legal, intimidating, democratic ones.

When this happens, mediation, facilitation, and consensus building may come to be seen, especially by those who feel oppressed, as *obstacles* to progress, or as Laura Nader brilliantly put it, "trading justice for harmony." By pursuing *only* settlement and compromise, mediation can be exploited by those with power to silence dissenting voices. Or, as in Munich before the outbreak of World War II, mediation can provide a cover for cowardly capitulation, and be manipulated to authorize injustice, compromise core values, obstruct change, and condone morally reprehensible policies, while masquerading as "justice," or "neutrality."

If we try to imagine how mediators and facilitators might have tried to bring about consensus, for example, between slaves and slave owners, in ways that could have prevented or minimized chronic conflicts between them, the *only* stable and lasting solution has to be one that *ends* the right to enslave others. It may be possible to reduce the economic impact of emancipation for slaves or slave owners through reparations, compensation, or other forms of assistance, but it is essential to recognize that the deeper source of these conflicts was the *system* of involuntary servitude forced on one group by another, and that chronic conflicts will inevitably continue until it ends.

It would also be possible to take a different approach and track the institution of slavery back to its origins in the collapse of a *prior* state of equality and social consensus that, had it been allowed to continue, would have granted equal status, wealth, and power to slaves, including citizenship and the right to vote, without leading to slave rebellions and armed resistance by slave owners who, *of course*, refused to surrender the profits, power, and privileges that flowed from trafficking their fellow human beings. This "tracking back" approach is not always convincing or successful in reducing resistance or overcoming impasse, as it requires an imaginative leap beyond what is immediate and compelling.

While mediation, facilitation, and consensus building might have been helpful in convincing slave owners to agree to return to a state of equality and social consensus, this could only happen if everyone accepted the end of slavery, based on a realization that the source of *all* conflicts regarding slavery throughout its' history originated not in the evil or personalities of the parties, or the brilliance or stupidity of their leaders, but in an unequal, unjust *system* that could either be tolerated and allowed to continue, or modified and reformed, or abolished entirely. Ultimately, every toleration, modification, reform, and permission for unjust conditions to continue simply *exhausts* everyone, distorts and undermines their authenticity, saps their resources, and postpones the inevitable, making emancipation the only authentic, lasting ground for consensus and resolution.

Some failures of consensus in large groups can similarly be attributed to a lack of skill in using mediation, facilitation, and consensus building to address and resolve systemic source of chronic conflict within the group. These skills may include the ability to facilitate dialogues between hyper-polarized parties; or organize large group, multi-stakeholder consensus building processes; or design *preventative*, interest-based dispute resolution systems; or exchange adversarial, zero sum, power-and rights-based processes for collaborative, non-zero-sum, interest-based ones that do not require victory and defeat.

DOING IT RIGHT AND DOING IT TOGETHER

My experience over four decades mediating and facilitating small, mid, and large group multi-stakeholder, consensus building processes has been one of trying to balance "doing it right" with "doing it together," and the two do not always coincide. There have been times when getting it right seemed at the time to require principled disagreement, which can aggravate conflicts and reduce group cohesion; and there have also been times when acting in concert seemed more important than having the right approach, which can lead to avoidance, accommodation, and less than optimal outcomes, and there is no clear, automatic, easy way of knowing when to do which.

It has sometimes been possible to successfully synergize these efforts, leading to exciting, energizing, *magical* outcomes that are simultaneously done right and done together. The key thing to remember is that what people say and do in splintered, distrustful, conflicted groups is sometimes just a superficial, distorted, first approximation and symbolic representation of what they *actually* feel and think, or want and mean, or need and desire, and it is important to avoid getting stuck in the *relatively* trivial issues of who said or did what to whom; or assume that the "facts" people cite and their emotional meanings are identical; and continue digging to discover what has been hidden, disguised, or subconsciously hinted at through the stories, narratives, metaphors, allegories, and parables people use to describe each other.

It is equally important to understand that *everything* is impermanent, especially large group, multi-stakeholder conflicts, which can be highly volatile and chaotic, causing the mood, attitude, energy, and cohesion in groups to shift rapidly — sometimes triggered by minor, unanticipated statements and events that spark something lying unnoticed beneath the surface that was *waiting* to be called forth when it was least expected, which can lead either to escalation, competition, and hyper-polarization; or to insight, collaboration, and creative outcomes that seem to come from nowhere and happen magically.

Lastly, as Ludwig Wittgenstein realized regarding philosophical difficulties — with equal relevance to group problem-solving, conflict resolution, dialogue, negotiation, mediation, collaboration, and consensus building–the key component in problem solving is how we *think* about the problem:

> Getting hold of the difficulty 'down deep' is what is hard. Because, if it is grasped near the surface, it simply remains the difficulty it was. It has to be pulled out by the roots; and that involves our beginning to think about these things in a new way. The change is as decisive as, for example, that from the alchemical to the chemical way of thinking. The new way of thinking is what is so hard to establish. Once the new way has been established, the old problems vanish; indeed, they become hard to recapture.

Mediation and facilitation have been *extraordinarily* effective in resolving small-scale conflicts between individuals, couples, families, neighborhoods, and work teams; and in many mid-scale disputes within groups, organizations, and institutions, and environmental and public policy disputes. It is now critical that we scale up these immensely successful methods to tackle much larger-scale global problems—as between highly polarized groups of political advocates, parties, and factions, and try to reach consensus on global warming, pandemic responses, and environmental protections; that we conduct dialogues between hostile political constituencies and rapidly de-escalate wars and potentially violent disputes between nuclear armed nation states.

What works on a small- or middle-scale may, of course, fail on a larger one, and *vice versa*. That is not what is important. What matters is that we *try;* that we be willing to fail in order to fail better and faster until we discover what works, and how, and why; that we *consecrate* our failures, and dedicate them to those with whom we failed, and the countless others who will come after and benefit from our failures. By doing so, we *redefine* failure as being overly preoccupied with success; and success as being willing to fail in searching for solutions.

Mary Parker Follett, an inventor of modern mediation, described the most important reason for helping groups build consensus this way:

> The potentialities of the individual remain potentialities until they are released by group life. Thus, the essence of democracy is creating. The technique of democracy is group organization.

What democracy needs to evolve and succeed are practical methods and skills that *simultaneously* strengthen diversity and unity, dissent and consensus; that support interest-based design processes that enable us to prevent chronic conflicts by resolving them at their systemic source. The need is apparent. What has been missing are first, the methodologies and techniques, which consensus building methods, collaboration skills, and conflict resolution provide; second, the courage to apply them, even half-baked, to reinvent them, and accept their ramifications and consequences; and third, the determination to see them through on all scales, knowing not only that they could fail, but more stunningly, amazingly, and magically, that they might actually succeed.

NINE

Mediation as a Change Process

FROM CONFLICT AND CRISIS TO COLLABORATION AND CONSENSUS

It is not the strongest of the species that survive, nor the most intelligent, but the one most responsive to change.

Charles Darwin

Any real change implies the breakup of the world as one has always known it, the loss of all that gave one identity.

James Baldwin

It is not possible to change anything until you understand the substance you wish to change. Of course people mutilate and modify, but these are fallen powers, and to change something you do not understand is the true nature of evil.

Jeanette Winterson

CHANGE IS CONSTANT, YET ITS' SPEED IS VARIABLE. SOMETIMES IT feels so glacial it is nearly unnoticeable, while at other times it feels so fast it is hard to encompass or keep up with. Today, not only are we changing rapidly in population size, economic wealth, scientific understanding, technological innovation, and global inter-dependency, but in divisiveness, inequality, polarization, destructiveness, vulnerability, and the catastrophic impact of change.

What is worse, the *rate* of change is also changing, becoming faster and faster, and catapulting us not simply from change to change, but from conflict to conflict and crisis to crisis, with less and less time to consider what we are doing, or whether this is the direction we *want* to be heading; leaving us unable to respond strategically, coordinate our responses, recover from our traumas, mourn our losses, or catch our collective breath.

Each of these disruptive changes, unresolved conflicts, and unremedied crises leaves us less able to solve the problems they generate, resolve the issues they stir up, and recover from the damages they create. They reduce our ability to learn, improve our skills and capacities, and plan how we might prevent and prepare for future disasters we can clearly see heading our way, even by trying too hard to prevent or fix them. And for many people, as the brilliant Rebecca Solnit correctly points out, "Perfection is a stick with which to beat the possible."

The social, economic, and political organizations and institutions, systems and structures, processes and relationships, cultures and contexts created over millennia to defend ourselves against the chaos of uncontrolled change, are becoming more cumbersome, obstructive, and outdated, triggering deadly consequences and hamstringing our ability to respond collaboratively, globally, and preventatively–not just to the Covid 19 pandemic, or the clearly catastrophic implications of climate change — but to massive species extinctions and the threat of ecological collapse; to war and nuclear brinkmanship; to global trade disputes and protective tariffs; to obscene disparities of wealth and hyper-competition; to fouling the air, land, and water on which our survival depends; to vicious biases, prejudices, and hatreds — and the list goes on.

The deeper problem presented by these escalating threats is not merely whether it is possible to find effective solutions to our problems, conflicts, and crises; but whether they can be implemented *in time*–in other words, whether we can change *ourselves,* our skills, and our relations with each other rapidly, sufficiently, and globally enough to combine and overcome them, before they combine and overcome us–that is, whether we can change the *way* we change.

If we are to overcome these obstacles, we need to recognize not only what isn't working, and what might work better, but be able to envision, articulate, and organize those who support these changes into a socially cohesive force that can convince others to implement it. As Yuval Noah Harari observed, "In order to change an existing imagined order, we must first believe in an alternative imagined order." At the same time, as Buckminster Fuller cautioned, we need to *act,* since: "You never change things by fighting the existing reality. To change something, build a new model that makes the existing model obsolete."

Yet imagination, belief, and new models are *still* not enough. It is equally important to understand the complex, paradoxical relationship between conflict and change; to invent ways of using conflict resolution techniques and methodologies to reduce resistance to change; and to implement collaborative, mediative, interest-based approaches to improving the way we change.

CONFLICT AND CHANGE

Much of what gets and keeps us stuck in problems, conflicts, and crises, whether local or global, personal or political, stems from the differing attitudes people bring to the thing being changed, and to the desirability and pace of change. These differences generate struggles for supremacy between advocates of change versus stasis, revolution versus reaction, progress versus resistance, hope versus fear, each feeding polarization, impasse, and intractability.

Every change takes place in time, and everyone who is touched by it experiences different levels of understanding and acceptance of why it is happening, why now, why it is necessary, how it is going to impact them, and what it means. As a result, there are differing degrees of willingness to accept its' real or imagined consequences; differing stages of readiness to let go of old and familiar patterns; differing intensities of fear and anxiety over what could go wrong; differing amounts of excitement, passion, and hope for improvement; and differing gradations of ownership and readiness for the change to occur.

These differences–sometimes over timing, without regard to disagreements about whether the change is desirable, predictably generate chronic, systemic conflicts, for example, between "progressives" who want the change to be implemented quickly, "moderates" who want to proceed slowly, "conservatives" who want to block the change altogether, and "reactionaries" who want to roll it backward to some idealized era that no longer exists.

As a result, much of what takes place for change efforts to succeed on all scales, consists of informal problem solving, strategic planning, facilitated dialogues, collaborative negotiations, consensus building, and mediated interventions that seek to clarify and reach agreement on the *specifics* of change, including why it is necessary, what *exactly* is going to change and what is not, how the change will happen, who will be responsible for making it happen, and when it will transpire.

While each of these interventions and approaches to change can succeed on a small- or mid-sized scale, they can also work on a grander, *global* scale, as each gives rise to a rich array of techniques for responding creatively to deeply entrenched destructive behaviors, and can be highly effective in reducing resistance to change, and altering systems that are outmoded or dysfunctional.

Mediators can assist not only in designing and facilitating small-scale change processes, but scaling-up diverse change processes, methodologies, and approaches, and applying them to large-scale, multi-party consensus building, problem-solving, and decision-making processes. Every variety of conflict resolution includes a range of techniques for overcoming resistance, intractability, and impasse that can be scaled-up and adapted to social, economic, political, and environmental disputes, perhaps improving our chances of survival.

Simply acknowledging that this is *possible* requires us to think more deeply about the relationship between conflict and change, and entertain the possibility that mediative approaches to resolving social, economic, political, and environmental conflicts, which assume many types, shapes, and sizes, could help us reduce resistance to much needed, long overdue changes, and design *interest-based* approaches that are less conflicted, regardless of the size or scope of the problem.

CONFLICT, CRISIS, CATASTROPHE, AND CHANGE

The coexistence of a pressing need to change and an unwillingness or inability to do so will *predictably* generate chronic conflicts. If conflicts are unresolved, they can lead to crises, which can turn into catastrophes. In reverse, catastrophes emerge from crises, which result from chronic conflicts, which flow from differences, which are often grounded in an urgent, deep-seated impetus to change, combined with an underlying source of resistance or reason for not changing, each of which can be prevented, resolved, transformed, or transcended.

To understand the logic and movement of this progression, we need to start with four sets of fundamental universal principles, or axioms:

1. The principles of impermanence, oscillation, complexity, and change

2. The principles of diversity and unity, individuation and integration, competition and collaboration, conflict and resolution
3. The principles of synergy, emergence, chaos, and creativity
4. The principles of evolution, adaptation, and the rise of higher forms of resolution, synergy, collaboration, and evolution

Given these core principles, we can predict that impermanence will make unity unstable and give rise to diversity. Diversity will deepen and lead to disagreements. Disagreements will trigger emotions and create conflicts. Conflicts will either be resolved, leading to conciliation, settlement, resolution, transformation, or transcendence, and higher, more complex sets of behaviors; or *not* resolved, become chaotic, and trigger crises and catastrophes. Thus,

1. When people lack the skills needed to respond to diversity, *disagreements* arise.
2. When people lack the skills needed to respond to disagreements, *conflicts* occur.
3. When people lack the skills needed to respond to conflicts, *crises* happen.
4. When people lack the skills needed to respond to crises, *catastrophes* follow.

It is therefore possible to prevent catastrophes, avoid crises, and dramatically reduce the severity and costs of conflict by strengthening our skills in responding to diversity, disagreements, and conflicts. Diversity, disagreement, and conflict are early stages in every change process, with the positive quality that they help us pinpoint or highlight what actually needs changing and what doesn't, without necessarily triggering entrenched opposition or obstructing improvement.

Mediation can then be defined simply as a method for surfacing the underlying diversities and disagreements that give rise to conflicts, unlocking them at their chronic source, defusing their emotional triggers, and searching for ways of satisfying the deeper interests that fuel and exacerbate them.

In other words, mediation is a *change process* that allows us to more skillfully respond to diversity and disagreement, thereby resolving conflicts, avoiding crises, and preventing catastrophes. This movement, or change process, I find takes place in the following rough chronological sequence:

1. Our responses to people and problems over time start to simplify and form patterns, which become simple and self-regenerating, creating systems that then slowly start to ossify, turning into customs and traditions, and eventually into ruts that generate a sense of security, commonality, continuity, and stasis.

2. Nothing, however, is permanent, and small, insignificant changes begin to accumulate in people, problems, relationships, systems, and the environment that do not match or support the patterned responses, customary approaches, and entrenched systems that no longer satisfy people, solve problems, fix relationships, repair systems, or evolve and adapt to changing environments.

3. Nonetheless, these antiquated responses, approaches, and systems continue to act as though nothing has changed, generating increasing friction, failure, dissatisfaction, and dysfunction among those whose interests are no longer being met by them.

4. These problems gather, cross-connect, intensify, and gradually become *personified* and are articulated — in the first place, by those who are dissatisfied with the old responses, approaches, and systems, and are more willing to

point out, often at some risk, that they are outdated and no longer work.

5. These "dissenters" find themselves increasingly at odds with those who have accommodated and accepted the old responses; or learned to tolerate and work around their chronic dysfunctions; or lack the energy, or do not understand, or are fearful, or do not have the skills needed to evolve and adapt to newer, less familiar ways of approaching and solving problems.

6. These people polarize, become increasingly defensive, personalize their differences, tell disrespectful stories and narratives about each other, form stereotypes, biases, and prejudices that diminish each other, and engage in repeated conflicts with one another.

7. Their conflicts gradually approach a "tipping point," a place both of impasse and possibility, where the old processes, relationships, systems, and environments begin to break down, both sides become stuck and seemingly unable to change, and the need to change becomes ever more compelling.

8. As the pressure to change mounts, problems increase, conflicts become more intense, issues get "politicized," and both sides resort to different forms of power or rights in an effort to *win* against the other side by denying or suppressing their differences and interests.

9. These conflicts turn into crises, as communication, trust, and collaboration falter and fail, leading to unreasoning rigidity and "hyper-polarization," undermining unity, discouraging dialogue, reducing diversity, denying complexity, stifling innovation, and blocking democratic, collaborative, win/win outcomes that seek to resolve the conflict, while encouraging autocratic, aggressive, win/lose solutions that seek to deny and suppress it.

10. These crises either go underground, dissipate, or are terminated — usually by *power*, through suppression,

violence, authoritarianism, war, and coerced obedience; or by *rights*, through legal coercion, litigation, voting, and disgruntled compliance. Occasionally, but increasingly, they are resolved by *interests*, through joint problem-solving, dialogue, consensus building, collaborative negotiation, mediation, restorative justice, and shared ownership of the problem.

Only the very last of these options is able to entirely avoid the catastrophe, end the crisis, and resolve the conflict, as power- and rights-based methods are unable to shift old, outdated paradigms or fundamentally transform the chronic, repetitive, systemic, and environmental conditions that gave rise to the conflict, and keep it going long after its' usefulness has disappeared.

This sequence suggests several important ways of defining conflict: first, it is simply the sound made by the cracks in a system; second, it represents a lack of skill in being able to handle the emotions, chaos, complexity, and disruptions of the change process; third, it is an inability to say good-bye, a refusal to let go of something that is dead or dying; and fourth, it is the voice of a new paradigm waiting to be born, a call for change in a system that has outlived its usefulness.

Mediation as a Collaborative, Interest-Based Change Process

Every mediation is therefore a *change process*. It is an effort to resolve conflicts over what, in organizational settings, is often called "change management"; that is, an attempt to identify the *sources* of the cracks in the system; clarify key elements in the new paradigm; help people work through the emotions triggered by the conflict; turn them in the direction of problem-solving; reduce the chaos, complexity, and disruption of the change process; and initiate dialogue, consensus building, strategic planning, collaborative negotiation, mediation, and similar processes that encourage people to let go of old patterns and reach agreements on what most needs to change, what doesn't, why, who will do what to make it happen, and how it can be done in an interest-based way.

We can then define conflict simply as a place where people are stuck and unable to change, and mediation as a collaborative, interest-based, consensus-driven, *change process* — one that searches for the precise places where people are stuck; identifies the communication patterns, emotions, ideas, behaviors, expectations, assumptions, systems, cultures, and conflict approaches that *keep* them stuck; and offers creative options, transformational skills, collaborative processes, ameliorative techniques, and a range of non-zero-sum, win/win methods people can choose from to end the impasse and work together to decide what, how, why, and when they are going to change.

These methods assume it is possible to transform the change process from power-based struggles for dominance that are unitary and mutually exclusive; or from rights-based battles for legal supremacy that are adversarial and competitive; to interest-based searches for solutions that are diverse, non-exclusive, and do not end with one side victorious and the other vanquished.

Interest-based approaches to change, however, require collaborative methods; complex, creative, participatory techniques; and higher order conflict resolution skills, including non-violent communication, empathetic listening, dialogue, consensus building, collaborative negotiation, and mediation, all of which affirm the diversity and non-exclusivity of *both* parties' complex needs, wishes, and desires; the truth and legitimacy of each individual's personal and emotional experiences; and a need to search for solutions that feel fair and just to everyone.

From Interests to Collaboration

In small-scale friendships, couples, and families; mid-scale communities, teams, and groups; and large-scale organizations and nation-states, conflicts start in earnest when people's needs and interests are unheard, unrecognized, and unmet, and they feel isolated, alone, frightened, sad, angry, competitive, and unable to listen to the needs and interests of others until *theirs* have been listened to, acknowledged, and satisfied.

As a result, people become mired in their conflicts and create crises because they lack the skills they need to alter, transform, or transcend the powerful, reciprocal, cyclical, adversarial dynamics that are triggered in every conflict on every scale. In short, they get stuck and cannot get unstuck without the aid of someone who is outside the conflict, or has the requisite skills and capacities to shift these dynamics and change the attitudes and behaviors that keep them at impasse.

Mediation can now also be defined not merely as a methodology for solving problems, resolving conflicts, ending crises, and avoiding catastrophes, but of equal importance, as a *collaborative change process* that seeks to reverse isolated, adversarial, zero sum, competitive approaches to transition, adaptation, evolution, and transcendence. It is a way of changing the way we change, and shifting the way we solve our problems by introducing collaborative, creative, caring conversations that acknowledge and affirm *everyone's* needs and interests, and diligently searching for just and fair ways of satisfying them for everyone.

The very first collaborative change brought about by conflict resolution consists simply of agreeing to come together in dialogue — which requires not just passive, neutral, dispassionate *hearing*, but active, empathetic, responsive efforts to listen, speak, and understand–and not simply the words, but the needs, interests, and desires that *precede* them, and give them power and meaning. Listening pays attention not just to the facts, or the stories of demonization and victimization, or narratives that bias and distance us from each other, but the unspoken requests for honesty and caring, authenticity and engagement that always underlie them.

A second collaborative change brought about by conflict resolution consists of mutual affirmation, acknowledgement, and acceptance—which come from realizing that the bitter, angry, frightened accusations and adversarial expressions of pain, loss, disappointment, and betrayal that pepper conflict conversations originate in deeper, more vulnerable, heartfelt wishes and desires, thoughts and feelings, needs and interests, whose frustration and loss gives rise to them.

A third collaborative change brought about by conflict resolution consists of inviting opposing sides to come closer, reveal themselves, and enter dialogue; to jointly design the agendas, processes, and questions that will invite them into empathy and problem-solving; to facilitate the interventions, consensus building efforts, joint actions, reflections and evaluations; and to transform "the problem" from a "you," "s/he," or "them;" into an "it," "I," or "us."

A fourth collaborative change brought about by conflict resolution consists of assisting the parties in negotiating non-zero-sum, interest-based, "win/win," "mutual gain" solutions, as described by Roger Fisher and William Ury in *Getting to Yes*. The balance, however, between helping one side maximize their self-interests and the other side maximize theirs can be precarious, challenging conflict resolvers to make certain that the collaborative nature of the process and relationship are kept primary, and that the long-term value of collaboration is not eclipsed by the parties' short-term desires for one-sided gain.

A fifth collaborative change consists of joint actions, perhaps in setting ground rules, researching problems, brainstorming solutions, reporting to others about what was learned, implementing agreements, evaluating what worked and what didn't, learning higher order skills, taking mutual steps to improve the relationship, and similar reciprocal, coordinated, cooperative acts.

In the process, it is helpful to realize that collaboration is an *outcome* of diversity, dissent, and honest communication of differences, which is undermined by efforts to suppress diversity, repress differences, blame others, or deny problems. Collaboration is a process in which differences are brought into dialogue with one another, given permission to express themselves fully and openly, then creatively combined in ways that could not have been imagined beforehand.

PERCEIVING THE NEED TO CHANGE

Perception of the *need* to change and actual change rarely occur in sync. Instead, people experience what neurophysiologists call "change blindness," which happens when physical alterations take place without accompanying perceptual changes, or some part of the environment changes slowly and incrementally, as in the example of the lobster in a pot of warm water that slowly comes to a boil.

The reverse can also take place, as when people get so caught up in the change process, or so focused on achieving their goals, or so concentrated on a task, that they miss important details altogether, as in the example of people who are so immersed in counting how many times a team playing basketball receives the ball that they fail to notice a person in a gorilla costume entering the court.

Our perception of the need to change often lags far behind the need to change, giving rise to dysfunctions, conflicts, crises, and catastrophes that could have been solved earlier at a vastly lower cost. This lag is especially pronounced where the change involves a loss, be it personal, emotional, and relational; or social, economic, political, and environmental. It is even *more* pronounced where those who have the most to lose from the change have the willingness, resources, and power to obstruct, obfuscate, or veto the problem-solving process.

When this occurs, as happened historically, for example, in seeking to solve the problem of British colonialism, or that of slavery in the U.S., causing the problem-solving process to turn violent, leading to revolution and civil war. Yet it is clear that far less costly solutions were readily available, but blocked by wealthy colonialists or slaveholders whose interests lay in perpetuating the problem.

While numerous efforts were made to mediate these disputes, virtually all of them were based on the false assumption that compromises could be found that would permit colonialism and slavery to continue without lasting conflict. This, however, was not genuine problem-solving or conflict resolution, but problem suppression, conflict avoidance, and compromise. The only real, genuine, lasting solution to both crises was to definitively transform the underlying systems that were regularly generating these problems and creating chronic conflicts. But because *true* resolution required a huge loss of dominance in status, wealth, and power by colonists and slaveowners, they not only tried to block and frustrate the change process, but to confine, distort, and constrain the *mediation* process so it could only result in compromises that failed to address the underlying problems.

EXPECTATION AND EXPONENTIAL CHANGE

There is a still deeper problem, which is that it is immensely difficult to understand, plan, and respond to systemic changes effectively, in time or in the right measure, when the *rate* of change is also changing, especially when that rate turns *exponential*, or when previously unconnected changes unexpectedly interact, multiply, and magnify; or conflicts arise that distract our attention, making it difficult to respond rapidly; or confuse people about where the change is heading; or crises compel us to address more immediate survival issues, leaving little time to respond to lower order priorities, or engage in planning or prevention.

Physicist Allan Albert Bartlett gave the following brilliant example of exponential change. Imagine a glass with two bacteria in it, which reproduce and double in number every minute, so that at the end of sixty minutes we know that they will fill the glass. How much warning time will the bacteria have that they are about to fill the glass? The answer is nearly none, because at 58 minutes before the hour, with only two minutes remaining, the glass is still only a quarter full. And at 59 minutes, the glass is just half full. Yet in one brief minute the glass will be entirely full, and in another, they will fill an entire second glass.

Many of the issues we face today are possibly of this character, as can be seen, for example, in the rapidly multiplying effects of global warming, climate change, and species extinctions; or in the rapid spread of pandemics, diseases, and drug-resistance; or in the escalation of conflicts between competing nation-states, each armed with enough nuclear warheads to destroy nearly all life on the planet; or in countless other problems of which we are still only dimly aware, as we are preoccupied with attention-catching issues elsewhere.

HYPER-POLARIZATION

One of the difficulties in responding to crises, conflicts, and changes arises in the form of hyper-polarization, excessive hostility, loss of trust, and ultra-adversarial responses that harden conflicts, making collaboration, problem-solving, planning, and resolution far more complex, arduous, and time-consuming, and requiring higher order skills to resolve them.

We often assume that polarization is inevitably destructive and undesirable, as it frequently is, especially when responded to with power- or rights-based tools. But it is equally important to recognize that polarization is a necessary *precursor* to change and an essential element in every evolution to higher forms of order. Whatever is new, innovative, and about-to-be must initially separate itself from what is old, habitual, and has-been. Increasingly, these are driven to differentiate, polarize, and stand apart from one another, creating a crossroads or watershed, a pivot or choice point, breaking the assumption that "there is no alternative," forcing collective energy to become binary and oscillate from one to the other.

By analogy with biology, complex life begins with cell division, or meiosis, in which chromosomes divide, separate, and *polarize*, enabling them then to cross over, replicate, and recombine; allowing maternal and paternal cells to mix and form a zygote that randomly combines, containing all the information needed to produce a brand new, entirely unique being.

Polarization plays a similar role in conflict — not just in personal, relational, and organizational settings, but social, economic, political, and environmental arenas as well. These are nearly always experienced by those on the opposite side as negative, undesirable, and destructive. Yet these very divisions and separations, which emphasize and exaggerate differences while minimizing and dismissing what they have in common, are essential precursors to change, and subtle indicators that an *evolutionary* process has *already* begun. Conflict can then be defined simply as the personalized voice of an evolution that is about to happen.

What many mediators seek to do in response is to weaken or compromise the polarization, including its' essential *creative* elements, or minimize the need for change. But they can also moderate and assuage only its *destructive* aspects that excessively personalize the issues, trigger unnecessary defensiveness and resistance, and mask or divert attention from what most needs to change.

In these ways, successful, *creative* polarizations can be valuable, by contrasting and pitting new ideas against old ones in ways that allow opposing parties to change their minds and jointly search for places where syntheses and unifications can occur — yet at a *higher* level, produced by the exploration and acceptance of new ideas; or by approaching old ideas empathetically and non-aggressively; or by seeking to recapture what was useful in each of them while building consensus on why change is needed; or by *perfecting* the choice between diverse options; and affirming the importance of learning, discovery, and improvement.

One of the critical roles played by dialogue, joint problem-solving, consensus building, collaborative negotiation, mediation, forgiveness, and reconciliation is marking the moment of transition from power- and rights-based change processes to interest-based ones, and the waning of polarization and conflict as dominant, defining principles in the parties' continually changing lives and relationships.

In these ways, polarization is merely a call to pay attention to whatever is not working effectively for someone, and often for everyone. Like conflict, it is a *request* for improvement, collaboration, and a disguised, oblique, unspoken wish for a deeper conversation. It is a hope for dialogue, problem-solving, negotiation, and mediation that will elevate and improve their processes, relationships, systems, cultures, and environments. In *form*, polarization is an *explicit* effort by one side to triumph aggressively over the other; while in *content*, it is an *implicit*, subtle desire to do so *collaboratively*, by satisfying the needs and interests of both.

The difficulties with polarization increase with the use of biases and prejudices, rewards for conformity, punishment of dissenters, and acts of bullying and aggression designed to unify supporters against a common enemy — sometimes castigating the *idea* of collaboration or dispute resolution as hopelessly naïve or traitorous. It routinely invites hatred of diversity, fear of creativity, suppression of openness, punishment of dissent, loss of empathy, ignorance of critical facts and opinions, stories of demonization and victimization, desensitization to cruelty and violence, brutalization of language, generalized distrust, cynicism, paranoia, apathy, irresponsibility, and the manufacture of elaborate defenses against understanding or learning anything from anyone on the opposite side.

These responses to polarization make it much more difficult to collaborate in solving complex problems by reducing the diversity of possible solutions and generating chronic conflicts that slip easily into crises. They effectively block peaceful, gradual, incremental, creative change, leading to violent, sudden, rigid ones, at incalculable cost. As U. S. President John F. Kennedy described it, "Those who make peaceful change impossible make violent revolution inevitable."

What we require, then, are interest-based change processes that allow us to capture the *positive* aspects of polarization, while acknowledging, appreciating, and affirming the commonalities, as well as the very real differences that fuel the opposition. This allows us to minimize, reframe, and transform the *negative* elements that discount or demonize these differences, turning them into sources of creativity by shifting their focus to dialogue, problem-solving, collaborative negotiation, and conflict resolution — i.e., to insight, learning, adaptation, improvement, transcendence, and evolution to more satisfying relationships.

CHANGE AND THE DYNAMICS OF INDIVIDUATION AND INTEGRATION

Two fundamentally opposing yet complementary systemic forces that impact the change process in relational conflicts, as in couples, families, teams, organizations, and communities, are those of *individuation* and *integration*, or differentiation and assimilation, separation and unification, independence and interdependence. While too much individuation can result in a loss of connection and collaboration, too much integration can result in a loss of diversity and uniqueness.

Small-scale relational conflicts often occur when the balance between these opposing forces shifts too far in one direction or the other, causing spouses, for example, to "need more space," or "want more time together." Yet the balance between these complementary forces is constantly shifting, requiring frequent fine-tuning. This allows both sides to learn from their chronic conflicts how to *calibrate* and fine-tune their skills in responding to change; to clarify and negotiate their expectations; to work more collaboratively and strengthen their relationship.

In mid-scale organizational disputes, these forces may take the form of individual as opposed to team responsibility, while in large-scale social, economic, political, and environmental conflicts, they may take the form of conflicts between personal liberty and social equality; individual rights and social justice; private autonomy and moral responsibility; or the freedom to decide for oneself and consideration for the rights of others.

Conflicts often occur over these issues because each side wants to shift the balance of power or rights in their favor; assume there is a single truth, which is theirs; feel justified in using power and coercion to impose their preferences on the other side; or believe theirs is the sole morally or legally correct position. Once either side decides to dismiss the other side's needs, interests, and wishes, the only remaining question is how far it will be acceptable for them to go to get the results they want. In religious, moral, ethnic, military, and political conflicts, the answer easily extends to genocide, war, and annihilation of the other.

The approach of mediation to these conflicts is to shift the parties' focus from serial monologues that seek to enforce fixed, overly simplistic, one-sided, zero-sum outcomes; to mutual dialogues that seek to synthesize malleable, complex, multi-sided, non-zero-sum interests, and collaboratively negotiate consensus-based outcomes that accept the legitimacy of both sides' concerns.

In other words, mediation seeks to transform the change process from one that is "either/or," into one that is "both/and"—not only in the adversarial *form* of the parties' communications and the *content* of their negotiations, but in the *context* of promoting *preventative* systems and structures, caring attitudes and relationships, and inclusive cultures and contexts, that transform what and how we change.

How Systems Resist Change

As neuroscientist Anil Seth has described it, "perception of change is not the same as change of perception." Indeed, most changes are gradual, incremental, unremarked, and extended over time, offering ample opportunities for denial, trivialization, discouragement, intractability, and the conscious and subconscious organization of a host of defenses against transformation and transcendence.

Indeed, systems *themselves* are defenses against change. If we define a system as anything that turns in a circle and is re-generating, the natural output of every system is repetition, giving rise to feelings of ease and comfort, safety and security, continuity and meaning. This, perhaps, led Swiss philosopher Henri Frédéric Amiel to insightfully declare: "Our systems, perhaps, are nothing more than an unconscious apology for our faults – a gigantic scaffolding whose object is to hide from us our favorite sin."

Systems are routines that slowly turn into ruts, which can be as complex and multi-faceted as the bureaucracies of large corporations and nation-states. These ruts give rise to methods systems can use to *resist* change, which vary widely, as can be seen, for example, in the following 15, which can be found in personal, relational, organizational, ideological, religious, and political systems:

1. *Marginalization*: Making ideas, people, perspectives, or insights that could threaten the system appear unimportant, irrelevant, irrational, or impossible to achieve.
2. *Negative Framing*: Using language that frames new ideas and critics negatively, so that nothing threatening to the system can be thought or communicated successfully.
3. *Exaggeration*: Stereotyping or exaggerating one part of an idea in order to discredit the other parts, and the whole.
4. *Personalization:* Reducing ideas to individual people or phrases, then discrediting them.

5. *Sentimentalization:* Using sentimental occasions, ideas, emotions, and language to enforce conformity and silence criticism.

6. *Seduction:* Describing the potential of the existing system in ways that unrealistically promises to fulfill people's deepest dreams and desires, while blaming the failure to achieve them on others.

7. *Alignment:* Communicating that in order to exist, succeed, be happy, or achieve influence, it is necessary to conform to the system, regardless of its faults.

8. *Legitimation:* Considering only existing practices as legitimate and all others as illegitimate.

9. *Simplification:* Reducing disparate, complex, subtle, multifaceted ideas to uniform, simplistic, superficial, emotionally charged ones.

10. *False Polarization:* Limiting people's ability to choose by falsely characterizing issues digitally as good or evil, right or wrong, either/or, with nothing in-between.

11. *Stereotype, Bias, and Prejudice:* Attaching derogatory, shaming, and hostile labels to anyone who does not accept the old system.

12. *Selective Repression:* Selecting individual critics as examples, bullying and shaming them for disagreeing or failing to conform, and criminalizing or ostracizing them.

13. *Double Binds:* Creating double standards that require people to live divided lives or compromise their beliefs, and make it difficult or impossible for them to act with integrity.

14. *Repeated Falsehoods:* Telling lies brazenly and repeatedly, confusing people about what is true, camouflaging what is dysfunctional, and encouraging irrational refusals to recognize the need to change.

15. *Chronic Conflicts:* Establishing rules and practices that are contradictory, generating chronic conflicts that keep people distracted and unable to function effectively.

The difficulty with all of these forms of resistance to change is that human systems are open and vulnerable to changes that occur naturally, either as a result of internal "mutations" or external shifts in the environment. When this occurs, conflicts and disorder become *essential* for the system to grow, adapt, evolve, and survive. George Ainsworth Land described the process this way:

> In any system, once a relative orderliness has been achieved, the only means by which a broader and more complex interrelationship among the various elements can be achieved is by introducing or generating disorder. The system can come apart to be put together in a much more integrated way. Any system that resists this creative disintegration and re-integration can only suffer the gradual erosion of its established order due to the energy required to protect the system from change.

This dynamic of "creative disintegration" and re-integration takes place in systems on all scales. Indeed, one of the principal reasons we resist change so passionately and energetically is because, as Octavia Butler wrote, "All that you touch, you change. All that you change, changes you." And changing ourselves or the systems we inhabit is always risky.

This risk can be seen in the strenuous resistance to change that is common in families, organizations, societies, and nation-states. At the same time, change is *mandatory*–how we handle it, what we do with it, and whether we turn it into learning, improvement, and more satisfying lives is *optional*, dependent on our attitudes, as well as our skills in responding to the conflicts and crises even the tiniest changes can stir up, and the losses they entail.

Anatole France believed that: "All changes, even the most longed for, have their melancholy; for what we leave behind us is a part of ourselves; we must die to one life before we can enter another." Yet by touching change and the conflicts it generates in the right way, i.e., with a high degree of empathy and caring, skill and attention, humility and wisdom, it becomes possible for people who are stuck in impasse and seemingly unable to change, to significantly alter its' outcomes, each other, and themselves.

Hence, every conflict is not only a place where change is frozen and unable to move, but an on-going search for ways of getting unstuck, and a potential miracle or magic that is always within our capacity to create. And as C. S. Lewis wisely advised, "You can't go back and change the beginning, but you can start where you are and change the ending."

RESISTANCE, REACTION, AND THE PHYSICS OF CHANGE

While power-based change processes trigger backlash, reaction, and rebellion; and rights-based methods strengthen bureaucracy, resistance, and weakened or compromised solutions; interest-based approaches overcome these obstacles by eliciting the underlying reasons for opposition, reducing emotional reactivity and fear of loss, and discovering creative ways of transforming hostile criticisms into suggestions for improvement, then incorporating them into the solution.

We can also learn a great deal about how things change, and about the dynamics of personal, relational, cultural, social, economic, political, and other forms of conflict, by considering the laws of change that operate in the physical world. For example, in Isaac Newton's classical three laws of motion, each can be seen to have a parallel as metaphor in the world of conflict resolution. Thus:

1. *Every object moves in a straight line unless acted upon by a force.* In conflict resolution, by analogy, the trajectory of polarization and hostility can continue in families for lifetimes; in societies for generations; and in cultures for centuries, unless the force of conflict resolution and peacebuilding are brought to bear on it.
2. *The acceleration of an object is directly proportional to the net force exerted and inversely proportional to the object's mass.* In

conflict resolution, by analogy, the intensity and
intractability of conflict are proportional to its' emotional
significance and "weight," or meaning to the parties, and
inversely proportional to its' proximity or intimacy.

3. *For every action, there is an equal and opposite reaction.* In
conflict resolution, by analogy, every adversarial action
leads to a cycle of retaliation and revenge, vendetta, and an
"eye for an eye and tooth for a tooth." But in interest-based
efforts at resolution, it is possible to shift these reactive
responses in ways that encourage empathy to resonate,
apology and forgiveness to be reciprocated, relationships to
be reconciled, and justice to be restored.

At a deeper level, in the world of conflict resolution, action and
reaction, cause and effect, fault and innocence appear separated, yet
they are also deeply united, interconnected, and equivalent. In this
sense, we can find a useful analogy in Einstein's "equivalence
principle," which equates gravitational attraction with acceleration
and the curvature of spacetime with the presence of mass. While in
conflict, as with Newton's laws of motion, the "mass" of emotional
significance and "weight," or meaning of the issues, distort the
personal, relational, systemic, and environmental space and time
within, between, and around conflicted parties, shrinking their
perceptions of distance, slowing time, separating their frames of
reference, and distorting or polarizing their perceptions of self,
other, and the issues that divide them.

Holocaust survivor Victor Frankel reminded us, "When we are no
longer able to change a situation, we are challenged to change
ourselves." Yet, as Leo Tolstoy insightfully put it, "Everyone thinks
of changing the world, but no one thinks of changing himself."
These two *arenas* of change are, of course, both unique and
inextricable. On many occasions throughout history, change agents
with the very best of intentions have denied, neglected, or papered

over the confused, amoral, and conflicted parts of their ideas, their systems, and themselves.

We have also seen what happened when some highly successful change agents, such as Mohandas K. Gandhi, Nelson Mandela, Malcolm X, Martin Luther King, Jr., Cesar Chavez, and countless others, even *partially* succeed in overcoming these divisions and were able to bring their own higher selves into the social change movements they led. This recognition led Tolstoy, with great insight, to observe:

> The changes in our life must come from the impossibility to live otherwise than according to the demands of our conscience ... not from the mental resolution to try a new form of life.

Searching for the right balance in the constantly shifting interplay between changing ourselves and changing the conditions that shape us is no easy task, since the same approach that leads to success in one set of circumstances can lead to failure in another. What is *constant* is our responsibility for resolving both. James Baldwin made this clear: "We are responsible for the world in which we find ourselves, if only because we are the only sentient force that can change it."

Conflict resolution methods allow us to improve the world, provided and to the extent that we also improve our own skills in recognizing what *actually* needs to change and what doesn't, and strengthen our capacity to coalesce, collaborate, and overcome our differences by affirming not only the value of unity and commonality with others, but the value of diversity and differences—even the value of *conflicts*, as matchless indicators of what most needs improving.

Mediation is a methodology for doing both, which is why it is important to regard it not only as a technique for settling disputes and resolving conflicts, but as a *change process* with immense transformational potential, and a useful adjunct to all attempts to bring about personal, relational, institutional, and social change.

Change stirs up conflicts, giving rise to a need to reconcile, reinvigorate, and redesign relationships, in part by drawing adversaries into dialogue, mediating their differences, and combining their interests synergistically in newer and more successful ways. By using these methods, we create a whole that is greater than the sum of its parts. Mary Parker Follett, in 1918, described how to do so:

> Instead of shutting out what is different, we should welcome it because it is different and through its difference will make a richer content of life; every difference that is swept up into a bigger conception feeds and enriches society; every difference that is ignored feeds *on* society and eventually corrupts it. ... Give *your* difference, welcome *my* difference, unify *all* difference in the larger whole — such is the law of growth.

TEN

Colonialism, De-Colonization, and Indigenous Restorative Practices

---

Blatant colonialism mutilates you without pretense: it forbids you to talk, it forbids you to act, it forbids you to exist. Invisible colonialism, however, convinces you that serfdom is your destiny and impotence is your nature: it convinces you that it's not possible to speak, not possible to act, not possible to exist.

Eduardo Galleano

The political in our time must start from the imperative to reconstruct the world in common ... a decolonization [which] is by definition a planetary enterprise, a radical openness of and to the world, a deep breathing for the world as opposed to insulation.

Achille Mbembe

There is no human failure greater than to launch a profoundly important endeavor and then leave it half done. This is what the West has done with its colonial system. It shook all the societies in the world loose from their old moorings. But it seems indifferent whether or not they reach safe harbor in the end.

Barbara Ward

EVERY HUMAN SOCIETY SINCE OUR EARLIEST BEGINNINGS HAS required skills in effective communication, collaboration, negotiation, and consensus building, along with socially accepted, culturally reinforced conflict resolution systems that help keep communities aligned and able to act in unison when conflicts or crises threaten to tear them apart. The larger, more diverse, and internally divided the group, the more advanced the dispute resolution skills and systems they require.

For this reason, it is not surprising to find that indigenous cultures around the world were the first and longest-lasting practitioners of a wide variety of dispute resolution techniques, and a rich source of wisdom and insight into systematic ways of understanding and defusing conflicts, transforming them into socially beneficial outcomes, and encouraging restorative outcomes, including restitution, redemption, forgiveness, and reconciliation.

Unfortunately, a prolonged history of colonial domination, environmental destruction, and systematic bias and discrimination directed against indigenous communities, bolstered by the widespread use of terror, military force, isolation of native cultures, and genocidal practices have all but eliminated much of this rich heritage, and continue to do so in countries around the world today.

While most indigenous, native, and aboriginal practitioners, communities, and cultures remain unrecognized, underfunded, and unsupported by the non-indigenous legal systems that try to dominate and control them, they have made, and continue to make, significant contributions to conflict resolution theory and practice, offering important insights and skills to mediators around the world.

INDIGENOUS MEDIATION PRACTICES AND TRADITIONS

There are strong, active, highly successful mediation practitioners in many indigenous communities today — for example, in many African tribes, among the Maori in New Zealand, Aboriginal communities in Australia, First Nation and Native American societies in North America, and others. These take many different forms even today — for example, the *panchayat* system in India, Pakistan, and Nepal; tribal communities using *palaver* in southern Africa, and many others.

Hundreds of cultural studies and extensive anthropological field work have shown that *every* society invents its own unique approaches to conflicts, and practices widely varied skills in resolving them. These include a wide array of conciliation, resolution, forgiveness, reconciliation, and restorative practices that deserve detailed and comprehensive study. Among them, the following five indigenous practices, in my view, deserve special mention, and as some of these may be unfamiliar, I will briefly review each, using my own personal labels, terminology, and examples.

1. "Spirit" or "Medicine" Wheel

In many indigenous communities, including a number of First Nation and Native American tribes, conflict resolution is highly regarded as an expression of wisdom, or "heart knowledge," and an integral part of each person's relationship, not only with themselves and others, but with the community as a whole, and with nature and the environment.

The fundamental approach these communities take to conflict resolution is sometimes described using the metaphor of the four cardinal directions: north, south, east, west, representing spirit, body, emotions, and mind, plus an additional two directions: one inner or *internal*, representing heart, intuition, wisdom, and subtle knowledge; and one outer or *external*, representing the environment, context, nature, and community, as illustrated in the following diagram of a "medicine" or spirit wheel.

**NATIVE AMERICAN MEDICINE
OR SPIRIT WHEEL**

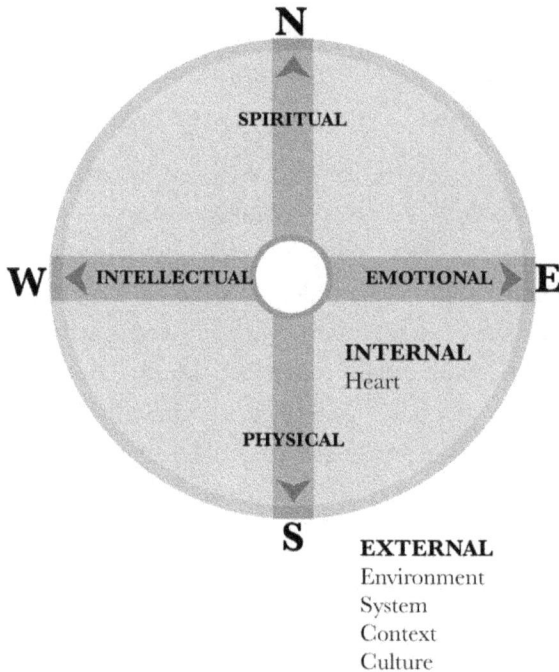

This diagram helps identify the principal *locations* and components of conflict *experience*, gain deeper insight into the sources of conflict, and envision an array of interventions, skills, techniques, and methods uniquely suited to each location. The English author Margaret Rumer Godden described these locations, based on her experience growing up in India using a different metaphor:

> There is an Indian belief that everyone is in a house of four rooms: A physical, a mental, an emotional and a spiritual. Most of us tend to live in one room most of the time, but unless we go into every room every day, even if only to keep it aired, we are not complete.

This diagram can also help mediators understand why the principal approach of many indigenous cultures to conflict resolution practice, while including skills and techniques in each location, routinely begins and ends by invoking spirit and heart, as well as the community and environment in which the conflicted parties live, on which they depend, and to which they belong.

By contrast, non-indigenous, U. S., and European mediations generally start with ground rules, then surface and analyze the issues, negotiate proposed solutions, and conclude with signed written agreements, all located primarily in the mind. While these mediators may pay attention to body language and emotions, few are skilled in spiritual or heart-based techniques, and rarely concern themselves with the environment or interests of the larger community that has been deeply impacted by the conflict.

Some of the specific techniques that naturally flow from the heart-based location or component of conflict, which often prove successful in mediation, generically include, for conflict resolution practitioners, the following steps:

- Welcome people with an open heart.
- Open with silence, or a question, invocation, prayer, meditation, or invitation directly to people's hearts.
- Ask each party to tell the others why they want to resolve the conflict, or what kind or relationship they would like to have.
- Elicit the heart-meaning of both parties' conflict stories.

- Open our hearts and use them to search for questions that invite the parties to speak and listen from theirs.
- Ask direct, honest questions that encourage integrity and trust.
- Be vulnerable and encourage vulnerability in others.
- Honestly communicate our own heartfelt insights, preferably in the form of questions.
- Encourage people to ask each other heart-felt questions and answer them openly and honestly.
- Focus attention and awareness on what is taking place at the center, core, or heart of the dispute.
- Bring insights, profundity, humor, and play into the conversation.
- Encourage participation in activities likely to result in positive, collaborative, open-hearted experiences.
- Ask each person what life lessons they learned from the conflict.
- Identify what each person is willing to do differently as a result.
- Encourage forgiveness and complete reconciliation.
- Jointly design new, more satisfying, consensual relationships.
- End with heart-felt acknowledgements and appreciations.

Similar sets of techniques and interventions can be identified for each of the other locations on the diagram. [See my personal lists of techniques for each of the six directions, in *The Crossroads of Conflict*, Second Edition (2010), Chapter 3.]

2. "Loving Confrontation"

All mediations take place within "conflict cultures," and the conflict cultures of non-indigenous, U. S., and many European countries are often intensely adversarial, competitive, self-centered, biased, and confrontational. These cultures "shape" our conflict communications, turning them into confrontations that are nearly always grounded in "negative" emotions such as anger, fear, jealousy, grief, shame, etc., which mediators then attempt to defuse and reframe, using a variety of psychological and emotionally informed interventions.

In most indigenous cultures, by contrast, there is widespread support for mediative processes that are more collaborative, socially centered, oriented to dialogue, focused on shifting people's approaches to conflict from negative to positive, and are more heart-based, empathy-inducing, poignant, and able to reinforce important social bonds and relationships. I think of these as "loving confrontations," because the people who engage in hostile, selfish, violent, and negative behaviors are not ignored or let off the hook, but confronted in a completely different, kinder, gentler, and more caring way.

Here, for example, is Alice Walker's account of the approach taken by people in the Baemba tribe in southern Africa to those who provoke conflict, or behave badly or aggressively toward others:

> [W]hen a person acts irresponsibly or unjustly, he is placed in the center of the village, alone and unfettered. All work ceases, and every man, woman, and child in the village gathers in a large circle around the accused individual. Then each person in the tribe speaks to the accused, one at a time, about all the good things the person ... has done in his lifetime. All his positive attributes, good deeds, strengths, and kindnesses are recited carefully and at length. The tribal ceremony often lasts several days. At the end, the tribal circle is broken, a joyous celebration takes place, and the person is symbolically and literally welcomed back into the tribe.

In another example, also from Africa, women who are about to give birth go into the bush or forest, accompanied by other women who will help and care for them. One of the tasks these women perform is to create a song that will welcome the child into the world and become their personal song. They sing this song during childbirth, and every year on the child's birthday. And when the child gets into conflict or behaves badly, members of the community sing the song to remind them of who they actually are, and that they can do better.

There are countless similar examples, all of which speak *directly* to the heart of the offender or perpetrator, and as a result, they are able to seamlessly support forgiveness and reconciliation, which are not artificially added on afterwards, but built into the culture. This is similar to, and a step beyond, Roger Fisher and William Ury's useful advice in *Getting to Yes*, to "separate the person from the problem," and be "hard on the problem and soft on the person."

These indigenous mediation practices represent a more *civilized* recognition that even those who are violent and aggressive, or are in pain and need care and acknowledgement, are part of the community, and vulnerable to approaches that express caring; and reinforce the parts of themselves that *know* that violence and aggression injure those it is used against, those who use it, and those they love and care about.

3. Palaver, or the "Talking Cure"

In several tribal communities and indigenous cultures, especially in Angola, Mozambique, and parts of southern Africa, mediations happen *collectively*, as when an entire tribe or community participates in discussing conflicts or problems and reaches consensus on solutions. This takes the form of "palaver," which is a kind of "talking cure," in which informal, unstructured conversations continue until everyone reaches agreement.

Tribal, elder, and village council meetings and similar practices are common in indigenous communities. Whatever they are called, these processes often consist of open, all-inclusive, non-stop dialogues, which may go through the night and last for several days, ending when consensus is reached concerning what happened and what needs to be done to fix or correct it.

It's interesting that in some European and colonial cultures, the word "palaver" is sometimes used to mean unnecessary, endless, useless conversations regarding topics that are unimportant, discounting its role in creating cohesion and coordinated responses. What matters for mediators is that conflicts are resolved *communally* by drawing diversity and dissent into open-ended dialogue in ways that naturally and incrementally give rise to fresh insights, alternative approaches, consensus-based agreements, and successful problem-solving.

4. "Self-Sentencing"

In a number of ancient indigenous cultures, if someone engages in conflict, or behaves badly, or breaks the rules, or commits a "crime," and it is believed necessary to impose some sanction or punishment on the one who did it in order to discourage future incidents, the first person who is asked to say what the punishment should be is the one who is to be punished.

If a miscreant, aggressor, or "perpetrator" suggests a penalty that is too weak, inconsequential, or self-serving, those in the community, including those who suffered, may see it as indicating a lack of remorse, denial of responsibility, insufficient empathy, or selfish attitude, and decide to impose a much harsher penalty as a way of communicating the unacceptability, not only of their conduct, but of their attitude toward the community and those they injured.

On the other hand, if the person proposes a penalty that is *too* severe, people in the community may see it as a sign of authentic remorse, acceptance of responsibility, empathy for those who suffered, an altruistic attitude, and decide to show mercy, welcome the perpetrator back into the fold, and be willing to forgive and reconcile.

A classic example of the first approach is the trial and execution of Socrates, who was asked at his trial before a 501 member Athenian jury composed of citizens selected randomly by sortition, what his punishment should be. According to Plato, he answered that he should receive "free meals for life," suggesting that he should be honored, rather than punished for what he had done. His apparent arrogance and hubris infuriated the jury, which voted 280 to 220 for his death, then paradoxically honored his request with a free cup of hemlock. Here is Plato's account of Socrates' speech in *The Apology*:

> What would be a reward suitable to a poor man who is your benefactor, and who desires leisure that he may instruct you? There can be no reward so fitting as maintenance in the Prytaneum [a dining commons in Athens where honored citizens ate for free], O men of Athens, a reward which he deserves far more than the citizen who has won the prize at Olympia in the horse or chariot race, whether the chariots were drawn by two horses or by many. For I am in want, and he has enough; and he only gives you the appearance of happiness, and I give you the reality. And if I am to estimate the penalty fairly, I should say that maintenance in the Prytaneum is the just return.

[For excellent accounts of the trial, see I. F. Stone, *The Trial of Socrates*, and Bettany Hughes, *The Hemlock Cup*.]

Somewhat later, perhaps as a result, Aristotle usefully defined justice as a fair or "due proportion," since too much punishment (or reward) is unfair, as is too little, because they both result in unequal outcomes for equal behaviors. Still later, the German philosopher Hegel took a somewhat different approach, arguing (also inspired, perhaps, by Socrates, who refused the offer to escape), that the criminal is a *citizen* who is responsible for making, following, and enforcing the laws, and therefore has an inalienable "right" to punishment, because any failure to impose punishment would strip citizenship of its meaning.

The indigenous practice of "self-sentencing," in this sense, is a far more just, civilized, democratic, respectful, dignified, empowering, mediative, effective, and unifying approach than the practice of judging and imposing penalties from outside and on high, stripping offenders of their citizenship and membership in the community; denying them the opportunity for restitution, forgiveness, and reconciliation; labeling them as perpetrators and *permanently* punishing them.

5. Restorative Justice or "Social Truth and Reconciliation"

Perhaps the most powerful and effective conflict resolution method, and one of the few to survive and successfully transition from indigenous to modern mediation practice, is restorative justice, which uniquely seeks to *heal* not only victims, but offenders, families, and communities. It does so by encouraging dignity and respect toward everyone, *including* the aggressor, wrong-doer, perpetrator, or criminal, and not out of fear, weakness, or promise of reward, but caring, empathy, compassion, and community.

Restorative justice, both as a value and a process, originated in native, indigenous, and tribal communities, especially among aboriginal and indigenous societies in New Zealand, Australia, First Nation communities in Canada, Native American tribes in the U.S., and in other countries of the global South. Among the Maori, "Utu" was an ancient practice used to resolve differences, reinforce integrity, and unite members of the community. In its modern, generic form, restorative justice is commonly based on five core ideas:

1. Conflict and crime are offenses — not just against the state, but more importantly, against victims, communities, and society as a whole.
2. Victims, offenders, relatives, neighbors, and communities, i.e., *everyone* impacted by a conflict or crime, should be able to participate in resolving it, understand why it occurred, agree on what needs to be done to repair the damage it caused, participate in the rehabilitation and redemption of

the offender, reach forgiveness and reconciliation, and restore normality for all.

3. Government's role should be limited to preserving safety, acting cooperatively, and supporting local communities in fostering peace and strengthening family and community ties.

4. Justice should not be based on revenge, retribution, and punishment, which only make people worse, but on restoring the victim, offender, community, and society as a whole, as far as possible, to fair, responsible, and productive lives.

5. The focus should not be exclusively on the past, but on the present and the future; not on humiliation, but on learning; not on facts, but on attitudes, heart, spirit, and caring; not on laws, but on values such as honesty, love, mercy, and compassion.

Modern restorative justice processes, in my experience, take place in six key steps. The first is *convening* a gathering or encounter, sometimes in the form of a "circle," in which a facilitated dialogue takes place between the victim, offender, relatives, neighbors, and members of the community. Everyone in impacted communities, neighborhoods, and families is welcome to attend, and informed about the nature and scope of the process. Process agreements may be reached–for example, that presence and participation are voluntary, that the process is confidential or not for attribution, that decisions will be reached by consensus, what will happen if consensus is not reached, that people agree to engage in open, honest, and respectful communication, and others.

A second step consists of the "victim" and "offender" telling stories about what happened, with members of the audience listening, asking questions, and adding their experiences and perceptions, sometimes having a facilitator or mediator elicit details and responses and keep the process on track so everyone can assess the truth, honesty, and contrition of the offender, recognize where he or she went wrong, and engage in dialogue that can lead to learning, forgiveness, reconciliation, and a better understanding of what happened.

A third step begins when the offender apologizes for the offense, acknowledges that it was wrong, and agrees to make amends to all who suffered. This means rejecting denials, excuses, half-hearted apologies, and rationalizations. But it also means understanding that the perpetrator, the community, the relatives and neighbors — even the victim — bear some responsibility for not having done more to prevent the offense, or correct the underlying conditions that contributed to it.

A fourth step consists of designing, fine-tuning, and reaching consensus on a program of restitution, reparation, or rehabilitation, in which the offender makes amends and agrees to compensate the victim, relatives, and community for the loss or harm they experienced. In many cases, full restitution is impossible. The object, however, is to encourage *symbolic* acts of restitution and *mutual* generosity as a demonstration of understanding, and the power of social collaboration.

A fifth step consists of designing and engaging in a ritual act or expression of forgiveness, reconciliation, redemption, and reintegration back into the community, as a strategic way of preventing repetition or recidivism, and healing traumas to the victim, offender, family members, neighbors, and society. This may include ceremonies of celebration, hugging, singing, dancing; or helping the offender find a job or treatment for drug or alcohol abuse; or on-going mentoring, supervision, counseling, and similar measures, based on a collective sense of what is needed and the creativity, energy, and commitment of the group.

A sixth step consists of *prevention* and conflict resolution systems design, in which the victim, offender, family members, and the community collaborate in trying to prevent future occurrences, and reach out to others before they become offenders or victims themselves. This may involve brainstorming, sometimes in mixed small groups, asking people in hindsight what they wish they had done differently or are willing to do differently in the future; asking the victim and offender if they would be willing to speak *together* to local groups, workplaces, or schools, and try to prevent or minimize the offending behavior at its' chronic, systemic source.

The overall goal of restorative justice is to ensure that responsibility for fixing the conflict or crime belongs principally to the *offender*, then the victim, their families, neighbors, and communities. Through open and honest dialogue, apology, acknowledgement, collaborative negotiation, creative problem-solving, mediation, and joint responsibility, those who were damaged by the offense begin to reclaim their lives, making justice both real and restorative.

OUT OF AFRICA

Restorative justice is only one of many indigenous, native, aboriginal conflict resolution practices that focus on restoring balance, harmony, and collaboration between the parties and within the larger community, resolving lingering resentments that people might otherwise hold on to, and actively encouraging forgiveness, redemption, and reconciliation.

It is widely recognized that human beings originated in Africa. What is less widely recognized is that, as a consequence, so did conflict, and so did skills in resolution. These skills then migrated several times out of Africa and spread across the world, evolving with the indigenous cultures that applied, modified, and improved them.

Many countries in Africa have produced a range of successful conflict resolution methods, based largely on dialogue, consensus building, arbitration by tribal chiefs or elders, interpretation of myths and legends, and mediative efforts by everyone in the tribe or community. Birgit Brock-Utne of the University of Oslo has written, for example, of the Acholi community in Northern Uganda, whose *"Mato Oput"* process involves:

- Acknowledgment of responsibility
- Repentance
- Asking for forgiveness
- Paying compensation
- Being reconciled through sharing a bitter drink, the *mato oput*

Brock-Utne cites the metaphor of weaving, with the warp and weft describing many tribal mediation practices in Africa:

> One of the two basic elements – the warp - is the tradition of family or neighbourhood negotiation, which is normally facilitated by elders. The other basic element – the weft - is the attitude of togetherness in the spirit of humanhood (kparakpor). Kparakpor is a Yoruba word for humanhood, ubuntu in the Zulu language of South Africa, ujamaa in Kiswahili (denoting – a family feeling of togetherness.) This concept points to the committedness [sic] to the community, as men and women of all ages are allowed to participate meaningfully in co-operation. The concept emphasizes association and relationships, as well as a collective goal, which is peace.

Similar studies have been done in many native, indigenous, and aboriginal mediation practices around the world. Wenona Victor, for example, in *Alternative Dispute Resolution (ADR) In Aboriginal Contexts: A Critical Review*, discusses three dispute resolution approaches that aboriginal communities appear have in common. The first uses "Western-based" paradigms, such as negotiation, conciliation, mediation, and arbitration; the second uses exclusively indigenous paradigms of dispute resolution; and the third consists of a combination of these approaches. Robert Neron adds to these distinctions, pointing out, in *ADR in the Aboriginal Context*:

[C]ertain concepts that form the bedrock of Western legal systems such as "blame" or "liability" and "punishment" largely do not exist in aboriginal languages. Accordingly, care should be taken not to rush blindly into the conclusion that aboriginal and non-aboriginal dispute resolution techniques can be harmonized without some difficulty.

We also find that the notion of hierarchies within the indigenous communities themselves may have an impact on how ADR sessions are conducted. The different levels of personal powers, spiritual or social, in the indigenous communities are sign of respect as opposed to oppression or control. The hierarchies between clan or community's members are based on the relations one has within the communities and their respective ability to contribute to the group... Also, the notion of time is different in the indigenous cultures than in the Western culture. For instance, the relationship building at the start of a meeting devotes to informalities of sitting together, talking and laughing are also ways in which most indigenous people interact with each other.

In my experience working with First Nation, Native American, Maori, African, and other indigenous mediators, and occasionally observing their practices, these reflections ring true. What was especially surprising to me as a non-indigenous observer at these sessions, were the following differences:

- Many hours were spent before the session began with everyone being greeted and welcomed, sitting in silence, passing a peace pipe, or expressing heartfelt concerns for the process.
- The respected role of elders included embodying and expressing the wisdom, cultural values, and *priority* of resolution, forgiveness, restoration of caring, and return to community.

- The ease and willingness of people to speak directly from their hearts was nearly universal.
- The ability to sit in silence and wait for insights or solutions to arise has almost no parallel in non-native Western cultures.
- There was a strong sense of collective responsibility for the success of the process.
- An immense amount of time was spent afterwards acknowledging, expressing gratitude, offering detailed examples, and celebrating the participants, which once included dances put on by children for the parties and the mediators, which sometimes lasted for hours.

It was remarkable to me, in the first place, how successful these practices were in reducing tensions, resolving conflicts, and returning people to collaboration, trust, and community; and in the second place, that they were able to do so in the context of colonial systems that had spent centuries trying to undermine and destroy them.

To more fully understand what modern, non-indigenous mediators can learn from these approaches to resolution and search for synergistic ways of combining them with native practices, it is important to grasp, even briefly and generically, the nature and legacy of colonialism, and how we can "decolonize" mediation, strip it of its' deep-seared biases, attitudes, and assumptions; and improve relationships between indigenous and non-indigenous peoples and cultures.

COLONIALISM AND CONFLICT

Colonialism is a vast subject with a lengthy history and many diverse forms critiqued by hundreds of writers whose work cannot be summarized adequately in a few pages. A smattering may suffice to expose the nature and destructive impact of colonialism, including its effect not only on indigenous communities, but on the subtle, unspoken assumptions that underlie conflict resolution practices in nations and cultures that practiced colonialism.

The German historian Jürgen Osterhammel defined colonialism, in *Colonialism: A Theoretical Overview*, not just as a program or policy, but as a *relationship* grounded in domination, superiority, and power:

> Colonialism is a relationship between an indigenous (or forcibly imported) majority and a minority of foreign invaders. The fundamental decisions affecting the lives of the colonised people are made and implemented by the colonial rulers in pursuit of interests that are often defined in a distant metropolis. Rejecting cultural compromises with the colonised population, the colonisers are convinced of their own superiority and their ordained mandate to rule.

Karl Marx viewed colonialism as a first step in the evolution of capitalism, which brutally exploited the gold, labor, and raw materials of less powerful countries, stripping their natural resources to feed large scale industrial production:

> The discovery of gold and silver in America, the extirpation, enslavement and entombment in mines of the indigenous population of that continent, and the conversion of Africa into a preserve for the commercial hunting of blackskins, are all things which characterize the dawn of an era of capitalist production. These idyllic proceedings are the chief moments of primitive accumulation.

In order to dominate the colonized, the colonizer had to erect clear barriers and divisions to keep them separate and apart, provoking a fear of violence, contamination, and disease to rationalize the barriers. Frantz Fanon wrote:

> The colonial world is a world divided into compartments. It is probably unnecessary to recall the existence of native quarters and European quarters, of schools for natives and schools for Europeans; in the same way we need not recall Apartheid in South Africa. Yet if we examine closely this system of compartments, we will at least be able to reveal the lines of force it implies. This approach to the colonial world, its ordering and geographical lay-out will allow us to mark the lines on which a decolonized society will be reorganized.

In the 20th century, after slavery was abolished in favor of free labor, colonial occupation gave way to *neo*-colonialism, a term introduced by Jean-Paul Sartre and Kwame Nkrumah, President of Ghana, to explain the system of economic dependence on former colonial powers, including favorable treatment for large multinational corporations, endemic corruption, national indebtedness, covert funding for military coups, regime changes to oust independent leaders, humanitarian crises, repression of civil society and labor unions, opposition to economic development, environmental pillage, and similar measures.

Nkrumah interestingly described neo-colonialism as "an attempt to export the social conflicts of the capitalist countries" to their poorer neighbors in the global South. If we think of colonialism and neo-colonialism as power-based relationships designed to strip resources from those less powerful and externalize their internal conflicts, we can imagine how these large-scale issues might scale down even to tiny interpersonal relationships and workplaces.

The essence of all forms of colonialism can be described quite simply as domination plus theft, with periodic efforts to suppress opposition and resistance, and *systematically* eradicate — not only the language, religion, and culture of the colonized, but the slightest tendencies toward self-determination, independence, equality, democracy, development, dialogue, and mediation. Each of these became a source of chronic, systemic, seemingly intractable conflicts.

Domination can take thousands of forms. It is not just physical, but psychological, emotional, spiritual, and environmental. What is stolen can include anything from land and agricultural or mineral resources to labor and free time, citizenship and self-determination, dignity and self-confidence, sexual expression and cultural identity, happiness and love. And the form of domination can be violent and non-violent, legal and extra-legal, genocidal and tolerant, patriarchal and infantilizing. All of these undermine traditional conflict resolution goals and practices, and impose instead the laws, languages, self-interests, and methods of the colonizers.

Ashis Nandy insightfully described British colonialism in India, explaining how it sought to resolve the conflicts it created by shaping even the ways people thought about resisting and rebelling against it:

> Conformity need not be monitored; dissent has to be. In any hegemony, dissent defines the limits and the final shape or legitimacy of a system, not conformity.... You are taught to fight established authorities according to the conventions authorized by the authorities themselves, so that rebellion gradually becomes a matter of apprenticeship and learning correct radical praxis according to texts produced in the global citadels of knowledge.

Indeed, as Albert Memmi wrote earlier, in his profound book, *The Colonizer and the Colonized*, the colonizers' approach to the colonized *guaranteed* that conflicts would turn chronic:

> The more oppression increases, the more the colonizer needs justification. The more he must debase the colonized, the more guilty he feels, the more he must justify himself, etc. How can he emerge from this increasingly explosive circle except by rupture, explosion? The colonial situation, by its own internal inevitability,

brings on revolt. For the colonial condition cannot be adjusted to; like an iron collar, it can only be broken.

Again, it is not difficult to refine, reframe, and extend these observations so they apply not only to large-scale geo-political institutions and policies, but to small-scale interpersonal relationships in marriages, families, neighborhoods, and workplaces, where neo-colonial attitudes and styles of communication produce similar patterns.

Another useful metaphor for describing the pervasively inhumane attitudes of colonizers to those they colonize, originates in artificial intelligence, which describes "catastrophic forgetting," in which AI learning programs routinely lose everything they previously learned with each new task they were given. Similarly, colonial relationships of domination, theft, and suppression require colonizers to "catastrophically forget" everything "human" about the colonized that might require them to act equally and fairly, or lead to ending the colonial relationship. At the same time, the colonizers force the indigenous colonized to forget their culture and everything they once knew or did, in order to encourage total reliance on the colonizer's cultures and practices.

One of the aims of colonizers in doing so is to reduce the colonized to a state of infantile surrender, social chaos, economic dependence, and political disorder that *retroactively* justifies colonial domination. In this way, as Jean-Paul Sartre wrote in his preface to Albert Memmi's *The Colonizer and The Colonized*, the colonizers systematically debased the colonized "in order to exalt themselves":

> Thus oppression justifies itself through oppression: the oppressors produce and maintain by force the evils that render the oppressed, in their eyes, more and more like what they would have to be like to deserve their fate. The colonizer can only exonerate himself in the systematic pursuit of the 'dehumanization' of the colonized by identifying himself a little more each day with the colonialist

apparatus... The engine of colonialism turns in a circle; it is impossible to distinguish between its praxis and objective necessity. ... The system wills simultaneously the death and multiplication of its victims.

One explanation for this pursuit of dehumanization, offered by Frantz Fanon in his classic study, *The Wretched of the Earth*, was that it forced the colonized to concede the validity of what the colonizers subconsciously *knew* was untrue:

[The colonizer] only ends his work of breaking in the native when the latter admits loudly and intelligibly the supremacy of the white man's values.

To which Albert Memmi added that the colonial system finds its' *complete* and highest expression in the brutal domination, authoritarian politics, supremacist stereotypes, aggressive provocations, and genocidal practices that are the core elements of fascist ideology:

Every colonial nation carries the seeds of a fascist temptation in its bosom. What is fascism if not a regime of oppression for the benefit of a few.

The recent discovery of hidden mass graves at religious schools for indigenous children in Canada and the U.S., and similar revelations in Australia involving Aboriginal children who were forcibly removed from their parents and communities, reinforce the need to understand the *culture* of colonialism, and the subtle ways it influences approaches to diversity, dissent, dialogue, democracy, and conflict resolution, even today.

The dynamics of colonial thinking are grounded in the idea that, for colonizers to defend their unequal status, wealth, and power, it is essential that they rigorously suppress any sense among the colonized that they are equal, or entitled to be heard and respected, and systematically disregard and dismantle any residual, subconscious recognition of their humanity. For this reason, Sartre added, "Oppression means, first of all, the oppressor's hatred of the oppressed."

Martin Luther King Jr. described nearly identical practices in the relationship between the U. S., which had itself been a colony of England, and its colonization of its' own indigenous populations:

> Our nation was born in genocide when it embraced the doctrine that the original American, the Indian, was an inferior race …. We are perhaps the only nation which tried as a matter of national policy to wipe out its indigenous population. Moreover, we elevated that tragic experience into a noble crusade. Indeed, even today we have not permitted ourselves to reject or feel remorse for this shameful episode. Our literature, our films, our drama, our folklore all exalt it.

One of the primary means by which this was accomplished was through the active *instigation* of social, economic, political, and territorial conflicts, which were used to justify the colonist in exercising violence and dictatorial power over and against the colonized, legitimizing the suspension of legal protections, and creating a *culture* of hatred and fear, bullying and submission, aggression and accommodation, cruelty and moral disengagement, to justify seizing native land.

Indeed, one of the many subtle sources of genocide is that the mere *existence* of those who have been treated cruelly acts as a mirror that reflects back and continually reminds the oppressor — not only of what they have done, but of who they have *become*, of the inadequately repressed falsity of their own justifications, and their complete alienation from empathy and kindness.

It is partly for this reason that colonialist and fascist governments invariably regard mediation, dialogue, empathy, compassion, and other conflict resolution methods as weak, coddling, and subversive; or, as in Munich immediately before World War II, as a crafty, consciously dishonest way of manipulating public opinion in order to achieve asymmetrical outcomes that favor only themselves.

Because mediation, dialogue, and conflict resolution are *inherently* egalitarian, empathetic, and empowering, colonists have nearly always refused to participate openly, honestly, and equally in them, and instead sought to manipulate, distort, and "cherry-pick" its practices to gain advantage over others, coerce compliance, and preserve their zero-sum superiority in status, wealth, and power.

DECOLONIZING MEDIATION

Because of the subtlety, depth, reach, and endurance of colonialism, successful decolonization requires not one or two, but *three* separate and distinct significant changes. First, there needs to be a complete, *unambiguous* ending of colonial policies and practices, which include not only their cessation and prohibition by law, but their *transcendence* through openness, honesty, and "truth and reconciliation" style conversations, open dialogues, sincere apologies, and sustained efforts to repair and restore the losses suffered by the colonized, in status, wealth, and power, or in the *interests* they represent.

Second, there needs to be a mutual transcendence of *relationships* of domination, theft, and suppression, in the form of increased expressions of empathy by those who were formerly colonizers, increased recognition of the dignity and pride of those who were formerly colonized, and increased unity in opposition to subtle, covert, on-going efforts to re-impose relationships of domination, theft, and suppression. Colonizer and colonized become humanized to each other through the *process* of completely freeing themselves from the colonial relationship.

Third, after these goals have been achieved, there needs to be a *transcendence* of the entire history and culture of colonialism, including both apology and pride, in opposition to those who would cling to them, or assert them as grounds for denying the rights of others to equal dignity and pride, and return to chronic conflicts based on colonial practices. It may then become possible for native and non-native people and cultures, for the first time, to genuinely appreciate and learn from each other. Frantz Fanon described it more dramatically:

> In decolonisation, there is ... the need of a complete calling in question of the colonial situation. If we wish to describe it precisely, we might find it in the well-known words: 'The last shall be first and the first last.' Decolonisation is the putting into practice of this sentence.

The goal, however, is not to create an "inverse colonialism" or colonize the colonizers. This, indeed, is the primal, subconscious fear of the colonizer, born of guilt and a desperate resistance to change. It is also a primal, subconscious desire of the colonized, born of pain and a desire for the colonizer to know for once what it felt like. But the *complete* elimination of colonialism requires a deeper, systemic, *mediated* transcendence of domination, and a lengthier iterative, cyclical process of learning how to communicate, interact, and build non-colonial relationships.

Decolonization is an effort to reverse colonial assumptions and practices—not just on a large scale by recognizing the political, economic, social, cultural, and environmental integrity and sovereignty of indigenous people; but on a small scale, by acknowledging personal boundaries and diverse perspectives; reframing the *language* we use to describe our differences; and designing conflict resolution *systems* that support the right to self-determination on all scales, including the right to independence. All of these are common goals in mediation.

One example of how we might reframe and de-colonize language has been suggested by Native American writer Steven Newcomb, who distinguishes patriotism from what he calls "matriotism":

> Matriotism is based on an appreciation of the fact that the source of life, air, food, and water and our very existence is Mother Earth, not the political construct known as the United States. When people talk about 'a country' in relation to 'patriotism,' they are talking about a political entity, not the Earth. ... A matriot is someone who loves, is loyal to, and promotes the interests of Mother Earth. I consider myself deeply matriotic.

Another example can be found in indigenous and cross-cultural conflict resolution practices. One of the reasons many non-native mediators are interested in native approaches to dispute resolution is that a great deal of what we regard as indigenous is, at a deeper level, simply *human,* which has been repressed, forgotten, lost, or covered over. These include native insights that are often experienced by non-natives as profound, heartfelt, and spiritual, yet feel familiar and are immediately subconsciously recognized. Part of what indigenous cultures therefore represent to the non-indigenous are the *externalized,* alienated, missing, holistic parts of *themselves* that can only be accessed and reclaimed by means of listening, empathy, dialogue, mediation, and similar practices–i.e., by de-colonization on the scale of *personal,* as well as social, economic, political, and environmental relationships.

This realization is an important step in the direction of decolonization. A related and equally essential step consists of looking honestly, unflinchingly, and critically at the ways our perceptions, ideas, feelings, and behaviors have been biased and skewed by *centuries* of rationalizations, defenses, justifications, and self-serving separations of self and other–especially for the colonizer, but also for the colonized, and the complex, multi-layered relationships between them.

These distortions have taken thousands of different forms, some buried so deep we are unaware of their influence. Among them is a loss of the *capacity* for openhearted dialogue, collaboration across cultural divides, joint opposition to the inhumane treatment of others, and a willingness to accept highly destructive environmental practices. More deeply, it is the subconscious acceptance of a false sense of superiority and inferiority. For this reason, as the famous South African anti-Apartheid activist Steve Biko trenchantly observed, "The most potent weapon in the hands of the oppressor is the mind of the oppressed."

If we want to reverse the impact of centuries of domination, theft, cultural erasure, environmental alienation, and systematic suppression of efforts to change them, it is essential that we take an additional step and make amends or reparations — just as we encourage people to do in restorative justice, victim/offender mediation, 12 step addiction programs, and similar processes — and that we do so in ways that address not only economic harm, but social, political, cultural, relational, environmental, and other kinds of harm as well. The perspective of the colonized on this issue was well captured by Frantz Fanon:

> Colonialism and imperialism have not settled their debt to us once they have withdrawn from our territories. The wealth of the imperialist nations is also our wealth. Europe is literally the creation of the third world.

It is, of course, not even *remotely* possible for former slave owning colonial powers to entirely repair or make up for the damage they caused during centuries of enslavement, plunder, and degradation, and the effort to do so focuses primarily on efforts to erase the past, rather than on securing a better present and future.

Instead, I believe the goals should be: first, to mark a clear, unambiguous, *symbolic* end to the ongoing, sometimes subconscious colonial practices of domination, exploitation, and control; second, to collectively own, apologize for, and commit to reversing the damage they caused; third, to use debt cancellation, social infrastructure investments, and economic and property transfers to jump-start native investments and equalize future negotiating power; and fourth, to begin creating the conditions for fundamentally transformed future interactions and relationships based on inclusion, mutual respect, equality, empowerment, self-determination, and collaboration.

There are significant psychological obstacles to remedying these relationships on both sides. For example, in his fascinating study of "the colonizer who refuses" colonialism, Albert Memmi describes the obstacles faced by humanitarians among the colonizers who empathize with the colonized and as a result, are seen by other colonizers as having gone over to the side of the enemy, yet are regarded by the colonized as outsiders, and not fully accepted by either camp.

Yet it is often the case that these individuals can play important roles as mediators, facilitators, witnesses, symbols, harbingers of future collaboration, and personal representatives of what William Ury calls the "third side," which supports neither one nor the other, but both; that is, is *simultaneously* "on the side" of everyone, which I described earlier as "omni-partiality."

Yet the role of mediators in highly polarized political conflicts is problematic because conflict resolvers can have one of two fundamentally different orientations: first, to seek compromise, conciliation, and settlement, which requires some degree of accommodation to a deeply dysfunctional system; or second, to seek resolution, transformation, and transcendence, and eliminate the chronic, systemic, underlying reasons that gave rise to the conflict.

The first form of mediation seeks a temporary accommodation between the colonizer and the colonized *without* addressing the system or structure of colonialism. The second seeks to accept the *person* of the colonizer while refusing to accept the *practice* of colonialism. It recognizes the dignity, equality, and suffering of the colonized, yet refuses to ignore, diminish, or erase the real harm experienced by both, and does not falsely equate them. It seeks to transcend colonialism as a *system* by drawing the parties into dialogue and negotiation, building consensus on the kind of relationship they would like to have with each other, and what each of them is prepared to do to make this happen. It is restorative justice applied to the system of colonialism.

In truth, this second, more complex form of mediation is *already* a transcendence of colonial intentions, assumptions, and expectations. Mediation is *inherently*, in its values and practices, implicitly and explicitly egalitarian, collaborative, and democratic, which colonial systems are forced to reject, as they systematically undermine the *project* of domination, and lead eventually to ending it.

Mediation is also important because the *last* step in decolonization, after all the others have been completed, is for both sides to affirm that their common humanity is stronger than the differences that have divided them. Doing so requires them to *invent* together the skills and methods they need to jointly turn their diversity and commonality in the direction of solving common problems.

One of the fundamental issues in every mediation is the relationship between Self and Other. On a personal level, colonialism consists of small acts that can be called "micro-dominations," which seek to dismiss–not only the other person's perceptions, thoughts, feelings, and experiences, but their *right* to perceive, think, feel, and experience differently, and *for themselves.*

In an intriguing comment, Jiddhu Krishnamurti distinguished the colonial division of people into separate, often adversarial, sometimes violent identities, from mediative inclusiveness, non-alienation of self from other, and the conflict resolution approach of "non-violent communication":

> When you call yourself an Indian or a Muslim or a Christian or a European, or anything else, you are being violent. Do you see why it is violent? Because you are separating yourself from the rest of mankind. When you separate yourself by belief, by nationality, by tradition, it breeds violence. So a man who is seeking to understand violence does not belong to any country, to any religion, to any political party or partial system; he is concerned with the total understanding of mankind.

The difficulty non-violent communication and conflict resolution techniques face is one of discovering in each distinct conflict how to reinforce the *context* of commonality and "total understanding" between hostile parties, while at the same time acknowledging and affirming the separate elements that make them unique, designing ways of creatively combining these elements, and turning their attention in the direction of jointly solving whatever problems they face.

The great advantage of conflict resolution is that it is possible to do so not only on a small-scale between individual disputants, but on mid- and large scales, within work teams and organizations, between communities and cultures, and among nation-states. The increasing success of conflict resolution processes in dismantling small- and mid-scale colonial-like behaviors helps us imagine how we might do the same in large-scale relationships.

As with the abolition of slavery and feudalism, it will not be easy or quick for people to surrender the superior status, wealth, and power that flows from colonial domination; or the cultural prejudices and privileges that promote satisfaction in one's supposed superiority; or the corrupt profits that proceed from exploitation, oppression, and environmental plunder.

Every day we see abundant signs that our destinies overlap, that the domination of others dominates us, that theft from others steals our integrity and peace of mind, that plundering our environment plunders our future, that the greatest problems we face cannot be solved using violence, exploitation, prejudice, and alienation, and that we are running out of time.

Indigenous conflict resolution practices, creatively combined with a wide range of successful non-indigenous mediation methods, can help us illuminate and orient the transition from small- to mid- and large-scale practices that will permit us to redress systemic power imbalances. We can start by improving our skills in listening empathetically and open-heartedly, communicating non-violently and spiritually, negotiating collaboratively and respectfully, meditating dangerously and caringly, and in these ways, *model* decolonized, inclusive, indigenous-informed approaches to diversity and dissent that invite us to walk together and carve new paths that others may follow. The Greek novelist Nikos Kazantzakis described this approach beautifully:

> As you walk, you cut open and create that riverbed into which the stream of your descendants shall enter and flow.

ELEVEN

Ending the War in Ukraine and All Wars

LONG-TERM LESSONS FOR MEDIATORS AND PEACE BUILDERS

If men hate each other, then there's no hope. We will all be victims of that hate. We will slaughter each other in wars we don't want and for which we're not responsible. They'll put a flag in front of us and fill our ears with words. And why? To plant the seeds for a new war, to create more hatred, to create new flags and new words. Is that why we're here? To have children and hurl them into the fiery furnace? To build cities and then raze them to the ground? To long for peace and have war instead? ... The day when we can build on love has still not arrived.

Jose Saramago

[T]he man of violence ... cannot exempt himself from suffering. His occasional efforts to destroy others are merely a roundabout route to his own destruction. Beneath his self-confidence, his braggadocio, lurks a fanatic of disaster. ... And we are all violent—men of anger who, having lost the key of quietude, now have access only to the secrets of laceration.

E. M. Cioran

No matter the paid parades, the forced applause, the instigated riots, the organized protests (pro or con), self- or state censoring, the propaganda; no matter the huge opportunities for profit and gain; no matter the history of injustice – at bottom it is impossible to escape the suspicion that the more sophisticated the weapons of war, the more antiquated the idea of war. The more transparent the power grab, the holier the justification, the more arrogant the claims, the more barbaric, the more discredited the language of war becomes.

Toni Morrison

WE UNDERSTAND THAT WAR IS CRUEL AND POINTLESSLY DESTRUCTIVE; that it is immensely costly on every level, that it brutalizes and traumatizes everyone and everything it touches–so why is there still war in the 21st century? Hannah Arendt, with special importance for mediators and peacebuilders, suggested a practical and strategic answer:

The chief reason warfare is still with us is neither a secret death wish of the human species, nor an irrepressible instinct of aggression, nor, finally and more plausibly, the serious economic and social dangers inherent in disarmament, but the simple fact that no substitute for this final arbiter in international affairs has yet appeared on the political scene.

Yet, if this is the case, we can suggest that mediation and peace building are improving rapidly, and nearly ready to appear on the political scene. Margaret Atwood offered an alternative, yet similar answer: "War is what happens when language fails." As mediators, we can add that war is what happens when people are demonized and disrespected; when needs are left unaddressed and interests unsatisfied; when pressing problems are ignored; when intense emotions are unheard and unacknowledged; when conflicts are allowed to fester, turning small, preventable, easily resolvable differences into unavoidable, intractable crises in which violence seems the only way out. And this happens on all scales. Every mountain was a molehill once. There was *always* an earlier time when opportunities to prevent disputes from becoming overwhelming or turning violent were readily available and more easily implemented, yet completely ignored. When mediators and peace builders were present, yet marginalized and dismissed.

Ukraine, like all violence and all wars, is a failure — not only of language, but of *caring*, listening, imagination, skill, determination, and our inadequate efforts as mediators to strengthen our conflict resolution capacity and transform the ways we think about, respond to, and *prevent* conflicts--and not just personally, relationally, and organizationally, but socially, economically, politically, culturally, and environmentally. Many interesting, important, useful, and insightful articles have been written exploring the war in Ukraine, but rather than focus on the particular history, background, incidents, and motivations that led to this devastating collapse of peace and civility, I want to consider the lessons and implications for mediators, peace builders, dialogue facilitators, collaborative negotiators, diversity professionals, restorative justice practitioners, and similar disciplines, who are becoming highly experienced— albeit on a smaller scale — in assisting committed adversaries and hostile parties to reach agreements and resolve their conflicts. What, then, are the *generic* lessons of the war in Ukraine, and all wars, for conflict resolvers? First, *numerous* advance warnings, predictable outcomes, and opportunities to mediate the underlying issues were present *long* before the invasion, as they are in conflicts on all scales. Second, as in all conflicts, these were ignored, repressed, and made worse by arrogance, bullying, demonization, insults, posturing, trivialization, dismissals of dialogue, and refusals to bargain or mediate–not only by the immediate parties, but their proxies, supporters, critics and detractors around the world. To solve these problems and prevent future wars, we need *higher order* skills in a wide array of political dispute resolution techniques, collaborative forms of *diplomacy*, new approaches to social justice, and innovative ways of *imagining* nation states that allow us to shift from competitive power- and rights-based methods to collaborative interest-based ones. [See Chapter 12.]. As journalist Anne O'Hare McCormick wrote following World War II, "the real test of power is not capacity to make war but capacity to prevent it."

WAR AS A CONTINUATION OF POLITICS

The Prussian military strategist Carl von Clausewitz famously defined war as "the continuation of politics by other means." The root causes of all wars can nearly always be found in the inability to resolve social, economic, political, and environmental conflicts; or to listen, acknowledge, collaborate, and satisfy both sides' interests in non-zero-sum ways.

The war in Ukraine, like most wars, is not the result of a single, solitary incident, isolated issues, or conflicted histories, but an escalation in a larger power contest to determine which countries, cultures, systems, and views of the world will win, dominate, and get to determine the future for others, or whether they will find ways of solving problems collaboratively, with lasting consequences for all.

Just as wars in Ethiopia, Manchuria, and Spain presaged World War II, and skirmishes in "Bleeding Kansas" foreshadowed the U.S. Civil War, the contest for dominance in Ukraine suggests an increasing willingness to bypass rights-based principles of international law, which, once weakened, can be cited to justify the aggressive, barbaric use of military, economic, and political force, sparking similar violations elsewhere. The most important of these legal rights aim to protect civilians from war crimes and to defend the principles of sovereignty, self-determination, and independence.

The war in Ukraine is thus deeply linked to a number of seemingly disconnected *political* conflicts between democracy and autocracy taking place around the world. In this sense the war represents a rejection by autocrats in and out of power — not just in Russia, but in the U.S., Hungary, Sudan, Israel, India, and elsewhere — of the core tenets of democracy, and the right of people to speak, debate, vote, dissent, legally regulate, and participate in their own governments.

This is because wars *require* governments to manipulate the ways people think and use language, and to censor media and distort communications in a power-based effort to *unilaterally* determine who will govern, which policies the victor will be able to implement, and the *limits* of what can be done to the vanquished. In these ways, war always makes the leaders of war-like countries seem cruel, unjust, and insane to anyone observing them from the outside. As George Orwell observed, "Every war when it comes, or before it comes, is represented not as a war, but as an act of self-defense against a homicidal maniac."

War is indeed a form of insanity, a loss of reason, a crime, an irrational, "evil" approach to problem-solving, all of which appears more clearly the more obvious and available solutions become. Yet the insanity, criminality, and evil we ascribe to our opponents in nearly every conflict can easily be turned into justifications for our *own* aggression, violence, and crimes against humanity.

There is thus a common thread linking what Russia and Ukraine *stand for* politically to each other with seemingly disconnected disputes, for example, over the January 6, 2021, insurrection in the U.S., masks and vaccines, restrictions on the right to vote, climate change, renewable energy, abortion, "critical race theory," LGBTQ+ issues, banning and burning books, the rise of white supremacy and antisemitism, police violence, gun control, and similar topics.

These divergent, hotly contested beliefs, attitudes, perspectives, and values point to deeper sources of conflict in our relationships with one another, leading to contrasting approaches to problem-solving, negotiation, and conflict resolution, and giving rise to vastly different futures for the planet. These differences, from a conflict resolution perspective, can be defined by their *orientation* either to competitive, adversarial, hierarchical, "zero sum," power- or rights-based processes, relationships, and cultures; or to shared, collaborative, heterarchical, "non-zero-sum" interest-based ones. Below is a rough, partial list of these differences.

ZERO-SUM ORIENTATION	NON-ZERO-SUM ORIENTATION
Autocratic	Democratic
Authoritarian	Collaborative
Aggressive	Accommodative
Hierarchical	Heterarchical
Domination/Superiority	Partnership/Equality
Power- or Rights-Based	Interest-Based
Rule Driven	Values Driven
Uniformity/Conformity	Diversity/Complexity
Monologues/Voting	Dialogues/Consensus
Focus on Order and Security	Focus on Equity and Justice
War, Violence	Diplomacy, Peacebuilding
Rigid Race, Class and Caste Roles	Fluid Race, Class and Caste Roles
Restricted Roles for Women	Gender Equality
Shaming of LGBTQ People	Inclusion of LGBTQ People
Hostility to Outsiders	Welcoming of Outsiders
Suspicion of Science	Respect for Science
Censorship of Books, Art	Literary and Artistic Freedom
Focus on Blaming, Fault Finding	Focus on Joint Problem-solving
Resistance to Change	Encouragement of Change
Norms of Secrecy	Norms of Transparency
Isolated, Divided, and Private	Interactive, Connected, and Social
Uniformity, Conformity	Diversity, Freedom
Conflict Avoidance/Aggression	Conflict Resolution/Prevention

These differences lead either to *divisive* attitudes that regard others as competitors and adversaries; or to *inclusive* ones that regard them as collaborators and allies. The first set *appear* to make sense when problems are seen as local, or there are scarce resources, or fierce competition for dominance or survival. The second set make more sense when problems are seen as global, there are sufficient resources to share, survival is not an issue, and collaboration, empathy, sharing, and fairness produce better and more satisfying outcomes.

Each of these competing orientations leads to profoundly different social values, economic systems, forms of government, and environmental policies. Each triggers different ideas and emotions; rewards and penalizes different attitudes toward others; utilizes different processes; encourages different relationships; and invites different approaches to dialogue, problem-solving, negotiation, and conflict resolution.

The first orientation leads to heightened perceptions of fear and loss, leading to increased willingness to use war and violence to win *over and against* "enemies." The second leads to heightened perceptions of commonality and increasing willingness to use mediation and peace building to win *with and for* others, strengthening unity and collaboration, and eliminating the need for enemies.

Power-based systems on all scales have a strong need to *create* enemies, both without and within, in order to justify fear, hatred, and suspicion of others. Diversity and dissent can then be cast as sedition, betrayal, and treason, which are "perfect" accusations, because they suggest sinister motives that justify duplicity, stereotypes, distrust of differences, hostility to dissent, a need to keep silent about things that matter, and a rationale for harming others. Peacemaking, conflict resolution, and interest-based political systems require the *surrender* of these adversarial assumptions, and with them, the need to create enemies.

The war in Ukraine, like many wars, is an escalating move in a competitive power contest. In this case, the contest is aggravated by the waning of a post-World War II "Pax Americana," as well as by increasingly polarized responses to climate change and migration, the rise of autocracies, a shift in global economic power and hegemony, escalating competition for natural resources and consumer markets, antiquated cold war thinking, a race for technological supremacy, and catastrophic environmental changes, each encouraging resort to military solutions where diplomacy and political solutions have failed to satisfy national interests.

CONFLICT AND THE NARROWING OF OPTIONS

If we consider just one of these issues, and imagine a dystopian future in which we fail to stop global warming, leading to a catastrophic collapse in the ability of hundreds of millions of people to survive in their countries of origin — like what is occurring today, but on a vastly larger scale–we can predict that massive numbers of people will begin to migrate in search of survival or a better life. The options available to nation states as a result will increasingly narrow down to two: First, they can pursue a policy of exclusion, selfishness, and "us first," resulting in walls, fences, hyper-competition, starvation, stereotyping, ostracism, fear, hatred, cruelty, violence, wars, and global genocides. Second, they can pursue a policy of inclusion, sharing, and "us together," resulting in triage and tremendous difficulties, but also in bridges, support, collaboration, openness, empathy, caring, mediation, peace building, social justice, and community.

The first option requires autocracy, enemies, hatred, distrust, elimination of independent journalism, censorship, book burning, cultures of enmity, conflict, and aggression, and cultures of permanent war. The second requires democracy, allies, empathy, trust building, journalistic freedom, open dialogue, conflict resolution, and cultures of peace and collaboration. Each of these paths demands fundamentally different skill sets, including our capacity for listening, empathy, dialogue, collaboration, negotiation, mediation, restorative justice, and other forms of conflict resolution. Each culminates in divergent futures, raising the stakes, and either increasing or decreasing the willingness of people to kill and die in their efforts to achieve them. If this perception is correct, efforts to support Ukraine, which is gaining momentum, will be opposed—not only by autocrats, nationalists, and militarists everywhere, for reasons that have little to do with Ukraine or Russia — but by those who seek the illusion of personal security through autocratically imposed political order, or simply feel they lack the skills to solve global problems collaboratively.

At a deeper, paradoxical, and counter-intuitive level, war is a form of conflict resolution—-one that seeks to resolve disputes by destroying the other side, without realizing that the other side also exists *inside us,* in the form of our *capacity* for empathy and collaboration. If we can activate these capacities in *any* conflict, people may begin to relate to their opponents as human beings, which will sap their will to kill and die for some distant cause, even within invading armies and the citizens of aggressor nations. A frequent justification for war and lesser forms of violence is that we have to put an end to conflicts caused by others, and the only effective options are to murder, crush, and silence those on the other side, whose very efforts at self-defense are seen as acts of aggression. Yet by doing so, we also, less obviously, murder, crush, and silence our capacity for trust, collaboration, honesty, empathy, compassion, integrity, wisdom, hope, curiosity, and caring—both in our opponents, and increasingly in ourselves as well.

As a result, war and violence make it nearly impossible to act fairly or jointly, or prevent and solve common problems, turning them into conflicts, crises, and catastrophes. Yet it is possible, *before* conflicts escalate, to replace zero-sum, power- and rights-based approaches with non-zero-sum, interest-based options, and encourage non-violent communication, dialogue, joint problem-solving, collaborative negotiation, consensus building, mediation, and restorative justice.

It will be far more difficult, but equally important, to replace autocratic forms of political decision-making: *first,* with formal, rights-based, *procedural* democracies that provide a floor made of law; and *second*, with informal, interest-based, *substantive* democracies that seek a ceiling made of hope, in which people are no longer regarded as political *objects* to be manipulated, but *subjects* entitled to voice their concerns both individually and collectively; and to participate *directly* in problem-solving, decision-making, and collaborative relations with others.

Wars *require* autocracies, which require passive, compliant, obedient, consenting citizens. The paltry excuses and flimsy justifications offered by politicians for autocratic rule, military aggression, invasion, and the murder of innocents *always* break down over time, even in dictatorial regimes. This initially leads merely to silence, then doubt, courageous dissent, increasing opposition, and a growing sense of the pointlessness and futility of applying military solutions to non-military problems. This malaise saps morale, not only among students, intellectuals, critics, and artists; but soldiers, civil servants, military leaders, and those who feel oppressed, or harbor an empathetic, or moral distaste for violence.

In a former life, I spent many years working to end the war in Vietnam, including with draftees, dissenting soldiers, and veterans. A significant contribution to stopping the war came from their outspoken opposition, and the unraveling of an unquestioned political consensus in the U.S. and its' allies—and not only among students, intellectuals, critics, and artists, but within the military itself, spreading outwards, and steadily weakening the ability to justify the war's escalating cruelty, or even *imagine* what it would mean to be victorious.

Rather than regard rigidly repressed civilians and fleeing émigrés as the sole source of anti-war sentiment in Russia, we need to consider the impact of increasing numbers of disaffected soldiers and draftees, who played a major role in convincing decision-makers in the US to withdraw from Vietnam. A major role can also be played by shifting international support, especially in Brazil, South Africa, and China, where the U. S. could easily offer trade and diplomatic inducements in exchange for their opposition to the war.

As Russian soldiers experience a significant collapse of their will to fight, which is already in progress, even in the mercenary Wagner Group, military and security officials will be forced to step in to save Russia from collapse. This could be the most important result of arming Ukraine, and calls for mediation and negotiation — *without* getting stuck on what the outcomes or positions of each side should be. As the Vietnamese demonstrated, fighting and negotiating can be combined in strategic ways that undermine support for invasion, war, and aggression.

Those who instigate wars, invasions, violence, bullying, and aggression on any scale, are *compelled* to punish those who disagree, or oppose their acts. Yet in doing so, they substitute obedience for thought, dogma for analysis, monologue for dialogue, autocracy for democracy, destruction for creation, and contempt for respect. These shifts undermine morale, motivation, and support, eventually reaching a critical mass that leads to a collapse of popular consensus, mutiny *within* the military, dissent inside the autocracy, and a decision to end the war.

In an effort to avoid these outcomes, and the loss of status, wealth, and power they entail, wartime governments try to repress disaffection by constricting the use of language, treating dissenters as traitors, and restricting the freedom of journalists, artists, and intellectuals. For this reason, among the first steps taken by Russia to suppress internal opposition was to criminalize any reference to it as a "war" or "invasion," insisting instead that it be called a "special operation." Interestingly, this took place at nearly the same time the Republican majority in Florida passed the "don't say gay" law making it illegal to refer to homosexuality in schools, banned books about "critical race theory" and racial bias, eliminated "woke" classes on systemic discrimination, and prohibited teaching history in ways that could "make people feel bad" about slavery and lynching.

BIAS, STEREOTYPING, AND WAR

In a similar way, Russia sought to prevent teaching that Ukraine is a separate nation, and declared it is not waging a war at all, but a glorious, patriotic, and justifiable defense against U.S. aggression and Ukrainian fascism. At the same time, we need to notice, even among *supporters* of Ukraine, an implicit set of biases—not only against Russia — but biases that inform much of the hostility toward migrants. Here, for example, are a few early responses by highly regarded news agencies to the war, contrasting it with wars in the Middle East:

- *BBC:* "It's very emotional for me because I see European people with blue eyes and blonde hair being killed."
- *CBS News:* "This isn't Iraq or Afghanistan... This is a relatively civilized, relatively European city."
- *Al-Jazeera:* "What's compelling is looking at them, the way they are dressed. These are prosperous, middle-class people. These are not obviously refugees trying to get away from the Middle East ... or North Africa. They look like any European family that you'd live next door to."
- *BFM TV (France):* "We are in the 21st century, we are in a European city, and we have cruise missile fire as though we were in Iraq or Afghanistan, can you imagine!?" "It's an important question. We're not talking here about Syrians fleeing... We're talking about Europeans." "To put it bluntly, these are not refugees from Syria, these are refugees from Ukraine... They're Christians, they're white. They're very similar to us."
- *The Daily Telegraph:* "This time, war is wrong because the people look like us and have Instagram and Netflix accounts. It's not in a poor, remote country anymore."
- *ITV (UK):* "The unthinkable has happened... This is not a developing, third world nation; this is Europe!"

The biases and prejudices are obvious: Ukrainian migrants do not fit the mold European cultures created to define refugees, so people could no longer distance themselves from their suffering. Indeed, global responses to similar wars and invasions in Iraq and Afghanistan, or Korea and Vietnam, did not produce *nearly* the level of outrage and opposition in the U S. and Europe, nor were refugees from those countries welcomed so warmly. These comments also reflect a kind of "empathy shock" created by the collapse of all but forgotten stereotypes in the presence of "real" human beings, and a sudden return of recognition of the subconscious moral and *human* connections between us that wars force us to forget. The novelist Carlos Ruiz Zafon wrote:

> Nothing feeds forgetfulness better than war. ... We all keep quiet and they try to convince us that what we've seen, what we've done, what we've learned about ourselves and about others, is an illusion, a passing nightmare. Wars have no memories, and nobody has the courage to understand them until there are no voices left to tell what happened, until the moment comes when we no longer recognize them and they return, with another face and another name, to devour what they left behind.

DEMONIZATION AND MORAL RATIONALIZATION

It is critical in every war that both sides create and sustain a sense of disconnect, distance, dread, and division, in order to separate "Us" from "Them," so we can paint "Them" as alien, evil, cruel, and insane; as enemies whose irrationality, perfidy, innate inferiority, and hostile intentions amply justify our use of violence to dominate, subordinate, domesticate, and punish their evil acts. Yet if we think globally, as a *species*, it is clear that there *is* no "them" — there is only us. The alienation and loss of empathy that emerge from easily triggered biases and stereotypes, together with the fear and anger that magnify them, coalesce into language, adversarial stories, and hostile narratives that demonize and diminish Them, and victimize and privilege Us. Yet these biases and stereotypes, fears and angers, stories and narratives arise in *all* wars, all acts of violence, and all conflicts, even petty, trivial, "ordinary" ones. This suggests that war is simply the large-scale organization of small-scale hatreds. Israeli novelist David Grossman wrote:

> From my experience I can say that the language with which the citizens of a sustained conflict describe their predicament becomes progressively shallower the longer the conflict endures. Language gradually becomes a sequence of clichés and slogans. This begins with the language created by the institutions that manage the conflict directly – the army, the police, different government ministries; it quickly filters down to the mass media that are reporting about the conflict, germinating an even more cunning language that aims to tell its target audience the story easiest for digestion; and this process ultimately seeps into the private, intimate language of the conflict's citizens, even if they deny it.

Many researchers, including Kurt and Kati Spillman, have studied the demonization process, and identified many common elements in the ways we create enemies and form biases against others. These include, in my view:

- *Assumption of Injurious Intentions* - they intended to cause the harm we experienced.
- *Distrust* - every idea or statement made by them is wrong or proposed for dishonest reasons.
- *Externalization of Guilt* - everything bad or wrong is their fault.
- *Attribution of Evil* - they want to destroy us and what we value most, and must therefore be destroyed themselves.
- *Zero-Sum Interests* - everything that benefits them harms us, and *vice versa.*
- *Paranoia and Preoccupation with Disloyalty* - any criticism of us or praise of them is disloyal and treasonous.

- *Prejudgment* - everyone in the enemy group is an enemy.
- *Collapse of Neutrality and Independence into Opposition* - anyone who is not with us is against us.
- *Suppression of Empathy* - we have nothing in common and considering them human is dangerous.
- *Isolation and Impasse* - we cannot dialogue, negotiate, cooperate, or resolve conflicts with them.
- *Self-Fulfilling Prophecy* - their evil makes it permissible for us to act in a hostile way toward them, and *vice versa*.

These scale-free assumptions help initiate a process that Albert Bandura calls "moral disengagement," which includes several steps or processes:

- *Rationalizing* the possible beneficial consequences of otherwise wrong behaviors are seen outweighing their negative consequences. ("If I make enough money by doing this, I can help people later.")
- *Obscuring* or lessening personal responsibility for participating in the wrongful activity. ("I just did what I was told." "I just played a small part." "Other people do the same thing, so why can't I?")
- *Denying* the seriousness of harmful effects on others. ("He won't mind." "He's going to be fine." "It was only a small thing." "He can claim it on his insurance.")
- *Blaming*, dehumanizing, or derogating the victim. ("He was stupid." "She was a bitch." "It served him right." "She shouldn't have …")
- *Demonizing* the perpetrator. ("He is vicious." "He's not human." "He should be shot.")
- *Magnifying* or exaggerating the harm that occurred. ("What he did [if a minor infraction] is intolerable.")
- *Distancing* or separating from both sides. ("A plague on both their houses." "It has nothing to do with me.")

The moral rationalizations people routinely offer in support of these mechanisms can be found in conflicts on all scales. According to Bandura, they include:

- *Moral Justification*: "He did it first."
- *Euphemistic Labeling*: "All I did was …"
- *Disadvantageous Comparison*: "He's much worse than I am."
- *Displacement of Responsibility*: "She made me do it."
- *Diffusion of Responsibility*: "Everyone is doing it."
- *Disregard/Distortion of Consequences:* "What I did wasn't that bad."
- *Dehumanization*: "He deserved it."
- *Blaming the Victim*: "She was asking for it."

It is possible, of course, to "reverse engineer" the "enemy-creating" process by stimulating biases and stereotypes, stories and narratives, fears and angers, demonizations and victimizations, *in order to* strip others of what rightfully belongs to them. Thus, anti-Semitic stereotypes were created by Nazis to justify the theft of Jewish property, jobs, art, and other resources; and racial stereotypes were created to justify slavery, exploitation, segregation, and imprisonment.

WAR AS THE HEALTH OF THE STATE

In these ways, war, violence, aggression, and unresolved conflicts undermine not only our *individual* integrity and capacity to engage in empathetic, compassionate, moral, and ethical behaviors, including our ability to oppose the inhumane treatment of others; but our *collective* capacity for democratic decision-making, twisting and distorting the nature of the individuals, groups, and nation-states that promote them. They do so by crushing empathy, creating a divided sense of self within the aggressor; punishing honesty, integrity, and integration; instilling a fear of ostracism, and with it, a repressed desire for connection.

In 1918, near the end of World War I, Sigmund Freud wrote an article entitled *Reflections on War and Death*, about the layered rationalizations nation-states establish during wartime to justify their actions:

> [T]he state forbids [the citizen] to do wrong not because it wishes to do away with wrongdoing but because it wishes to monopolize it... A state at war makes free use of every injustice, every act of violence, that would dishonor the individual. It employs not only permissible cunning but conscious lies and intentional deception against the enemy, and this to a degree which apparently outdoes what was customary in previous wars.

> The state demands the utmost obedience and sacrifice of its citizens, but at the same time it treats them as children through an excess of secrecy and a censorship of news and expression of opinion which render the minds of those who are thus intellectually repressed defenseless against every unfavorable situation and every wild rumor. It absolves itself from guarantees and treaties by which it was bound to other states, makes unabashed confession of its greed and aspiration to power, which the individual is then supposed to sanction out of patriotism.

Hannah Arendt added, based on Hitler's lies leading up to World War II:

> If everybody lies to you, if everybody always lies to you, the consequence is not that you believe the lies, but rather that nobody believes anything any longer... And a people that can no longer believe anything, cannot make up its mind. It is deprived, not only of its capacity to act, but also of its capacity to think and to judge. And with such a people, you can then do what you please.

The state does these things, in part, to achieve its' highest goal, which is the *complete* unification of the nation, total loyalty to its' leaders, and absolute obedience to its' will. This is the great dream of autocrats, dictators, and power-mongers everywhere. Also writing in 1918, Randolphe Bourne described the role of war in achieving these goals, reaching similar conclusions to Freud's. In an article provocatively entitled, *"War is the Health of the State,"* Bourne wrote:

> Minorities are rendered sullen, and some intellectual opinion, bitter and satirical. But in general, the nation in war-time attains a uniformity of feeling, a hierarchy of values, culminated at the undisputed apex of the State ideal, which could not possibly be produced through any other agency than war. Other values such artistic creation, knowledge, reason, beauty, the enhancement of life, are instantly and almost unanimously sacrificed and the significant classes who have constituted themselves the amateur agents of the State are engaged not only in sacrificing these values for themselves but in coercing all other persons into sacrificing them.

Bourne described the energy, righteousness, and certainty that are encouraged by war, creating a *passive* consensus in support of violence, militaristic solutions, authoritarian leadership, repression of dissent, and rationalizing the rejection of dialogue, negotiation, and mediation, likening them to treason:

> War — or at least modern war waged by a democratic republic against a powerful enemy - seems to achieve for a nation almost all that the most inflamed political idealist could desire. Citizens are no longer indifferent to their Government but each cell of the body politic is brimming with life and activity. We are at last on the way to full realization of that collective community in which each individual somehow contains the virtue of the whole. In a nation at war, every citizen identifies himself with the whole, and feels immensely strengthened in that identification. The purpose and desire of the collective community live in each person who throws

himself whole-heartedly into the cause of war. The impeding distinction between society and the individual is almost blotted out. At war, the individual becomes almost identical with his society. He achieves a superb self-assurance, an intuition of the rightness of all his ideas and emotions, so that in the suppression of opponents or heretics he is invincibly strong...

Beneath the drive to war and hatred of the enemy lies, paradoxically, a desire for *unity* and togetherness—not in the complex, problematic, conflicted form of diverse individuals with different needs and unique interests; but in the far simpler, less troublesome, ego-satisfying form of unquestioned loyalty, blind obedience, uniformity, and surrender to the dominant status, dictates, and punitive power of the absolutist State, as embodied in the One True Leader. As Adrienne Rich reminds us,

> War is an absolute failure of imagination, scientific and political. That a war can be represented as helping a people to 'feel good' about themselves, or their country, is a measure of that failure.

We can mitigate that failure, first: by supplementing the "fight, flight, or freeze" response — not only with "*fawning*," or currying favor with an adversary, which Anna Freud called "identification with the enemy," — but second: I suggest, with "*flocking*," or seeking safety by refusing to be or have an enemy, and aligning with everyone. As Edwin Markham nicely put it:

> They drew a circle that shut me out,
> Heretic, rebel, a thing to flout.
> But Love and I had the wit to win,
> We drew a circle that took them in.

The addition of "flocking" to our typical responses to stress accurately reflects what we and many other species do, and suggests that unity and connection can be transformed from a *negative* process of picking enemies and seeking victory "over and against" *people*; to a *positive* one of joining others, collaborating to solve *problems*, and seeking victory "with and for" everyone.

How to Create an Enemy

Our innate desire for unity and connection when faced with a threat leads politicians and conflicted parties to *personalize* their fears, angers, biases, and war-like feelings, and transfer them; first, from problems to people; and second, from one enemy to another, enabling former opponents to cease their hostilities and make common cause against a new common enemy. In the U.S., for example, hatreds shift quite easily internally from Blacks to Native Americans, Mexicans, Jews, Muslims, Asians, Irish, Italians, etc., and externally from Russians to Chinese, Cubans, Iranians, Iraqis, etc. How does the process of enemy creation work? At a subtle, subconscious level, we can break the logic for individuals and groups down to 10 discrete steps that can be recognized, acknowledged, seen as mutual, and reversed through dialogue and mediation. The *internal* logic, reasoning, and moral rationalization for all wars, violence, and conflicts, at the simplest level, seems to me to begin like this:

1. I am /We are decent, reasonable, and nice.
2. Therefore, I/we do not *deserve* to be treated badly.
3. If someone treats me/us badly, it cannot therefore be because of something I/we did, but about who *they* are.
4. The hostility directed against me/us is therefore imbalanced, disproportionate, unfair, and unjust, as I/we did not deserve it.
5. The only reason he/she/they would engage in such hostile behavior against me/us can only be because he/she/they is/are cruel, insane, immoral, and evil.
6. His/her/their cruelty, insanity, immorality, and evil justifies me/us in suppressing our empathy and behaving hostilely in response.

7. Since he/she/they are cruel, insane, immoral, and evil, there is no use trying to communicate, negotiate, or mediate with him/her/ them.
8. Indeed, doing so would mean *condoning* his/her/their cruelty, insanity, immorality, and evil, and permitting it to continue.
9. I/we am/are therefore not morally or ethically responsible for communicating, negotiating, or mediating an end to the conflict.
10. Since he/she/they have ignored my/our needs, wishes, and interests and spurned my/our innate decency, reasonableness, and niceness, I/we are justified in acting unilaterally and autocratically, and using war and violence to force him/her/them to provide what I/we reasonably want or need.

Wars and conflicts create enemies in ways that are personal, ahistorical, and specific, and also in ways that are impersonal, trans-historic, and generic. Wars and conflicts are lose/lose exchanges, caused not only by events, but by frustrated emotions, unexamined logic, socially unacceptable behaviors, political perfidy, disgraced or humiliated cultures, and hostile, unresponsive, disrespectful, uncaring relationships, which are *always* able to mutate and find fresh targets. For these reasons, *we* are the enemy in every war and conflict, and we are also the perpetrators and victims. It is therefore in *all* our interests to help end the war in Ukraine, and prevent future ones that will follow, by dismantling and reversing the demonizing stories and narratives that fuel the enemy-creation process.

How Mediators Can Help End the War in Ukraine and Those that Will Follow

As Desmond Tutu advised, "There comes a point where we need to stop just pulling people out of the river. We need to go upstream and find out why they're falling in." *Of course*, we need to support

Ukrainians and their rights to independence and self-determination, and do what we can to stop invasions and aggressions wherever they occur, yet if we are also to prevent future wars, we need to better understand how they begin, and develop the skills that will help us avoid and dismantle them at their deeper, systemic sources.

Doing so, however, requires higher order skills in communication, dialogue, peace building, political problem-solving, mediation, and other conflict resolution methods, at levels that are *exponentially* greater than we presently practice. Yet this is *exactly* what each of these methods seek to accomplish, every day, in every nation, in every conflict, no matter how small or relatively insignificant.

Only four ways of ending the war in Ukraine, or any war or conflict, are possible. First, one side (Ukraine) defeats the other (Russia). We know, however, that this is extremely unlikely, as Russia is too vast and powerful to be defeated by a country as small and dependent as Ukraine, even with extensive military and financial support. Second, Russia defeats Ukraine. This also is highly unlikely, as the will to fight in Ukraine is strong and lasting, and military and financial aid, combined with deteriorating morale in Russia and the impact of economic sanctions have created a near stalemate on the battlefield. Third, the war escalates to include nuclear options and other nations, which is possible, but simply returns us to options one, two, and four. Fourth, there is a negotiated or mediated ceasefire, followed by collaborative efforts by many countries, especially China, to help the parties reach either a temporary or long-lasting peace. This seems far more likely, as U. S. funding for Ukraine depends partly on the 2024 presidential elections that are uncertain, and could result in cutting aid.

The difficulty with nearly all competitive, adversarial, power-based conflict negotiations is that the parties and their supporters *immediately* put forth a set of "non-negotiable" demands, which the other side "unconditionally" rejects, making it appear impossible to

358 • THE MAGIC IN MEDIATION

reach an agreement. Collaborative, mutual gain, interest-based negotiations, however, work differently. Instead, they initially seek agreement on "side" issues, like ground rules, or what each side has suffered, or what their interests and priorities are, or what kind of relationship they would *like* to have with each other, etc. [For more on interest-based negotiations, see Roger Fisher and William Ury's *Getting to Yes*, and the chapter on negotiation in my book with Joan Goldsmith, *Resolving Conflicts at Work* (3rd edition, 2010)]

It is, of course, axiomatic, as antiwar U. S. Representative Jeanette Rankin observed, that "You can no more win a war than you can win an earthquake." What, then, can mediators do to help the parties end this war *without* acquiescing to the conditions that created it. This will not be easy, but if the issues include not only who gets what territory, but whether sanctions are lifted, what happens to NATO, whether UN monitored plebiscites should be held in occupied territories, reconstruction, trade, and similar topics, it is possible to imagine a mixture of solutions that might do the trick. A call to negotiate or mediate is not a call to surrender, but a search for less costly and damaging ways of solving problems.

We also need to think preventatively about what mediators might do to help prevent the next war and those that will follow: How might we help halt, even at their tiniest, least significant beginnings, the metamorphoses of molehills into mountains? How might we, in the midst of violence, help people *imagine* peace, and strengthen the skills, capacities, and conditions that allow it to flourish?

The easiest answer is to assume that wars are simply scaled-up conflicts, and whatever has succeeded in resolving scaled-down, everyday conflicts between people might also be effective in settling large-scale disputes between heads of nation-states. This relatively easy answer inspires us to realize that we can begin *immediately* advancing a wide range of resolution techniques, and applying them, with minor modifications and adjustments, to virtually all international conflicts.

The more difficult answers require us to recognize that part of what makes mediation and related resolution processes successful is that, on a small-scale, the stakes are relatively insignificant; whereas between nation-states, they can be far more devastating, impactful, and difficult to resolve. What interest-based negotiators call the "best alternative to a negotiated agreement," or BATNA, in small- and mid-scale disputes may just be litigation, while the worst alternative, or WATNA, may be minor financial loss. But in disputes between nations, the best alternative may be an ineffective, inconclusive, diplomatic stalemate leading to continued fighting; while the worst may be nuclear war, massive civilian deaths, near total destruction, genocide, and loss of freedom for generations.

Moreover, the orientations of nation-states to adversarial, competitive, win/lose, power-based outcomes *predictably* favor the election of leaders who actively pursue war-like goals and may be more skillful and successful in achieving them, turning the political process in a circle and generating systems that are *always* inclined to war-like results. As Israeli novelist David Grossman observed:

> It is highly rational for a nation always in a state of war to elect combatants as its leaders. But could it be possible that the fact that those combatants are the nation's leaders decree that the nation be in a constant state of war?

The same point can be made, first, regarding international institutions, such as NATO, SEATO, the global military-industrial-political complex, etc., which create an unending stream of enemies; second, regarding unequal social hierarchies, inequitable economic systems, autocratic governments, and selfish environmental policies that resist democratization and treat reformers as enemies; and third, regarding stereotypes, prejudices, and biases, militarized languages, divisiveness, polarization, exploitative attitudes, and cultures of violence that support them.

There are many simple, sensible, and sane solutions to the destructiveness of modern warfare that nonetheless seem impossible to implement, such as *complete* disarmament, starting with nuclear arsenals, fighter jets, missiles, tanks, bombs, gas, biological agents, etc., down to assault rifles, grenades, and similar weapons. Similarly, nations may someday be persuaded to cede their "sovereign" right to wage war to a global body, such as the United Nations, that could mandate mediation, arbitration, or adjudication *without* predetermining what the outcome will be. None of these, however, is at all likely any time soon.

On a smaller scale, many years ago I spent several weeks in Ukraine mediating and facilitating dialogues between Ukrainians and Russians, and training them in conflict resolution skills. One of the Russians said that the *idea* that there could be a third party in conflict, or an unbiased mediator, or a mutually agreeable solution that satisfied both sides' interests, *did not exist*. It barely exists today, and needs to be supported and strengthened by creating a kind of "moral" or "ethical" second front, targeting the *citizens* of aggressor nations.

It is possible, for example, for mediators to create small, mid-, and large-scale dialogues with citizens of hostile countries; speak directly from afar by internet with citizens of both nations, even in wartime; encourage empathy, compassion, and non-adversarial, communications; and "fraternize" with the "enemy."

THE "MEDIATION BUTTERFLY EFFECT"

Wars, like conflicts, are chaotic, unique, surprising, and unpredictable, frustrating analysis, as Tolstoy described in his novel, *War and Peace*; yet their underlying dynamics reveal elements that are eternal, unsurprising, and all too predictable. As mediators and peace builders we need to pay attention to both.

This chaos, or "sensitively dependent on existing conditions," leads to a kind of "butterfly effect, as with the weather, which routinely magnifies small perturbations into large-scale effects, producing not just unforeseen, but *unforeseeable* consequences. This realization led Winston Churchill to warn:

> Never, never, never believe any war will be smooth and easy, or that anyone who embarks on the strange voyage can measure the tides and hurricanes he will encounter. The statesman who yields to war fever must realize that once the signal is given, he is no longer the master of policy but the slave of unforeseeable and uncontrollable events.

But there is also something I call the *"mediation* butterfly effect,"* which weakens adversarial and aggressive resorts to force and violence by strengthening both side's abilities to see the other side as human, and thereby, as Martin Buber put it, transforms a "you" into a "thou." This happens frequently on a small- and mid-scale, encouraging conflict resolvers to develop large-scale collaborative peace-building skills and global mediative capacities that focus preventatively on peoples, cultures, and nations that are moving toward war.

This is already happening on a small scale in several places around the world, leading to a collapse of acquiescence and support for war by ordinary citizens. Dismantling hostility and hatred in any conflict is not quick or easy, yet mediators do so in small-scale conflicts around the world every day. At the level of large-scale nation-states, more is required to shift the ways of thinking and reacting that fuel warlike responses. Leo Tolstoy, considering this issue, concluded that:

> To abolish war, it is necessary to abolish patriotism, and to abolish patriotism it is necessary first to understand that it is an evil. Tell people that patriotism is bad and most will reply, 'Yes, bad patriotism is bad, but mine is good patriotism.'

From a mediation perspective, what is important is *not* that people should not love their countries, but that they should not do so blindly, violently, aggressively, or in ways that do not allow other people to love theirs. The famous cellist Pablo Casals expressed this idea beautifully: "The love of one's country is a splendid thing. But why should love stop at the border?"

Mediators can help prevent future wars by identifying and addressing early warning signs, such as subtle shifts in language, micro-escalations, the rapid spread of hostile stereotypes, demonizing stories, and dehumanizing narratives. We can look for signs of softening resistance to peacebuilding. We can facilitate dialogues, build consensus, solve problems, negotiate collaboratively, and mediate—even on a person-to-person basis. We can design interest-based early interventions and conflict resolution systems that prioritize prevention and provide a rich array of methodologies for de-escalation.

Mediators can, as is being done today, use artificial intelligence to model conditions in Ukraine and Russia and recommend negotiating points and creative approaches to problem-solving. We can help create massively parallel, multi-faceted, multi-disciplinary, *integrated* approaches to peace negotiations, using techniques like "single document/multiple draft" that worked well in the past.

Former Ambassador John MacDonald, who helped pioneer the idea of "multi-track diplomacy," emphasized the importance of Track 2 "back channel" methods that enroll conflict resolvers and non-state actors *directly* in de-escalating conflicts and coordinating with other tracks. Here is an overview of the multi-track approach by the Institute for Multi-Track Diplomacy:

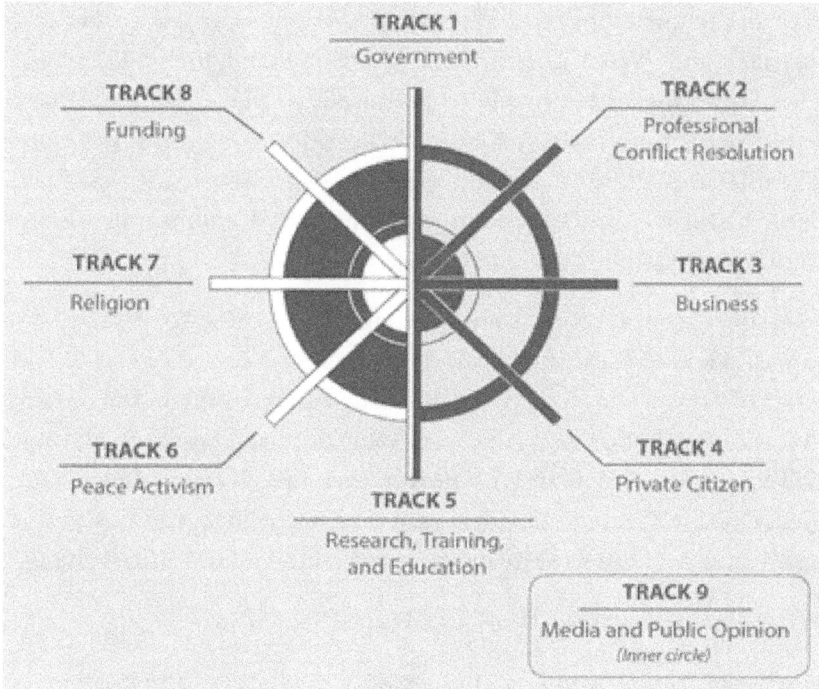

TRACK 1
Government

TRACK 8
Funding

TRACK 2
Professional
Conflict Resolution

TRACK 7
Religion

TRACK 3
Business

TRACK 6
Peace Activism

TRACK 4
Private Citizen

TRACK 5
Research, Training,
and Education

TRACK 9
Media and Public Opinion
(Inner circle)

IMTD Institute for Multi-Track Diplomacy

Diverse multi-track approaches work best when teams are formed combining tracks 2 and 3, and then build links to all the others. Experienced mediators could, for example, work alongside international peace building organizations as "shadow consultants" to coach and assist heads of state in the mediation process. We could train civil society actors and organizations in a broad range of de-escalation and impasse resolution skills; facilitate dialogues and restorative justice circles, and conduct "trauma informed mediations" among vulnerable civilian populations before, during, and after negotiated cease-fires and settlements.

Mediators can assist people on both sides in better understanding the cultures, metaphors, and subtle meanings that are often missed by opponents, yet profoundly impact the ways they act in conflict.

We can ask questions like: "What does Ukraine *mean*, or stand for in Russia?", and "What does Russia mean or stand for in Ukraine?" These questions are unlikely to be raised, addressed, or negotiated at the bargaining table, yet Russia's hostility toward the West and Ukraine; and Ukraine and the West's hostility toward Russia, have deep historical roots, hidden meanings, and intense emotional significance for both sides.

Mediators can create forums on multiple scales to discuss hot topics, such as "asymmetrical," and "cyber" warfare; shifts in the *forms* of power and divergent ways each side uses them; the parties' diverse perceptions of powerlessness, disempowerment, and willingness to use forms of power that are deemed illegitimate, illegal, or immoral by the other side; or how to "balance" power and encourage collaborative forms of negotiation and problem-solving.

WHAT PEACE BUILDING DOES AND DOES *NOT* MEAN

Wars, like conflicts on all scales, require mediators to recognize the *trap* of professed neutrality, which can lead to complicity, condonation, and implied permission to invade and attack others, as occurred in Munich immediately before World War II. Being unbiased, "omni-partial," and on both parties' sides at the same time, as discussed in Chapter 1, does *not* mean agreeing with either side's biases, prejudices, hatreds, positions, demands, historical assertions, factual representations, or legal claims. Nor does it require the condonation of violence, aggression, invasion, genocide, and war crimes.

As mediators, it's important to treat *people*, cultures, and nations with equal respect, but this does not require us to *equally* respect their kindness and their cruelty, their fairness and their bias, their defense and their invasion, their freedom and their slavery, their dignity and their contempt. Nor does it require us to stop at condemning acts of cruelty, which often just replicates them, and try to dismantle them at their *source* by revealing the pain that gave rise to them.

Listening, empathizing, acknowledging, negotiating, mediating, and searching for joint solutions and mutual understanding do *not* mean justifying, or giving permission, or rationalizing, or condoning violence and aggression. Rather, they are *affirmations* of the universal principles of respectful communication, unconditional kindness, collaborative problem-solving, restorative approaches to justice, and their extension to *every* party in every mediation. They are efforts to prevent the next war by deconstructing the process of enemy-creation, identifying the legitimate underlying interests of all sides, and redirecting their energies and attentions to collaborative problem-solving and win/win outcomes.

Increasingly, global problem-solving requires trans-national cooperation, which war, ultra-nationalism, and competition for global dominance undermine and obstruct. Therefore, *by necessity*, mediators have two goals to achieve: first, to help stop existing wars, violence, and aggression; and second, to encourage preventative cross-border dialogues, problem-solving, collaborative negotiations, truth and reconciliation sessions, mediations, and restorative justice circles.

Mediators in all countries, on all scales, and at all levels of expertise, can contribute to these goals, and help halt present and future wars in many multi-scale, rich, diverse, and powerful ways, a *few* of which are to:

- Support victims and refugees from all countries, not only with material, medical, and humanitarian assistance, but emotional support, expressions of solidarity, trauma services, and reach out however we can.
- Listen to *people* on both sides and help design and facilitate mutual multi-track dialogues, storytelling sessions, empathy building, restorative circles, living room conversations, and similar exchanges with those on "the other side."
- Strengthen the United Nations, European Forum for Restorative Justice, Centre for Humanitarian Dialogue,

Mediators Beyond Borders International, and similar peacebuilding organizations.

- Aid, protect, and assist members of local mediation organizations in hostile countries, and help them connect, communicate, de-escalate, and solve common problems.
- Advocate for peace, ceasefire, dialogue, negotiation, and mediation, always and everywhere.
- Point out how hostile stereotypes, biases, and prejudices prepare the way for future violence, and help design and facilitate bias awareness and prejudice reduction dialogues.
- Respect national differences, encourage cultural diversity, and do not assume that "our" ways, interests, and factual truths are the only ones possible.
- Connect in person and through social media with mediators and citizens of warring countries, help strengthen their conflict resolution skills, capacities, and conflict cultures.
- Try to reduce nuclear proliferation, "Mutually Assured Destruction" (MAD), nuclear threats, political posturing, brinksmanship, war profiteering, and preparations for aggression and genocide.
- Convene joint, collaborative problem-solving teams of professional mediators and negotiators from both sides to offer consensus-based suggestions to the leaders of both sides.
- Publicize, in the languages of hostile countries, articles and videos on the power and effectiveness of conflict resolution processes.
- Set up joint "blue ribbon" commissions, mock peace negotiations, citizens assemblies, town hall meetings, restorative circles, war crimes tribunals, truth and reconciliation commissions, etc.
- Uncover the complex, hidden sources of war and violence in every conflict, large and small, and jointly discuss and improve them.

Mediators can also help disputing parties discover, discuss, and disseminate proposed answers to several important and profound questions:

1. Where and how, exactly, do the lines get drawn that separate us irrevocably from one another, even for a moment, in any conflict?
2. How can democratic nations, organizations, and groups participate in principled ways in dialogues, collaborative negotiations, mediations, and other forms of courageous, constructive, creative contention, alongside autocrats, dictators, militarists, chauvinists, neo-Nazis, and armed opponents?
3. What are the limits of conflict resolution, and the sources of its' hidden magic?
4. If we cannot work directly, top-down, and from the inside out, how can we work indirectly, bottom-up, sideways, and from the outside in, so the passive acquiescence and coerced consensus to war starts to unravel?
5. How do we resist censorship, stereotyping, dehumanization, demonization, and the distortions of language that are essential parts of the "war building" process?

As C. Wright Mills perceptively wrote many years ago, in *The Causes of World War III*, "[T]he immediate causes of World War III are the preparations for it." Among nation states, *vast* resources and efforts are devoted to nothing else. We cannot continue funding wars and expect them not to occur, yet our military- industrial complex is constantly preparing to wage them. A poem written by Lawrence Ferlinghetti on the bombing of Hiroshima reads, as I recall, "pinned on the drawing board/are plans for the destruction of petunias and violins ..."

This does not mean that Ukraine's military opposition to invasion should not be funded, but that it should not be the *only* thing that is funded. Trillions are being spent for war — which is essential if self-determination and freedom from invasion are to be more than mere words — but how much is being spent to strengthen mediation, negotiation, peace building, and prevent future wars? Nearly nothing.

Every defeat in every war is a tragedy, not merely for the nations and citizens who have been defeated, denied freedom, or died, but for *all* of us everywhere–and not just abstractly, but as a very real, very personal loss of humanity and caring, a crushing of hopes, a dismissal of dialogue and mediation, a brutalization of language and culture, a freezing of imagination and possibility, a collapse of empathy and compassion, an inability to solve pressing problems, a closing of our hearts and minds to others.

None of this will be easy, and as May Sarton reminds us, "Sometimes it is necessary to be a hero just in order to be an ordinary decent human being." Yet we need to begin, no matter how daunting and difficult the task. Mary Parker Follett, one of the founders of modern mediation in the U.S. in the 1910's and 20's, wrote, inviting us to cherish the simple, yet profound heroism of *every* effort at peacebuilding and mediation:

> We have thought of peace as passive and war as the active way of living. The opposite is true. War is not the most strenuous life. It is a kind of rest cure compared to the task of reconciling our differences... From War to Peace is not from the strenuous to the easy existence; it is from the futile to the effective, from the stagnant to the active, from the destructive to the creative way of life. ... The world will be regenerated by the people who rise above these passive ways and heroically seek, by whatever hardship, by whatever toil, the methods by which people can agree.

TWELVE

Imagining an Interest-Based State

MEDIATION, CIVIL SOCIETY, AND THE
TRANSFORMATION OF POLITICAL CONFLICTS

While we can't guess what will become of the world, we can imagine what we would like it to become. The right to dream wasn't in the 30 rights of humans that the United Nations proclaimed at the end of 1948. But without it, without the right to dream and the waters that it gives to drink, the other rights would die of thirst.

Eduardo Galeano

[I]t is not merely that we must be allowed to govern ourselves, we must learn how to govern ourselves; it is not only that we must be given 'free speech,' we must learn a speech that is free; ... [I]t is not only that we must invent machinery to get a social will expressed, we must invent machinery that will get a social will created.

Mary Parker Follett

Imagine a circle of compassion. Then imagine nobody's standing outside that circle.

Father Gregory Boyle

HERE IS THE PROBLEM. AS WE CONFRONT EACH NEW SET OF CONFLICTS and crises, from the Covid 19 pandemic to bias and prejudice, war and nuclear proliferation, global warming and species extinction, it is increasingly obvious that the most powerful problem-solving mechanism created in human history, the nation-state, is no longer capable of solving the increasingly complex, potentially catastrophic difficulties we face as a species, partly because the most pressing of these difficulties are *global* in nature, and well beyond the reach of even the most powerful nation-states to correct.

Moreover, the dominant social, economic, and political systems that shape the abilities of these nation-states to respond to these global problems are increasingly polarized, competitive, adversarial, militaristic, insular, resistant to change, and weakened by chronic conflicts and an unequal distribution of status, wealth, and power. As a result, nearly all nation-states are constricted and dominated by a combination of wealthy elites with a compelling interest in maximizing their dominance, in alliance with politicians who seek power and are beholden to them.

The political leaders of these states are elected, and required to represent deeply divided parties, factions, groups, and tendencies, usually in hostile, "winner-take-all," adversarial electoral contests that are highly vulnerable to wealth, favoritism, biases and prejudices, demagoguery, and a host of politicized conflicts that can render them ineffective as problem solvers. This is especially true when their problems reach higher levels of complexity, intensity, breadth, and seriousness, or require coordinated, collaborative, sustainable, long-term global responses.

The inability to rise above these divisions, resolve internal and external conflicts, and collaborate across borders and political divides to solve common problems makes them seem hopeless, increasing their danger, and turning minor differences into major rifts, opponents into enemies, and relatively simple disagreements into conflicts, crises, and catastrophes, that could culminate in systemic collapse.

THREE APPROACHES TO POLITICAL PROBLEM-SOLVING

From a mediation perspective, problems can be solved, and conflicts resolved — be they small and interpersonal or large and social, economic, political, and environmental — using one of three fundamentally distinct processes or approaches:

1. Using *Power:* In power-based approaches, those with the greatest status, wealth, and power decide dictatorially, autocratically, and hierarchically what the outcome will be, often without considering what others might want. Power-based organizations, including monarchies and military organizations, operate primarily by commands, orders, and pronouncements, and ultimately rely on violence, threats, prejudices, hatred, and bullying. And, as Lord Acton famously observed, "All power corrupts, and absolute power corrupts absolutely." Or as Alan Watts wryly put it, "Governments are always led by the most successful group of gangsters."

2. Using *Rights*: In rights-based approaches, those with superior positions in the hierarchy and bureaucracy decide what the outcome will be based on legally enforceable principles, often after an adversarial legal process that at least "hears" and considers what other "recognized" parties are legally "entitled" to. Rights-based organizations, like *procedurally* democratic states and administrative bureaucracies, operate by coercion and control, restrict voting, adjudicate conflicts, and rely on positional negotiations, arm-twisting diplomacy, and temporary compromises. As Saul Alinsky aptly concluded: "A free and open society is an ongoing conflict, interrupted periodically by compromises." John Kenneth Galbraith described it

differently: "Politics is not the art of the possible. It consists in choosing between the disastrous and the unpalatable."

3. Using *Interests*: In interest-based approaches, everyone who has an interest in the problem is invited to participate in deciding what the solution will be using a variety of methods and processes, including dialogue, joint problem-solving, consensus building, collaborative negotiation, mediation, and facilitation. Power asks what we want, rights ask what we are entitled to, and interests ask *why* we want it. Interest-based approaches therefore depend less on compromise than collaboration, creativity, empathy, and consensus. Interest-based organizations, like direct, participatory democracies and civil societies operate primarily by open and honest communication, egalitarianism, collaboration, altruism, and shared values.

While the outcome, content, and *explicit* meaning of the solution may be identical in all three approaches, the processes and *implicit* meanings of the methods used in each case are vastly different. Power-based decision-making can work quite well when there is a clear, compelling need for quick, unified action; where the problem is relatively simple; where the decision does not significantly impact others; where peoples' interests largely coincide; where other peoples' independent participation is not essential for the problem to be solved, etc.

The *inherent* message of power as a process, however, is inevitably divisive, top-down, and hostile to openness, honesty, democracy, diversity, participation, dissent, collaboration, and consensus, simply because the interests of those without power are disregarded — until the reasons for power disappear or begin to ebb, wane, and dissipate. Power-based political systems therefore *create* enemies, especially enemies within, to justify their fear, hatred, and suspicion of others, and legitimize the use of power and violence over and against them. Internal enemies suggest duplicity, sinister motives, secret conspiracies, distrust of others, suspicion of ordinary communications, and a need to remain silent about things that matter. Interest-based systems have no need to create enemies, conspiracies, or distrust.

Power- and rights-based approaches clearly communicate that superior privileges, wealth, and elite status in the chain of command, hierarchy, or bureaucratic pecking order entitle some to dictate, dominate, control, and get rich, while disregarding the legitimate *human* needs of others, who are required merely to accept their inequality, powerlessness, and cruel, callous, inhumane treatment by others.

Power-based hierarchies can also be imagined as having *dimensions*, in which, for example, a one-dimensional line of individuals is arranged in a vertical pecking order; a two-dimensional plane expands the line to put all in-group members on a plane over and above out-group members, as by advancing, for example, men over women, whites over people of color, etc.; and a three-dimensional cube that turns hierarchies into *policies* that are either open and compulsory, as with fascism, or *systematic*, superficially democratic, and culturally repressive, as by passing laws that prohibit teaching about racism or slavery as prejudiced against whites.

Even where a solution or decision is *substantively* correct, the way it is made can suggest and perpetuate social, economic, and political inequality, leading to a usurpation of *citizenship*, a lack of interest by those who are excluded in solving the problem, and inadequate skills and capacities in complex, collaborative, dialogic, consensus-building, problem-solving, and conflict resolution. Novelist Salman Rushdie presciently wrote, with special relevance to power and political ideas:

> [A]ny idea is asked two questions. When it is weak: will it compromise? How do you behave when you win? When your

enemies are at your mercy and your power has become absolute: what then?

TOWARD MULTI-SCALE METHODOLOGIES

In trying to imagine a *generic* interest-based design for nation states that could improve their ability to solve pressing internal and external problems more effectively, collaboratively, and globally *without* relying on power-based coercion or short-lived rights-based compromises, it is useful initially to scale-*down* the problem, by reducing it to one that is smaller, simpler, and more familiar.

We can begin, for example, by considering how problems are solved and conflicts resolved on the smallest possible scales, between friends, couples, and family members; then on a somewhat larger middle-scale within neighborhoods, schools, and workplaces. We can then consider how the most successful of these methods might be "scaled-up" to address larger-scale problems confronting political players and nation states.

From a historical or evolutionary perspective, there are three minimally essential goals, stages, or purposes in solving problems and resolving conflicts that can be found in the natural world, as well as in human societies. The first goal is simply to survive; the second is to succeed; and the third is to adapt and learn, in order to maximize the other two in continually changing environments.

These goals are similar to the lower rungs in Abraham Maslow's famous "hierarchy of needs," each of which corresponds to a hierarchy of personal problem-solving and conflict resolution skills. What is missing in Maslow's scheme, from a multi-scale problem-solving or conflict resolution perspective, are:

1. A recognition that each higher stage requires an
   exponentially higher order of skill in solving problems and
   resolving conflicts between people who have both similar
   and dissimilar needs and interests; that is, in

communicating, collaborating, dissenting, negotiating, and synthesizing disparate ideas.

2. An understanding that while lower order power- and rights-based processes can satisfy lower order physiological and safety needs, they may *undermine* the ability to satisfy higher order needs without introducing higher order interest-based processes.

3. An identification, inclusion, and detailed exploration of the social, economic, political, and environmental consequences of satisfying higher order needs in relation to the skills needed to sustain them.

There are three fundamentally differing approaches to satisfying these needs, goals, or purposes: first, there is *selfishness* (looking out for oneself); second, there is *altruism* (looking out for others); and third, there is *collaboration* (looking out for self and others). The first two have been written about in detail (see, e.g., Richard Dawkins, *The Selfish Gene,* or *Selfish Gene Theory and Altruism*; Matthieu Ricard, *Altruism*; Peter Singer, *The Most Good You Can Do.*)

The third is a complex, constantly shifting, higher order, interest-based synthesis of the first two, and has received far less attention, yet is the *ground* and defining character of all small- and mid-scale collaborative problem-solving and transformational conflict resolution practices, from consensus building and mutual gain bargaining to restorative circles and mediation.

If we regard the nation state as a large-scale problem-solving and conflict resolution mechanism, we can consider how these problem-solving and conflict resolution processes might be scaled up from issues faced by friends, couples, and family members, and how *both* might benefit from higher order skills in active listening, empathy building, emotional intelligence, creative problem-solving, dialogue, consensus, collaborative negotiation, mediation, and similar methods.

These small-scale methodologies can be modified and adapted to work on multiple scales; for example, in resolving mid-level disputes in neighborhoods, workplaces, groups, teams, civil societies, organizations, and other complex, multi-stakeholder conflicts [see discussion in Chapter 9]; as well as in large-scale conflicts between nation states, political parties, and their factions.

On each of these scales, we face common problems in figuring out how to balance, learn from, integrate, transform, and synthesize contrasting *values,* principles, ideas, feelings, perceptions, histories, and "complementarities"; and how to reconcile competing forces, such as unity and diversity, integration and individuation, altruism and selfishness, collaboration and competition. The first questions we want to ask, at each level and scale, are:

1. What is the binding force, source of attraction, and organizing principle that holds these opposing forces together?
2. How much space is available within each for diversity, differentiation, and dissent?
3. How much flexibility and creativity are permitted or required by internal or external circumstances?
4. How are differences, problems, and conflicts resolved between them?
5. Are there creative ways of combining, synthesizing, and transcending them?

In seeking answers to these questions, we discover that there are three fundamental roads to unity that are present on every scale; three divergent approaches to problem-solving and conflict resolution; three discrete methods for drawing people into orbit around a common center, then spiraling upward:

1. First, there is the affirmation and reinforcement of *integration,* unity, conformity, and cohesion, which may lead

to the suppression of individuation, diversity, difference, and dissent–sometimes through violence, authoritarianism, conformity, and negative expressions like anger and fear.

2. Second, there is the affirmation and reinforcement of *individuation*, difference, diversity, and dissent, which may lead to the suppression of integration, unity, conformity, and cohesion — sometimes through cynicism, anarchy, separation, egotism, and negative expressions like alienation, sociopathy, and loneliness.

3. Third, there is the affirmation and reinforcement of *both*, collaboratively and creatively combined, which may lead to discovery, transformation, synergy, transcendence, and the emergence of higher, more complex forms of order and relationship–sometimes through exploration, dialogue, collaboration, and positive expressions like camaraderie, playfulness, and love.

Throughout history, human societies have vacillated between the first two options, and only rarely been able to acquire the skills needed to continually balance and integrate their opposites, which are essential to reaching the third option. Too great an emphasis on integration will predictably and automatically trigger an intense desire for individuation, and *vice versa*, leading societies and individuals to cycle or fluctuate from one to the other.

When we consider small-scale problem-solving and conflict resolution processes between friends, couples, spouses, and family members, where the desire for unity and connection can overwhelm individual differences and diversity, and there is not enough separation to allow for non-conformity and dissent. And when the desire for "space" and ability to be oneself overwhelms unity and connection, there is not enough togetherness to allow for collaboration, which can trigger unhappiness, separation, or divorce. These dynamics are similar on all scales.

The core problem in all relationships, regardless of scale, is how to balance and integrate the centrifugal and centripetal forces that either crush the individuality and unique characteristics that make us interesting and inventive; or break the collective commonalities, intimate bonds, love, and heartfelt connections that draw us to one another and sustain us. Indeed, in the final analysis, as Dr. Martin Luther King Jr. reminds us, power and love are interconnected:

> What is needed is a realization that power without love is reckless and abusive, and that love without power is sentimental and anemic. Power at its best is love implementing the demands of justice, and justice at its best is love correcting everything that stands against love.

What keeps us from achieving these ends is, I believe, the same on all scales. In part, it is the absence of higher order problem-solving and conflict resolution skills; for example, in valuing diversity, eliciting interests, acknowledging emotions, engaging in dialogue, exploring complexity, building consensus, negotiating differences, learning from dissent, strengthening collaboration, reconciling, designing preventative systems, and resolving the conflicts that get triggered as a consequence of the belief that there *is* no third way. Instead, we can say that there is no *simple*, easily accessible, lower order third way for those who lack the skills and experience needed to construct a complex, *integrated* one out of thin air.

Every nation state, every organization, every family, every marriage, every friendship is, in essence, a mediation. One of its' critical functions is to connect diverse people by preventing minor differences from escalating into disagreements, conflicts, crises, and catastrophes–that is, to hold naturally unique, diverse, dissenting individuals in relationships that increase their ability to solve common problems, resolve disputes, and achieve common goals. Once this has been recognized, we can ask several questions, starting with:

- How good are they as mediators?
- What skills might be added to their repertoire that would allow them to be even better mediators?
- What exactly is being mediated?
- Between whom, and how, and why?
- How are their structures and systems, cultures and environments influencing their conflicts, and their capacity for resolution?
- How might these be re-designed to improve their effectiveness as mediators?

To consider how we might begin answering these questions, improving the mediative, interest-based skills and capacities of people in groups of all sizes, and imagining how to apply them to the nation-state, we first need to consider how to understand and navigate the complex relationship between nation-states and civil societies, especially in relation to mediation.

ARISTOTLE ON MEDIATION, CIVIL SOCIETY, AND THE STATE

The idea of civil society, as an informal, public, egalitarian, diverse, voluntary, self-organized "political community" existing *outside* the state, originated in ancient Athens, at least with Aristotle, who viewed people in general as naturally political and social animals who wished to participate in making decisions that impacted their lives.

This belief supported the development of *direct* democracy and the Athenian method of "sortition," which enlisted *every* citizen (excluding "women, children, slaves, and barbarians") to serve periodically in nearly every role in government. A modern version of sortition is being used in a number of countries today, and in citizens' assemblies in the U.S. [See e.g., Ariel Procaccia, "A More Perfect Algorithm," *Scientific American*, November 2022.]

In his book, *Politics*, Aristotle defined politics as "a search for the highest common good," which is an excellent description of mediation, and a key element in his view of "corrective justice," in which judges and statesmen reinforce equality or parity between disputing parties by acting as a mediator or "intermediary between loss and gain," and an unbiased guide in their search for justice.

Yet in Socrates' view, because justice, virtue, and truth were multifaceted and complex, the only way democracy could work was through an ongoing "dialectic," or dialogue between people with contrasting political views. In this way, civil society was linked with democracy, which Aristotle, Plato, Democritus, and others, plus several events in Athenian history, revealed to be highly vulnerable to manipulation by autocrats, despots, dictators, tyrants, populists, and demagogues.

Historically, civil societies, or *political communities*, began in families and clans, and gradually expanded in ancient Greece to include farmers, artisans, ex-slaves, merchants, aristocrats, and other social classes or divisions of labor. These combined to form local "associations of associations" in the form of city-states, which evolved centuries later into nation-states that were shaped and organized not only according to status, wealth, and power, but historical circumstances, including prevailing forms of communication, problem solving, decision-making, and conflict resolution.

To hold these increasingly diverse elements of society together, solve social problems, make decisions that impacted everyone, defend themselves against hostile city states with competitive military forces, resolve divisive conflicts, and protect their status, wealth, power, and property–especially slaves–from being redistributed, usurped, or emancipated, it became necessary to develop "universal" rules, or codes of law, and enforcement mechanisms that were *ostensibly* neutral and the same for everyone, yet upheld the rights of slave owners over slaves, men over women, citizens over barbarians, etc.. These inequalities and asymmetries created deep divisions between civil society and the state.

FROM ARISTOTLE TO HEGEL

Many centuries later in 1820, the German idealist philosopher Georg Wilhelm Friedrich Hegel published the Philosophy of Right, becoming one of the first in the modern world to examine the relationship between mediation, civil society, and the state. Hegel began by identifying three fundamental spheres of "ethical life" and human activity, each with a different orientation to self and others, each on a different scale, each leading to the emergence of the next, and each combining opposites in ways that gave rise to chronic conflicts requiring mediation. For Hegel, (simplifying his complex philosophical analysis) these spheres were:

1. The *Family* or clan, characterized by "particular altruism," consisted of the willingness of individuals to act altruistically, but only toward a limited, *particular* group of people related by blood or marriage.
2. *Civil Society*, including commerce, characterized by "universal selfishness" or egoism, consisted of individuals acting in their own self-interests, yet finding ways of compromising or negotiating solutions with others.
3. *The State*, characterized by "universal altruism," consisted of the willingness of individuals to act altruistically toward a universal group of their fellow citizens, for example, through legally regulated processes like voting, military service, or taxes.

Hegel described the historical progression and evolution from family to civil society to the state partly as a consequence of increasing population and complexity. He showed how each successive level contradicted, dissolved, and disintegrated the previous one, giving rise to a transcendence by *antithesis* to successively higher forms of order and disorder, each requiring mediation to remain united — as, for example, a family dissolves when its' members cease to act altruistically and begin caring only for themselves; or a civil society dissolves when its members become too diverse to connect to each together, other than through a higher (i.e., state) form of altruism.

Hegel then identified three distinct "moments" or aspects of each stage that impacted its' capacity to develop, solve problems, and evolve. Families, he wrote, were grounded in the "mediation of need and one man's satisfaction through his work and the satisfaction of the needs of all others–the *System of Needs*." Civil societies, on the other hand, were cooperative and grounded in consensual mediation through the law and administration of justice. Finally, states required the coercive mechanism of the police and the "corporation," and mediation through the activities of government.

From the perspective of conflict resolution, the family, civil society (which, for Hegel, included commerce), and the state *all* practiced mediation, as each sought to satisfy *particular,* diverse, individual needs and interests within the context of a *universal,* united, collective effort to satisfy the needs and interests of everyone. Each sought to do so in similar yet unique ways, as each acted on different scales, from small to middle and large.

On all scales, mediations seek to be generic, timeless, and universal, yet also to produce unique, evolving, individual outcomes, making every family, civil society, and state simultaneously alike and different, with each possessing universal forms and structures that arise out of, are conditioned by, operate semi-independently of, and are sensitively dependent on the unique, complex, evolving individual interests and relationships that give rise to them.

Each distinct combination of dependence and independence produces contrasts, antagonisms, and conflicts between *particular,* living, evolving, complex individuals; and *shared,* non-living, relatively fixed, simplified structures, processes, and relationships. These, in turn, impact families, civil societies, and states, generating a rich variety of *chronic* disputes that demand periodic adjustments, compromises, settlements, and resolutions, which require *repeated* mediations to keep them in sync. For this reason, the desire for continuity and stability in families, civil societies, and nation states *organically* gives rise to different, successively more advanced mediation skills and capacities.

In the absence of advance mediation skills and capacities, diversity and dissent give rise to differences that, if left unaddressed and unresolved, can turn into chronic conflicts and dysfunctions, which start to accumulate, sparking increased polarization, growing hostilities, crises, and catastrophes. Conflicts are, in essence, merely cries for help, confessions of inadequacy in handling disputes, calls for resolution, desires for reconciliation, and frustrations over failed efforts to evolve and adapt to changing conditions.

When mediations fail, so do the bonds that hold people in relationships on all scales, leading to personal alienation, separation, and divorce; or to political resistance, rebellion, and revolution, generating desperate, coercive, violent, ultimately failed efforts to *forcibly* preserve the *status quo* and block any changes that might lead to the creation of a new one. [See Chapter 9.]

We can then extend Hegel's description of mediation of the family's "system of needs," civil society's "administration of justice," and the state's reliance on "police and corporations," reflecting his view of the forms and processes required to mediate conflicts in each successively larger, more complex formation, so as to roughly represent, in inverse order, the three fundamental evolutionary approaches to dispute resolution I described: interests, rights, and power.

We can then ask: Are there interest-based approaches that could link individuals, families, civil societies, and nation states? Are there scale-free methods that can support both unity and diversity, consensus and dissent, dependence and independence, and do so on all three scales and formations in ways that allow each level to learn from, feed, and improve on the others?

An alternative way of describing mediations on all three scales is that they seek to elicit, reframe, and encourage dialogue; to creatively combine and *synthesize* the potentially contradictory self-interests of unique individuals, cultures, and principles; they acknowledge, validate, and work through people's self-protective emotional responses to conflict on all levels; they try to overcome perceived adversarial attitudes toward others; and they transform conflicts by asking questions that create opportunities for individual and group learning, evolutionary improvement, and transcendence to more satisfying, higher order relationships.

In principle, these outcomes are all possible whether the conflict takes place on a small-scale between friends, couples, and family members; or mid-scale between communities, organizations, and actors in civil society; or large-scale between citizens, factions, political parties, and nation states. In attempting to imagine how, it will be helpful for us to identify, in Hegel's view, the most common generic elements and characteristics of political institutions, and consider how, where, and to what extent universal, scale-free mediative principles are possible.

HEGEL'S THEORY OF MEDIATION

Hegel saw the family and civil society as culminating and reaching their highest expression in the state, which he saw as consisting of an executive—at that time, a Monarch; and a legislature—at that time, the Estates, representing the clergy, the nobility, and the common people—at that time, primarily agricultural and handicraft laborers. Hegel saw each playing a mediative role that served to resolve conflicts and keep the whole from fragmenting or dissolving.

In T. M. Knox's translator's notes to *Hegel's Philosophy of Right*, the importance of the mediation process in distinguishing between civil society and the state becomes clearer, as in Hegel's view, there *is* no state without a mediative "middle term" to hold its opposing parts together:

What essentially differentiates the state from civil society and makes it rational, is the parliamentary organization which mediates between particulars [i.e., different elements in civil society] on the one hand and the individual monarch on the other. ... [T]he monarch and the classes constitutive of civil society are opposed to one another as the one and the many, or as the abstract individual and the abstract universal. ... These opposites become fused into a unity only if some middle term comes into existence to mediate between them. ..."

For this reason, as indicated earlier, the state is necessarily *itself* a mediation, because it seeks to combine contradictory sets of interests *within* the Estates, as well as between them and the monarchy, because its' autocratic, power-based nature would otherwise completely overwhelm the more democratic, rights-based legislature, and the more communal, interest-based orientation of civil society's lower classes, and *vice versa*. Hegel viewed mediation as the glue that held them all together–but *only* if it was performed in a relatively superficial, non-transformational "neutral" way that did nothing to resolve the systemic and structural sources of social inequality, economic inequity, and autocratic political conflict that were engrained in their relationship.

Marx's Critique of Hegel's Theory of Mediation

Hegel's view of the relationship between mediation, civil society, and the state was critiqued by Karl Marx, in terms that are important for mediators today to consider. Marx was a student and close follower of Hegel's philosophy, and an active leader of the "Young Hegelians." Hegel had argued that the three Estates, [the *substantial* estate (agriculture), the *formal* estate (trade and industry), and the *universal* estate (civil society)] were unified, aggregated, and brought into alignment with the state through an on-going mediation process. Marx disagreed.

In 1843, Marx wrote his *Contribution to a Critique of Hegel's Philosophy of Right* (adopting Hegel's philosophical categories), arguing that the estates were political stand-ins for social classes, which together formed civil society. The legislature, or estates, "not only *mediate* nation and government," as Hegel described, they also used mediation as a camouflage to prevent the "monarchical authority" from appearing as an "arbitrary tyranny" or isolated "extreme," and the oppressed classes from appearing, or becoming, a revolutionary mass or "aggregate."

In critiquing Hegel's analysis, Marx described how the mediative function of the estates was used to obscure the deeper divisions and sources of chronic conflict within civil society and the state, and to regard the mass of the people as an integral part of the organization of the state:

> This mediating function is what the Estates have in common with the organised executive power. In a state in which the position of the Estates prevents individuals from having the appearance of a mass or an aggregate, and so from acquiring an unorganised opinion and volition, and from crystallising into a powerful bloc in opposition to the organised state, the organised state exists outside the mass and the aggregate; or, in other words, the mass and aggregate belong to the organisation of the state.

Marx then asked,

> What is it then that makes the Estates appear to be the mediation against this extreme? It is merely the isolation of the particular interests of persons, societies and Corporations; or the fact that their isolated interests balance their account with the state through the Estates while, at the same time, the unorganised opinion and volition of a mass or aggregate employed its volition (its activity) in creating the Estates and its opinion in judging their activity, and enjoyed the illusion of its own objectification.

In this way, Marx argued that mediation helped *preserve* the monarchical state against the creation of a republic, and defended it against the opposition of the third estate through a counter-process of "disorganization" directed by the state against the formation of a unified, organized opposition to the state within civil society. To strengthen his analysis, Marx began by quoting Hegel:

> The manner and means of the state's mediation with the family and civil society are 'circumstance, caprice, and personal choice of station in life'. Accordingly, the rationality of the state has nothing to do with the division of ... the state into family and civil society. ...

> These circumstances, this caprice, this personal choice of vocation, this actual mediation are merely the *appearance* of a mediation which the actual Idea [of the State] undertakes with itself and which goes on behind the scenes. Actuality is not expressed as itself but as another reality. Ordinary empirical existence does not have its own mind but rather an alien mind as its law, while on the other hand the actual Idea does not have an actuality which is developed out of itself, but rather has ordinary empirical existence as its existence. [Emphasis added.]

Marx therefore concluded that "All the contradictions of modern state-organisations converge in the Estates. They mediate in every direction because they are, from every direction, the middle term." Yet Marx believed there were two very different aspects, or ways of understanding how the state approached mediation, as Hegel described it:

> It should be further noted that, while the Estates, according to Hegel, stand between the government in general on the one hand and the nation broken up into particulars (people and associations) on the other, the significance of their position ... is that, in common with the organised executive, they are a middle term.

Regarding the first position, the Estates represent the nation over against the executive, but the nation *en miniature*. This is their oppositional position.

Regarding the second, they represent the executive over against the nation, but the amplified executive. This is their conservative position. They are themselves a part of the executive over against the people, but in such a way that they simultaneously have the significance of representing the people over against the executive.

For this reason, the nation state, as a *mediator*, could not be a "universal," a whole, a neutral, or a "totality," as Hegel described it, but was rather always a *duality*, a contradiction, a partisan in the conflict, an effort to define an external "mean," and a "mere representation" in opposition to the *real* source of mediation, which was civil society.

In the on-going state-sponsored mediation of political disputes, Marx asserted that the estates or social classes, legitimized by their mediative role and presence in the legislature, simultaneously represented two entities, rather than one – not only:

(1) the extreme of the nation over against the executive, but (2) the mean between nation and executive; or, in other words, the opposition within the nation itself. The opposition between the executive and the nation is mediated through the opposition between the Estates and the nation. From the point of view of the executive the Estates have the position of the nation, but from the point of view of the nation they have the position of the executive. The nation in its occurrence as image, fantasy, illusion, representation — i.e., the imagined nation, or the Estates, which are immediately situated as a particular power in dissociation from the actual nation - abolishes the actual opposition between the nation and the executive. Here the nation is already dressed out, exactly as required in this particular organism, so as to have no determinate character.

Hegel cast the monarchy, the executive, the legislature, and the Estates as mediators in their conflicts with each other and with civil society, alternately casting the sovereign as "the middle term in the legislature between the executive and the Estates; … [and] the executive [as] the middle term between him and the Estates, and the Estates between him and civil society." This led Marx to rhetorically ask,

> How is he to mediate between what he himself needs as a mean lest his own existence become a one-sided extreme? Now the complete absurdity of these extremes, which interchangeably play now the part of the extreme and now the part of the mean, becomes apparent. They are like Janus with two-faced heads, which now show themselves from the front and now from the back, with a diverse character at either side. What was first intended to be the mean between two extremes now itself occurs as an extreme; and the other of the two extremes, which had just been mediated by it, now intervenes as an extreme (because of its distinction from the other extreme) between its extreme and its mean. This is a kind of mutual reconciliation society.

To make his case regarding the absurdity and impossibility of Hegel's description of an internally divided state acting as a mediator for itself a bit less abstract and somewhat clearer, Marx offered several examples, which are closer to what mediators commonly encounter today:

> It is as if a man stepped between two opponents, only to have one of them immediately step between the mediator and the other opponent. It is like the story of the man and wife who quarreled and the doctor who wished to mediate between them, whereupon the wife soon had to step between the doctor and her husband, and then the husband between his wife and the doctor. It is like the lion in *A Midsummer Night's Dream* who exclaims: 'I am the lion, and I am not the lion, but Snug.' So here each extreme is sometimes the lion of

opposition and sometimes the Snug of mediation. When the one extreme cries: 'Now I am the mean', then the other two may not touch it, but rather only swing at the one that was just the extreme. As one can see, this is a society pugnacious at heart but too afraid of bruises to ever really fight. The two who want to fight arrange it so that the third who steps between them will get the beating, but immediately one of the two appears as the third, and because of all this caution they never arrive at a decision. We find this system of mediation in effect also where the very man who wishes to beat an opponent has at the same time to protect him from a beating at the hands of other opponents, and because of this double pursuit never manages to execute his own business.

Marx cited three fundamental errors in Hegel's thinking about mediating political conflicts that, in his view, would have allowed him to avoid these dilemmas. Put in more modern terms, these can be described as a set of correctable attitudes and assumptions that underlie many political conflicts:

1. Since, for each side in political conflicts, only their own extreme is true, "every abstraction and one-sidedness takes itself to be the truth."
2. Since political opposites naturally polarize and form extremes, "which is nothing other than their self-knowledge, as well as their inflammation to the decision to fight," they are viewed as harmful to the state, which tries to avoid and obstruct extremes wherever possible.
3. Since whenever political mediations are attempted, for each side, "no matter how firmly both extremes appear, in their existence, to be actual and to be extremes, it still lies only in the essence of the [*other* side] to be an extreme, and it [loses, as a result,] the meaning of true actuality."

Marx applied this analysis to the deeper difficulties faced by many political mediators today, which impact their ability even to *imagine* the formation of a mediative, interest-based approach to resolving political conflicts — that is, where polarization is *not* accidental, superficial, or purely individual, but based on real, substantive, vital, social, economic, political, and environmental differences.

> Actual extremes cannot be mediated with each other precisely because they are actual extremes. But neither are they in need of mediation, because they are opposed in essence. They have nothing in common with one another; they neither need nor complement one another. The one does not carry in its womb the yearning, the need, the anticipation of the other.

Marx was not opposed to political mediations in general, but to the idea that hierarchically divided, class-based, monarchical *state* institutions could mediate the highly conflicted, contradictory, antithetical conditions in republican, democratic civil society that gave rise to them, without also seeking to resolve the underlying adversarial systemic or structural reasons for their conflict, and revealing the revolutionary truth of what was in common between them.

Marx ultimately asked the question: Why did Hegel propose mediation with the Estates at all? He answered, that while the sovereign "exists within the state," civil society does not — *except* through its formal, artificial, *mediated* representation in the Estates. Thus, in the on-going mediation that constitutes the state, civil society plays no role, and therefore has "no political existence." He concluded,

> The legislature, therefore, needs mediation within itself, that is to say, a concealment of the opposition. ...The Estates are supposed to be the mediation between the crown and the executive on the one hand, and the crown and the people on the other. But they are not this, but rather the organised political opposition to civil society. ... Indeed, only the legislature is the organised, total political state; yet,

precisely in it appears, because it is in its highest degree of development, the open contradiction of the political state with itself. ... Either the Estates must be established as the sovereign will or the sovereign will be established as the Estates. ... The Estates, at this moment, are the romanticism of the political state, the dreams of its substantiality or internal harmony. They are an allegorical existence.

Marx viewed Hegel's dream of internal harmony and the allegorical existence of the Estates as not only romantic, but a camouflage and cover for the *real* conflict, which could *not* be addressed in a state-conducted mediation, because the true parties were not present — except in an abstract, desiccated form. He believed that if Hegel had viewed class distinctions as the true source of political conflict, social classes and the civil society they constituted would have been included as independent, active participants in a genuinely mediative approach to political conflicts; and if a *real* mediation were to occur within civil society, or between it and the state, why would any other mediation be necessary?

After he has developed the political Estates as a specific element, as a transubstantiation of the unofficial class into state citizenship, and precisely because of this has found the mediation to be a necessity, by what right does Hegel dissolve this organism once more into the distinction of the unofficial class, ... and then derive from it the political state's mediation with itself? If civil classes as such are political classes, then the mediation is not needed; and if this mediation is needed, then the civil class is not political, and thus also not this mediation.

In language that anticipates his colleague Friedrich Engels' description of the obsolescence and famous idea of the "withering away" of the state, Marx expanded this point, arguing:

Here then, the political state no longer exists as two opposed wills; rather, on the one side stands the political state (the executive and the sovereign), and on the other side stands civil society in its distinction from the political state (the various classes). With that, then, the political state as a totality is abolished.

Engels described it in similar, but somewhat different language:

The interference of the state power in social relations [i.e., in civil society] becomes superfluous in one sphere after another, and then ceases of itself. The government of persons is replaced by the administration of things and the direction of the processes of production. The state is not "abolished", it withers away.

It is possible, therefore, to regard mediation itself as the *withered away judicial* state, and if so, it could provide a model for imagining how the process might work in connection with other state activities. In Marx's view, it was precisely the necessary division between state and civil society, and the inability of any internal, *state-sponsored* mediation to resolve the chronic, *systemic* conflicts between them, that drove authoritarians, demagogues, and tyrants *within* the state to adopt violent, coercive, autocratic, conflict-inducing, dictatorial methods — all in an effort to artificially maintain the unity and superiority of the state, and through it, the unity and superiority of its ruling elites, over and *against* civil society and its' essential, yet politically subordinate social classes.

Marx added that the *simultaneity* of mediation and the contradictory, entrenched, dominating, adversarial interests of these opposing social classes would continually get in the way of successful mediations:

... these elements which mediate 'in common' seem quite prone to get into one another's hair.... In the Estates on the one hand, and the executive element of the legislature on the other, which together would mediate between civil society and the sovereign, the opposition thus appears to have become, first of all, a refereed opposition, but also an irreconcilable contradiction.

From Marx's comments, it logically follows that there will be profound, systemic difficulties in all political mediations that are conducted by the state and do not include civil society or its' subordinate social classes, whose very real, *existential* conflicts may certainly be *vocalized* and argued by the leaders of political parties, yet these same parties seek to channel and distort the mediation process to achieve their own narrower ends, because any genuine resolution could require them to surrender some of their status, wealth, or power.

This is similar to the ways attorneys in litigated cases sometimes mediate, translating their clients' experiences into legal categories that require a lawyers' expertise, and negotiating in ways that are likely to result in higher legal fees, while largely ignoring the emotional and relational elements, as well as the systemic and structural reasons for disputes that often lie directly beneath the narrow issues being litigated.

In short, if we are to use mediation to collaboratively search for ways of resolving, transforming, and transcending political issues, facilitating systemic and structural improvement, and affirming social justice and fundamental fairness, then the mediation process needs to take place within the context of *systemically* divided parties, civil societies, and those who are most impacted by the conflict; address the sources of systemic and structural unfairness; and resist being diverted or co-opted by parties with superior status, wealth, or power.

The great advantage of mediation in seeking to resolve chronic social, economic, political, and environmental conflicts is that it is *naturally* inclusive, inherently fair, ethically oriented to "power-balancing," systemically and structurally motivated to resist unequal outcomes based on privilege or hierarchies of status, wealth, and power; and as a result, is far closer to civil society than to the state.

SOME DIFFERENCES BETWEEN CIVIL SOCIETY AND THE STATE

Hegel and Marx were deeply impacted by the French Revolution, writing at the end of feudal absolutism, overthrow of hereditary monarchies, dissolution of slavery and serfdom, rise of capitalism, and creation of national republics with publicly accountable executives, democratically elected legislatures, formally independent judiciaries, and professional administrations. At the same time, civil society became increasingly separated from the state, controlled by it, and *opposed* to its' continued oppressive, hierarchical, adversarial, and bureaucratic practices. While Hegel believed these differences could be mediated *within* the state, Marx saw them as emerging naturally from feudalism and capitalism, which created alienated social classes *outside* the state. Since property qualifications for voting were virtually universal at the time, the state would have had a natural, built-in bias in favor of landowners, slave masters, feudal lords, and merchant capitalists, which created *legal* ways of excluding the propertyless, including slaves, serfs, and factory workers, from gaining or exercising political power. This in turn meant that the state could never be any more than *abstractly* neutral and *ceremoniously* mediative in resolving political conflicts between opposing social classes. This implicit bias toward those with the most wealth and property led Marx to imagine an alternative *outside* the state in which these conflicts were fully resolved:

> In place of the old bourgeois society, with its classes and class antagonisms, we shall have an association in which the free development of each is a condition for the free development of all.

The *idea* that the free development of each — *including* former opponents — might be considered a condition for the free development of all, could be applied not only to small-scale conflicts in relationships between friends, couples, family members, and work teams, where its' significance is clear–but to mid-scale conflicts in communities, workplaces, and organizations; and large-scale conflicts in civil societies, political factions, and nation states–helps create a philosophical foundation for scale-free, mediative, holistic, interest-based, non-zero-sum, *systemic* approaches to problem-solving and conflict resolution. The core ethical principles underlying this philosophy are commonly recognized and can be easily stated. It is: "An injury to one is an injury to all;" "We're all in the same boat;" "A house divided cannot stand;" "All for one and one for all;" "No man is an island;" etc. In conflict resolution, these phrases translate into efforts to satisfy *all* parties' interests — not merely by reaching consensus, but identifying and resolving the deeper, *systemic* inequalities and dysfunctions that gave rise to the dispute, and will continue to generate new disputes until they are resolved. If we can imagine extending this interest-based philosophical principle from resolving political conflicts to satisfying deeper sets of interests — to eliciting and strengthening the parties' capacity for empathy, caring, compassion, and connection; if we can imagine scaling these qualities up from couples, families, and work teams to communities, workplaces, and organizations, and from there to civil societies and nation states — what might happen on each scale as a result? How might the practical functions performed by nation states be redesigned? What might a mediative, interest-based nation state *look* like? The answers require us to dig deeper into the differences between civil societies and nation states, especially in relation to problem-solving and dispute resolution.

CIVIL SOCIETIES VS. NATION STATES IN PROBLEM-SOLVING AND DISPUTE RESOLUTION

[Some of what follows in the next two sections has been drawn and adapted from my previous book, *Conflict Revolution: Designing Preventative Systems for Chronic Social, Economic and Political Conflicts (2nd Edition) 2015.*]

Civil society can be defined quite simply as an informal, voluntary, self-organized community of people. It consists of the spontaneous, unofficial, social, economic, political, cultural, and environmental *activities* and *relationships* of people who interact informally *alongside* the formal, involuntary, hierarchically organized state, yet remain private individuals and public citizens whose lives are largely independent of it.

Whereas the state is in essence a formality, a structure, a system, an intricately woven illusion, an abstract, impersonal legal entity with no concrete physical existence, other than through acts of governance, domination, and control; civil society is a real, informal, multi-systemic, loosely structured, sometimes chaotic set of self-regulated, networked social relationships and experiences, engendered by people interacting informally, individually, and in concert — for the most part collaboratively and democratically, but also competitively and autocratically.

Broadly speaking, and with notable exceptions, the distinction between nation states and civil societies can be clarified through the following rough generalizations and distinctions:

- While the state relies on a separate class of elected leaders, legal and bureaucratic experts, and political professionals; civil society relies on an integrated network, or spontaneous community of informal leaders and volunteers.
- While the state is generally stable, ongoing, formally objective, and electorally responsive to public needs; civil society is continually evolving, fluctuating, subjective, and responsive to personal needs.
- While the state is artificially designed and oriented to pre-set rules, systems, and *hierarchical* structures, self-consciously reflecting the dominant goals and ideals of the times; civil society is "naturally" designed, "*heterarchically*" structured, and oriented to human values and relationships,

which naturally and un-self-consciously reflect its true, diverse, and complex inner nature.

- While the state is largely objective, emotionally distant, and rational; civil society is largely subjective, emotionally present, and "gestalt," holistic, non-linear, and human in thinking.
- While both make mistakes, civil societies more readily acknowledge their errors, and are more accepting of chaos, diversity, ambiguity, paradox, subjectivity, and human frailty than states, which routinely deny all errors and wrongdoing and accept natural disorder.
- While the state is predominantly competitive, adversarial, win/lose, and a "zero sum" game in which the whole is "sub-additive" and never greater than the sum of its parts; civil society is predominantly collaborative, non-adversarial, win/win, and a non-zero-sum game in which the whole is "super-additive" and often greater than the sum of its parts.
- While the state can be regarded metaphorically as the "ego" of civil society, civil society can be regarded as the "soul" of the state.
- While violence, competition, legal coercion, bureaucratic controls, and restricted voting are the principal methods adopted by predominantly power- and rights-based states to settle political conflicts and solve social problems; interest-based civil societies use non-violent communication, collaboration, dialogue, consensus-building, conflict resolution, inclusion, and participation.

While it is *possible* for civil societies to perform many of the problem-solving and conflict resolution functions of nation states, states hardly ever perform the qualitatively different functions of civil societies. In conflict resolution, for example, states rarely send criminal cases to mediation, ask offenders to pronounce judgment on themselves, promote forgiveness, encourage "truth and reconciliation," or allow communities to act as judges and impose sentences. They almost never support personal transformation and transcendence through risky, open, honest, public dialogues, collaborative negotiations, restorative justice circles, or submit even low-level political conflicts to mediation, yet civil societies are able to do all of these.

While it is possible for civil societies to adopt and enforce rules or sit in judgment, like parties in mediation, they *design* their rules based on subjective, as well as objective criteria, and are more likely to act with mercy and compassion; whereas states fear that doing so will lead to accusations of bias or corruption, entail electoral defeat, or undermine their pretense of "neutrality."

Civil societies rarely enforce rules uniformly, especially when they are unjust, unfair, or there is no clear and compelling need to do so. States, on the other hand, try to enforce rules uniformly and bureaucratically for everyone *without* regard to their justice or fairness, even when there is a clear and compelling need *not* to. In short, states routinely enforce *rule-driven values*, while civil societies seek consensus on *value-driven rules*.

States historically claim to represent civil societies, while superimposing themselves and seeking to dominate and control them, yet are silently subservient to the wealthiest elements of it– i.e., to slave owners, feudal lords, monarchs, rich merchants, factory owners, and wealthy campaign contributors. States are therefore *grounded* in domination, *required* to use force, violence, coercion, control, and deliberately manipulate electoral processes to maintain hierarchical power. This, however, makes them suspect mediators, because civil societies include slaves, serfs, subjects, workers, consumers, citizens, and those who are poor, making them more open, fluid, egalitarian, and suspect by the state.

Mediation, by definition, seeks to equalize and balance the interests of dominators with those they dominate. Yet this forces mediators to stand *outside* domination, making the process not exactly "neutral," but *capable* of regarding domination as a *systemic* source of chronic conflict, and understanding and affirming the deeper, *human* interests of everyone, dominator and dominated alike.

This simple stance *outside* of domination, however, turns political mediators into potential critics, obstacles, and alternatives to unfettered domination *within* the state, leading autocrats, dictators, and tyrants everywhere to periodically turn the full force of state repression against civil society and *block* or resist its mediative activities, or restrict it to silencing and placating the opposition.

As a result, efforts to expand freedom and equality continually and *inevitably* arise within civil society, where they are initially repressed and transformed into conflicts, which leads them to demand greater democracy, which stimulates calls for regime change, which periodically accelerate into polarizations and political crises — and also, *implicitly*, into requests for problem-solving and mediation.

State Functions and How Civil Societies Perform Them

Given these differences between states and civil societies, we can start to imagine how the most common state functions might be performed differently by civil societies–i.e., how these differences might translate into civil society-oriented, and therefore mediative, interest-based "states," and what the consequences might be for political problem-solving and conflict resolution.

In general, and without regard to their specific content, nationality, history, culture, socio-economic-political-environmental differences, and similar factors, the most common functions of nation states, as distinguished from those routinely performed by civil societies, generally include the following eight:

1. Defense of national sovereignty and territory against external enemies.
2. Protection of the established social, economic, and political order against internal strife, discord, and rebellion.
3. Unification of disparate and competing ruling factions.

4. Prevention of private violence.
5. Creation of mechanisms for the peaceful resolution of chronic, systemic conflicts.
6. Promotion of economic well-being and competitive advantage in pursuit of national economic interests.
7. Regulation of domestic economic practices in the interest of health and "fair competition."
8. Establishment of orderly mechanisms for conflict resolution, and for social, economic, and political change.

Nation states around the world and throughout history have carried out these seemingly neutral functions in unique and diverse ways that have differed markedly, not only from one another, but from the ways their *own* civil societies might have approached or performed or them. They have done so, I believe, in at least the following noteworthy and consequential ways:

1. *Defense of national sovereignty and territory against external enemies.* In defending sovereignty and territory, states typically create standing armies led by a hierarchical officer corps recruited from social elites, staffed by the lower classes, relying tactically on aggression, centralized command, hierarchical organization, coerced obedience, and superior military force. Civil societies, on the other hand, typically create volunteer civilian militias with officers recruited from below, relying tactically on defense, mobility, guerilla maneuverability, and superior unity, motivation, and morale. While large standing armies are often considered preferable to civilian militias, their military advantages have significant weaknesses, as can be found in their defeat in Vietnam, Afghanistan, Iraq, and elsewhere. Moreover, standing armies are an enormous burden on the economic resources and moral conscience of a people. They can readily turn to aggression, bullying, and *coups d'etat*; undermine efforts to reduce global warming and

protect the environment; and discourage the use of less costly, damaging, and violent methods of dispute resolution. As these burdens increase, the purely defensive, mediative, interest-based approaches typical of civil societies can provide strategic advantages and support reductions in the use of bullying and brinksmanship as means of resolving civil and international disputes.

2. *Protection of the established social, economic, and political order against internal strife, discord, and rebellion.* While the state exists partly to preserve a "pecking order" in status, wealth, and power; civil societies aim for a more equal distribution and sharing of resources. Therefore, states tend to favor elites; reinforce hierarchies, bureaucracies, and autocracies; and suppress diversity and dissent. Civil societies, on the other hand, tend to treat their members more equally; reinforce heterarchies, citizen participation, and direct democracies; and are more welcoming of diversity and dissent, seeing them as sources of learning and change.

3. *Unification of disparate and competing ruling factions.* States seek to unify competing groups and factions under a single dominant political leader and faction, or coalition of factions, using autocratic methods, rights-based compromises, "formal" neutrality, and coerced conformity to avoid splits and civil wars. Civil societies seek to unify competing groups and factions through interest-based dialogues, informal democratic methods, participation in decision-making, and voluntary community. They use collaboration, diversity, and dissent, and encourage self-determination, including the right to independence, while proactively working together to reduce or eliminate the reasons for leaving.

4. *Prevention of private violence.* States are concerned with restricting or punishing resort to private violence so as to maintain their monopoly over the use of force. They seek to minimize differences, suppress intense emotions, and use

military, police, and bureaucratic agencies to discourage social experimentation. Civil societies, because they are less formal, indirect, and impersonal, act preventatively to redress the deeper, underlying emotional and systemic reasons for violence, promote forgiveness, truth and reconciliation, victim-offender mediation, and restorative justice programs, and offer a broader range of effective, inexpensive alternatives to violence.

5. *Creation of a mechanism for the peaceful resolution of chronic, systemic conflicts.* States principally resolve conflicts by selecting one party as the winner through adversarial litigation or negotiation, *after* the dispute has become seriously disruptive and costly, biasing the process toward those who can afford to pay attorneys. Civil societies try to *prevent* conflicts through informal problem-solving, early mediation, and conflict resolution systems design, which help to shrink or eliminate the need for litigation. Instead, they use voluntary, participatory, egalitarian, private, confidential, subjective, non-coercive, empathetic, consensus building processes that allow people to reach higher levels of resolution and reconciliation.

6. *Promotion of economic well-being and competitive advantage in pursuit of national economic interests.* States seek to promote economic expansion in part by managing competitive economic activity, setting tariffs to protect domestic industries, offering subsidies and reduced taxes to favored interests, and encouraging "trickle down" development in ways designed to distribute wealth primarily to those who already have it. Civil societies, on the other hand, seek to maximize everyone's personal and socio-economic well-being by encouraging global collaboration and trade, eliminating protective tariffs, supporting equitable economic activity, promoting social, environmental, and local "free trade" markets; encouraging "trickle up" investments, micro-lending, and community development;

and re-distributing profits and surpluses to those most in need.

7. *Regulation of domestic economic practices in the interest of health and "fair competition."* States attempt to regulate the most extreme forms of consumer gouging and endangerment, political corruption, and corporate greed, but are limited in doing so by their vulnerability to wealthy individual and corporate campaign contributors, and their reliance on formal bureaucratic regulations that primarily penalize only the crudest, poorest, and least sophisticated violators. Civil societies, on the other hand, tend to promote truth in advertising, strong consumer protection efforts, active citizen involvement, insulation of regulatory officials from undue influence, minimization of corruption and economic abuse, and blocking unsafe products and unfair practices at their source.

8. *Establishment of orderly mechanisms for conflict resolution, and for social, economic, and political change.* Modern states use elections and lawsuits as non-violent mechanisms for resolving political conflicts, maintaining continuity, and discouraging deep, systemic, structural, or transformational changes, by promoting candidates, parties, and institutions that are focused on image, gesture, and spin. Civil societies are more grounded in substantive, participatory, *direct* democracy and meritocracy, and tend to encourage systemic and structural changes, invite leaders and policies to be improved, not only by voting for candidates, but public dialogue, consensus-building, and political mediation. Its methods are less formal and more concerned with the *content* of issues than with image or spin.

In sum, the state is organized around the competitive, adversarial, and acquisitive exercise of political power, mirroring its' equally competitive, adversarial, and acquisitive relationship with social status, economic wealth, political power, and willingness to exploit the environment, which value possessions more highly than the human beings who create them and the relationships that give them meaning.

Consequently, states tend to define success by acquisition, control, winning and losing, and domination over and against others, all of which generate chronic conflicts. Civil societies, on the other hand, while often hierarchical, are more open to sharing, collaboration, and democracy, valuing human beings and social relationships over possessions, encouraging political power sharing, discouraging adversarial attitudes toward status, wealth, power, and the environment, promoting mutual gain, and seeking to transform and prevent chronic conflicts.

These distinctions are, of course, rough, generic, abstract, and variable. Their purpose is not to sanctify civil society or demonize the state, but to suggest that mediation and other interest-based "arts and sciences," if they are to result not only in compromise, conciliation, continuity, and stasis; but resolution, reconciliation, transformation, and transcendence; are probabilistically far less likely to reach higher order outcomes in contexts and settings that are power- or rights-based, as nation states have traditionally been; than in contexts that are pluralistic, mediative, and interest-based, as civil societies are far more able to become. The philosopher Isaiah Berlin brilliantly described the inevitable, unending conflicts that arise whenever we seek political balance between people with opposing values, such as liberty and equality, individuality and collectivity, chaos and order, and similar "intrinsic, irremovable" elements in human life. Our aim, he believed, should be to maintain a "precarious equilibrium that will prevent the occurrence of desperate situations, of intolerable choices," by recognizing that political truths are *not* abstract, scientific, unitary, or exclusive; but empirical, subjective, diverse, and pluralistic:

> So long as only one ideal is the true goal, it will always seem to men
> that no means can be too difficult, no price too high, to do whatever

is required to realize the ultimate goal. Such certainty is one of the great justifications of fanaticism, compulsion, persecution ... If there is only one solution to the puzzle, then the only problems are first how to find it, then how to realize it, and finally how to convert others to the solution by persuasion or by force. But if this is not so ..., then the path is open to empiricism, pluralism, tolerance, compromise. Tolerance is historically the product of the realization of the irreconcilability of equally dogmatic faiths, and the practical improbability of complete victory of one over the other. Those who wished to survive realized that they had to tolerate error. They gradually came to see the merits of diversity, and so became skeptical about definitive solutions in human affairs.

Interest-based approaches like dialogue, collaborative negotiation, consensus building, mediation, and restorative justice, allow us to consider the possibility of translating these rough, generic distinctions between nation states and civil societies into *higher order* forms of problem-solving and conflict resolution that do not end simply in tolerance, compromise, or stalemate over deeply held, critically important values, but in the *affirmation* of diversity and dissent, collaboration between "teams of rivals," and the discovery that better, *transformational* solutions can emerge and evolve through mutual exploration, synthesis, and dialogue.

MARY PARKER FOLLETT AND THE "NEW STATE"

What would a practical, interest-based, civil society-oriented, transformational approach to political conflicts actually look like? In 1918, at the end of the First World War, Mary Parker Follett, one of the founders of modern mediation, wrote *The New State: Group Organization, the Solution for Popular Government*, in which she advocated an earlier form of what later became known as "participatory democracy." Follett powerfully declared:

> We talk about the evils of democracy. We have not yet tried democracy. Party 'interests' govern us with some fiction of the

'consent of the governed' which we say means democracy....
Government by the people must be more than the phrase. We are
told – The people should do this, the people should do that, the
people should be given control of foreign policy, etc. But all this is
wholly useless unless we provide the procedure within which the
people *can* do this or that.

Follett's key insight was that, to create such a state, we require not
only self-governance, free speech, and institutional responsiveness
to social conditions, but an understanding of what governance
properly *consists* of, the creation of a *language* that allows people to
speak freely, and the invention of institutions that *proactively* elicit,
express, and improve those social conditions. As she brilliantly
wrote in the epigraph cited at the beginning, in a passage that
deserves repeating:

> [I]t is not merely that we must be allowed to govern ourselves, we
> must learn how to govern ourselves; it is not only that we must be
> given 'free speech,' we must learn a speech that is free; ... [I]t is not
> only that we must invent machinery to get a social will expressed,
> we must invent machinery that will get a social will created.

This means moving beyond *exclusive* reliance on the ballot box,
which creates "a mere phantom of democracy" and takes attention
from the real task, which is the creation of a "genuine union of true
individuals;" in other words, it asks us to bring about through
interest-based processes a unification that is authentic because it is
founded on the diversity of real individuals whose differences
augment and *increase* their sense of community, rather than
reducing or subtracting from it.

To achieve these results, we require a higher order of skills than
those typical of political and government institutions–skills in
communicating non-violently, managing diversity, reframing and
learning from dissent, facilitating dialogues, building consensus,

exploring paradox and ambiguity, negotiating collaboratively, resolving conflicts, restoring justice, and designing *preventative* conflict resolution systems that teach and reinforce these skills.

Doing so, Follett believed, required the creation of "a new principle of association" that can "maintain difference within unity, conflict within integration." It is this principle that, in my view, is the heart, soul, fundamental meaning, and "spirit" of democracy; that lies at the heart of its' "core operating system" and can lead us to a more mediative, interest-based approach to politics and political conflicts.

For any government to continuously reflect and represent a diverse and constantly changing group of people, Follett believed it was essential to develop a *process* that could help people "learn how to live with each other." On a small scale, in the communities where she worked, she found this process expressed in the dialogues that took place during meetings conducted by local committees. She wrote,

> The object of a committee meeting is to create a common idea. I do not go to a committee meeting merely to give my own ideas. If that were all, I might write my fellow members a letter. But neither do I go to learn other people's ideas. If that were all, I might ask each to write me a letter. I go to a committee meeting in order that all together we may create a group idea, an idea which will be better than any one of our ideas alone, moreover which will be better than all of our ideas added together. For this group idea will not be produced by the process of addition, but by the interpenetration of us all. This subtle psychic process by which the resulting idea shapes itself is the process we want to study.

For this to work, people need to be supported in putting forth their own unique individual ideas; disagreements need to be reframed as contributions to the greater good; dissent, dialogue, and the search for win/win solutions need to be actively encouraged; and conflicts need to be transformed through an interest-based process of discovery, creative contention, and consensus building. Done correctly, this approach can lead people to higher order syntheses and holistic integrations of a broad array of partial, polarized, even contradictory truths that, once they are seen correctly, can be regarded as *complementary* to each other. Follett wrote,

> [A majority vote or] even the passing of a unanimous vote by a group of five does not prove the existence of a group idea if two or three (or even 1) out of indifference or laziness or prejudice, or shut-upness, or a misconception of their function, have not added their individual thought to the creation of the group thought.

This meant that "a readiness to compromise must be no part of the individual's attitude." Instead of compromising principles and sacrificing unique individual truths, opposing views needed to be acknowledged, discussed, integrated, synthesized, and creatively combined in ways that reveal *larger* holistic, composite, higher order truths. What Parker described can be seen today as a description of the effort most mediators, collaborative negotiators, dialogue facilitators, consensus builders, and restorative practitioners make every day in seeking qualitative, synthesized, transformational, "win/win" outcomes, as opposed to quantitative, averaged, compromised, "lose/lose" solutions that simply add two sums together and divide by two.

Power-based political systems, while democratic in name, are hierarchical, and prone to corruption, dictatorship, autocracy, and the use of violence and coercion to enforce obedience. Rights-based political systems are bureaucratic and based on elections in which people vote for representatives in adversarial factions and political parties, who verbally battle with one another for swing voters and make decisions almost entirely by compromise—indeed, politics is often described as "the art of compromise"—in order to ensure compliance and a grudging unity.

But compromise always boils down to a numbers game and is fundamentally digital–that is, voting is limited to choices that are either for or against, this candidate or that, this party or that, this solution, value, principle, and future or that. These methodologies may succeed where the problems to be solved are simple, static, insular, and short-term; but they will predictably fail when these problems become complex, changing, global, and long-term.

What is therefore required for genuine, participatory, substantive, direct democracy is the creation of a pluralistic, inclusive, participatory, interest-based political system that is capable of using *analogue* forms of problem-solving, decision-making, and conflict resolution, as these rest on the realization that political issues are inherently non-linear and non-digital, because nearly all are complex, have more than one correct solution, and therefore require processes that encourage diversity, dissent, creative contention, principled engagement, exploration, inquiry, collaboration, consensus building, and the discovery through dialogue and synthesis of solutions that are *at least* as complex as the problems they seek to solve—in other words, difference within unity, conflict within integration, and self within other. Interest-based approaches view democracy not merely as an institution, or an outcome, but as an evolving *process*, and as a network of fluid, egalitarian social *relationships*. Again, Mary Parker Follett writes,

> Majority rule rests on numbers; democracy rests on the well-grounded assumption that society is neither a collection of units nor an organism but a network of human relations. Democracy is not worked out at the polling-booths; it is the bringing forth of a genuine collective will, one to which every single being must contribute the whole of his complex life. ...Thus the essence of democracy is creating. The technique of democracy is group organization. Many men despise politics because they see that politics manipulate, but make nothing. If politics are to be the highest activity of man, as they should be, they must be clearly

understood as creative … [In this process, t]he fallacy of self-and-others fades away and there is only self-in-and-through others, only others so rooted in the self and so fruitfully growing there that sundering is impossible.

This is a beautiful description of the real, *practical* magic of mediation, which is also found in dialogue, collaboration, consensus building, restorative circles, and similar processes that draw opposites into conversation, creative contention, and collaborative problem-solving with each other. It then becomes possible for diversity to discover its latent unity; for individuation to transition into integration, and for the Other to be revealed as nothing other than a previously unnoticed element of the Self.

When this happens in friendships, couples, and families we call it love, or we may say that people "click," "sync," or "connect" with each other. But it can also happen during sporting events, ecological disasters, and political crises. It can occur in work teams, neighborhoods, and communities, as well as in organizations, nation states—even on-line between otherwise disconnected individuals around the world. It can happen in a flash, without any indication that it is even conceivable.

In the political arena, as Follett revealed, there is on-going tension and occasional conflict between the individual and society, the person and the people, the solitary being and the masses, the one and the many. This tension, or conflict, as a matter of logic, can only be resolved in the following six fundamental ways:

1. By elevating (for example) personal liberty over social equality
2. By elevating social equality over personal liberty
3. By rejecting both
4. By fluctuating back and forth between them
5. By seeking a middle ground through compromise

6. By bringing them into creative contention, collaborative negotiation, and mediation, and attempting to synthesize better, higher, more satisfying outcomes than either could achieve on their own

Mary Parker Follett referred to the last of these as "the group," whereas today we would more likely use the word "team" or "community," as they reflect the presence of an animating energy or "spirit"— a quality of caring that makes a house different from a home, a block from a neighborhood, a group from a team, a city from a community, and a whole that is greater than the sum of its parts.

While we can easily recognize the difference between a house and a home, a block and a neighborhood, a group and a team, or a city and a community, we also understand that the latter are more often the exception than the rule, which raises the question: why is it so difficult to create unity out of diversity, or wholes that are greater than the sums of their parts, and what does this mean for the *project* of democracy in general? What are the obstacles or *flaws* in rights-based democratic systems that return them to power and autocracy, rather than propel them towards participatory, interest-based solutions?

Obstacles to the Creation of an Interest-Based State

The world's already immense and increasing difficulties, including wars, global warming, nuclear proliferation, famines, mass extinctions, hatreds, intolerance, environmental degradations, and many others, face additional, more immediate obstacles in the near complete dependence of international problem-solving on the voluntary cooperation of nation states, each of which is different, with unique needs, perceptions, and interests, and little desire to use interest-based forms of cooperation with feared or hated rivals, as these methods are commonly viewed as signs of weakness or disloyalty, and lacking any clear promise that they will deliver significant short- or long-term advantages.

Moreover, most nation states are led by governments that change completely every few years. Many are rife with dishonesty and corruption, and dependent on political donations and campaign contributions from entrenched elites, large corporations, defense contractors, and wealthy interests, which earn immense profits by promoting nationalist "us-first" rhetoric, protectionist trade policies, military brinksmanship, and environmentally destructive practices.

These corporations and wealthy individuals form part of a much larger global capitalist system, which is intensely competitive, highly resistant to regulation, driven by short-term profits, and historically hostile — not only to spending money on social and environmental improvement, but to any measures that might dilute their social status, economic wealth, or political power, as a consequence of government oversight and regulation, consumer protection, community collaboration, economic and environmental planning, shared decision-making, and substantive, direct, participatory, interest-based forms of democracy.

Many nation states are therefore internally divided, often between a dominant minority with a vested interest in *resisting* global cooperation, collaborative problem-solving, popular democracy, and healthy, sustainable environmental practices; versus a subordinate majority with an interest in promoting them as essential elements in expanding our collective capacity for global problem-solving and conflict resolution.

These internal divisions are aggravated, not only by privately owned media with an interest in stirring up conflicts to sell advertising, but by powerful, well-funded, entrenched political parties and factions, which make it nearly impossible for genuinely democratic leaders to actively encourage global problem-solving without being dishonest, or jailed, attacked, and accused of disloyalty or treason.

Moreover, the primary ways nation states are held democratically accountable, vested interests are blocked, and governments are stopped from engaging in these destructive practices, is through the organized political opposition of individuals and groups *within* civil society, and the transformation of *opposition* into *aspiration* for a fundamentally better system. This recognition leads autocratic, hierarchical, and bureaucratic elements within the state to regard diversity, dissent, and democratic rights, including the right to vote, as *inherently* subversive and hostile to their self-interest in continued domination and control.

It can also lead vulnerable nation states to resist efforts at global collaboration, participatory problem-solving, and conflict resolution, as they require more than mere passive consent, and are profoundly undermined by apathy, cynicism, perceptions of unfairness, social inequality, economic corruption, demagogic leadership, biases and prejudices, and political demonization. Efforts to overcome these barriers create even *more* political divisions, both within and between nation states, which fuel still deeper suspicions and increased resistance.

As a result, many otherwise intelligent efforts to solve global problems are opposed, resisted, frustrated, delayed, or ignored by sovereign, independent, competitive, and hostile nation states, each with strong nationalist, chauvinist, "us-first" factions that are vying for power and trying to placate constituents. Moreover, many nation states are run by immense bureaucracies, created to sideline civil society-based efforts to bring about systemic change or alter the status quo — for example, by propounding formal, slow-moving rules and regulations that obscure their intentions, insulate their operations from public scrutiny, and channel change efforts into dank, slow-moving swamps. Yet these procedures are regarded as compulsory for all but the most privileged, making them vulnerable to corruption, anti-democratic, and difficult to change.

Many nation states also have large, entrenched, corrupt, arms-trading military-police-industrial complexes that profit immensely from the fear and anger triggered by external enemies, internal threats, and unresolved conflicts. The mere presence of hostile armed forces in any country *creates* fear and anger among their neighbors, who feel threatened and provoked, leading them to organize opposing military and political forces that *also* use fear, anger, and patriotic fervor to advance the hegemonic aspirations of their own national elites.

In these ways, opposing nation states *cooperate* in fueling each other's worst fears and suspicions, inventing and spreading one-sided demonizing stories and narratives, punishing calls for collaboration, dialogue, and mediation as weak or treasonous, and providing each other with backwards-justifying moral rationalizations for mutual hostility, distrust, and renewed cycles of escalation. These tit-for-tat escalations offer useful arguments for allocating significant tax revenues to strengthening both states' destructive capacities, rejecting dialogue and mediation, and keeping their populations separated, angry, frightened, obedient, and ready to die for their country.

They also, of course, provide the resources required by aggressive elements within nation states to forcibly invade, colonize, and cannibalize the wealth of less powerful states, making their fears real, and forcing those who wish to avoid this fate to fight back, further strengthening their cultures of violence and devaluing the possibilities of cooperation, dialogue, and mediation. In short, for divided, *formally* democratic governments to maintain their power and perceived legitimacy, it is sometimes necessary to *manufacture* conflicts, automatically giving rise not only to useful enemies, but to a sense of injury, perfidy, and injustice at the hands of others, with compelling reasons for uniting against common foes. These produce a convincing set of excuses, rationalizations, and justifications for unilaterally imposing their will on others, even by violence, turning the process into a regenerating cycle. Yet, as Israeli novelist David Grossman recognized,

> [S]omewhere deep inside, every person knows when he is committing or colluding with an injustice. Somewhere deep in the heart of any 'reasonable person' of sound mind, there is a place where he cannot delude himself regarding his acts and their implications. The burden created by the injustice – even if it is repressed – is there, and it has effects and it has a price. And what a relief, what a feeling of repair … there must be in a release from the … open and hidden conflicts it engenders.

Each of these obstacles to mutual problem-solving and mediation adds to this burden, wastes precious time, and diverts valuable resources from strengthening internal and external collaboration, allowing unsolved problems to mutate into unresolved conflicts, which can become crises, connect, and turn into catastrophes. There are many possible solutions to this dilemma, but what is essential is to recognize that strengthening global problem-solving and conflict resolution are *critical* among them. These efforts cannot be exclusively or entirely global, but must begin with the polarization of internal political factions, and the collapse of trust and hope that turn democracies into autocracies. And, in politics, as the Polish writer Leszek Kolakowski observed, "being deceived is no excuse."

THE OBSTACLE OF FACTIONS

Nearly all nation states are deeply internally divided between hostile, competing factions and intensely adversarial political parties, each with its own distinct interests and constituencies, loosely joined by a fragile commitment to patriotism, or the common good, and a set of rules of engagement, framed as legal principles that can be enforced by judges, who are selected by the faction in power at the time to bias the system in its favor.

In the United States from its' inception, and in the drafting of its' Constitution, warnings were issued by many leaders on the dangers of political factions. In 1787, James Madison, famously writing in the *Federalist Papers* Number 10, defined a faction as follows:

> By a faction, I understand a number of citizens, whether amounting to a minority or majority of the whole, who are united and actuated by some common impulse of passion, or of interest, adverse to the rights of other citizens, or to the permanent and aggregate interests of the community.

From a mediation perspective, a faction is simply a party acting in its' own interests, rather than in the interests of all, which means in *opposition* to the interests of others. What much of the critique of factions has obscured is that the deepest factional disputes in the U. S. at the time were the contests for power between diverse groups of property owners regarding whose rights the Constitution was meant to protect: slave owners, merchants, farmers, landowners, or manufacturers. Madison suggested that there were two ways of "curing the mischiefs of faction":

> The one, by removing its causes; the other, by controlling its effects. There are again two methods of removing the causes of faction: The one, by destroying the liberty which is essential to its existence; the other, by giving to every citizen the same opinions, the same passions, and the same interests.

Madison explained why, in his view, neither method was advisable:

> It could never be more truly said than of the first remedy, that it was worse than the disease. Liberty is to faction what air is to fire, an

aliment without which it instantly expires. But it could not be less folly to abolish liberty, which is essential to political life, because it nourishes faction, than it would be to wish the annihilation of air, which is essential to animal life, because it imparts to fire its destructive agency.

The second expedient is as impracticable as the first would be unwise. As long as the reason of man continues fallible, and he is at liberty to exercise it, different opinions will be formed. As long as the connection subsists between his reason and his self-love, his opinions and his passions will have a reciprocal influence on each other; and the former will be objects to which the latter will attach themselves. The diversity in the faculties of men, from which the rights of property originate, is not less an insuperable obstacle to a uniformity of interests. The protection of these faculties is the first object of government.

From a mediation perspective, it will be useful for us to imagine what an interest-based approach, or set of approaches, for responding to the problem of political factions and the conflicts they create might look like. We might, as in Chapter 8:

1. Assign factions to mixed small groups or circles with facilitators.
2. Ask questions that deepen or broaden the issues, elicit empathy for others, and cannot be answered factionally.
3. Invite all participants to engage in open, public dialogue regarding their experiences and perspectives on the nature of the problem.
4. Search for ways of combining their diverse perspectives.
5. Engage in joint problem-solving, brainstorm, and prioritize possible solutions.
6. Ask small groups to report on their solutions, and search for commonalities.
7. Reach consensus on as many options as possible.

8. Where consensus fails, ask small teams representing all factions to work together, jointly research and prioritize options, etc.

While these and similar methods have been highly successful in solving similar problems, reaching consensus, and resolving conflicts in small- to mid-scale groups and organizations; and while social media and AI programs might certainly help modify and adapt them to large-scale interventions, a far deeper transformation will be required to introduce sustainable interest-based ways of thinking in conflicts between hostile factions, political parties, and nation states.

We can also consider Madison's approach to factions from the perspective of the three divergent orientations to problem-solving and conflict resolution described earlier, that is:

1. An orientation to *power*, resulting in minority rule, which may take the form of sham democracy, autocracy, and violent repression — all of which seek extra-judicial control over electoral outcomes and a *forced* simplification of political conflicts through the marginalization, manipulation, or attempted elimination of diversity and dissent

2. An orientation to *rights*, resulting in majority rule, which takes the form of purely procedural democracy, bureaucracy, legislative promulgation of electoral rules, judicial review of electoral outcomes, and coerced compliance with results–all of which *publicly* affirm the value of diversity and dissent, while *privately* discounting and discouraging them

3. An orientation to *interests*, resulting in popular participation in decision-making, which takes the form of substantive, direct, or participatory democracy, with an orientation toward joint, interest-based, collaborative problem-solving,

> public dialogue, mediation, and pluralism–all of which
> actively support, encourage, learn from, and elicit improved
> solutions through diversity and dissent

When the principal orientation of government is to *power*, the whole of politics and the public good become the private property of a dominant few. When the principal orientation is to *rights*, as Madison recognized, the state may strip dictatorial power from despots and tyrants, while at the same time using the state to protect the unequally distributed property of the wealthy few from the redistributive intentions of the impoverished or less-propertied many. When the principal orientation is to *interests*, there is broader participation in direct political decision-making, allowing a less-propertied majority—especially slaves — to seek more equitable economic redistribution through the electoral process.

Madison explicitly connected political factions and the *form* of democracy with property rights, motivated especially by political conflicts in the nascent republic between slave owners, large landowners, merchants, financiers, and industrialists; and the slaves, family farmers, consumers, borrowers, and workers whose interests they sought to minimize; and unite them all in a single nation state:

> From the protection of different and unequal faculties of acquiring property, the possession of different degrees and kinds of property immediately results; and from the influence of these on the sentiments and views of the respective proprietors, ensues a division of the society into different interests and parties.... [T]he most common and durable source of factions has been the various [forms of] and unequal distribution of property. Those who hold and those who are without property have ever formed distinct interests in society. Those who are creditors, and those who are debtors, fall under a like discrimination. A landed interest, a manufacturing interest, a mercantile interest, a moneyed interest,

with many lesser interests, grow up of necessity in civilized nations, and divide them into different classes, actuated by different sentiments and views. The regulation of these various and interfering interests forms the principal task of modern legislation, and involves the spirit of party and faction in the necessary and ordinary operations of the government.

He therefore concluded that government should be structured to favor the "minority of the opulent" over the majority of the propertyless:

> In England, at this day, if elections were open to all classes of people, the property of the landed proprietors would be insecure. An agrarian law would soon take place. If these observations be just, our government ought to secure the permanent interests of the country against innovation. Landholders ought to have a share in the government, to support these invaluable interests, and to balance and check the other. They ought to be so constituted as to protect the minority of the opulent against the majority.

The fundamental problem, as with all power- and rights-based forms of government, is that power is *acquired* through people acquiescing, agreeing, or being forced to cede it to those who, as a result, possess more of it, become their "leaders," and can then coerce or manipulate more people into at least tacitly agreeing to obey or follow them. Yet democracy also *implicitly* conditions the right to govern on the consent of the governed, who can resist, withhold, withdraw, or reclaim their power, either individually or *en masse*.

The same can be said of rights, which are simply legislated *limitations* on the exercise of power. Interest-based approaches, on the other hand, directly empower people and *invite* them to withhold their consent if they disagree, which raises a series of problems, as it can also be used to shift diverse or dissenting groups away from a battle for fundamental values and towards compromise or cooptation, rather than collaboration, consensus building, conflict resolution, and the difficult task of searching for solutions that work for everyone.

Social theorist Niklas Luhmann suggested that social systems perform "immunological" functions, and that the role of the law and the state is to "vaccinate" society "in anticipation of possible conflicts." They do so by grounding themselves in the past and promulgating rules for resolving similar disputes in the future. Conflicts, he argued, are social systems that are *parasitic,* in the sense that they cause attention and resources to be redirected toward the conflict and away from what is taking place inside and around the system. In this way, politics simultaneously avoids and promotes conflicts, allowing those who dominate to regard their beliefs and behaviors as correct, reject critical feedback, and punish or sanction those who dissent or seek innovative ways out.

THE OBSTACLE OF *KNOWING* WE ARE RIGHT

Any effort to imagine an interest-based approach to resolving political conflicts has to come to terms with the many subtle, covert ways that civil society is unequally divided and search for ways of re-uniting it. Indeed, it is *axiomatic* in mediation that bringing both sides into authentic communication and collaboration requires "power balancing," a "level playing field," "mutual gain bargaining," and an effort to "satisfy the interests" of all sides.

As a thought experiment, let's imagine what would likely happen if we tried to introduce modern conflict resolution principles into a power-based slave-owning society. It would be impossible for any genuine dialogue to take place between slaves and slave owners, as doing so would *automatically* undermine the fundamental principles of domination and subordination on which the entire system of slavery rested. Similar difficulties can be found in many modern, non-slave owning, power-based systems.

In the context of slavery, or any other form of systematic domination, the nation state, which maintains a monopoly on the means of violence and coercion, can play one of only three fundamental roles:

1. It can enforce slavery and domination, represent solely slave owners and dominators, become a power-base instrument of support for those who seek to enslave and dominate others, and be compelled to use violent, autocratic, coercive methods to preserve minority rule.
2. It can seek various forms of compromise that permit slavery and domination, while recognizing minor, limited rights among slaves and the dominated, become a rights-based, "neutral," "Hegelian" mediator and arbiter between them, pretend to represent both sides, and use bureaucratic and legalistic methods to defuse conflicts.
3. It can reject slavery and domination, seek the liberation of slaves and the dominated, become an interest-based instrument of support for those who wish to end slavery and domination, and use democratic methods that encourage diversity, dissent, and dialogue.

Beyond these three, there is a hypothetical fourth, which is the form we might imagine would be taken by an interest-based state *after* slavery and domination have completely dissipated and disappeared. Even regarding slavery, we have not yet reached this stage.

Since their earliest beginnings, internally divided democracies have been held together by varying combinations of internal cohesion and external threat; of loyalty to insiders and fear of outsiders; of love for some and hatred for others. These democracies have largely lacked the skills and capacities, methodologies and techniques needed to sustain consensual political relationships when they become chronically conflicted, or experience traumas or losses, or even great gains and successes. The skills and capacities needed to sustain these democratic states consist partly of interest-based techniques for improving communications and relationships, transforming dissent into suggestions for improvement, turning diversity into higher forms of unity, building consensus between highly polarized, passionately conflicted parties, and mediating unresolved problems.

Participation, democracy, and political freedom, as Plato recognized, always give rise to diversity and dissent, which inevitably coalesce into hostile factions and parties that *know* they are right. On the one hand, these can temporarily increase loyalty, adherence, and electoral successes by provoking internal differences, stoking passions and hatreds, denying commonalities, and turning people against each other. On the other hand, after achieving victory, they necessarily seek to assuage the opposition, assert the need for unity, moderate their passions, accept that they may not be exclusively right, and claim to represent everyone. This can lead people to conclude, as Mary Parker Follett did in the 1920's, that:

> ... the aim of all party organization is to turn out a well-running voting machine. The party is not interested in men but in voters... The basic weakness of party organization is that the individual gets his significance only through majorities.

What Follett omitted from her catalogue of power- and rights-based failures, is that individuals, factions, and parties that are failing and unable to achieve a majority can often be convinced by autocrats, despots, demagogues, and tyrants to *falsely* claim they constitute a majority, disregard previously accepted rules and laws governing the electoral process, and assert their dominance through rigged elections, power-based putsches, and effective *coups d'etat*.

The difficulties for mediators in imagining interest-based solutions to these political problems are many and diverse, and among them is figuring out how to apply the values and principles that guide small scale mediations to a full range of political processes, including electoral design, political dialogues, strategies for reducing hyper-polarization, etc.; and use them to guide multilateral problem-solving, consensus building efforts, and collaborative negotiations.

It is equally important to figure out how to avoid the false, simplistic, superficial, amoral, "plague on both your houses" political distancing, with its moral posturing, pretentious rhetoric, and cowardly neutrality; as well as the adversarial, overly simplistic, one-sided political languages and cultures that are *incapable* of listening, collaborating, or extending empathy to fellow citizens on the other side.

Fixing the Flaws in Power- and Rights-Based Democracies

Over two thousand years ago, Plato wrote in *The Republic* that "Dictatorship naturally arises out of democracy, and the most aggravated form of tyranny and slavery out of the most extreme liberty." His argument went as follows:

> Democracy, by permitting freedom of speech, opens the door for a demagogue to exploit the people's need for a strongman; the strongman will use this freedom to prey on the people's resentments and fears. Once the strongman seizes power, he will end democracy, replacing it with tyranny.

Plato has been proven right numerous times, and his ideas are being tested today, but he is unclear about whether, or how it might be possible to have free speech and at the same time offer interest-based ways of addressing peoples' deepest concerns, desires, resentments, and fears, so that they would be significantly less willing to be preyed upon by strongmen.

In the early 1800's, Alexis de Tocqueville insightfully described a different way democracy could be turned into despotism:

Let me imagine the various ways in which despotism could manifest itself. I envisage a host of people, all more or less alike and in similar situations, who move round and round in a circle without pause in search of trivial, everyday pleasures which fill their lives. Each stands alone, isolated, heedless of the fate of all the others. As far as he is concerned, the human race consists simply of his family and those around him. He stands side by side with his fellow men but he does not see them. He touches them but he does not feel them. He exists solely in and for himself.

Here again, implicit in de Tocqueville's description of social fragmentation and alienation it is possible to spot a potential fix: what if these same people could be brought into regular, direct, non-trivial, *substantively* democratic relationships with one another, in ways that could reduce the ability of despots to isolate them, turn their unacknowledged pain into hatred, and. increase their desires, skills, and *capacities* for hope, trust, empathy, solidarity, and collaboration with others?

In addition to these routes to despotism, the famous mathematical logician Kurt Gödel, after escaping fascism in Europe, applied for US citizenship, and in preparation, carefully studied the US Constitution. He claimed to have found an "inner contradiction" or logical loophole that would allow the US to be legally turned into a fascist dictatorship. When he appeared before a judge to be admitted to citizenship, accompanied by Albert Einstein and Oscar Morgenstern, the judge commented that the Nazi dictatorship in Gödel's Austria could not happen here, and Gödel immediately responded, "Yes it can, and I can prove it!"

Einstein and Morgenstern reportedly quickly changed the subject and there is no record of what Gödel thought the contradiction was, but following the insurrectionary events on January 6, 2021, several possibilities can be imagined. These include the power of the President, as Commander in Chief, to declare a national emergency, impose martial law, and cancel elections; the ability to amend the

Constitution to permit a dictatorship; and the ability of a President, a majority of the Senate, and a 5-4 majority of the Supreme Court to suspend or overturn long-accepted Constitutional protections, as occurred, for example, with the overturning of <u>Roe v. Wade</u> and the Constitutional right to an abortion.

Based on these various flaws, to which others might be added, it is clear that purely procedural, digital, highly conflicted, rights-based representative democracies will *always* find it difficult to escape the possibility that unresolved, hyper-polarized political conflicts could trigger a rapid regression to dictatorial, power-based rule, from which it would be exceedingly difficult to escape. Yet it is equally clear that substantive, analog, mediative, participatory, interest-based democracies would stand a much better chance of avoiding that fate — in part because they are more skilled at resolving political conflicts and removing the reasons for reversion to power-based politics as a way of ending them.

To find out whether these assumptions are correct, it may be helpful to describe four fundamental flaws that are baked into rights-based political operating systems in ways that are extremely difficult to alter:

1. Wealthy elites in any representative, rights-based democracy in which decisions are not made by the people directly, but by their elected representatives, can easily "game the system" by legalizing unequal campaign contributions, regarded by the U. S. Supreme Court as Constitutionally protected "free speech," thereby excluding from office everyone who can't afford the cost of running, and converting procedurally fair, nominally democratic elections based on "one person, one vote," into procedurally unfair, substantively plutocratic elections based on "one dollar, one vote."

2. The democratic promise to all citizens of a right to equal participation in open, public, political decision-making can

be systematically manipulated, undermined, and even eradicated by hyper-polarized, ultra-competitive, adversarial, biased, conspiratorial, zero-sum, hierarchical political *cultures* which are *grounded* in fear and scandal, dependent on advertising revenues from social, economic, and political elites, and ready to stir up prejudices and political conflicts, in part to justify and preserve their own hierarchies. Tyrants can then easily silence isolated opponents, reinforce domination, and bully and coerce voters into unquestioning loyalty to autocratic leaders.

3. The widespread use of adversarial, highly centralized, power- and rights-based problem-solving, decision-making, and conflict resolution processes that *fail* to examine or resolve the underlying or systemic issues that divide people, make it vastly more difficult to freely and openly discuss ideas, learn from diverse perspectives, communicate with dissenting groups, and collaborate in solving political problems. In these and other ways, they turn citizens into alienated, conformist, apolitical followers who are discouraged from uniting, except ineffectively, even to address life-threatening crises.

4. A related difficulty, which I described in more detail in *Politics, Dialogue, and the Evolution of Democracy*, is that rights-, and interest-based methodologies require *exponentially* more advanced, complex, higher order skills, and without support these tend to degrade over time, each more rapidly than the last, due to a kind of "social entropy," in which the number of ways conflicted communications and relationships can break down *enormously* exceeds the number of ways they can come together to create higher order outcomes.

To avoid the fates Plato, de Tocqueville, Gödel and others warned against, we need to re-imagine democracy from an interest-based perspective and consider how we might bake into its' foundations a rich, robust array of self-replicating higher order systems and structures, processes and relationships, attitudes and approaches, skills and capacities, each of which may have the potential to significantly reduce or overcome these flaws.

IMAGINING AN INTEREST-BASED APPROACH TO POLITICAL CONFLICTS

The best way to imagine anything is not to start with what already *is* and try to improve it, but with what does not *yet* exist but could, and try to elaborate it. As Mark Twain pointed out, "You can not depend on your eyes when your imagination is out of focus." The fundamental reason for trying to imagine an alternative future was brilliantly captured by Greek novelist Nikos Kazantzakis: "By believing passionately in something that still does not exist, we create it. The non-existent is whatever we have not sufficiently desired."

It should not be difficult for mediators to imagine that a more evolved, collaborative, cohesive, and caring form of conflict engagement is possible. If we begin with small-scale everyday experiences resolving conflicts in couples, families, neighbors, and work teams, we can see how mediators routinely help parties imagine better outcomes. Many mediators have scaled up those experiences and applied them to mid-scale conflicts, facilitating dialogues, envisioning workshops, strategic planning sessions, and joint problem-solving in communities and organizations, and can vividly recall the moments when they witnessed a couple, team, group, community, or entire nation unite and pull itself together to solve a problem, confront a disaster, or celebrate a significant achievement.

With this knowledge, it is possible to imagine and *redefine* politics from a scaled-up, interest-based perspective, as I sought to do in *Politics, Dialogue, and the Evolution of Democracy*, where I suggested the following three interest-based definitions, each offering ways we might imagine responding to political issues:

1. *Politics is a social problem-solving process.* As a result, a diversity of views about the nature of the problem and social collaboration in finding creative ways of solving it will predictably result in better, more sustainable solutions.

2. *Politics is a large group, consensus-building, decision-making process.* As a result, the greater the consensus, the stronger the democracy, and the more people agree with a decision, the more likely it is to be owned by the group, and be lasting and effective.

3. *Politics is a conflict resolution process.* As a result, the amount of chronic, adversarial, hyper-polarized, destructive conflict can be dramatically reduced by assuming that there is more than one correct answer to political questions, and that a complex, interest-based approach can result in no one having to lose so that others can win.

Each of these alternative definitions repositions conflict resolution skills as central to the creation of higher, more evolved, interest-based forms of democracy. We can also describe six scale-free ways of reframing how we think about, approach, and *experience* politics that can help us shift the language and culture of politics in a more malleable, fluid, interest-based direction, supporting a more mediative, dialogic process of problem solving. We can regard politics, for example,

1. As an *attitude*–for example, toward problems, opponents, or social change

2. As a *process*–for example, in how we approach problem-solving

3. As a *relationship*–for example, our responses to diversity, dissent, and difficult behaviors

4. As a *practice*–for example, in mediation and restorative justice

5. As a *dialogue*–for example, in addressing family, community, and workplace, or social, economic, political, and environmental issues

6. As a *search*–for example, for authenticity, dialogue, open-hearted relationships, shared meaning and values, satisfaction, and closure

10 PROCESS PROPOSALS FOR IMAGINING AN INTEREST-BASED STATE

If we adopt these ideas and imaginings as *core design criteria*, then apply the principles of conflict resolution systems design [as described, for example, by William Ury, Steven Goldberg, and Jeanne Brett in *Getting Disputes Resolved;* or Cathy Costantino and Christina Sickles Merchant in *Designing Conflict Management Systems*; or by Janet K. Martinez, Lisa Blomgren Amsler, and Stephanie E. Smith in *Dispute System Design*; or in my book with Joan Goldsmith, *Resolving Organizational Conflicts: A Course in Mediation and Systems Design*], we can start to identify the rough outlines of a civil society-informed, interest-based, mediative nation state that *proactively,* preventively, and collaboratively addresses social, economic, political, and environmental conflicts by identifying, resolving, transforming, and transcending their underlying chronic causes.

Conflict resolution systems design, in my view, can be successful on three distinct levels, evolutionary stages, "generations," or orders of magnitude, each more expansive and far-reaching than the last:

1. The first level or generation, described by Ury, Goldberg, and Brett, focuses on strengthening conflict resolution systems in groups and organizations, and designing conflict resolution systems for handling grievances, complaints, arguments, difficulties, problems, and conflicts inside an organizational system.

2. The second level or generation regards groups, organizations, and institutions as *conflict resolution*

mechanisms; considers all their internal systems from an *integrated* conflict resolution perspective, including feedback and evaluation, reward and compensation, leadership, and similar systems that impact or are influenced by conflict; evaluates how well each system is doing in preventing and resolving it, and how these systems might be improved.

3. The third level or generation undertakes to redesign the systems design process *itself* in fluid, scale-free ways, allowing us to apply it not only to small-scale relational and family systems, or mid-scale community and organizational systems, but large-scale social, economic, political, and environmental institutions and practices.

Interest-based processes are not utopian or infallible, but require considerable effort to modify and maintain. Still, as Henry David Thoreau advised, "If you have built castles in the air, your work need not be lost; that is where they should be. Now put the foundations under them."

The creation of less-conflicted nation states will not always prevent or resolve conflicts. Instead, just as city states were driven to collaborate and evolve into nation states in order to better respond to higher order problems, nation states are being driven to collaborate and evolve in order to address higher order global difficulties that are beyond the capacity of single nations to solve. And just as cities continued to exist afterwards, it is likely that nation states will as well.

But rather than cite the countless *substantive* ways we might use systems design principles to improve democracy in nation states, or propose specific interest-based structural and systemic alternatives, or suggest concrete ways of working globally to resolve chronic political conflicts, as I have attempted in previous books, I want to focus more narrowly here on a few simple, easy to implement process improvements that, without regard to issues, entities, or parties, could help create a scale-free, interest-based, *infrastructure*, a set of integrated complex self-correcting systems, and an increased capacity to address divisive political conflicts. In so doing, it is important to heed poet Mary Oliver's advice, and "Keep some room in [our] heart[s] for the unimaginable."

Of the hundreds, if not thousands, of possible ways of applying interest-based processes, improving their functionality, strengthening skills, and building the capacity of political organizations and institutions to resolve hyper-polarized social, economic, political, and environmental conflicts, here are my Top 10:

1. Conduct open, collaborative "conflict audits" or "root cause analyses" at all levels of government to identify the primary sources of conflict, their causes, and how much they cost– not only financially, but morally, emotionally, culturally, politically, environmentally, etc.

2. Form facilitated task forces representing all political constituencies at every level of government, and empower them to jointly investigate, discuss, recommend, and implement a broad range of consensus-driven policies designed to resolve, transform, and transcend political conflicts of every kind.

3. Bring in skilled, independent mediators and facilitators to help design processes, convene constituencies, facilitate dialogues, evaluate root causes, reach consensus on proposals for implementation, and recommend ways of improving *all* government meetings, interactions between political opponents, and discussions of potentially divisive issues, including in Congress.

4. Recruit experienced dialogue facilitators to conduct strategic planning, problem-solving, team building, empathy and consensus building dialogues over hot political topics–not just *after* issues have become hyper-polarized; or solely between high-level political advocates; or without

recommending concrete changes — but *before* issues become divisive and intractable, in local neighborhoods and communities, building consensus, and implementing solutions.

5. Enlist seasoned mediators and conflict resolution professionals to assess and try to resolve on-going social, economic, political, and environmental conflicts using the full range of dispute resolution processes.

6. Create a cabinet-level Mediation and Ombuds office, with branches in all agencies and departments; assign ombuds professionals to advise and assist every government office, and train volunteer peer mediators who are *elected* in every workplace and institution.

7. Weave mediation, dialogue, and similar methods into the entire electoral process; convert adversarial debates into socially constructive dialogues about issues, and make consensus-based recommendations; introduce online voting on candidates and mediated proposals for resolving divisive issues; and election review boards with a power to mediate, arbitrate, and disqualify candidates who grossly or repeatedly violate the rules.

8. Fund "multi-door courthouses," as proposed by the late Harvard Law School Professor Frank E. A. Sander, and encourage informal problem-solving, facilitated negotiation, early neutral evaluation, summary jury trials, mediation, and arbitration before, during, and after litigation.

9. Draft generic language requiring parties to use mediation or other alternative dispute resolution processes *before* litigation, and include it in all contracts, agreements, legislation, executive orders, and treaties, and at every level of government.

10. Fund education in conflict resolution for all students from kindergarten through college, with special courses for aspiring political candidates, as well as public sector

employees, managers, and supervisors *before* they run for office or start work, with refresher courses periodically to improve their skills.

While none of these proposals addresses the serious substantive, structural, and systemic issues that divide us, and much more is obviously needed, these measures, and many more like them, are quicker, easier to implement, and better able to convince hostile opponents that democracy need not be scrapped simply because we lack the higher order skills we need to turn political animosity in the direction of social problem-solving.

James Baldwin was clearly right when he wrote that, "Not everything that is faced can be changed; but nothing can be changed until it is faced." It may be helpful to add that not everything can be changed immediately; but without a sense of immediacy nothing can change.

We face problems today that force us to rapidly figure out how to solve a growing number of divisive, complex, life-threatening, global issues. Chief among these is our inability to solve them *together* because we lack the skills and capacities, processes and relationships, systems and structures needed to turn hyper-polarized political conflicts into collaborative social problem-solving. Yet these skills and capacities are now available and well within our grasp.

Even a *grossly* insufficient, dreadfully underfunded, half-hearted effort to implement just a *fraction* of these 10 proposals could have a dramatic, transformational effect, and point us decisively in the right direction. All we need to begin is an interest-based orientation, a diverse set of skills and processes that can be scaled-up or down, and a willingness to risk drawing people into dialogue, collaborative problem-solving, negotiation, and mediation.

Will we succeed, and will we be able to do so in time? No one knows. But we do know that there will be little hope of succeeding if we don't try. We also know, as Rebecca Solnit reminds us, that the hope of doing so resides in all of us:

> The grounds for hope are in the shadows, in the people who are inventing the world while no one looks, who themselves don't know yet whether they will have any effect, in the people you have not yet heard of.

Mary Parker Follett was right, we have not yet experienced *real* democracy; not the genuine "government of the people, by the people, for the people" that Lincoln hoped would not perish from the earth. We couldn't, and can't, until we develop the skills we need to make it work. We now have these skills, and it's time to put them to work.

THIRTEEN

Economic Conflicts

ECOLOGY, TECHNOLOGY, AND EVOLUTIONARY
LIMITS OF CAPITALISM

In the long term, the economy and the environment are the same thing. If it's unenvironmental, it is uneconomical. That is the rule of nature.

Mollie Beattie

That knowledge has become the *resource, rather than a resource, is what makes our society 'post-capitalist'. It changes, ... fundamentally, the structure of society. It creates new social dynamics. It creates new economic dynamics. It creates new politics.*

Peter Drucker

It is failure that guides evolution; perfection provides no incentive for improvement.

Colson Whitehead

OF THE MANY SOURCES OF HOSTILITY AND CHRONIC DYSFUNCTION IN the world, one of the greatest, deepest, and most difficult to resolve are conflicts over economic issues. Whether they impact individuals, groups, organizations, classes, or nation states, vast portions of the world's population are suffering or deeply upset over the unequal, unfair, inequitable, and unjust distribution of wealth; or unregulated growth and runaway technological innovation; or hyper-competition and economic warfare; or financially inspired layoffs and hostile mergers; or the consequences of adversarial competition; or the ruthless pursuit of profits.

If we were to imagine shrinking the global economy down to the size of a single couple or family, or team or community, and ask: "What would happen if each person regarded themselves as a private corporation in largely unregulated competition with others, and behaved as giant global corporations typically do?" The dysfunctional, inhumane, catastrophic results would immediately become apparent. If we were then to imagine scaling these results up to larger and larger dimensions, we would be able to predict many of the chronic social, economic, political, and environmental difficulties we currently experience. We might then ask: "What would happen if we scaled *up* the caring of couples and families, the participation of teams, and the collaboration of communities?"

More profoundly, the ability to scale these negative and positive effects up or down suggests the presence or absence of an underlying competitive, conflict-prone economic *system* that is grounded in adversarial, zero-sum games; and the operation of an individualistic algorithm with destructive impacts that richly rewards selfish and self-serving behaviors, even when they injure or destroy others — and sometimes, even the system itself.

Finally, let's imagine that this couple, family, team, or community is facing a serious *shared* problem, such as the Covid 19 pandemic, global warming, environmental destruction, nuclear proliferation, war, famine, prejudice, etc., each of which requires consensus, collaboration, and coordination to solve; and then ask: "How *useful* is this large-scale separate, anarchic, competitive drive to maximize individual economic self-interests likely to be in solving these problems?", we could quickly predict the global crises we are actually experiencing.

Many years ago, when I was working as a mediator and consultant in school and educational reform, I learned of a lecture by a professor of education titled "The Devil Made Me Do It," in which he asked the question: "If the devil were to design an educational system with maximum destructiveness and evil intent, what would he do?" The professor proceeded to argue that it would result in *exactly* the kind of educational system we have. The same question would likely produce a similar answer in economics.

An alternative approach to crisis analysis and prediction would begin by understanding that chronic, intractable conflicts are simply the *sound* made by the cracks in a system. They are chronic, built-in dysfunctions, made worse by our failure or unwillingness to recognize and confront deeper, systemic problems and adapt, change, and evolve in an effort to fix them. Economic conflicts are partly a result of differences, divisions, disagreements, and tensions that have accumulated over time, creating lines of polarity that separate people, pit them against one another, draw them into conflict, and periodically spark collisions in which they battle over alternate futures, opposing possibilities, and evolving opportunities. Yet most of these conflicts are based on an unspoken assumption that economics is *inherently* an unequal, adversarial, zero-sum game; that wealth is limited, so that if you receive 60%, I will receive 40%, and for me to receive 60% you must receive 40%. The result is economic conflict, including class conflict, and as billionaire investor Warren Buffet trenchantly observed, "There's class warfare all right, but it's my class, the rich class, that's making war, and we're winning."

THE ECONOMICS OF CONFLICT AND THE CONFLICT OF ECONOMICS

Economics is a set of choices about the ways goods or services are produced and circulated, wealth is accumulated and distributed, resources and surpluses are allocated, and labor is organized and compensated. Yet it is also, less obviously, the ways each of these generates its' own unique, chronic conflicts, how much these conflicts cost us in various ways, and how they can be resolved.

While traditional capitalist economies are deeply concerned with conducting cost-benefit analyses and calculating financial "bottom lines," there are *many* significant costs and bottom lines in conflict that can result in incalculable losses, yet these are rarely included in the calculations that inform our choices, or how they might most effectively be handled.

Consider, for example, the costs incurred as a result of conflicts that occur at work. Research in the emerging field of conflict resolution systems design has so far generated a partial list of these costs, which include:

- The time spent by employees arguing rather than working
- The time spent by managers responding to conflicts
- The time spent by human resources and personnel department investigating and trying to settle conflicts
- The time spent by lawyers investigating complaints and defending the organization against grievances and lawsuits
- The time lost due to reduced morale and motivation, not only by the parties, but everyone impacted by the conflict
- The time lost due to fatigue, emotional upset or trauma, and increased tension at work
- The time lost due to industrial injuries and psychological stress
- The time spent by co-workers and colleagues discussing, gossiping, and taking sides in the conflict
- The time spent by human resources, lawyers, managers, and witnesses in disciplinary proceedings punishing or firing people for engaging in conflict-related behaviors, or in mediations, arbitrations, and lawsuits afterwards

- The time spent recruiting, hiring, and training new employees to take the place of those who were fired, or who simply left because of the toxic atmosphere created by unresolved conflicts
- The income lost due to missed opportunities, reduced creativity, waste, mistakes, and diminished productivity due to conflict
- The income lost from prospective customers and clients who were turned off by the conflict and decided to go elsewhere
- Etc., etc., etc.

If we were to calculate the number of employee and managerial hours spent on conflict, multiply this by the number of hours employees and managers lost being impacted by it, and multiply the result by their average salaries, the total would be staggering, and far exceed the cost of the most elaborate and expansive conflict resolution program possible. [For more, see *Resolving Conflicts at Work: 10 Strategies for Everyone on the Job* (3rd Ed.), 2010; and *Resolving Organizational Conflicts: A Course in Mediation and Systems Design*, 2021.].

The question then arises: if conflicts are so costly and destructive, why wouldn't financially prudent individuals, groups, and organizations — be they couples, communities, corporations, or governments — seek to reduce these deficits by introducing *demonstrably* superior, far less costly conflict resolution systems to efficiently and effectively settle, resolve, transform, transcend, and prevent them? What could *conceivably* justify the waste of *not* doing so? While it is certainly true that sophisticated conflict resolution methodologies are relatively recent, untried on a large scale, and only superficially understood, it is important to acknowledge that there are also a number of deeper, more profound, *unspoken* reasons for resisting widespread implementation of interest-based dispute resolution procedures. Among these is a subconscious suspicion that they represent a significant paradigm shift with profound consequences for organizations on all scales — i.e., that their operations and processes are *naturally* not only non- but *anti-*hierarchical; that they are *innately* collaborative and democratic; that they are welcoming and friendly to subjective, personal, and emotional experience; that they rely on open and honest dialogue, rather than secrecy and "need to know"; that they operate by consensus, rather than command or fiat; that they are inclusive and egalitarian, regardless of diversity or differences; that they do not reinforce privileges based on hierarchies of status, wealth, or power; that they are oriented to value-driven rules rather than rule-driven values; that they do not end with "winners" and "losers," but strive for "win/win" outcomes. These paradigm shifts run counter to many widely accepted corporate practices, established organizational processes, customary workplace relationships, autocratic leadership styles, hierarchical structures, and bureaucratic self-reinforcing systems, making what people say and do in mediation and other dispute resolution processes seem counter-intuitive, "touchy-feely," costly, time consuming, and vaguely subversive.

In many corporate, autocratic, and hierarchical cultures, there are at least *tacit* patriarchal celebrations of aggression, toughness, and combative, adversarial behaviors; there are hiring and promotional practices that advance people into leadership who act condescendingly and disrespectfully toward those "beneath" them; there are feedback and evaluation systems that punish people for whistle-blowing, pointing out failures, or criticizing their bosses; there are reward and compensation systems that reinforce hyper-competitive, selfish, conflict-creating behaviors, as opposed to collaborative, altruistic, resolution-creating ones.

Alternative Economic Systems

There are two *fundamental* approaches to economics, each of which is expressed in divergent choices, characterized by different behaviors, and represented classically by contrasting economic systems and structures. These are:

1. *Competition,* based on zero-sum assumptions, characterized by personal gain and selfishness, with the goal of winning over and against others; represented classically by capitalism; and
2. *Collaboration,* based on non-zero-sum assumptions, characterized by collective gain and sharing, with the goal of winning with and for others; represented classically by socialism.

Each of these disparate approaches to economic problem-solving and decision-making differs from country to country and era to era, strives for unique goals, works successfully under varying circumstances, and generates its' own particular sources of conflict. Competition and capitalism, for example, have (in general) been highly successful in sparking innovation, and worked effectively in conditions of scarcity, maximizing "primitive accumulation" and amassing capital. They have also generated countless conflicts between rich and poor, management and labor, and routinely prioritize profits over people. Collaboration and socialism, on the other hand, have (in general) been effective in reducing economic inequality, and worked successfully under conditions of abundance, maximizing collaboration and building teamwork. They have also generated conflicts over "free riders," those who do not pull their own weight, and a range of what are called "tragedy of the commons" behaviors.

In addressing these deficits, Elinor Ostrom won the Nobel Prize in Economics for demonstrating, in contrast to orthodox, competitive economic principles, that even within capitalist economies, groups of people are completely capable of managing their common economic and natural resources collaboratively whenever the following eight conditions are met:

1. The group and its purpose are clearly defined.
2. The costs and benefits are shared equally.
3. Decisions are made by consensus.
4. Misconduct is monitored.
5. Sanctions start out mild and escalate only as needed.
6. Conflict resolution is fast and fair.
7. The group has the authority to manage its own affairs.
8. The relationship of the group with others is appropriately structured.

Notably, these eight (especially number six) are *precisely* what we would expect a list of mediated agreements on all scales to include, but with the addition of more detail on exactly how each might be achieved. Ostrom's work suggests three new and important ideas:

1. It is possible to use these elements to improve the effectiveness of collaboration on all scales and prevent or reduce the severity of conflicts that may arise when people work together and share resources, in capitalism as well as socialism.
2. It is possible to introduce these elements, either piecemeal or as a whole, as partial, non-systemic, scale-free, *mediated* solutions to chronic conflicts that are triggered by competitive, selfish, zero-sum economic behaviors.
3. It is possible to regard these elements as core steps in the construction of small-, mid-, and large-scale collaborative projects, from families, teams, and workplaces to global organizations and nation states.

Indeed, it is possible that many failed socialist experiments might have turned out differently had Ostrom's steps been taken—not rigidly or uniformly, but with room for flexibility and innovation. Moreover, each of these radically democratic elements has broad applicability and profound social, economic, political, and environmental consequences. As Economist Hazel Henderson points out:

> Economics is politics in disguise. It is simply a way of rationalizing certain decisions about how to allocate resources from the point of view of the people who have the money to pay economists: the powerful interest groups like military contractors, politicians, trade associations, and the like. Consider the way ... economic resources are divided up and distributed, particularly in government budgets: how much goes toward the military versus programs for the homeless. The homeless don't have very much lobbying power, and the military contractors have a whole lot.

The introduction of a multi-scale collaborative, consensus based, *mediative* approach to economic decision-making, including allocation of resources, production and distribution of wealth, and similar economic choices, is increasingly necessary and possible– not only to solve immensely challenging global problems, but to stop actively *rewarding* people for making them worse.

CAPITALISM AS A CAUSE OF CLIMATE CHANGE AND ECOLOGICAL CONFLICT

A clear example of economic choices making problems worse is global warming and its impact on local economies and ecological imbalances. It has, for a considerable time, been beyond dispute that fossil fuels produce greenhouse gases that raise earth's temperature, resulting in *catastrophic* warming and ecological damage, yet oil and gas companies and the banks and shareholders who fund them continue making immense profits and pretend it isn't happening, while most politicians and media pundits obfuscate, bureaucratize, "greenwash" their activities, and resist real efforts to solve the problem.

We have now passed eight billion people on the planet, forests are being felled to make pastures for homes and raise cattle; extractive industries and plastics are polluting our water, air, and soil, and the delicate ecological balance that has sustained countless species for millennia is being pushed off-balance in the name of progress. These events are giving rise to increasing conflicts — for example, between herders or pastoralists and farmers in Africa over access to water and grazing land; between oil, gas, and mining corporations who would exploit natural ecosystems and the indigenous communities whose livelihoods and cultures depend on them; between migrants, whose work and wealth have disappeared as a result of climate change, and the citizens of countries where they seek to travel.

In addressing these problems and conflicts it's best to follow Mark Twain's humorous advice: "When you find yourself in a hole, the first thing to do is stop digging." The difficulty, as climate change activists and eco-defenders increasingly argue, is that capitalist enterprises seem unable to stop digging.

Writer and journalist Naomi Klein has written insightfully, about how capitalist competition and the prioritization of profits, especially in unregulated environments, drive corporations to exploit natural resources and cut costs, partly by ignoring the environmental destruction they cause, and partly by paying politicians and pundits to disregard and marginalize environmental efforts.

The insightful Native American leader Chief Joseph commented in the 19th century, about the white European settlers, that "The love of possessions is a disease with them." Writing at nearly the same time, Karl Marx connected capitalism as an economic system with environmental destruction, writing:

> All progress in capitalistic agriculture is a progress in the art, not only of robbing the labourer, but of robbing the soil: all progress in increasing the fertility of the soil for a given time, is a process towards ruining the lasting sources of that fertility. Exploitation and

squandering of the vitality of the soil take the place of conscious rational cultivation of the soil as eternal communal property, an unalienable condition for the existence and reproduction of a chain of successive generations of the human race.

Professor Kohei Saito at Tokyo University revised, reinterpreted, and expanded these ecological ideas to promote a "degrowth" alternative to the drive of capitalist economies to "exploit and squander" natural resources for profit. Saito *reversed* the traditional assumption that economic growth makes us richer, and argued instead that the historic success of capitalism is increasingly turning into a failure, making us *poorer* by destroying the very things that keep us alive, help us prosper, and give us pleasure. Saito explained:

> Since the earth is finite, it is obvious that there are absolute biophysical limits to capital accumulation. Despite knowing this, capital is incapable of limiting itself. On the contrary, capital constantly attempts to overcome these limits only to increase its own destructiveness against society and nature. Hence arises the 'necessity of social control' to put an end to the wasteful survival and preservation of the natural environment. Such social planning of production is, however, incompatible with the basic logic of capitalist production.

While the privatization and commodification of natural resources can temporarily raise a country's gross domestic profit, partly by turning what was once free and available to all into something that is saleable, it does so by transforming the wealth of everyone into the riches of a few. The law of supply and demand then incentivizes global corporations and industry groups like OPEC to monopolize and control oil and gas output to *create* scarcities that artificially inflate prices.

The same system leads pharmaceutical companies to exploit science and nature to create medicines that only the wealthiest can afford, jack up prices during pandemics, and refuse to share their technologies with poorer countries, even to save lives. It also leads privately owned corporations to increase their short-term profits by cutting health and safety costs for employees; dumping waste products into water, soil, and air; and ducking environmental protection expenses.

Saito calls degrowth "a conscious downscaling of the current 'realm of necessity'" created by capitalism, and sees it as a democratic, collaborative, planned effort to improve the quality of life by automating work, downscaling levels of production and consumption, and redefining wealth to create an economy that is abundant *without* focusing entirely on commodities, thereby reducing environmental pressures and reversing global warming and environmental destruction.

What is clear, however, in works by Naomi Klein, Andreas Malm, and many others who have advanced environmental critiques of capitalism, is that a *profound* polarization is taking place, leading predictably to far deeper and more intense economic conflicts in which trillions of dollars and the fate of the planet and its' people are understood to be at stake.

In Klein's view, this realization has led those on the political right to oppose efforts to halt global warming and accelerated the rise of anti-democratic, autocratic political movements, like those of Donald Trump in the U. S., Jair Bolsonaro in Brazil, and others. It has also led those on the political left to embrace "Extinction Rebellion" and other acts of militant resistance–as suggested by the title of Andreas Malm's recent book, *How to Blow Up a Pipeline.*

The question all of us, including conflict resolvers, need to consider is this: Is it *possible* to use conflict resolution, dialogue, collaborative negotiation, mediation, and similar methods to help shift these increasingly hostile, highly polarized, deeply consequential disputes in the direction of collaborative, creative, democratic problem-solving?

To answer this question, we need to look closely at what is taking place within capitalist economies, the principles by which they are organized, and how cyber-technologies such as artificial intelligence, quantum computing, robotics, and what has been called the "Singularity" are transforming capitalist priorities and their social and political impacts in profound and unexpected ways.

CAPITALISM, TECHNOLOGY, AND CONFLICT

Over the course of millennia, seemingly fixed and stable economic systems like hunting and gathering, slavery, feudalism, etc., have repeatedly risen, been shaped, and forced to evolve, not only as a consequence of changing environmental conditions and social or political constraints, but more often as a result of the creation, invention, and discovery of transformational technologies.

This succession of economic systems, each with its' own distinct technological methods and processes, helped define the social relationships and political formations that supported and sustained each system — sometimes by significantly altering what people could imagine was possible. Each of these seemingly stable social, economic, and political systems rested on mutually reinforcing technologies that had a ripple effect on *what* was done, and *how* and *why*–i.e., on processes, relationships, cultures, behaviors, attitudes, and expectations.

Not every technological innovation is transformative, and each depends on many factors. Yet it is clear that the shift from hunting and gathering to nomadic herding to settled agriculture depended on the domestication of animals and plants, which relied on the development of genetic breeding, plows, fertilizers, irrigation, crop rotation, means of storage, and similar technologies.

These, in turn, led to increased stability and food surpluses, which permitted the development of more advanced divisions of labor, the growth of settled communities and city-states, and the rise of slavery and large-scale agriculture. These needed to be protected by professional soldiers, prayed over by priests, and unified by politicians—i.e., by *non*-productive classes who were needed to keep slaves in bondage, defend private property against social redistribution, and resolve conflicts between increasingly diverse groups, needs, and perspectives.

This encouraged the more rapid development of technology, not only in food production, but metallurgy, ceramics, weaving, and other handicraft industries, which resulted in still greater surpluses that were turned into commodities and sold in distant markets. These, in turn, led to the rise of a new class of merchants, the need for legal systems, rights-based approaches to dispute resolution, ostensibly neutral, democratic governments to promulgate and enforce them—and conflicts with autocratic, dictatorial, monarchical, power-based alternatives.

With the growth of markets, improvements in transportation and shipping, and enormous increases in profits from the sale of commodities, an emerging class of wealthy merchant-capitalists began to organize the process of production in ways that would maximize their profits. Here is how I described it, and how merchants became capitalists, in *Conflict Revolution: Designing Preventative Solutions for Chronic Social, Economic and Political Conflicts*:

> While feudal markets for commodities in the Middle Ages were limited by product availability, rigid castes, onerous forms of taxation, brigandage and feudal obligations, they nonetheless served as engines of transition to more efficient merchant-capitalist systems that promoted production for profit. These new mercantile systems created fresh sources of obligation and markets that were freer, yet remarkably similar in some respects to those that plagued feudalism....
>
> Merchants increasingly transported salable items from distant regions by ships or caravans, creating marketplaces in cities near

trade routes, natural harbors and navigable rivers. These early traders, for example, brought English wool to weavers in Italy and returned with finished cloth to England, selling the surpluses in France, Holland and Germany. Gradually, local weavers were no longer able to compete and began to disappear. Merchants soon realized that they could make more money paying weavers to work from their homes in England rather than import finished products from Italy. It was then quite simple to gather weavers in a factory, impose a division of labor, institute assembly line techniques and install gigantic looms that produced cloth far cheaper than any local weaver could offer.

The factory system dramatically lowered the costs of transportation and reduced the time it took for products to be produced, taken to market and sold, thereby cutting the costs of production and speeding up the conversion of money into commodities and back into money again. In doing so, it weakened the bargaining power of weavers in negotiating wages and working conditions and dramatically increased factory owners' profits.

These innovative technologies rapidly transformed the features of capitalism, redefining what constitutes wealth, and connecting people globally across national, racial, religious, gender, and class lines. These shifts reopened the question of how social surpluses ought to be invested and distributed. They also fundamentally transformed social, economic, political, and environmental relationships, giving rise to *fierce* battles over the purpose and orientation of democratic political institutions, and the responsive rise of creative, collaborative, interest-based, *technologically compatible* approaches to conflict resolution.

We can see a similar revolutionary re-alignment taking place today in the expansion and private use of computer-based technologies, especially personal computers, smart phones, and the internet; as well as the rapid development of artificial intelligence, quantum computing, robotics, natural language algorithms like ChatGPT;

and the exponentially escalating *pace* and sweep of their applications, which are also rapidly altering the field of conflict resolution.

The convergence of these stunning, transformational, scientific and technological innovations is sometimes referred to as "the singularity," referring to a hypothetical yet foreseeable point in the not-too-distant future when artificial intelligence will surpass any *individual* human intelligence; and not long after, the collective intelligence of *all* human beings on the planet. [See e.g., Ray Kurzweil's provocative and data filled book, *The Singularity is Near.*]

The singularity has also been described as the ability of AI programs to construct and design improved versions of themselves faster than human beings could do on their own. We can see this trend already emerging in the ability, for example, of generative AI programs like ChatGPT — not simply to speak and interpret natural languages and quickly return with what are often highly intelligent responses; or to fix their often erroneous, fantasized, prejudicial responses; or to pass medical licensing and bar exams; but in their ability to turn ordinary language into software programs of all kinds, including their own, and control a wide range of robots based on simple text commands from people who lack engineering and programming skills.

At the same time, versions of ChatGPT have been trained to answer questions with a politically conservative or ultra-right bias, with prejudices and disinformation other versions would reject; and have been trained in the opposite direction to edit out biased and prejudicial responses found in the database they were trained on.

Many of the fears and concerns regarding the expanded use of generative AI programs and similar advanced technologies, seem to center around the following eight issues:

1. Expansion of government surveillance, leading to loss of privacy

2. Elimination of jobs and reduction of wages or working conditions

3. Perpetuation of biases, prejudices, fantasies, and hallucinations

4. Sale of personal data for corporate profit and commercial advantage

5. Use by autocratic governments to encourage conformity and silence dissent

6. Increased effectiveness of weapons, policing, and warfare, leading to new fears, unnecessary deaths, and environmental destruction

7. Ethical issues around acquisition of sentience or consciousness

8. Potential to decide to exterminate the human race

Each of these concerns originates less in the scientific *content* or technological nature of AI, computers, robots, and similar technologies, than in the social, economic, political, and environmental applications and contexts in which they may be put to use, including the attitudes and intentions of those who may use them to achieve evil or repressive goals. Each requires careful consideration.

Yet it is important to recognize that nearly *every* technology we have invented has been a means that could be converted to selfish and destructive ends. The difficulty is not merely that these technologies are being loosed on the world without adequate safeguards, but that political and economic rivalry and the drive for domination in zero-sum contests encourages nations and companies to introduce these game-changing technologies, nearly always without sufficient thought, planning, testing, transparency, regulatory oversight, damage control—or indeed, *any* idea whatsoever about how they learn, what hidden information they rely on, or what the long-range impact of their use will be.

These concerns led to the publication of an open letter from Elon Musk and hundreds of highly regarded AI experts recommending a pause in research until better safeguards can be put in place; an article by Yuval Noah Harari and others arguing for "mastering AI before it masters us;" and similar dire warnings. Yet in the context of cold war-like global competition, especially with China; or unregulated hostility between AI competent countries like Russia and Ukraine, Israel and Iran, India and Pakistan, and others, there will always be more reasons to push research forward than to stop it. A recent example is the condemnation of Israeli spyware and cyber-attacks, together with secret government use of them.

If it is correct, as neuroscientist Gulio Tononi has suggested (with Kristof Koch, Max Tegmark, and others) that consciousness is simply a byproduct of information processing with high levels of complexity, plus integration or cross-linkage ("integrated information theory"), then at our current rapidly accelerating rate of innovation, it will not be long before sentience, or some close semblance, creates irreparable harm, or compels recognition that the "invisible hand" of capitalist market economies cannot adequately contain the problem, and some form of global collaboration, demilitarization, and agreed-upon ethics and principles will be needed—perhaps even designed by AI itself.

At the same time, as Thomas Friedman and others have correctly pointed out, AI and similar technologies *can* be applied in an ethical, humane, transparent, and scientifically appropriate way, and used to help solve significant social, economic, political, and environmental problems, allowing us to test solutions to determine which approaches work best. This possibility also exists in conflict resolution.

For example, in an interesting research study of options for addressing economic inequality, the UK-based AI company, DeepMind, conducted a test among more than 4000 people using a computer simulation in an online, four-player economic game.

Players were given different amounts of money and asked to decide how much to contribute to a pool of common funds that they would receive a share of in return. Players then voted on their favorite policies for doling out these funds.

The AI reduced disparities in wealth by redistributing the money according to how much of the starting pot each player contributed. It discouraged free riders by giving back nearly nothing to players who had not contributed about half of their starting funds. Interestingly, this policy won *more* votes from players than either an "egalitarian" approach of redistributing funds equally regardless of how much each person contributed, or a "libertarian" approach of handing out funds according to the proportion each person's contribution to the pot.

When there was the greatest inequality between players at the start, a "liberal egalitarian" policy that distributed money according to the proportion of funds each player contributed, but did *not* discourage free riders, was as popular as the AI proposal, garnering more than 50 per cent of the vote. [See: *Nature Human Behaviour*, DOI: 10.1038/s41562-022-01383-x]

What is interesting is that these choices matched well with Elinor Ostrom's Nobel Prize winning research cited earlier, as well as with the macro-economic policies of what has been described as the "first stage" of socialism, or "from each according to their ability and to each according to their work" — except in the case of great inequality, when "free riders" received equalizing money, corresponding to a "second stage" distribution of wealth "according to their need."

What is also interesting is that the study intuitively validated preferences for a nuanced, mediative, socially unifying approach to reducing economic inequality, resulting in increased satisfaction and fewer social and economic conflicts, while the less preferred approaches of pure uniformity or pure individuality were seen as less fair, and resulted in more conflicts.

Whether these innovative technologies will be successful, and whether AI programs will ultimately become sentient or conscious and surpass human thinking and creativity is, of course, unknown; but what *is* known is that they are already having a transformational impact on society, economics, politics, and the environment, and fundamentally altering the way we think about, experience, and act in the world.

A simple example can be seen in the video meeting platform Zoom, which allowed people to work from home during the Covid pandemic, and *immediately* shifted the way employees thought about their work, the time they needed to commute to distant locations, the nature of their work relationships, the levels and types of workplace conflicts, the roles and powers of management, etc.; while simultaneously demonstrating that it is possible to work together globally, enormously reduce the use of fossil fuels, positively impact climate change, and dramatically reverse the pollution of air, soil, and water, just by meeting online.

If we consider these technological shifts only from a conflict resolution or problem-solving perspective, we can easily imagine using advanced technologies to supplement and support parties and dispute resolution practitioners in complex problem-solving, collaborative negotiations, consensus building, and other conflict resolution processes, as in public policy, health care, commercial, and environmental mediations — by gathering data, generating options, researching best practices, suggesting ways of "expanding the pie," proposing appropriate criteria, creating rubrics, identifying interests, critiquing potential bargaining strategies, recommending creative solutions, and similar acts.

MEDIATION AND THE EVOLUTIONARY LIMITS OF CAPITALISM

A more subtle and far-reaching set of issues concern, first: the potentially disruptive impact these innovative technologies may have on previously dominant economic forces, structures, systems, relationships, and processes that arose and were shaped by earlier technologies; second, on the ability of capitalism as a *system* and organizing principle to successfully evolve and adapt in sync with these changes; and third, on the likely costs and results of its' failure to do so.

In 1942, Joseph Schumpeter, in his classic text, *Capitalism, Socialism, and Democracy*, coined the phrase "creative destruction" to describe the capitalist "process of industrial mutation that continuously revolutionizes its own economic structure from within, incessantly destroying the old one, incessantly creating a new one." Schumpeter wrote:

> Capitalism ... is by nature a form or method of economic change and not only never is but never can be stationary. ... The fundamental impulse that sets and keeps the capitalist engine in motion comes from the new consumers' goods, the new methods of production or transportation, the new markets, the new forms of industrial organization that capitalist enterprise creates.... The opening up of new markets, foreign or domestic, and the organizational development from the craft shop and factory ... illustrate the process of industrial mutation that incessantly revolutionizes the economic structure *from within*, incessantly destroying the old one, incessantly creating a new one.

Some of the most important questions posed by the process of creative destruction in today's economies include these four:

1. Growth and innovation, but at what cost, and with what controls?
2. Is it likely, given these costs and current trends in technology and the environment, that capitalism can continue creatively destroying forever?
3. If not, what are the likely evolutionary limits of capitalism?
4. Given these costs, trends, and limits, what sort of economic system might be designed to reform or replace it?

John Maynard Keynes satirically defined capitalism as "the extraordinary belief that the nastiest of men for the nastiest of motives will somehow work for the benefit of all." Even the economically conservative, staunchly pro-capitalist U.S. President Woodrow Wilson grudgingly admitted, "The truth is, we are all caught in a great economic system which is heartless."

There are countless social, economic, political, ecological, technological, and humanistic critiques of capitalism, each of which can help us assess the *reducible* costs to those who have been negatively impacted by it. But few of these critiques explore how the *advantages* of capitalism over other economic systems might paradoxically prevent it from adapting and evolving when presented with new and changing conditions; and how this inability might increasingly give rise to conflicts that point in the direction of more socially, economically, politically, ecologically, and technologically sustainable alternatives in economic decision-making.

In his 1995 book *Beyond Capital*, the Hungarian philosopher and economic theorist István Mészáros connected this issue with the exploitation of nature under capitalism, but also, and what is important for our purposes, with *mediation*:

> [H]uman individuals must always fulfill the inescapable material and cultural requirements of their survival through the necessary *primary functions of mediation* among themselves and with nature at large. This means securing and safeguarding the objective conditions of their productive reproduction under circumstances which inevitably and progressively change under the impact of their own intervention through productive activity ...

Mészáros described these primary functions as "first order mediations" between human beings and nature, which included the social regulation of reproduction, organization of the labor process, establishment of exchange relations, development of coordination and control, allocation of resources, and enactment and administration of rules and regulations. With the appearance of capitalism, these gave rise to "second order mediations" in which,

> ... every one of the primary forms is altered almost beyond recognition, so as to suit the self-expansionary needs of a fetishistic and alienating system of social metabolic control which must subordinate absolutely everything to the imperative of capital-accumulation.

These second order mediations were now characterized by the rationalization of exploitation, domination, and control of nature — no longer simply in an effort to live and reproduce, but to transform natural resources into private wealth — and no longer entirely for the benefit of small families and clans, but of corporations, nation states, and wealthy individuals. The only *natural* limit to the continuation of this exploitation is the depletion and/or destruction of nature itself.

While Mészáros did not mention it, from a purely conflict resolution perspective, we can imagine "*third* order mediations" between human beings and nature, in which newer, higher order, transformational outcomes become possible. Human beings are, after all, both an inextricable part of, and in active "metabolic" *relationship* with nature, and like all relationships, requires continual mediation.

These relationships, and the mediations that keep them synchronized, manifest themselves in at least three ways, building on Hegel's description of the stages of political formation discussed in Chapter 12, which evolved historically from families to civil societies to nation states. That is, they evolved from:

1. *"Particular altruism,"* or first order mediations, consisting of the willingness of individuals to act altruistically in families

or toward nature, but only toward a limited, particular
group of people; to

2. *"Universal selfishness,"* or second order mediations, consisting
of the desire of individuals to act in their own self-interests
in civil societies, polities, and corporations toward nature; to

3. *"Universal altruism,"* or third order mediations, consisting of
the willingness or desire of individuals to act altruistically
toward a universal group, which Hegel believed was the
state, but can instead be seen as human beings relationships
with nature, requiring the collaborative evolution of civil
societies, polities, and corporations in their relations, both
with each other and with nature.

We can then adapt the distinction between these three orders of
relationship between human being and nature to equally describe
the transition from:

1. "First order" hunter-gatherer beliefs that we are dependent
on, beneficiaries of, and scientifically in the dark about
nature; to

2. "Second order" capitalist beliefs that we are independent of,
scientifically superior to, and in competition with nature; to

3. "Third order" post-capitalist beliefs that we are partners
with, scientifically inseparable from, and stewards for,
defenders of, and collaborators with nature.

Each of these three orders of belief and approaches to nature gives
rise to unique difficulties, limits, problems, and conflicts; yet each
also leads to unique forms of conflict resolution and problem-
solving, and generates unique relationships, processes, cultures,
outcomes, and resolutions. These difficulties, limits, problems, and
conflicts lead "first order" economies to gradually encounter their
evolutionary limits in the form of problems or conflicts that *cannot*
be solved or resolved within the confines of those systems, and
increasingly compel them to evolve into "second order"

relationships, processes, cultures, outcomes, and resolutions. This history encourages us to ask:

1. What limits the ability of "second order" capitalist systems to adapt and evolve in sync with rapidly changing ecological and technological conditions?
2. What role is likely to be played by "third order" attitudes, ideas, processes, and mediations in this evolutionary process?
3. What more can we say about the characteristics of this "third order" toward which we may be evolving?

What Limits the Ability of Capitalism to Evolve?

Every system on every scale, whether in marriages and families, communities and organizations, or nation states and global economies, is an effort to trade some degree of flexibility and adaptability for continuity, stability, and predictability in a constantly evolving environment. Systems make this exchange through *mediations* — for example, in marriages, by both spouses promising, implicitly or explicitly, to behave in reciprocally agreeable ways.

In doing so, systems become both buffers against change, and *limits* on the ability to evolve in response to changes that occur internally, as the system inevitably grows and evolves; or externally, as its environment changes; or as a consequence of ongoing interactions between them. This makes systems similar to paradigms, which *stabilize* belief systems—at least until anomalies appear that accumulate until they undermine the old beliefs and give rise to a new paradigm.

An analogous word for "anomaly" in evolving social, economic, political, and environmental systems, is *conflict*, which is created on the one hand by a need to adapt, evolve, and change; and on the other hand, by a reactivity, rigidity, inability, or resistance to change. Where systems are tightly interwoven, these conflicts can trigger a fear that the entire structure, which has been reinforced and counted on to remain the same, will now crumble into anarchy and chaos.

In small-scale workplaces, mid-scale organizations, and large-scale economies, systems are stabilized and reinforced by laws, government regulations, customary practices, corporate structures, managerial hierarchies, and a variety of social, economic, political, and cultural mechanisms that reward "business as usual" behaviors, punish efforts to fundamentally alter the system, and obstruct, channel, or bureaucratically sideline any changes that might threaten it.

The difficulty, however, is that these systems are *open* rather than closed, making it nearly impossible to isolate and defend them against internal growth, scientific discoveries, technological inventions, demographic and social shifts, political realignments, market swings, climate change, environmental degradation, and ecological imbalances.

12 SOURCES OF CHRONIC CONFLICT AND 10 LIMITS IN CAPITALISM

The principal characteristics of capitalism vary considerably from country to country and decade to decade, yet overall seem to me to include the following 12 elements, each of which can trigger chronic economic conflicts:

1. Intense competition for market dominance
2. Unceasing efforts to maximize sales and profits
3. Primacy of the financial bottom line
4. Constant innovation in technology, almost regardless of consequences
5. Dependence of profits on costs of production, especially wages, rents, taxes and raw materials
6. Unequal distribution of profits

7. Hierarchical control over investments, wages and management decisions
8. Separation and division of labor
9. Centralized organization of work processes
10. Increasing dependence on employee motivation and participation in decision-making
11. Unending search for inexpensive raw materials, cheap labor and markets for finished products
12. Globalization of production and distribution

In *Conflict Revolution: Designing Preventative Systems for Chronic Social, Economic and Political Conflicts* (2015), I described how many of these characteristics, when combined, can lead to chronic, predictable, costly, and preventable conflicts:

> Based solely on these few characteristics, it is easy to anticipate that, at a certain point in its evolution, capitalism will begin to become an obstacle to its own collaborative, participatory, democratic development. There is an obvious limit, for example, in the ability to grow and expand that finds its boundary in environmental ruin, just as there is a limit in the globalization of production that finds its boundary in the ability of other countries to negotiate for a larger share of the profits. Indeed, each of these characteristics of capitalism can be seen to contain the seeds of chronic conflicts that, if resolved, would require significant systemic modifications, up to and including its evolution to some higher order of economic functioning. Indeed, it is possible to discern this same process in earlier transitions from hunting and gathering to slavery, feudalism and capitalism.
>
> Moreover, the inconsistency between ever-increasing social equality, economic equity and political democracy, together with inevitable efforts to block their full expression, predictably give rise to a unique set of chronic conflicts that can be regarded as markers revealing the inherent limits of capitalism as a conflict-generating

system and the hidden places where sources of resolution and evolutionary change may most likely emerge.

If we look at these characteristics of capitalism from a *conflict resolution*, rather than an economic perspective, the following question arises: What are the systemic, paradigmatic, innate characteristics of capitalism that may limit it, or keep it from evolving in response to changes in its environment, or prevent it from solving higher order problems, generating chronic economic conflicts? Here are my "Top 10" answers, explained in more detail below:

1. Capitalism is often zero sum, adversarial, and power- or rights-based.
2. Capitalism is often competitive, hegemonic, and monopolistic.
3. Capitalism is often profit-driven, greedy, and selfish.
4. Capitalism is often expansive, driven, and dependent on continual growth.
5. Capitalism is often exploitative, unequal, and inequitable.
6. Capitalism is often acquisitive, materialistic, and possessive.
7. Capitalism is often hierarchical, autocratic, and domineering.
8. Capitalism is often divisive, biased, and discriminatory.
9. Capitalism is often inauthentic, inhumane, and bureaucratic.
10. Capitalism is often unscrupulous, manipulative, and oriented to short-term gain.

Of course, no two nations or capitalist economies or corporations are the same, so while there are certainly exceptions to each of these limits, it is the *intrinsic* nature of capitalist enterprises to periodically behave in these socially, politically, and environmentally destructive ways, each of which offers economic advantages, yet at the same time generates chronic conflicts, undermines collaboration, and depending on the circumstances, limits its' evolutionary options.

1. Capitalism is often zero sum, adversarial, and power- or rights-based. That is, any increase in the wealth of a few is matched by a corresponding reduction in the wealth of the many, and *vice versa.* Moreover, the gross disparity in economic wealth between the top few billionaires and rest of the world's population is accelerating, as Thomas Picketty has demonstrated, creating inhumane conditions for many. For example, the Forbes' Billionaires List for 2021 listed 2,755 billionaires in the world, with a combined net worth of $13.1 trillion; and the Global Wealth Report in 2021 by Credit Suisse showed the bottom 50% of the world's population with less than 2.4% of global wealth, while the top 10% had 82.4%.

An alternative, non-zero-sum, non-adversarial, interest-based economic system might begin by recognizing additional, expanded, alternative forms of wealth, including, as Martin Hägglund and others have suggested, the availability of free time. Hägglund writes:

> The deepest reason capitalism is a contradictory social form is that it treats the *negative* measure of value as though it were the *positive* measure of value and thereby treats the *means* of economic life as though they were the *end* of economic life. The real measure of value is not how much work we have done or have to do ... but how much disposable time we have to pursue and explore what matters to us ... to enable us to lead our lives.

If we define wealth in multiple, diverse, non-zero-sum, non-adversarial, interest-based terms, including not only disposable time, but the experience of nature, family and social relationships, art and cultural enrichment, beneficial purpose, and creative play, then the systemic sources of inequality begin to shrink and dissipate, leaving diversity, creativity, and the "pursuit of happiness." It then becomes possible to treat purely financial wealth as a means, rather than an end.

2. Capitalism is often competitive, hegemonic, and monopolistic. That is, its' competitive orientation carries over into individual lives, cultural norms, social relationships, political communications, and attitudes toward nature and the environment, reducing our *capacity* for collaboration and joint problem-solving, encouraging hyper-competition, increasing alienation and social isolation, rewarding bias and prejudice, aggravating hatreds, manufacturing pointless enemies, and triggering violence and wars.

Competition paradoxically leads both people and corporations to try to *stifle* their competition, largely through efforts at hegemonic control such as monopolization, mergers, acquisitions, buy-outs, price fixing, selective regulation, vertical and horizontal integration, and similar anti-competitive tactics. Competition then becomes a demand made to those above or outside, and rarely or voluntarily granted to those below or inside.

Unregulated economies easily turn hyper-competitive, which can quickly give rise to "robber baron"-like conditions, leading not only to the *absence* of any willingness to engage in joint problem-solving or conflict resolution, but behaviors that *generate* problems and conflicts, as part of a disguised strategy to achieve monopolistic or hegemonic control.

Competition, or more accurately, *collaborative competition*—as can be seen, for example, in sporting competitions, where the rules are collaboratively designed and adopted by consensus—can be quite positive, but only to the extent that competition is regulated fairly and equally — *except* in one area, that of skill—or in the case of corporations, in sales, based on the quality and desirability of their products or services.

In the world as a whole, collaboration is becoming increasingly indispensable as we attempt to mitigate potentially catastrophic global crises, such as climate change, nuclear proliferation, pandemics, wars, ecological destruction, and many others. *None* of these crises can be solved by solitary nation states, or by economic systems that reward selfishness, domination by the wealthy and powerful, and the competitive pursuit of narrow, relationally destructive, personal or corporate advantage.

While capitalist economies frequently collaborate voluntarily, their innate competitive orientation often forces a regression to "looking out for number one," which undermines trust and the consistent, systemic, creative teamwork that is essential for problem-solving and conflict resolution capacities to evolve; or respond more rapidly, proactively, fairly, justly, and effectively; or avoid creating these problems in the first place.

3. Capitalism is often profit-driven, greedy, and selfish. That is, each privately owned capitalist enterprise must earn more than it spends or go out of business. This can be achieved, for example, all else being equal, by reducing the cost of raw materials; lowering the amount spent on wages, rents, equipment, and taxes; decreasing the amount of time required for communication and transportation; or minimizing health care costs, safety requirements, environmental protections, and similar expenses.

It can also be accomplished by making politicians and the media dependent on advertising, financial loans, campaign contributions, and outright bribes; by infiltrating and weakening regulatory agencies, etc.–i.e., by effectively *privatizing* political decision-making and social problem-solving, and thereby preventing democracy from reducing, interfering with, or redistributing corporate profits.

These measures represent the prioritization of profits over people, which encourages selfishness and greed, undermines trust and teamwork, and generates countless chronic conflicts. It then becomes extremely difficult for profit-driven corporations to spend money on *anything* that is unlikely to result in financial gain, even if it is morally, ethically, emotionally, scientifically, socially, politically, culturally, logically, and environmentally the right thing to do–as can be seen, for example, in pharmaceutical and fossil fuel corporate responses to Covid and climate change.

While it is certainly possible on a simple tactical level to use consumer activism, political pressure, and media coverage to boycott or publicly shame recalcitrant corporations and encourage them to act responsibly, none of this is easy, quick, or likely to fundamentally alter the economic system that routinely encourages and reinforces these behaviors, especially where laws require corporate management to serve the interests of shareholders before those of employees, the public, or the environment.

While no economic system can succeed for long if it isn't able to remain solvent, this is a far cry from the *addiction* to profitability built into capitalist enterprises, even in "non-profit" corporations, as can be seen, for example, in the intense scramble for private donations and shift in programming at U. S. public broadcasting corporations.

Alternatively, it is possible to publicly finance endeavors that serve the public interest *without* stifling creativity, suppressing free speech and dissent, or becoming strangled by bureaucracy. It is especially important to do so where, as with public parks, libraries, fire departments, roads and highways, public utilities, product safety, space exploration, and similar areas, profits are unlikely and core public values or interests are at stake.

It is equally possible to do so in ways that support non-zero-sum, collaborative, democratic, mediative, interest-based approaches to economics, and *require* socially responsible practices. For example:

- We can require all corporations, non-profits, and publicly owned enterprises to include on their boards of directors and top leadership teams representatives of employees, the communities they impact, consumer advocacy groups, and environmental defenders.

- We can require their boards, leadership teams, and work forces to reflect the genders, races, classes, and other demographics in the areas they are located.
- We can require equal treatment, due process of law, and freedoms of speech, press, assembly, religion, and association, even in privately held corporations.
- We can mandate them to make decisions wherever possible by consensus, to use professional facilitators, and to include everyone who will be significantly impacted by the decision.
- We can establish "excess profits" taxes, reduce pay differentials between highest and lowest paid employees, and make employees and members of the community shareholders who can vote and share in economic successes.
- We can mandate them to build integrated conflict resolution capacity in their organizations, including peer mediation, and put an ombudsman on all boards of directors.
- We can direct them to conduct "conflict audits" and use conflict resolution systems design to prevent chronic conflicts wherever possible, and transform them into organizational learning and improvement.

None of these examples requires the government to nationalize privately owned corporations, or transform the nature of government, or the dysfunctional ways organizations typically operate. Yet these and similar measures could help achieve the *implicit* goals of nationalization, without triggering costly and uncertain battles in an effort to achieve them.

4. Capitalism is often expansive, driven, and dependent on continual growth. That is, remaining the same size, even if profitable, can be insufficient to ensure survival, in part because a common competitive tactic is to *intentionally* reduce profit margins by lowering prices to drive out smaller competitors and seize their market share; or introduce some new technology, service, or twist that renders older, established enterprises archaic, costly, and obsolete, even at the risk of social, economic, political, and environmental collapse.

Growth and expansion thereby become *compulsory* under capitalism, as nearly every outmoded corporation, product, technology, and service can attest. With unlimited resources, this would not be a problem, but natural resources are limited and shrinking. This creates an added problem, as the shifting ratio of supply to demand makes disappearing resources *more* profitable, and therefore more likely to be driven to extinction in the absence of government intervention. This, in turn, incentivizes private companies to bribe, corrupt, and "influence" government officials to "deregulate," ignore problems, and finance their own destruction.

In these ways, unlimited growth can turn malignant, causing countless chronic conflicts — for example, between corporations, developers, government officials, and the military or police on the one hand and local communities, residents, environmentalist, and nature defenders on the other. These conflicts fracture communities, pitting those who are seeking simply to survive or for a better quality of life or future for their children against each other — worse, they obstruct efforts to solve these problems, leaving fear, distrust, hatred, and more egregious conflicts in their wake.

Alternatively, it would be possible to shift from creating "more" to creating "better," to collaboratively planning how we can all live more enjoyable, creative, equitable, and environmentally sustainable lives without exhausting limited natural resources, fouling our nest, and upsetting the delicate ecological balance that keeps us alive.

5. Capitalism is often exploitative, unequal, and inequitable. That is, it seeks to gain as much as possible while paying as little as possible — especially for raw materials and labor power. In the process, it creates relationships with nature, employees, and communities that consist of taking from others without equal, reciprocal, and equitable compensation.

In this sense, capitalism is a *theft*, both from nature and from communities, as it converts public natural resources to private non-natural uses, and pays less than the value of what was taken. This produces profits through one-sided extraction for corporate gain, while creating an ethos and culture that are exploitative, unbalanced, and conflicted.

Alternatively, it would be possible to act with *reciprocity* toward nature, for example, by cleaning and replenishing air, soil, and water and enriching habitats; by distributing profits to employees in ways that decrease poverty and inequality, by increasing opportunities for learning and enjoyment, or by funding universal basic income programs for the under-employed.

6. Capitalism is often acquisitive, materialistic, and possessive.; That is, it shapes and commercializes people's innate needs and desires, turning them into marketable solutions, then fetishizes, imbues, packages, and promotes its commodities and services as socially "hip," fashionable, exclusive, purely material ways of satisfying them.

In *The Gift: Imagination and the Erotic Life of Property*, Lewis Hyde brilliantly distinguishes between property as *logos* or calculation, aimed at personal gain, ego, hoarding, and possession; and property as *eros* or pleasure, aimed at social connection, altruism, circulation, reciprocity, and giving, which are diminished by market thinking and the production of commodities and services solely for exchange.

In a similar way, people in conflict often become possessive, ego-driven, and "hoard" their issues, emotions, suggestions for improvement, problem-solving skills, and resources, thereby magnifying their suffering and freezing their relationships in hostility, antagonism, and chronic, unresolved conflicts.

Alternatively, through mediation and other forms of conflict resolution, people can be encouraged to share their issues and emotions, offer suggestions for improvement, and participate in solving the problem, thereby reinvigorating their relationship, rebuilding trust, encouraging altruism, and promoting reciprocity by making concessions that lead to their becoming unfrozen, cooperative, flexible, and able to collaborate.

There is no reason why similar outcomes could not be achieved on a large-scale by approaching chronic economic policy disputes as though they were ordinary conflicts, then applying a wide range of dispute resolution methodologies that systematically strengthen and encourage the use of higher order collaborative skills, techniques, and processes.

7. Capitalism is often hierarchical, autocratic, and domineering. That is, it produces "pecking orders" based on zero-sum attitudes regarding status, wealth, and power, then ranks people internally and externally along a one-dimensional, hierarchical line, allowing only those who are regarded as "superior" at the top to set policy, while those who are regarded as "inferior" at the bottom are required to comply or obey.

These hierarchies and pecking orders, once established, can easily be applied to races, genders, religions, ages, nationalities, ethnicities, and similar categories, providing a useful *scaffolding* for every kind of bias, stereotype, prejudice, and discrimination, whose innate assumptions of superiority and inferiority can be cited as *backwards* justifications for domination, as was done during slavery and the Holocaust.

In global trade, while capitalism preaches openness, equality, and democracy — mostly in an effort to gain access to other nations' natural resources and consumer markets — it acts surreptitiously, unequally, and autocratically to preferentially protect its *own* natural resources, and imposes tariffs and sanctions that favor its' corporations, products, and services over those of others. In today's high-tech world, it uses AI to replicate the pecking order described above. Political Science Professor Jodi Dean described the process more harshly:

> What happens when capitalism is global? It turns in on itself, generating, enclosing, and mining features of human life through digital networks and mass personalized media. This self-cannibalization produces new lords and serfs, vast fortunes and extreme inequality, and the parcellated sovereignties that secure this inequality while the many wander and languish in the hinterlands.

In many corporations, non-profits, and government institutions, managers and supervisors *routinely* act hierarchically, autocratically, and inhumanely toward employees, rarely collaborating, and often treating them disrespectfully, as though they were inferior beings. These hierarchically driven, autocratic behaviors generate countless costly conflicts, undermine democracy, disincentivize collaboration, dissipate morale, and discourage creativity, consensus building, problem-solving, and conflict resolution.

Alternatively, it would be possible to work *heterarchically*, collaboratively, and democratically, by rejecting domination and abandoning the project of controlling others, including nature, in favor of the far more difficult task of learning the higher order skills needed to participate in creative, collaborative, egalitarian relationships on all scales, and still get one's interests satisfied. To do so, as Eleanor Roosevelt concluded, "... we must get rid of is the idea that democracy is tantamount to capitalism."

8. Capitalism is often divisive, biased, and discriminatory. That is, it divides people *vertically* into social classes, paying women less than men, people of color less than Whites, etc., partly in order to increase competition below, raising the demand for jobs and lowering the price of labor for those above. Along with these economic antagonisms go similar distinctions in social status and political influence, which reinforce differences in wealth and income.

Capitalist competition generates zero-sum thinking, encouraging people to try to raise their position in the pecking order by getting in-group members to unite against outsiders in order to more successfully dominate them and gain access to the wealth, status, power, and privileges they would otherwise have been entitled to enjoy.

In a similar way, corporations divide employees *horizontally* into silos and fixed job descriptions, each with its' own rights, privileges, and self-interests, thereby reducing their capacity to unite, find common ground, and jointly participate in planning, strategizing, coordinating, collaborating across internal boundaries, and able to engage in diverse, democratic, creative, synergistic problem-solving and resolve their chronic conflicts.

Hence, it is possible for organizations to shift to more unifying, collaborative, democratic, non-zero-sum forms of organization, such as self-managing or self-directed teams, employee cooperatives, labor-management decision-making councils, employee membership on corporate boards, employee stock ownership plans, "worker control" proposals, and similar measures. [For more, see my book with Joan Goldsmith, *The End of Management and the Rise of Organizational Democracy*.]

9. Capitalism is often inauthentic, inhumane, and bureaucratic. That is, corporations often suppress truthful information about their products and services, and in some cases seek to camouflage their actual ingredients or characteristics in order to project an image that will sell its' products and services while hiding their harmful or deleterious consequences, even to the extent of adding known carcinogens to baby food, baby powder, and baby toys, then covering it up.

While large corporations often *pretend* in public to care about people, it is clear to nearly everyone else that this is a fantasy designed to obscure their readiness to sacrifice ethics, democracy, decency, health, nature, human lives, and the environment for profits, so long as they think they won't get caught, and their acts won't become public, resulting in reduced sales.

Bureaucracy then becomes the *legal* form taken by indifference, cruelty, obfuscation, dishonesty, corruption, greed, and rapaciousness. As Hannah Arendt memorably described *political* bureaucracy, yet in terms that apply equally in the economic world:

> [T]he latest and most formidable form of ... domination [is] bureaucracy ... which could be properly called rule by Nobody. If, in accord with traditional political thought, we identify tyranny as government that is not held to give account of itself, rule by Nobody is clearly the most tyrannical of all, since there is no one left who would even be asked to answer for what is being done.

Alternatively, it would be possible to reduce inauthenticity, inhumanity, and bureaucracy by, for example, requiring open book transparency, even in accounting; or including ethicists and "consumer watchdogs" on boards of directors, or "chief ethical officers" on leadership teams; or by requiring publication of customer reviews, including on company websites; or by mandating the use of process mapping, quality improvement teams, and similar efforts to reduce and simplify unnecessary bureaucracy.

10. Capitalism is often unscrupulous, manipulative, and oriented to short-term gain. That is, it frequently prioritizes rapid results at the expense of long-term social, economic, political, and environmental sustainability and ethical improvement. In many indigenous communities, such as First Nation people in Canada, tribal decision-makers routinely consider the impact of environmental decisions far into the future, even to seven generations.

It is common to read about the punishment of corrupt politicians who accept bribes, but rare to read about anyone fining, firing, or arresting the corporate leaders who ordered the bribing. And while many of these bribes are solicited by politicians, the lure of profits and fear of loss to competitors has often proved more powerful than laws, ethics, or principles.

It is not, however, the large, overt, *blatant* corruption and readiness to disregard what everyone recognizes as proper business practices that is most destructive, but the little, covert, *patent* transgressions — the routine affronts, minor manipulations, petty self-aggrandizements, sociopathic dishonesties, and secret coverups that happen every day in global businesses that sap integrity, discourage authenticity, distort corporate cultures, and render them unethical and inhumane.

These are exacerbated by a widespread focus on short-term gains, even when it is clear that doing so leads to long-term losses, as is presently the case with the production of fossil fuels that exacerbate climate change and undermine environmental sustainability. This is also true (although somewhat less clear) with the introduction of innovative technologies such as AI without adequate consideration for their long-term consequences.

Alternatively, it would be possible to strengthen personal and organizational commitment to ethics, values, and integrity; bring transparency to all corporate processes and relationships; reduce rewards for bribery and manipulation; and require boards of directors and managers to consider the long-term consequences of corporate decisions on all levels, especially their social, economic, political, and environmental impacts.

[For more on designing economic and organizational alternatives, see *Conflict Revolution: Designing Preventative Systems for Chronic Social, Economic, and Political Conflicts* (2nd Ed., 2015); *The End of Management and the Rise of Organizational Democracy* (2002); and

Resolving Organizational Conflicts: A Course in Mediation and Systems Design (2021).]

None of these 10 evolutionary limits is primarily oriented to purely economic issues or challenges, although many of the critiques of capitalism address these problems, and it would be possible to expand this list by including them. [See, for example, Daniel Schmachtenberger in 'Design Constraints for a Viable Economic System'.] Instead, I opted to focus on attitudes, behaviors, processes, and relationship — i.e., on characteristics that occur often, but not always or everywhere, and in ostensibly socialist economies as well. Yet each can be recognized as a source of chronic, destructive economic conflict, for which countless collaborative, interest-based alternatives are available. Indeed, the labels "capitalist" and "socialist" conceal more than they reveal, so I have focused on *behaviors* instead.

As a consequence of these "top 10" limits, capitalism is driven to simultaneously promote and resist its own evolution, thereby becoming chronically conflicted. These endless conflicts and the violence they sometimes inspire led Mohandas K. Gandhi to conclude that: "Centralization as a system is inconsistent with a nonviolent structure of society. By the nonviolent method, we seek not to destroy the capitalist, we seek to destroy capitalism."

Because of these limitations, the most powerful and effective problem-solving, collaborative, consensus building, and conflict resolution practices encourage organizational behaviors that lie *beyond* the present ability of capitalism as a system to successfully implement, as they each require higher order solutions to resolve lower order conflicts. Raymond Williams saw resistance to this evolution as the source of paradoxical conflicts:

> The whole of public policy is an attempt to reconstitute a culture, a
> social system, an economic order, that have in fact reached their
> end, reached their limits of viability. And then I sit here and look at

this double inevitability; that this imperial, exporting, divided order is ending, and that all its residual forces, all its political formations, will fight to the end to reconstruct it, to re-establish it, moving deeper all the time through crisis after crisis in an impossible attempt to regain a familiar world. So then a double inevitability: that they will fail, and that they will try nothing else.

The difficulty is that socialist experiments have *also* generated chronic economic conflicts, yet none of the analyses of both that I am familiar with examine them from a conflict resolution perspective. As a consequence, no one knows exactly what will emerge from this evolutionary process.

It is important to remind ourselves that inexorable evolutionary forces, driven partly by conflicts that cannot be fully resolved within the old system, offer multiple ways out of these conflicts, yet *none* of them is inevitable. While it is difficult right now to imagine how such significant transformational outcomes might occur, similar changes have occurred countless times in the past. This idea was expressed succinctly by Ursula K. Le Guin: "We live in capitalism. It's power seems inescapable – but then, so did the divine right of kings."

In considering this issue, Wolfgang Streeck argued in *How Will Capitalism End?* that capitalism "permanently revolutionizes the society that it inhabits," instilling fear and greed as successful drivers of innovation; yet it also creates "continuous uncertainty in social relations" that "permanently put established ways of life at risk," commodifying and seeking ownership over what economist Karl Polyani described as three "fictitious commodities": labor, land, and nature.

In my view, having spent many decades mediating conflicts inside hundreds of large organizations, including Fortune 100 corporations and large government institutions, it is *entirely* possible for employees to design and build more successful collaborative, democratic, interest-based, non-zero-sum organizations and institutions by applying alternative conflict resolution principles and processes to economic life, and thereby both prevent chronic economic conflicts before they become costly and destructive, and resolve them more fully. I have witnessed, facilitated, and mediated it on a small- and mid-scale, countless times.

The brilliant Russian novelist and journalist Vasily Grossman, writing in the 1920', 30's, and 40's, raised what may be the deepest and most profound issue of all, in the form of a simple question:

> What I want to know is — do you believe in the evolution of kindness, morality, mercy? Is man capable of evolving that way?

The answer lies partly in our ability to create collaborative, democratic, humanistic, heartfelt, interest-based, non-zero-sum economic processes, relationships, systems, and cultures that are able to *invent* and design the means by which we can reward and promote these behaviors and apply them to the whole of economic life—including our relationship with nature, technology, and the ways we work and interact with each other. Erich Fromm phrased it nicely:

> By the very fact of his being human, man is asked a question by life: how to overcome the split between himself and the world outside of him in order to arrive at the experience of unity and oneness with his fellow man and with nature. Man has to answer this question every minute of his life. Not only — or even primarily — with thoughts and words, but by his mode of being and acting.

FOURTEEN

Mediating Death, Dying, Trauma, and Renewal

"CONFLICT IS DEAD, LONG LIVE CONFLICT!"

One night or one morning a man crosses a boundary, reaches his peak and takes his first step downwards, toward death. Then the question arises: should he descend proudly with his face turned towards the darkness, or should he turn around towards what was, keep up an appearance and pretend it isn't darkness, but just that the light in the room has been extinguished?

Olga Tokarczuk

The death of the contemporary forms of social order ought to gladden rather than trouble the soul. Yet what is frightening is that the departing world leaves behind it not an heir but a pregnant widow. Between the death of one and the birth of the other, much water will flow by; a long night of chaos and desolation will pass.

Alexander Herzen

The death of human empathy is one of the earliest and most telling signs of a culture about to fall into barbarism.

Hannah Arendt

A PERSONAL NOTE

We have all had brushes with death, and I have had many, but the most recent felt closer and lasted longer, prompting me to write this chapter. In 2022, I was diagnosed with prostate cancer that had spread to my lymphatic system. I began hormone deprivation therapy with shots and pills and high-dose radiation, which have so far been successful in stopping the cancer.

As Dr. Samuel Johnson famously remarked, "… when a man knows he is to be hanged in a fortnight, it concentrates his mind wonderfully." This proximity to death enabled me to experience what it feels like — first, to be *entirely* without male hormones (giving rise to hot flashes, extreme fatigue, and other menopausal effects experienced by women); second, to lose control over my basic bodily functions; and third, to recognize my own personal death as no longer taking place in some distant, hard to imagine, infinitely postpone-able future, but *immanently*, unarguably, and insistently, in ways that commanded my attention and re-prioritized everything. Marcel Proust described it brilliantly:

> We say that the hour of death cannot be forecast, but when we say this we imagine that hour as placed in an obscure and distant future. It never occurs to us that it has any connection with the day already begun or that death could arrive this same afternoon, this afternoon which is so certain and which has every hour filled in advance.

Leo Tolstoy recounted the same experience in detail in his novel, *The Death of Ivan Ilyich,* in which Ilyich was fully willing to accept the idea that "man in the abstract" was mortal. Nonetheless, "he was not an abstract man, but a creature quite, quite separate from all the others ... for me, little Vanya, Ivan Ilich ... it's altogether a different matter."

The cancer forced me to abruptly end my four decades-long, wide-ranging, exhilarating mediation practice, and it was only once I stopped that I realized how much energy it takes to hold together in civil and constructive dialogue parties, groups, organizations, and communities that are deeply divided and often hate each other; assist them in gaining insights into the sources of their conflicts; and help them find mutually satisfying ways out of impasse that *feel* magical, but don't require wishful thinking, denial, cover-up, or rose colored glasses.

As a result, one of the deeper realizations I came to, already acknowledged in most meditation practices, is that the magic in mediation — as with peace, wisdom, insight, and enlightenment — is *already* implicit in each of us, and all we need to do is figure out how to let go of everything else. It is difficult, of course, to divest ourselves of our foibles, flaws, bad habits, false expectations, and addictions.

But what we can do, using meditation and other profound and poignant conflict resolution practices, is become more finely and acutely aware of them; cease being so reactive in response to them; trace them to their underlying sources in traumas, family patterns, social systems, and environmental conditions; discover higher order paths that teach us how to side-step them by always coming from a place of authenticity, integrity, and caring; and allow everything else to die within us. Buddhist teacher and writer Pema Chodrun described it this way:

> For me the spiritual path has always been learning how to die. That involves not just death at the end of this particular life, but all the falling apart that happens continually. The fear of death — which is also the fear of groundlessness, of insecurity, of not having it all together – seems to be the most fundamental thing that we have to

work with. ... We have so much fear of not being in control, of not being able to hold on to things. Yet the true nature of things is that you're never in control. ... You can never hold on to anything. ... So my own path has been training to relax with groundlessness and the panic that accompanies it ... training to die continually.

Both meditation and mediation have helped me by showing how easy it is to get stuck, and how it is possible to become unstuck from a vast range of denial, avoidant, and diversionary behaviors. For mediators, I believe this begins with realizing that we are no different from the people we are mediating with; and that, while working with them, we are also simultaneously working on ourselves.

Conflict resolution is beautiful, powerful, inspiring, noble, and magical work, but progress in addressing our own conflicts feels a lot slower; less powerful, inspiring, noble, or magical; and always two steps forward, one step back. Illness made me realize how *exhausting* this work is, and how we carry it with us, and how we don't do nearly enough to recover, and how deeply it impacts our creativity and ability to be present and insightful and daring and magical; and how important it is to let it all go, in order to come back a hundred times stronger. That is why I have had to give it up, at least for now, with humility and gratitude for all it has given me, and allowed me to do and be. I am still able to coach and teach and write and meditate, and search for ways of transforming and transcending the internal and external barriers that keep me, and all of us, in conflict; and to remember, as one Buddhist teacher optimistically observed, "You can transform your life with your very last breath." The brilliant Zen poet Basho put it exquisitely: "Every moment of life is the last, every poem is a death poem."

"Conflict is Dead, Long Live Conflict!"

The obvious, immediate, *ostensible* purpose of all conflict resolution is to end conflict. But if we end it without resolving the underlying reasons that gave rise to it; if we fail to learn the lessons it took place to teach us; if we are to remain unable to evolve, or develop new skills, or transcend the lower order behaviors that got us stuck in the first place, the conflict will have occurred in vain, and be compelled to return, like a ghost, to remind us of something unspoken, yet broken and unhealed in ourselves, our relationships, systems, and environments — our world.

At every stage of our lives, we encounter conflicts, every one of which takes place at a crossroads, defined on the one hand by a problem we are now required to solve; and on the other by the fact that we do not yet have the skills we need to solve it. [See discussion in *The Crossroads of Conflict*.]. After we have learned these higher order skills, not only do *those* conflicts begin to dissipate and disappear, so do *all similar conflicts*, because *we* have evolved, and are now able to experience more advanced conflicts that require higher skills to resolve, and so on till we die.

Indeed, the last, deepest, most poignant and profound conflicts in life are those we experience in death and dying. *Every* conflict represents the death of *something*, just as every resolution is a kind of rebirth, re-emergence, and renewal, in the sense that whatever it was that kept us stuck has now been worked through, transformed, risen above, transcended—often by some new awareness, insight, skill, or capacity that magically frees us from lower order constraints.

That is why, on the one hand, we strive and struggle and hope that our conflicts will end; yet on the other hand, we want the lessons they teach us to continue forever, because it is principally through conflict that we evolve and acquire the higher order skills we need to live better lives, cultivate more satisfying relationships, and graduate to higher order conflicts. Albert Camus wrote, "Face up to death. Thereafter anything is possible." This is true not only for the one great death we all face, but the thousands of little deaths we experience throughout our lives. Alan Watts explained why:

Nothing is more creative than death, since it is the whole secret of life. It means that the past must be abandoned, that the unknown cannot be avoided, that 'I' cannot continue, and that nothing can ultimately be fixed. When a man knows this, he lives for the first time in his life. By holding his breath, he loses it. By letting go, he finds it.

And is this not the case with every little abandonment of the past, every earlier "I" that no longer exists, every false expectation that could never be met—in other words, with everything that has kept us in conflict? If so, is it not apparent that among the principal sources of resistance, impasse, and intractability in conflict are the fear of loss, the immature strivings, the superficial attachments, the systems that are dying, the demise of what we wanted so badly? And what happens in conflict when these fears, strivings, attachments, systems, and desires turn fragile, lose their grip, no longer succeed, and the idea of moving beyond them begins to grow and take shape inside?

Conflicts about Death, Dying, Grief, and Loss

One alternative definition of conflict, among those offered in earlier chapters, and in *The Crossroads of Conflict,* is a lack of awareness of the immanence of death or sudden catastrophe. Why? Because if we know we are about to die, or that our opponent is dying, or that either of us is facing a sudden catastrophe, our conflicts start to feel trivial and unimportant. We then realize that conflicts are simply false priorities, ones that matter far less than life, and that we have simply forgotten what matters most. Conflict is therefore not only a *denial* of the imminence of death, as Ernest Becker recognized in his aptly titled classic, *The Denial of Death*, it is also a denial of *life*, yet one that can paradoxically be transformed into a justification or rationalization for causing or contributing to the deaths of others. Becker wrote:

The irony of man's condition is that the deepest need is to be free of the anxiety of death and annihilation; but it is life itself which awakens it, and so we must shrink from being fully alive.... What is the ideal for mental health, then? A lived, compelling illusion that does not lie about life, death, and reality; one honest enough to follow its own commandments: I mean, not to kill, not to take the lives of others to justify itself.

This "taking of the lives of others" happens both on a large scale, as in war, and on a small scale, in the little ways we block, and insult, and punish others, simply for being themselves; or try to stop them from growing, because if we didn't, they might leave us, forcing *us* to grow, let go of whatever we have been holding on to, and move on. In short, conflict is a fear of *loss*, a grieving, a trauma, a death or dying that is hidden in nearly every issue. This can be glimpsed in the subconscious, camouflaged, distorted ways people deny what is real, both for themselves and others; the ways they resist resolution; the ways they become angry, scared, sad, ashamed, jealous, lonely, and guilty; and the ways they avoid honesty, vulnerability, open heartedness, caring, and authenticity in each other's presence. We can see this connection vividly in the subconscious beliefs, attitudes, assumptions, and feelings people experience and express toward death and dying, many of which have direct applicability to conflict. These attitudes toward death are especially apparent in children, and while they vary from culture to culture, I find many of us secretly harbor similar ideas, including these twenty:

1. We believe death and conflict must have been caused by some outside agency or force.
2. We believe we (or others) *caused* it to happen by wishing it, or by being bad.
3. We believe it will not happen to us, unless we have been bad. It's our fault if we die or experience conflict with others.
4. We are privately relieved that it was the other person who died or experienced conflict, and not us.

5. We subconsciously believe death and conflict are "unfair."

6. We hope and wish that death and conflict will not be permanent, that we will return to "normal" afterwards, and that our suffering will be recognized and rewarded.

7. We forget the problems caused by those who died, and remember only their good points. The opposite happens in conflicts.

8. We tend not to celebrate people's accomplishments until they die, or the conflict is over.

9. We feel angry at those who die, but since we cannot publicly express it as anger, it comes out as passive-aggressive grief. We are also angry at our opponents in conflict, but since we cannot express it as grief, it comes out as passive-aggressive anger.

10. We are afraid of dying and conflict, and shun those who are in the grip of either because it feels bad, or for fear that we will "catch" it.

11. We are afraid of the *look* of death, and have undertakers make over corpses in an attitude of sleep or repose. In conflict, we wear masks that project attitudes of stoicism, lack of caring, and inner strength.

12. We lie to children about both and keep them secret, as though we were ashamed of them.

13. We are torn, and debate whether to tell the person who is dying or their spouse or relatives of their impending death. In conflict, we keep our deepest feelings from our opponents, as well as our allies.

14. We seek to preserve life through technical support and hospital care, which fail to recognize or satisfy the emotional or spiritual needs of the dying person. In conflict we search for compromises, which do the same thing.

15. We do not know what to say or how to act with people who are dying, or stuck in emotionally intense, intractable conflicts, so we avoid them both.

16. We trivialize the risk of death for people undergoing surgery, or conflict for people undergoing change, in order not to upset them, making them unprepared when they do not recover, or when the change reaches an impasse, or triggers conflict.

17. We make decisions for dying people without asking their opinions, and ignore their requests, and even in opposition to their express wishes. We sometimes do the same with those who are in conflict.

18. We fail to recognize or celebrate people in life for who they actually are, and measure them, even in death and conflict, by their status, wealth, or power, rather than their kindness, caring, and humanity.

19. We glorify death and combat, but briefly and artificially, encouraging others to sacrifice their lives, as we did, for things that don't really matter.

20. We want our deaths, traumas, and conflicts to *mean* something, to make a difference, to express who we see ourselves to be, and what we want our lives to have been about.

These commonly held subconscious beliefs and attitudes toward death and conflict are often silenced, suppressed, camouflaged, or projected onto others, making it more difficult for us and them to do the *work* that is required for us to move on, reach closure, end the pain and suffering, evolve into higher order skills, and acquire the wisdom needed to navigate these complex, convoluted, spiritually meaningful pathways in the future.

STAGES, EXPERIENCES, AND PHASES IN RESPONDING TO DEATH AND DYING

Elisabeth Kübler-Ross in her classic, immensely useful book, *On Death and Dying*, identified five stages we commonly experience in facing our own deaths, or the death of someone we love. I prefer to think of these not simply as *stages*, which implies that they occur in a strict sequence, but also as emotional *experiences* that can mix together and be felt in different ways; or as *phases*, suggesting that we can transcend, overcome, and move through and beyond them. Here are the most widely recognized five, which also occur in conflict:

1. *Denial*
2. *Bargaining*
3. *Anger*
4. *Depression*
5. *Acceptance*

To these, when viewed from a conflict resolution perspective that considers *every* conflict a kind of death, it makes sense to tack on a number of similar, corollary experiences, including common conflict responses (in italics), plus a critical sixth stage that ends the cycle not just by accepting the old cycle, but starting a new one:

1. Denial, False Optimism, Refusal to Listen, and *Avoidance*
2. Anger, Guilt, Suppression of Fear and Pain, and *Aggression*
3. Bargaining, Manipulation, Efforts to Control, and *Compromise*
4. Depression, Self-Isolation, Loneliness, and *Accommodation*
5. Acceptance, Letting Go, Closure, *Forgiveness and Self-Forgiveness*
6. Rebirth, Love, Collaboration, and *Reconciliation*

This sixth stage, experience, or phase completes the cycle by showing that it starts again, and like the other stages, experiences, or phases, can occur even for those who are dying, in the period leading up to their death. In conflict, this is especially important, as impasse and resistance can quickly give way to resolution, which can lead to forgiveness and self-forgiveness, and culminate in reconciliation, renewal, and the ability to collaborate in redesigning dysfunctional systems, solving common problems, and renegotiating relational expectations.

A somewhat more detailed, elaborate, and emotionally nuanced list of fourteen responses can then be derived from these six. Here, for example, is my modestly expanded list, identifying under each stage five extra, frequently experienced aspects or sub-stages in relation to death and dying or conflict:

1. Denial:

- Disbelief — the feeling that this is not really happening
- Not listening or paying attention to "negative" information
- Avoidance, changing the subject
- False optimism, assuming it will all magically go away
- Distraction and focus on trivia

2. Shock:

- Numbness
- Bodily reactions – i.e., palpitations, panic, confusion, agitation
- Loss of mental alertness and awareness
- Emotional distancing
- Withdrawal from contact

3. Anxiety:

- Feelings of helplessness
- Exaggerated fears
- Continual insecurity
- Feelings of desertion and betrayal
- Distrust

4. Pain:

- Feelings of physical pain due to separation, loss of connection
- Intense longing
- Pain of emptiness
- Increased (or decreased) empathy for the pain of others
- Use of drugs or alcohol to dampen the pain

5. Resentment:

- Feeling stuck having to deal with problems
- Sense of futility about effectiveness
- Dismissal of past efforts
- Rejection of unhelpful or inappropriate responses by others
- Negative attitude toward everything done to help

6. Anger:

- Feelings of rejection and betrayal
- Blaming the one who left for leaving
- Trying to keep the connection alive through anger and "negative intimacy"
- Transferring anger to others, especially those who remind us of the one who is gone
- Self-anger for causing them to go, or being unable to help

7. Bargaining

- Thinking it will go away if only … [whatever]
- Trying to manipulate and tinker with circumstances
- Seeking to control what can't be controlled
- Looking for compromise solutions
- Searching for magical interventions

8. Guilt:

- Blaming or punishing oneself
- Feeling that "It's all my fault"
- Externalizing guilt and blaming others
- Wallowing in self-pity
- Finding subconscious ways of inflicting self-harm

9. Depression:

- Deep sadness over what has been lost
- Negative self-esteem
- Pessimistic world view
- Feeling that there is no hope for anything
- Despair and self-isolation

10. Sadness:

- Missing them and fondly recalling their good qualities
- Feeling we will never find anyone to replace them
- Accommodating to the wishes of others
- Constant little reminders of what has been lost
- Loneliness that feels permanent

11. Forgetting:

- Loss of some memories
- Waning of emotional fatigue
- Inability to experience the same emotional intimacy or intensity with others
- Gradual disappearance of pain, anger, guilt, and sadness
- Starting to focus on new events and experiences

12. Acceptance:

- Letting go of the past
- Searching for closure

- Forgiving the other person for leaving
- Forgiving oneself for not having been able to prevent it
- Deciding to go on with life

13. Relief:

- Feeling glad that the negative emotions have waned
- Experiencing pleasure in being able to live one's own life
- Having balanced memories of the other person
- Releasing ourselves from old roles, behaviors, and patterns
- Beginning to feel good again

14. Rebirth:

- The return of love, joy, and the celebration of life
- Being grateful for what our opponent or the conflict taught us
- Viewing the experience *spiritually*, as from a distance, as one of growth, insight, transcendence, renewal, and the constant interplay of gain and loss
- A return to openheartedness, unconditional kindness, emotional generosity, and playful collaboration
- Reconciliation with others, and forgotten parts of ourselves

Looked at in these ways, the experience of death and dying, conflict, or any kind of loss, requires us to acquire an ordered, graduated, advanced set of skills and understandings to process the physical, mental, emotional, spiritual, and heartfelt dimensions of trauma that result from feeling ripped apart and separated from those we love, as well as from the parts inside us that love them, and ourselves.

It is possible to find *all* of these stages, experiences, and phases in ordinary, everyday mediations that seem far removed from death and dying — suggesting that they are *scale-free* experiences that range from the very large to the very small. As a result, many of the methods and techniques for dealing with the experience of death and dying can help people process even small-scale losses, and *vice versa*.

WHAT HELPS PEOPLE PROCESS GRIEF AND LOSS?

Of course, the great advantage of conflict over death is that, in the vast majority of cases, it is possible to live long enough to process, work through, transform, and transcend grief and loss, and thereby begin our transition to recovery, rebirth, resurrection, renewal, and reconciliation. Yet processing death or conflict requires us to confront and work *through* our grief and loss, which may consist simply, as in conflict, of releasing ourselves from the burden of our own false expectations.

If we think about working in mediation — not only with people who are directly experiencing death and dying, but any type of conflict — a number of approaches can be taken to help mitigate even small-scale traumas. These may include, for example, comforting, consoling, acknowledging, validating, listening, reframing, and sharing. Or, they may take the form of verbalizing the loss, ventilating the anger, normalizing the sadness, empathizing with those who have suffered, and relieving the guilt people feel for causing or contributing to the loss, or not having done enough to mitigate and assuage it.

Later, in steps that require still greater skill, it may involve designing rituals of release, completion, and closure; helping people let go of their losses, get to acceptance, clarify the meaning of their suffering, and focus on their recovery. Sometimes, it may mean envisioning a positive future, or ways of moving on with their lives, or telling or writing positive stories about each other, or learning from what happened, or *consecrating* the pain it produced and dedicating it to those who suffered most, or those who will come after.

It may consist of helping people express regret, or reach forgiveness for whatever they or others did or did not do; or recognize that they are not alone, and that others have suffered as well, even those who triggered their grief and loss. It may consist of choosing to let the suffering end with them, or discovering meaning in the loss, or completing whatever was unspoken or unperformed, or identifying something positive they can do to prevent whatever happened from happening again, or dedicating some part of their lives to making sure no one will suffer as they did, and that it won't happen again.

Responding to Catastrophic Loss

Sometimes, when the loss is truly catastrophic and the grief and trauma are deep, profound, cumulative, and unresponsive to efforts to strengthen people's capacity to evolve and process what happened, it may be necessary to approach the experience entirely differently, even in counter-intuitive ways that paradoxically *ask* something of those who are suffering. [See *The Crossroads of Conflict.*]

With such deep, catastrophic loss, the *idea* of renewal can feel not only impossible, but painful, and *itself* traumatic, as it is a reminder of the immensity of what has been lost. In these cases, I sometimes find it helpful to shift from working through the stages, experiences, and phases of grief and loss, and focus instead on ways of making the trauma *meaningful* — often by helping others; or finding companionship in a community of people who have been traumatized; or working collaboratively and *systemically* to help make sure that others do not experience the same loss.

This can sometimes be done by volunteer work, organizing support groups, advocating legislative changes, visiting the afflicted, giving talks, writing articles and blogs, offering coaching, and similar methods that allow those who suffered to transform their trauma into a *gift* to others. These may involve, for example:

- Telling personal stories about what happened, expressing the pain that was experienced, and how it was handled.
- Expressing open regret and self-forgiveness for whatever they did or did not do that contributed to their suffering, or that of others.
- Speaking, performing, or becoming whatever feels unspoken, unperformed, or repressed, as a result of the traumatic experience.
- Identifying something positive people can do to prevent it from happening again.
- Committing some significant part of their lives to making sure it doesn't happen again.
- Choosing that the trauma and suffering will end with them.

These steps are sensitive, complex, easily misunderstood, and can sound like "blaming the victim" if they are not done with the right person, at the right time, and with the right skill and intention. It is always risky for conflict resolvers, but riskier still for those who have experienced the loss. As Buddhist teacher Pema Chodrun describes it:

> To be fully alive, fully human, and completely awake is to be continually thrown out of the nest. To live fully is to be in no-man's-land, to experience each moment as completely new and fresh. To live is to be willing to die over and over again.

The deeper the grief and loss, the more essential it is to be *unconditionally* authentic, and to avoid the platitudes and false or superficial expressions of grief, like "I know exactly how you feel," or "You'll get over it," or "Life must go on." Edna St. Vincent Millay wrenchingly described the grief experience:

> *Time does not bring relief; you all have lied*
> *Who told me time would ease me of my pain!*
> *I miss him in the weeping of the rain;*

I want him at the shrinking of the tide;
The old snows melt from every mountain-side,
And last year's leaves are smoke in every lane;
But last year's bitter loving must remain
Heaped on my heart, and my old thoughts abide.
There are a hundred places where I fear
To go,—so with his memory they brim.
And entering with relief some quiet place
Where never fell his foot or shone his face
I say, "There is no memory of him here!"
And so stand stricken, so remembering him.

A MEDIATIVE APPROACH TO END-OF-LIFE CONFLICTS

While dying is widely recognized as emotionally intense and profoundly important, it is rare that people who are in the process of dying sit down with their families and friends to talk about what they are feeling, or plan the way they want to be treated as they die. Here are the results of a 2013 survey:

- 90% of people said that talking about end-of-life care is important, but only 27% of people have actually had these conversations.
- 82% of people said it's important to put their wishes in writing, but only 23% have actually done it.
- 80% of people said that if seriously ill, they would want to talk to their doctor about end-of-life care, but only 7% of people said they had that discussion.
- 60% of people said that making sure their family is not burdened by tough decisions is "extremely important", but 56% had not communicated their end -of-life wishes.

[Source: The Conversation Project National Survey 2013, cited in Kimberley Best's excellent book, *How to Live Forever*]

While a great deal has been written about processing the deaths of others, little has been written of a practical nature about how to *mediate* disputes that arise in the course of dying. These begin with the marginalization, disempowerment, and infantilization of the elderly, sick, and dying, who are often sidelined and excluded from making decisions about their own death and dying. Stephen Jenkinson writes:

> When people are elderly or dying, they are forced to identify themselves as no longer quite alive; their citizenship in the land of the living becomes iffy. And we, the living, conspire in that, because we ask less and less of the dying, to the point where we ask nothing of them at all: no alertness, no courtesy, no work, no testifying – nothing. This is all a way of engineering their failing health. It's not the disease that ends their well-being, it's our unwillingness to number them among the living.

A second source of conflict is with family members and close friends over unresolved conflicts from the past, inheritance issues, palliative care, and many other issues, all of which are aggravated by dysfunctional family patterns that have never been discussed or resolved. Yet mediators, conflict coaches, small group facilitators and others are able to assist people who are dying and their families and friends in creating comprehensive, integrated, collaborative approaches to communicating, negotiating, and resolving these issues, by:

- Helping the dying plan a "good death"
- Offering conflict coaching to aid them and others in understanding and accepting death and the process of dying
- Celebrating those who are dying, and facilitating "anticipatory mourning," including recognition, gratitude, and celebration of life
- Mediating and assisting families in letting go of past conflicts

- Working with attorneys to draft wills and trusts that prevent survivors from "inheriting" conflicts
- Planning legacies and bequests that resolve or repair old conflicts and prevent new ones
- Facilitating family dialogues and rituals around death and dying
- Mediating decisions about end-of-life care and family assistance
- Partnering with health care providers and Hospice, in mediating conflicts over end-of-life choices during the last stages of dying
- Designing rituals of release, completion, and closure that help end family and relational conflicts
- Facilitating end-of-life apologies, forgivenesses, and reconciliations
- Helping design what I call "Durable Powers of Attorney for Conflict Management" that allow a named mediator to step in when disputes arise, and be paid out of the estate
- Mediating conflicts over wills, trusts, and estate administration
- Facilitating interviews and creating oral histories of the lives of the dying, or completing genealogies, or helping family members ask questions they always wanted to ask, but never had time to
- Designing conflict resolution systems for surviving family members

In discussing and mediating these issues, it is helpful to ask people to speak from their hearts, with full awareness of the immanence of death, and remind them of the importance of kindness. I find it useful to celebrate the life of the dying person, and ask, "If this were the last conversation you were going to have with each other, what is the very last thing you would want to say?" And ultimately, it is often true, as novelist Leslie Marmon Silko wrote, that "The only cure ... is a good ceremony."

WHAT IS TRAUMA?

All conflict is traumatic, and every conflict restimulates and reminds us of earlier traumas, even ones we do not recall from infancy and childhood. And, as Judith Herman pointed out in *Trauma and Recovery*, traumas become *complex* through repetition, as during times of war—but also as a result of living in societies that are racist, sexist, homophobic, anti-Semitic, etc.; or are brutal and unkind; or people are *systematically* disrespected; or subjected to autocracy, bullying, and violence.

Trauma is often thought of simply as an injury, but can be more deeply understood as an injury that results from experiences that overwhelm our belief in our ability to defend or protect ourselves, or to remain safe. Trauma is a loss of *resiliency* to injury that can be physical, mental, emotional, relational, spiritual, or heart based. And trauma can be impacted by social, economic, political, and environmental injuries, grounded in organizational, institutional— even generational experience, and take multiple and diverse forms.

Gabor Maté, who has studied, worked with, and written deeply about trauma, defines it in his book, *There is No Normal*, as "an inner injury, a lasting rupture or split within the self, due to difficult or harmful events; ... [it] is not what happens *to* you but what happens *inside* you." It can be regarded as an injury together with a sense of powerlessness, failure, and loss of self-esteem.

Maté considers the cause of trauma to be a consequence, byproduct, or outcome of *conflict*–most often between our fundamental need for being and authenticity, *versus* our need for belonging and attachment. He explains it this way:

> [There is an] inescapable tension, and for most of us an eventual clash, between two essential needs: *attachment* and *authenticity*. This clash is ground zero for the most widespread trauma in our society: namely, the 'small-t' trauma expressed in a disconnection from the self even in the absence of abuse or overwhelming threat.

Regardless of its source, emotional trauma is thought to contain four key elements:

- It was unexpected.
- The person was unprepared.
- There was a direct threat to survival and preservation.
- There was little or nothing the person felt could be done to prevent it from happening.

It is not the nature of the *event* that alone determines whether something is traumatic, but how each individual subjectively *experiences* the event, so that it is unpredictable how anyone will react in response, or what kind of event will result in trauma. For someone who is used to being in control of emotions and events, it may be surprising–even embarrassing — to discover that an accident, illness, loss, or experience of conflict, including social, economic, political, and environmental conflicts, can be so debilitating that it becomes traumatic.

What Is Trauma-Informed Mediation?

Many years ago, I co-founded and became first President of Mediators Beyond Borders (MBB), (originally Mediators Without Borders, later Mediators Beyond Borders International, or MBBI), an organization dedicated to strengthening conflict resolution skills and capacities in underserved communities around the world. Among our first projects was work with former child soldiers in the Bududuram refugee camp in Ghana, and with conflicted Hutu and Tutsi communities in Rwanda, Somali refugees in the U.S., and many others.

In these cases, while teaching mediation skills, we realized that not only was everyone we worked with *deeply* traumatized by violent experiences, each fresh conflict re-triggered these earlier traumas. In response, several members began developing what we call "trauma informed mediation," which is being advanced in Ukraine,

Sudan, and elsewhere by Prabha Sankaranarayan, MBBI's current President, and other members.

Trauma Informed Mediation (TIM) differs from traditional approaches to trauma (T) in four primary ways, based on an analogy with "trauma informed care":

1. Understanding the trauma:

- (T) Trauma is seen as a single event and symptoms as predictable. Survivors see themselves as victims who are powerless. Conflicts are rarely mediated or resolved, and if so, it is done separately.
- (TIM) Trauma is often cumulative and unpredictable. Survivors see systems, conditions, and environments as sources, and themselves as able to challenge them. Conflicts are resolved as part of an *integrated* response.

2. Understanding the survivor:

- (T) The individual and their problem are considered synonymous, and their identity is defined by their trauma. Emphasis is on the past, and people are seen as having separable parts.
- (TIM) People and problems are separated, identity is defined by one's response to trauma. Emphasis is on the whole person and the context in which he or she is living.

3. Understanding the process:

- (T) Trauma is addressed individually within a set time frame. Focus is on managing risk and medicating symptoms. Outcomes are focused and stabilization is the primary goal. Conflicts are treated separately.
- (TIM) Trauma is addressed socially as well as individually. The primary goal is to return a sense of control and

autonomy through a resilience-based focus on building skills. Conflict resolution is an integral part of the process.

4. Understanding the relationship:

- (T) People are viewed as passive participants, while professionals are seen as having universal solutions and superior knowledge, that hinder innovation and collaboration.
- (TIM) There is open and genuine collaboration between participants and professionals. Participants engage in dialogue and decide on solutions, processes, and relationships.

TRANSFORMING AND TRANSCENDING TRAUMA IN MEDIATION

Gabor Maté, with special significance for mediators, defined healing from trauma as "a natural movement toward wholeness;" as a "direction, not a destination;" and as "self-retrieval," rather than self-improvement, that can take years to process. This is especially important where the source of the trauma is not entirely interpersonal, but has been impacted by chronic social, economic, political, and environmental disputes, or systemic conditions that have deepened, reinforced, or replicated the trauma, allowing it to ripple outward and be passed on to others.

One element in healing from trauma consists in a return to the *authentic* Self. Another is to enter into collaborative, enjoyable, integrative relationships with the "authentic Other"–that is, to first figure out how to individuate and be oneself, and then integrate and connect with those who are substantially different. Solving this problem requires significant, higher order skills in mindfulness, empathy, communication, emotional intelligence, collaboration, and conflict resolution.

Echoing Tolstoy, every conflict is traumatic, but in its' own way, and it is helpful for those who have been traumatized to be brought together to share their experiences, insights, reflections, and desires for the future—discovering in the process that they are not alone; that they have mistakenly blamed themselves and each other for their suffering; and that they can act together to solve their present and future problems, resolve their conflicts, and recover their wholeness.

Another effective approach to working with trauma — for example, by George A. Bonanno in *The Other Side of Sadness* — identifies the principal "trajectories" of grief and trauma as follows:

1. *Resilience:* "The ability of adults in otherwise normal circumstances who are exposed to an isolated and potentially highly disruptive event, such as the death of a close relation or a violent or life-threatening situation, to maintain relatively stable, healthy levels of psychological and physical functioning" as well as "the capacity for generative experiences and positive emotions."
2. *Recovery:* When "normal functioning temporarily gives way to threshold or sub-threshold psychopathology (e.g., symptoms of depression or Post-Traumatic Stress Disorder (PTSD), usually for … several months, and then gradually returns to pre-event levels."
3. *Chronic Dysfunction:* Prolonged suffering and inability to function, usually lasting several years or longer.
4. *Delayed Grief or Trauma:* When adjustment seems normal, but distress and symptoms increase months or years later.

One key element in determining which trajectory traumatized people will pursue is the presence of unresolved conflicts—especially *chronic* conflicts that reappear and block healing. Yet an obvious remedy for the feeling of powerlessness in conflict-related trauma is the use of higher order resolution skills, especially in responding to intense "negative" emotions, such as grief, guilt, fear, and anger. Equally important is the ability of trauma-informed mediators to step *outside* the conflict, gain perspective and emotional distance from it, then step back *inside* the conflict to gain insight and emotional empathy; then *combine* these experiences to locate a potential synthesis that might lead to more skillful interventions with greater likelihood of success.

These skills bolster self-confidence and can be acquired, even by people who have suffered from serious traumas — as we learned working with child soldiers and victims of genocide. Yet it is the ability to move in and out of traumatic experience that seems to have the greatest impact on people who feel trapped by their traumas, as doing so is a way of practicing mediation and mindfulness skills, and demonstrating to trauma survivors that it is possible for them also to:

1. Step outside the places where they feel stuck, confused, untrusting, and are experiencing intense emotions.
2. Look back at their conflict or trauma as though from the outside.
3. Realize that the one who is looking back is *not* the one who is stuck, confused, untrusting, or experiencing intense emotions.
4. See with greater clarity and compassion what *others* may be feeling or experiencing.
5. From this improved vantage point, step *back* into the conflict or trauma, without surrendering these insights.
6. Apply these insights, especially in the form of questions that invite others into a conversational space that is emotionally honest, authentic, caring, and free.

HISTORIC, SYMBOLIC, IDENTITY-ALTERING TRAUMAS

Deeper, more entrenched, longer-lasting difficulties arise in families, groups, and communities that have experienced massive, profound, "historic" traumas, which have come to symbolize their mistreatment and become part of their identity for generations. These traumas have been described as "chosen," or universally held within the community of victims, as the brutality of these events allows them to be held up to others, especially their former oppressors, and force them to look at what they did, in hopes that doing so will ensure that it doesn't happen again.

Vamik Volkan, a psychiatrist working with communities that have experienced serious, sustained ethnic, religious, and political violence, described the formation of these "chosen traumas," defined by cultural critic Lewis Hyde, in *A Primer for Forgetting: Getting Past the Past,* as an "identity-informing ancestral calamity whose memory mixes actual history with passionate feeling and fantasized grievance and hope." The choice and fantasy do not refer to *whether* the calamity occurred, but *why* it happened, and the possibility that it will happen again.

The central question raised by Volkan and Hyde is how individual people and oppressed communities can recover and heal, when their collective trauma constantly reminds them of how horrifically they were treated, and indeed, how, in the absence of an agreed-upon memory, they can easily be treated again. Here are a few interesting initial questions on chosen traumas, suggested by Volkan:

- How can the symbols of chosen traumas be made dormant so that they no longer inflame?
- How can group members "adaptively mourn" so that their losses no longer give rise to anger, humiliation, and a desire for revenge?
- How can a preoccupation with minor differences between neighbors become playful?
- How can major differences be accepted without being contaminated with racism or prejudice?

Deeper transformational questions might be added to these, especially in the context of facilitating direct communications between former adversaries, for example, in dialogue, mediation, restorative justice, and truth and reconciliation commissions, where memory, truth telling, and *responsibility* for inflicting the harm are *essential* for healing to happen, and reduce the fear that it could happen again.

Unfortunately, as Holocaust survivor Ruth Kluger has insightfully pointed out, "A remembered massacre may serve as a deterrent, but it may also serve as a model for the next massacre." As a result, a trauma can *always* return, as the memory of it preserves not only the horror of what was inflicted, but the implicit power to inflict it, along with the stereotypes, prejudices, and rationalizations that fuel it.

Indeed, communities that reinforce their memories of past traumas can inadvertently lock themselves into chronic conflicts for generations, freeze both the past and the future, and prevent themselves evolving and becoming any more than the sum of how they were once treated. And, as Jean-Paul Sartre aptly expressed it: "Freedom is what you do with what's been done to you."

Memories of trauma, whether explicitly or implicitly, take the form of *accusations*, which in time are directed not at the *actual* perpetrators, who are often no longer alive — but at their descendants, silent supporters, and complicit enablers, who are seen as guilty by association, and regarded as evil for acts they themselves did not commit — as can be seen in the refusal of former slave-owning families and segregated states in the U.S. to teach children about racism—bizarrely, because they would feel bad about it, yet thereby permit it to continue.

Through experience, and in mediation, we learn that insulting the one who insults us does not terminate the insult, but redoubles it, justifies it, and turns the process in a circle. We can't bully the bully and hope to stop bullying. Instead, we need to see that the one who is bullied and the one who bullies are *both* trapped, trying to use simplistic, adversarial, shaming and blaming, and other lower dimensional skills to solve a complex, shared, higher dimensional problem.

We may then recognize that the effort to end slavery is not entirely for the purpose of freeing the slave, which of course is its' primary goal, but to also free the master–and more profoundly, *all* of us from the countless ways we were enslaved and traumatized without even noticing it; to free us from hate-filled politics, traumatized relationships, divided cultures, and the traumatizing *system* of domination and enslavement. As Gabor Maté observed:

> The closer I look at the political landscape ... the more I see the wounded electing the wounded, the traumatized leading the traumatized and, inexorably, implementing policies that entrench traumatizing social conditions.

The difficulty is that *not* remembering and teaching about traumas like slavery and genocide denies or minimizes them, allowing oppression to win, and giving *implicit* permission for it to happen again, while recalling it accentuates and prioritizes the past, permitting it to cancel or dominate the present, obscure shared memories, and weaken the ability to reunite and imagine alternative futures. In this way, "chosen traumas" constrict *identity*, linking it only and always to trauma and oppression.

The difficulty, then, is to figure out how to participate in *forms* of remembering that do not remain fixed in the past, but use it to improve the ability of both sides to live in harmony in the future–*including*, most importantly, the children of former oppressors. Otherwise, the trauma never truly ends, and is passed on down the generations in ways that, paradoxically, invite it to recur.

Examples of this transformational approach can be seen in many mediations, especially juvenile victim-offender mediations and restorative justice circles, which begin with the assumption that *everyone* has been traumatized by the conflict, perpetrator and victim alike. Yet if there is no acknowledgement, contrition, empathy, or ownership of what happened by the perpetrator, the victim will have a far more difficult time reaching forgiveness; and without forgiveness by the victim, it will be far more difficult for everyone to let it go, reconcile, and create the kind of community in which these sorts of traumas no longer occur.

What Is "Vicarious Trauma"?

Traumas are experienced primarily, secondarily, and vicariously. Secondary traumas are experienced as though the person impacted had actually taken part in the experience or was emotionally injured by the traumatic feelings of others. Vicarious traumas are those of caregivers, where the trauma was experienced or felt through a profound imaginative, poignant, compassionate, or empathetic sensitivity to the traumatic experiences of others.

Charles Figley, Chair of Disaster Mental Health at Tulane, defined vicarious trauma as the "natural consequent behaviors and emotions resulting from knowing about a traumatizing event experienced by a significant other; it is the stress resulting from helping or wanting to help a traumatized or suffering person." Those most likely to experience vicarious trauma are often present in the families, workplaces, communities, or social and political environments that are filled with real or anticipated threats and dangers, or with terrible suffering, emotional upset, terror, horror, disgust, rage, pain, and fear. They may be living or working inside dysfunctional familial, social, economic, political, or environmental systems, and include medical caregivers, mental health professionals, and, of course, mediators.

Vicarious trauma is often experienced by mediators, facilitators, and other conflict resolution professionals in the form of burnout, empathy or compassion fatigue, cumulative stress, physical and mental illness, heightened sensitivity, "relief worker PTSD," shellshock, sympathetic traumatic conditions, hostile judgments about oneself or others, depression, quitting, "soul sadness," and other post-traumatic stress disorder (PTSD) symptoms. What I have found most successful over many decades in reducing my own vicarious trauma symptoms, and those of other mediators and conflict resolvers, are these 10 activities:

1. Engage in regular meditation, exercise, yoga, and other stress reduction activities.
2. Participate in a variety of reflective practices, both individually and with others.
3. When in conflict, seek the calm at the center of the storm, where stress starts to dissolve and disintegrate.
4. Be as fully present in the conflict as possible, and observe closely what is taking place beneath the surface.
5. Be willing to take risks and mediate "dangerously."
6. Abandon judgments, and practice "radical acceptance," empathy, and forgiveness, both of others and ourselves. [See, e.g., Tara Brach, *Radical Acceptance*.]
7. Turn the trauma into a search for deeper meaning, understanding, improved skills, and innovative approaches that might work better.
8. Release all forms of attachment to outcomes, and empower other people to make choices that belong to them.
9. Always act with integrity, humility, kindness, and genuine caring.
10. Dedicate and consecrate mistakes to those who will come after.

If we regard mediations as "first order" practices, we can imagine "second order" practices, as the brilliant physicist Heinz von Foerster invented for the field of cybernetics. These second order practices, which we call the "mediation of mediation," consists largely of collaborative, "reflective practice" activities in which conflict resolvers collectively examine their successes and failures, and work to improve their skills, but also to identify the sources of their vicarious trauma, and collaboratively seek to heal and repair them. A "third order" practice might consist of removing the sources of suffering inside us so that trauma has little or nothing to stick to, as Mother Theresa is said to have done.

Conflict, Lying, and the Creation of a Divided Self

Among the reflexive behaviors characteristic of people who experience vicarious trauma, or seek to escape the experience of trauma, or are in denial about death or dying, or are trying to avoid conflict, is *lying* about it–mostly to others, but also to themselves. Lying creates a divided, inauthentic, conflicted self, a self that actively either avoids or *seeks out* conflicts, as an inverted, externalized, unsuccessful, *negative* effort to return to wholeness. By externalizing *half* of one's divided self, flipping it, projecting it onto an opponent, and trying to defeat it, they are using the conflict to teach themselves the skills they need to heal their internal divide.

We learn how to lie in childhood when we discover that we can protect ourselves and avoid conflicts, with their accompanying shame and guilt, their implied threat of familial death or dying, their fear of being blamed or punished. We do so by making up stories that excuse our mistakes, rationalize our cruelties, and soothe our wounded vanities.

We grow up in families where people lie about all sorts of things, especially about death and conflict. We watch grownups lie about their disputes, relationships, work, thoughts, feelings, histories, and who they are. We grow up in societies where advertising is a constant series of lies, where giant corporations and government leaders routinely lie about their mistakes and failures; where politics consists almost entirely of lying about what has been, is being, or will be done, and why; where religious hypocrisy and pressures to conform socially, sexually, and ideologically, are all disguised by a broad array of dishonesties.

We lie to others, and we lie to ourselves, even about whether we are lying. We lie because we are afraid, or do not have the courage to face the truth, or we think others won't know, or to gain momentary advantages, or our self-esteem is fragile, or our self-confidence is weak, or our fear of being abandoned is too great. We tell "little white lies" to avoid hurting other people's feelings with the truth, or to protect ourselves from their harsh judgments—yet always at the cost of our authenticity and integrity, instigating conflicts between parts of ourselves that we then externalize and project onto others, resulting in a division, a dying, even a death of our *capacity* to be unified, undivided, holistic selves.

Our lies implicitly suggest that there are two primary arenas of narrative truth: factual and emotional. Through conflict stories, we learn that it is common, effective, and permissible to distort *factual* truths in order to accurately describe deeper and far more important *emotional* truths; so if we have a choice about how to describe a conflict experience, we will nearly always sacrifice factual truths for emotional ones in order to create a more compelling story.

In short, we lie not only to survive and avoid trauma, blame, and self-loathing, but to *create* images of ourselves by telling stories that mask our avoidant or aggressive intentions, rationalize our harmful behaviors, and make us look better than we actually are. What we do not understand, at least at first, are that the consequences of lying extend far beyond the obvious impact our lies have on others.

The first, most important impact of lying is the creation of a divided self, consisting on the one hand, of the part of us that lied; and on the other hand, of the part of us that *knows* we lied. The presence of these two *automatically* produces a third, a self that buries, masks, camouflages, and distorts the other two, defending them from discovery by disguising or trivializing the issues, or refusing to talk about what actually happened for fear of being found out.

Excuses for Not Talking about What Actually Happened

When people face death and dying, or experience trauma, or get stuck in conflict, they are often reluctant to talk about their feelings, especially with each other. Instead, they cite a variety of seemingly plausible reasons for *not* doing so. Yet when we look *beneath* those reasons, we find attitudes of avoidance, accommodation, aggression, and compromise that are grounded in subconscious perceptions that they may be hurt if they tell the truth, or lack the skills they need to be honest, or are afraid of risking disapproval, or are reluctant to be vulnerable, or don't feel they have the strength to engage in deep listening, or are unprepared for change, or don't know how to achieve collaborative, win/win outcomes.

Thus, if I am worried that the other person will disagree with me, disrespect me, yell at me, or punish me, it probably means I have: 1.) *accurately* understood that they will not like or agree with what I want to say, and may decide to "shoot the messenger;" 2.) I want to avoid their anger, disapproval, rejection, disrespect, and/or my own, and 3.) I don't feel I have the skills I need to avoid becoming reactive, or trigger an intense emotional reaction, or get my message across.

Yet these very realizations can help me to 1.) identify more precisely what they are likely to become angry *about* and why; 2.) reframe my message so they will be more likely to hear it without getting upset with me; and 3.) plan more strategically what I am going to say and how I am going to say it — to set the stage, timing, mood, and location for the conversation; anticipate their objections; listen actively, empathetically, and responsively to their concerns; summarize them back so they will feel heard; and offer concessions designed to satisfy their interests without giving up my own, getting emotionally plugged in, or experiencing a loss of authenticity and open communication.

If I rationalize my reluctance to talk with them and avoid meeting or discussing my concerns, I will not improve my skills. If I charge into the conversation without recognizing the validity of the subtle information my intuited fears are based on, I may trigger more anger than I need to, miss their deeper concerns, and be less prepared to respond constructively and collaboratively. But if I accept both truths simultaneously: the one my reluctance to speak to them is pointing to, and the one my desire to communicate suggests, I may find a *middle* path that incorporates both possibilities, identifies skills I can use to overcome these obstacles, and suggests ways of being both authentic and strategic.

More deeply, there is a set of core conflict resolution skills that are missing in nearly every case of conflict avoidance, accommodation, aggression, and compromise. At the risk of exaggerating, these are the skills of communicating — not just honestly and authentically, but *caringly* and kindly with those who upset us--and not just the emotional skills of empathy, or social skills of collaboration, but the spiritual and heart-based skills of kindness, forgiveness, and reconciliation.

These are also the most important skills in experiencing death and dying, or trauma and loss, all the way from denial and anger to rebirth, renewal, and reconciliation. They are the skills of open, honest, empathetic, vulnerable, and caring communication; of resilience and emotional intelligence; of *unconditional*, consummate, impeccable integrity; and of resolving, transforming, and transcending conflicts in interest-based, non-polarizing, non-zero-sum ways.

THE MEDIATION IS THE MESSAGE

Communication theorist Marshall McLuhan famously wrote that "the media is the message" to call attention to the diverse *content* of different *processes* of communication. In a similar way, there is a content to the diverse processes we use to resolve conflicts, and outcomes can differ radically based on which process we use to achieve it. The essence of interest-based conflict resolution is the open, humble, humanistic, *caring* content of collaboration, dialogue, consensus building, reconciliation, restorative justice, and similar processes. Mediation can be defined, both in nature and in human interactions, as what happens naturally at the places where opposites connect. It is the co-existence of contrasting *meanings,* diverse people, dissenting ideas, unique feelings, and different experiences of the world. The *forms* of this communication have evolved over millennia, and with them, the forms of meaning and relationship that arise between hostile individuals, and the bonds that unite them, as can be seen in every family, community, organization, society, and nation state. These forms have changed as the technology of communication has evolved — as described, for example, by McLuhan, for whom the invention of electronic media created not only radically new possibilities for thought and social relations, but new forms of *mediation,* by extending our nervous system "… in a global embrace, abolishing both space and time." This new technology:

> … requires utter human docility and quiescence of meditation such as befits an organism that now wears its brain outside its skull and its nerves outside its hide. Man must serve his electric technology with the same servo-mechanistic fidelity with which he served … all other extensions of his physical organs.

Media theorists Jay David Bolter and Richard Grusin extended this idea, connected it with the use of "immediacy" and "hypermediacy," which give rise to "remediation," in which one type of mediation informs and is represented through another. Abstracting their description of media, we can translate their core ideas into conflict resolution practices as follows:

- *Remediation is the mediation of mediation:* Each act of mediation depends on other acts of mediation and mediates them continually.
- *Remediation is the inseparability of mediation and reality:* All mediations are real and all reality is mediated, so it is impossible to end one without ending the other.

- *Remediation is the reform of reality:* The goal of remediation is to refashion, rehabilitate, and reform, or transform and transcend reality.

In these ways, we can think about remediation, together with "second order" mediation described earlier, as scale-free approaches to the much larger problem of the relationship between how people learn and evolve in the midst of conflict–especially over death and dying, grief and loss, trauma and renewal–and *globally*, with individuals, families, communities, and nation states. Immanuel Kant's well-known "categorical imperative," for example, asserts that one should act only on the basis of principles, morals, laws, or values that are *universal*, and always treat other human beings, and oneself, as *ends*, rather than mere means. For conflict resolvers, these ideas suggest that each of us is responsible for resolving conflicts locally as well as *globally*; for doing whatever we can to strengthen our skills and capacities; and for contributing to the scale-free arts and sciences of dispute resolution, and the magic that lies within them.

Reconciliation, Rebirth, and Renewal as the Last Phase of Conflict

While conflict is a clear sign of dysfunction, it is also an *invitation* to remedy or fix it. It is the problem, yet it is also the opening, the gateway, and the means by which we discover and invent solutions. It is the first step in a cycle of learning, growth, evolution, and transcendence that does not end until there has been rebirth, renewal, and reconciliation, whose possibility is always immanent in conflict.

Conflicts feel fixed and unmovable, as though they were nailed to the floor. But nails are merely stories of demonization and victimization that keep us stuck, and the floor is a complex mixture of emotions, attitudes, assumptions, and intentions, each of which is malleable, vulnerable, and evolving as it discovers there is yet another, still deeper floor beneath it, to which *nothing* can be nailed.

Mediation is the means by which these discoveries occur. It represents the unifying principle and the celebration of diversity. It is the *precise* point where yin meets and dissolves into yang. It is the heart of heartlessness, the place where light emerges from darkness. It is the unspoken request for kindness that lies beneath every cruelty. It is the discovery of the other within the self, and the self within the other. It is the sacred at the center of the profane, the ice awaiting the thaw. It is patience and openness and caring in the presence of suffering. It is the whole that is greater than the sum of its' parts. It is the way in, and the way out. It is the gateway to higher order conflict resolution practices, and the inspiration for us to declare: "Conflict is dead, long live conflict!"

We celebrate soldiers who risk their lives in battle and thank them for their service, but rarely celebrate, or are even *conscious* of the countless mediators, collaborative negotiators, dialogue facilitators, and peace builders around the world who risk trauma, and work passionately and tirelessly every day to save these same lives. It is an honor to belong to this community, and when one of us is acknowledged, we are all honored. It is therefore important to thank those whose trauma and suffering have taught us new ways to alleviate them; those who venture each day into darkness and try to rekindle the light; those who have failed and wondered why; those who have succeeded and wondered why not. We need to celebrate the magical, challenging work we have done and continue to do — all so we can face, with the deepest commitment, humility, and audacity, the work that remains for us to do.

FINAL LESSONS FROM A LIFETIME SPENT LEARNING FROM CONFLICT

Here are a few final lessons, drawn from a lifetime meditating conflicts, my own and others; ideas on searching for ways of finding, feeding, and fomenting magic; on working for social, economic, political, and environmental justice; on experiencing the practical methodology, heart knowledge, and profound wisdom of transformation and transcendence.

- *Everything* we do outside or to others we do inside and to ourselves.
- Once we find the place where there is not just a single Truth, but multiple, complex, overlapping, even contradictory truths, the goal is not to choose between them, but to reveal the symmetries, synergies, and insights that emerge from their creative combination.
- Everything large, important, meaningful, and profound is contained, in miniature and holographically, in something small, trivial, meaningless, and profane. That is where they live and die.
- We are all filled beyond overflowing with emptiness, which is not nothing, but our ground state, rest energy, and subtle meaning.
- For every judgment about others, there is some part of ourselves we can no longer touch, feel, learn about, or become. For every declaration and fixed assumption, there is some unasked question that is a hundred times more powerful.
- The most important contribution we can make in all our relationships and conversations is to *show up*, be as fully present as possible, and ready for *anything* at every moment, as though *our* lives were about to change as a result.
- Anything one touches *correctly*, with the right spirit, leads to the center; or rather, from the center one can reach back to the center, while from the periphery one can touch only the periphery.
- Success mostly consists in not being afraid to fail, while failure consists in being overly concerned with success.
- What matters most is the simplicity, kindness, and generosity of our intentions; the skill, enjoyment, and

artistry of our ceremony; and our *impeccable* willingness to accept the same truths about ourselves.

- Conflicts teach us how to hold on to what is important, let go of what isn't, remember who we are, and search for the magic, even in the midst of pain and trauma, grief and loss, death and dying.
- Most conflicts appear to take place between "us" and "them," but there is no "them," there is only us.
- The most profound step we can take in resolving conflicts is to open our hearts *unconditionally*, both to our opponents and to ourselves.

Novelist Louise Erdrich described the core lesson of conflict more dramatically:

> Life will break you. Nobody can protect you from that, and living alone won't either, for solitude will also break you with its yearning. You have to learn how to love. You have to feel. It is the reason you are here on earth. You are here to risk your heart. You are here to be swallowed up. And when it happens that you are broken, or betrayed, or left, or hurt, or death brushes near, let yourself sit by an apple tree and listen to the apples falling all around you in heaps, wasting their sweetness. Tell yourself you tasted as many as you could.

Or, as the magnificent poet Mary Oliver expressed it:

> ... *if the heart has devoted itself to love, there is*
> *not a single inch of emptiness. Gladness gleams*
> *all the way to the grave.*

About the Author

Kenneth Cloke is Director of the Center for Dispute Resolution and for over forty years has been a mediator, arbitrator, facilitator, coach, consultant and trainer, specializing in communication, negotiation, and resolving complex multi-party disputes, including marital, divorce, family, community, grievance and workplace disputes, collective bargaining negotiations, organizational and school conflicts, sexual harassment, discrimination, and public policy disputes; and designing preventative conflict resolution systems.

His facilitation, coaching, consulting, and training practice includes work with leaders of public, private and non-profit organizations on effective communications, dialogue, collaborative negotiation, relationship and team building, conflict resolution, leadership development, strategic planning, designing systems, culture and organizational change.

His university teaching includes mediation, law, history, political science, conflict studies, urban studies, and other topics at several colleges and universities. He is or has recently been an Adjunct Professor at Pepperdine University School of Law; Southern Methodist University; USC, Global Negotiation Insight Institute at Harvard Law School; Omega Institute; Albert Einstein College of

Medicine, Cape Cod Institute; University of Amsterdam ADR Institute; Saybrook University; Massey University (New Zealand).

He has done conflict resolution work in Armenia, Australia, Austria, Bahamas, Brazil, Canada, China, Cuba, Denmark, England, Georgia, Greece, India, Ireland, Japan, Mexico, Netherlands, New Zealand, Nicaragua, Pakistan, Puerto Rico, Scotland, Slovenia, Spain, Thailand, Turkey, Ukraine, USSR, and Zimbabwe. He is founder and first President of Mediators Beyond Borders.

He served as an Administrative Law Judge for the California Agricultural Labor Relations Board and the Public Employment Relations Board, a Factfinder for the Public Employment Relations Board, and a Judge *Pro Tem* for the Superior Court of Los Angeles. He has been an Arbitrator and Mediator for over forty years in labor management disputes, and is a member of a number of arbitration panels.

He received his B.A. from the University of California, Berkeley; J.D. from U.C. Berkeley's Boalt Law School; Ph.D. from U.C.L.A.; LLM from U.C.L.A. Law School; and did post-doctoral work at Yale University School of Law. He is a graduate of the National Judicial College and has taken graduate level courses in a variety of subjects.

Index

www.ingramcontent.com/pod-product-compliance
Lightning Source LLC
Chambersburg PA
CBHW020843270326
41928CB00006B/358